REFORMIST
VOICES OF
Islam

REFORMIST
VOICES OF
Islam

MEDIATING ISLAM
AND
MODERNITY

— SHIREEN T. HUNTER, EDITOR —

M.E.Sharpe
Armonk, New York
London, England

Library of Congress Cataloging-in-Publication Data

Reformist voices of Islam : mediating Islam and modernity / edited by Shireen T. Hunter.
    p. cm.
  Includes bibliographical references and index.
  ISBN 978-0-7656-2238-9 (cloth : alk. paper)
  1. Islam—21st century. 2. Islamic renewal—Islamic countries. 3. Globalization—Religious
aspects—Islam. 4. Religious awakening—Islam. 5. Islamic modernism. I. Hunter, Shireen.

BP163.R44 2008
297.09'0511—dc22   2008010863

Printed in the United States of America

The paper used in this publication meets the minimum requirements of
American National Standard for Information Sciences
Permanence of Paper for Printed Library Materials,
ANSI Z 39.48-1984.

BM (c)   10   9   8   7   6   5   4   3   2   1

Contents

Detailed Table of Contents

Foreword

During the last three decades, Western observers and analysts of the Muslim world have been preoccupied mainly with the rise of a variety of radical interpretations of Islam and with groups promoting them. This preoccupation has been understandable in light of threats that the followers of these extremist readings of Islam have posed to the stability of their own countries, the negative impact on sensitive regions such as the Middle East and the Persian Gulf, and the intensely anti-Western sentiments that they cultivate. The tragic events of September 11, 2001, followed by other acts of terror in Europe and Asia, clearly showed the depth of these extremists' animosity toward the West, their geographic reach, and their lack of scruples in targeting innocent civilians, including many Muslims.

In addition to extremist discourse, in recent decades the Muslim world has also witnessed the rise and spread of ultra-conservative and literalist readings of the Qur'an and practices that flow from such readings. The behavior of the Taliban regime in Afghanistan was the most vivid actualization of this discourse.

But however damaging the emergence of this discourse and its proponents has been both for the Muslim world and the West, it is important to recognize that they do not represent the entire spectrum of intellectual space in the Muslim world. On the contrary, during the past fifteen years a robust reformist discourse has emerged in many Muslim countries and among Muslims living elsewhere. This discourse offers a reading of Islam based on a more rationalist and contextualist approach, which, if broadly adopted in the Muslim world, could enable Muslims to reconcile the requirements of building modern and vibrant societies with democratic and law-based political systems. This would entail both respect for the basic rights of all human beings and retention of Muslims' cultural and spiritual heritage. It would also enable Muslims to enter into constructive relationships with other cultures and make a significant contribution to ongoing debates regarding serious challenges facing humanity that require collaboration among all countries and peoples for them to be met successfully.

A variety of factors have contributed to the emergence of this debate within the Muslim world. These include the failure of Islamic governments, like Iran's, to deliver on promises of economic prosperity and political freedom, the disastrous rule of the Taliban regime, and the devastating consequences for Muslims stemming from radical actions, including the unleashing of military conflicts in Afghanistan and Iraq.

However, the roots of this reformist discourse go deep into Islam's early history, when a rationalist school battled with a literalist reading of the faith only to lose to the latter. The next flourishing of reformist discourse in Islam dates from the mid-nineteenth century. The impetus was the European advance into the Muslim world and Muslims' encounter with modernity. This advance showed Muslims how far they had moved away from their early achievements and generated soul-searching among them about the causes of their decline and how to reverse it. A main conundrum was how Muslims can modernize without totally losing their own identity and culture. Islamic reformism was one response.

This reformist discourse was overtaken in later decades by modernizing secularist and conservative Islamic discourses. However, both have proved to be ineffective in Muslim societies. As interpreted and implemented in the Muslim world, secularism and modernity have led to authoritarianism, repression, and perpetuation of Muslims' inferior economic conditions. Conservative and mostly radical Islam has no major, sound, long-term, rational, humane, or democratic solutions to fix the historical, economic, and social factors that have led to the stagnation, repression, and instability prevalent in many Muslim societies.

Secular models of modernization as imported phenomena have often not succeeded because they have not been rooted in Muslims' own national and cultural traditions. What today's Muslim reformers want to do is to mediate between the requirements of modernization and the maintenance of indigenous cultures. They aim to show that Islamic principles—properly understood, interpreted, and implemented—are compatible with modernity, democracy, and human rights, and that Muslims do not have to choose between their faith and the need for modernization. In short, the reformers' goal is to develop a version of modernity rooted in Islamic principles and traditions.

The stakes involved in the outcome of the conflict between these divergent views within the Muslim world are high both for Muslims and for the West. It is therefore important to understand the views and positions of reformist thinkers throughout the Islamic world, to identify the common traits of their thinking as well as their differences, and to understand why the reformist discourse and Muslim reformists have so far not fared well in the Muslim world. Equally important is the need to assess the impact of Western policies and other international events in determining the fate of Muslim reformists and to determine what policies on the part of Muslim and Western governments are more likely to help advance the reformist discourse.

The editor and the contributors to *Reformist Voices of Islam: Mediating Islam and Modernity*, all noted scholars, have done excellent work in analyzing the current Islamic reformist discourse and the writings of its major protagonists, many of whom are not well known in the West. More important, the editor and contributors put the current debate into its proper historical context, and they also offer advice on what needs to be done to ensure that the outcome of the current debate in the Muslim world favors a reformist rather than either radical or obscurantist Islam.

These are goals that are very much in keeping with the mission of Carnegie Corporation of New York, which was created in 1911 by Andrew Carnegie to promote "the advancement and diffusion of knowledge and understanding." The foundation carries out Mr. Carnegie's mandate by focusing on the two areas that he devoted himself to during his lifetime—advancing education and international peace. Both efforts will certainly be served by deepening the breadth and scope of our collective awareness and understanding of Islam as a religion, Islamic civilizations, and Muslim states and societies. Hence, in our grantmaking, and in particular, through our Scholars Program, we have integrated an emphasis on increasing public knowledge about the diversity of thought, cultures, and history of Islam and Muslim communities, including those in the United States. This book is an outstanding contribution to achieving these important objectives; indeed, I can think of few that are as critical or timely.

Vartan Gregorian
President
Carnegie Corporation of New York

Preface

Since the mid-1970s, discourse on Islam in the Islamic world has been dominated by a revivalist trend with a wide spectrum of intellectual and operational tendencies, ranging from varying shades of conservative, fundamentalist, and literalist to revolutionary, extremist, and jihadist.

Groups belonging to this broad revivalist trend differ significantly in terms of their readings of Islam, their objectives, and their methods of achieving them. The jihadists, best represented by Al Qaeda and its affiliates, combine a literalist and conservative reading of Islam with a violent mode of operation. Some revolutionary Muslims combine a relatively progressive reading of Islam with violent methods, if necessary, to reach their goals. Iran's Revolution of 1979 is the embodiment of the revolutionary trend within the revivalist movement.

What all revivalist groups have in common is strong animosity toward the West and its allies and friends in the Islamic world. They have demonstrated this animosity by engaging in violent acts against Western interests in the Islamic world and against Muslim governments friendly to the West. The Iranian hostage crisis of 1979–80 and the 9/11 attacks by Al Qaeda on U.S. targets are the most dramatic manifestations of this type of anti-Western operations undertaken by supporters of revolutionary and jihadist trends within the revivalist movement.

It is thus understandable that, during the past three decades, most Western scholarship on Islam has been preoccupied with the extremist trend within the broader revivalist movement. It is equally understandable that this preoccupation has become stronger since the events of 9/11, subsequent acts of violence committed by Muslim extremists and jihadists in Europe and Asia, and the continued challenges they pose to Western powers in Afghanistan and Iraq since the start of military operations in those countries in 2001 and 2003, respectively.

Not surprisingly, the emergence of extremist trends in Islam has encouraged the appearance of formulations such as Samuel P. Huntington's "clash of civilizations." This theory views Islam as unable to accommodate modernity and as posing a long-term civilizational and security challenge to the West, thus painting a dark picture of future relations between the West and the Islamic world.

Less understandable is the lack of adequate recognition by Western scholars, journalists, and other observers of the Islamic world of the fact that extremist discourses have not represented the entire spectrum of Islamic thought in the last three decades. On the contrary, even in this period, moderate and reformist discourses on Islam have been developed and expounded by Muslim intellectuals, religious leaders, and political activists and parties. Nor has there been enough recognition in the West of the fact that it is by no means certain that the extremists will succeed in dominating the intellectual and operational fields in the Islamic world.

The proponents of a moderate Islamic discourse advocate a nonviolent approach to the Islamization of Muslim societies and a less rigid interpretation of certain Islamic injunctions and laws, notably those pertaining to family law, gender rights, and the penal code. Their ultimate goal is either gradually to introduce fundamental reforms into these laws or at least to encourage restraint and leniency in their application. The moderates also reject confrontation with other faiths, cultures, and governments, notably those of the West; instead, they promote dialogue.

Reformist Muslim thinkers and activists are even more ambitious in their objectives. They are not satisfied with slow and gradual reform of those aspects of Islamic law and praxis that they see as no longer adequate to Muslims' needs and conditions. They want through their discourse to reconcile faith and reason and to mediate between Islam and modernity. They propose a more rationalist and contextualist approach to the interpretation of Islamic scriptural and legal sources, an approach that opens the way to new readings of Islamic sources. These new readings, they hold, would better reflect Islam's true spirit and its foundational principles of justice and mercy, and hence would be more relevant to Muslims' current needs and conditions.

Through this methodology, the reformists also aim to demonstrate that Islam's basic ethos and spirit are compatible with modern notions of human rights, democracy, pluralism, and tolerance. By doing so, they challenge simplistic theories that claim that Islam is incompatible with modernity, facing Muslims with the stark choice of either abandoning their faith or forever remaining on the margins of the modern world. Through their embrace of pluralism, tolerance, and constructive interaction and dialogue with other cultures, the reformists question the validity of theories predicting an inevitable clash of civilizations between the Islamic world and the West, and they present a less cataclysmic view of the future character of their relations.

The reformists' ultimate ambition is to provide an intellectual basis and framework, inspired by and embedded in Islam's basic ethos, for development of an indigenous concept of modernity that can satisfy Muslims' twin needs for modernity and authenticity. They believe that such a concept of modernity would stand a better chance of success in the Muslim world because it would be rooted in Muslims' own spiritual, cultural, and intellectual ethos and heritage. By achieving this goal, the reformists hope to counter the influence of utopian, radical, literalist, and excessively nativist readings of Islam.

During the last fifteen years, several factors have strengthened both moderate and reformist discourses: disenchantment with the revolutionary Islam's experience in Iran and the conservative jihadist Taliban rule in Afghanistan; disappointment with radical and utopian readings of Islam; and fundamental changes in the dynamics of the international political system that were triggered by the Soviet Union's collapse and the dramatic erosion of communism's credibility. However, the strengthening of moderate and reformist discourses has not occurred uniformly throughout the Muslim world, nor has it yet reached a point where it can be considered either dominant or irreversible. On the contrary, the proponents of conservative, literalist, extremist, and jihadist discourses of Islam retain significant influence in the Islamic world, and are active in spreading their particular readings of the faith. They have been helped by growing resentment in the Muslim world of Western policies in Afghanistan, Iraq, and Palestine. Meanwhile, the cause of reformists who advocate a conciliatory approach to the West has suffered from these same events.

Despite the importance of the reformist discourse for the evolution of Muslim societies and their relations with the Western world, neither the works of most reformist thinkers nor the intellectual evolution and political activities of reformist and moderate political groupings have received much attention in the West. Further, the new generation of reformist thinkers and activists is virtually unknown to Western audiences. Even the few studies that have dealt with the ideas of the more prominent reformist thinkers have not put their work in the context of Islam's intellectual history, especially its more rationalist traditions, nor in the context of their respective countries' historical experience of modernity. Moreover, these works do not offer sufficient analysis of the reasons behind the failure of reformist ideas to take root in Muslim countries and what this failure implies for the prospects of the current wave of reformist discourse.

In light of these critical gaps in Western study of reformist Islam and the need for broader knowledge and understanding of what is taking place, this volume has the following principal objectives:

1. to provide a comprehensive survey of the works and ideas of Muslim reformist thinkers and selected moderate and reformist political and civic groups in key Muslim countries and within Muslim communities in the West;
2. to introduce the lesser-known and younger generation of Muslim reformist thinkers to Western audiences;
3. to explain the methodology of reformist and moderate thinkers and groups as applied to the interpretation of Islamic religious and legal sources, along with their views regarding such vital issues as democracy, human rights, gender and minority rights, and freedom of conscience and expression;
4. to place the works and ideas of key contemporary reformist thinkers within the broader context of the history of reformist discourse in the Islamic world during the last century and a half, including the primary impetus

behind its emergence and the classical Islamic tradition of reform and renewal;

5. to identify both the common features of reformist thinkers in different Muslim countries and differences that derive from particular conditions and concerns, thus permitting a comparative analysis of the reformist discourse;

6. to identify causes of the failure of reformist discourses thus far to gain greater popular acceptance and to translate ideas into concrete reforms;

7. to assess the outlook of current reformist thinkers and activists, based on experience; and

8. to identify factors most likely to help or hinder the success of the current reformist wave, thus providing guidelines for strengthening the reformist trend.

To achieve these goals, contributors to this volume were chosen from among the best scholars around the world, with high accomplishment and standing in the fields of Islamic, Middle East, South Asian, and Southeast Asian studies. Some of them are themselves prominent Muslim reformist thinkers. In order to enhance the comparative dimension of the project, the authors have dealt with a range of fundamental issues and questions within the different historical, sociopolitical, and cultural contexts of key Muslim countries and regions.

This study was made possible by the generous support of Carnegie Corporation of New York. Accordingly, I express my deepest thanks to the Corporation, and especially to its president, Dr. Vartan Gregorian, for unfailing confidence and support. My thanks also go to Prince Al Waleed Bin Talal Center for Muslim-Christian Understanding and its founding director, Professor John Esposito, its associate director, Professor John Voll, and to the Edmund A. Walsh School of Foreign Service and its dean, Ambassador Robert Gallucci, for enabling me to complete this project at Georgetown University. I am also grateful to professors Esposito and Voll for their advice in the process of completing this work. I thank my research assistant, Katherine Pitsch, for her help in providing research material and a wide range of other assistance. And special thanks go to my husband, Robert Hunter, for his support, patience, and encouragement throughout the preparation of this work.

However, the greatest thanks are due to the contributors to this volume, without whose excellent work, spirit of collaboration, and patience in responding to my many requests this work would not have been completed.

Despite all the help and support that I have received in completing this work, I am solely responsible for any errors of fact or judgment.

Shireen T. Hunter

REFORMIST
VOICES OF
Islam

Introduction

Shireen T. Hunter

In the Islamic world, two different discourses on Islam are currently competing to win the hearts and minds of Muslims and to determine the course of Muslim societies' evolution. One discourse is generally referred to as reformist, or occasionally as liberal Islam, and the other is variously referred to as conservative, traditionalist, or literalist Islam.

Within each of these broad trends, there are different tendencies in terms of philosophical outlook, methodology, and modes of operation. Reformist thinkers vary in their methodology of analyzing Islamic scriptural and legal sources, in their view of the allowable scope for interpretation, and in their opinion regarding what aspects of Islamic scripture and laws may be reinterpreted. Some reformists favor only a limited reinterpretation of these sources and exclude the fundamentals of the Faith. They may use traditional methodologies in their interpretations, such as those embodied in the *usul al-fiqh*, and they may prefer a gradual approach to changing those Islamic laws seen as no longer responsive to Muslims' current needs and conditions. Other reformists advocate a broader scope for rereading basic Islamic sources in light of new circumstances, the application of modern methodologies derived from the social sciences in addition to traditional methods, and the extensive revision, even abolition, of those Islamic laws which they consider outdated and irrelevant to Muslims' current needs and aspirations.

Within the conservative/traditionalist/literalist trend, the major difference lies in the preferred mode of operation of different groups. Some are politically non-active and even quietist. Others seek to impose their version of Islam, and a social and political organization based on it, on their respective societies. A radical minority within this tendency is prepared to use force to achieve its goals. Philosophically, however, both groups to varying degrees adhere to literalist and narrow interpretations of Islam's major scriptural and legal sources, oppose changes to the existing laws, notably the penal code, and even oppose exercising caution and leniency in the application of existing laws through a more liberal interpretation.

More fundamentally, supporters of these two broad tendencies disagree on the definition and meaning of key terms such as "reform," "conservatism," "traditionalism," or "literalism." All these terms are highly contested and are understood differently by various groups. What some may consider as "reform" others may see as *bid'a,* an innovation that is harmful, an unacceptable departure from established practices. Some define reform as the reinterpretation of fundamental sources, leading to changes in existing laws and making Islam more compatible with the requirements of modernity. Others define reform as the elimination of exogenous influences on Islam, the adoption of a literalist reading of sources, and the restoration and maintenance of the laws and practices of early Islam.

Yet both conservatives/literalists and reformists claim that they want to restore the original and pure Islam of the time of the Prophecy. However, reformists emphasize the restoration of Islam's spiritual rather than ritualistic dimension, the recapturing of its true spirit, which they believe has been buried under layers of ritual and legal constructs, and the achievement of its ultimate, and so far forgotten and unaccomplished, mission, which is to establish justice, mercy, and respect for human dignity.

To those unfamiliar with Islam's intellectual history, the current debate may appear as a new phenomenon. This latest debate has many novel features, and it has been generated by new factors. Yet the issue of reform and renewal and the debate about what constitutes reform are nothing new and date to Islam's early history.

Reform and Renewal in Islamic Thought: Origins and Evolution

According to the prophetic tradition, in every century God will send a leader (*mujaddid*) to the Muslim community to renew its faith. In Islamic tradition, this is known as *tajdid* (renewal).[1] Another and closely related concept is that of *islah.* It means "reform" in the sense of eliminating any harmful exogenous factors that may have influenced Muslims' religious and ethical values and practices, thus leading to their societies' moral deterioration.

The main reason for the existence of these traditions is the belief that, with the passing of time and under the impact of alien influences, Islamic principles become misinterpreted, misused, or—worse—forgotten, eventually leading Muslims away from the Straight Path (*sirat al-mustaqim*) and toward corruption and disbelief. Over time, this deviation from the Straight Path results in Muslim societies' decline, the disunity of the *umma* (the community of Muslims), and their increased vulnerability to external predatory forces.

Throughout their history, Muslim communities have been subject to such corrupting forces and have suffered from their negative consequences. This fact accounts for the continued appeal of the concepts of reform and renewal for Muslims and the periodic appearance of individuals within different Islamic traditions claiming to be the renewers and reformers promised by the Prophet. However, Muslims have never agreed on exactly what constitutes reform and renewal and therefore on who is a reformer. Some who have considered themselves reformers have been viewed by others as guilty of innovation (*bid'a*), and hence heretics. Others have been seen as reactionaries hampering Islam's intellectual and scientific flourishing and condemning it to ossification and irrelevance.[2]

Nevertheless, until the nineteenth century, reform and renewal had generally meant the elimination of what were seen as exogenous influences on Islam, return to the essentials of the faith, and often a restrictive interpretation of the two major Islamic sources, the *Qur'an*, the holy book containing the revelations of God to Muhammad, and the *sunna*, the practice and sayings of the Prophet, as recorded and related in *hadith*.[3] The proponents of this type of reform and renewal believed in the immutability and eternality of the Qur'an and the *sunna*. They refuted the view that some content of these sources was bound to a specific time (that of Muhammad's Prophecy) and a particular place (Arabia of the time of Revelation) and thus potentially subject to reinterpretation according to changing times and circumstances.

Methodologically, although championing *ijtihad* (independent interpretation of scriptural and legal sources) against *taqlid* (imitation, or the blind following of the rulings of earlier *ulema,* the scholar-arbiters of Islamic law), the proponents of this type of reform defined *ijtihad* in a narrow sense and allowed a limited role for reason in the interpretation of key sources. They used *ijtihad* only to decide whether certain practices and views of other *ulema* and the broader community correctly reflected the injunctions of the Qur'an and the *sunna,* which they often interpreted in a literalist fashion.

By the mid-nineteenth century, however, the terms *tajdid* and *islah* acquired the added meaning of reform in the sense of reconciling Islam with rationalist and scientific thinking and restructuring Muslim countries' educational and sociopolitical institutions more or less along the lines of European institutions. The nineteenth-century Jadid movement in Russia and Central Asia, spearheaded by the Tatar reformists Ismail Bey Gasprinsky and Shihabeddin Marjani, was the embodiment of this new meaning of *tajdid*.[4] The Indian Muslim reformer Sir Sayyid Ahmad Khan's movement, especially his educational reforms, was also close to this conception of reform. *Islah* in this sense is primarily associated with the Egyptian religious scholar and reformer Sheikh Muhammad Abduh and his disciples. Abduh is viewed, at least in the Arab world, as the founder of the Islamic modernist school of thought.

Since the nineteenth century, with certain variations, these two different conceptions of reform and renewal have coexisted and competed in the Muslim world. However, the main motivation and the ultimate goal of all renewers and reformers, despite differences of opinion regarding what constitutes reform, the essentials of Islam, and the best methodology for the interpretation of major Islamic sources, have always been the following: (1) return to the basic sources of Islam, namely the Qur'an and the *sunna*; (2) restoration of Muslims' faith and morality; (3) intellectual, economic, and political revitalization of the Muslim world; (4) strengthening the Islamic community and defending it against internal and external enemies; and (5) ensuring Islam's continued relevance to Muslims' lives in all its dimensions.

Those who are engaged in the current debate, despite their many philosophical, methodological, and operational differences also pursue similar objectives. What distinguishes earlier and current reformists from others is their belief that these goals, especially the last objective, can only be achieved through appropriate reforms that would enable Islam to provide viable answers to Muslims' changing questions and needs.[5]

Reform Movements as Responses to External Threats and Internal Crises

Historically, reform movements in the Islamic world, in both senses described above, have emerged in response to two challenges or a combination of them: (1) external threat, especially foreign conquest; and (2) actual or perceived departure from moral and religious observance, often followed by a period of overall decline of Muslim societies. Reformers have often seen foreign conquest as resulting from the erosion of religious and moral standards and the ensuing decline of Muslim societies. Since the mid-nineteenth century, departure from Islam's rationalist and scientific spirit and traditions has been added to the causes of Muslims' decline. Among the early renewers and reformers, the views of the thirteenth-century Hanbali scholar Ibn Taymmiyya, especially those related to political leadership and the right of Muslims to revolt against rulers who did not live and govern according to Islamic injunctions, were formed by a combination of those factors.

The external threat was dramatically manifested in the Mongol conquest of Baghdad in 1258 and the end of the Abbasid Caliphate. Ibn Taymmiyya saw this defeat as the direct result of Muslims' decline, which he believed had occurred because of Islam's contamination by other cultures, such as the Persian, the Byzantine, the Turkic, and finally by the Mongols, whose conversion to Islam he believed to have been superficial.[6]

The reform movement initiated in the early eighteenth century by Muhammad Ibn Abdul Wahhab, also a Hanbali and a disciple of Ibn Taymmiyya, was primarily in reaction to what Abdul Wahhab considered to be creeping idolatrous practices in his native Najd, and large-scale injustices and low moral standards in many Muslim lands that he witnessed in his travels.[7]

The nineteenth-century reform movements were different in nature and character from earlier movements. But, like their predecessors, they were responses to external threats manifested in the European powers' imperial expansion into Muslim lands, along with Muslim societies' moral, intellectual, and material decline. Muslim reformers and renewers of the twentieth century, too, have been influenced by similar factors, notably a sense of moral and spiritual decline of Muslim societies and humanity in general. The Egyptian Sayyid Qutb (1906–1966) was one influential thinker whose views were deeply affected by this sense of moral decline, which he believed had resulted in the dispiritualization of human societies and greater unhappiness despite material advances. Qutb wrote:

There is no doubt that man has attained great conquest by virtue of science. He has made immense progress in the field of medicine and the treatment of physical diseases. In the same way, man has also made tremendous progress in the field of industrial products. But despite all these, the question arises what man has actually got out of all these struggles and progress. Have they caused any spiritual growth? Has he gained the wealth of peace, comfort, and satisfaction? The answer to all these questions is nothing but an emphatic "No." As a result of this material progress, instead of getting peace and ease man is confronted [by] troubles, restlessness, and fear.[8]

Qutb also believed that Islam as practiced in most Muslim countries, especially by the ruling elites, was not the real Islam. Rather, Muslims had gone back to the dark days of injustice, ignorance, passivity, and impiety (*jahiliya*) that had prevailed before the dawn of Islam.[9] In other words, they had regressed morally and spiritually. In the Shi'a context, Ayatullah Murtaza Mutahari (1919–1979), the Iranian reformist cleric and thinker, also argued that material progress is not sufficient for human happiness.[10]

Ali Shariati (1933–1977), the highly influential Iranian thinker, was more concerned about the socioeconomic disparities and political despotism in the Muslim world and more generally in developing societies.[11] Nevertheless, he, too, expressed views similar to those of Qutb regarding the despiritualizing and alienating aspects of modern socioeconomic systems, as reflected in the following passage from his lecture on "Modern Calamities":

The modern calamities that are leading to the deformation and decline of humanity may be placed under two headings: (1) social systems and (2) intellectual systems. Within the two outwardly opposed social systems . . . capitalism and socialism what is tragically felt is that man['s] primary and supra-material essence has been forgotten. . . . [B]oth these social systems . . . regard man as an economic animal. . . . [T]echnological prodigies, who ought to have freed mankind from servitude to manual labor and increased people's leisure time, cannot do even that much. . . . [H]umanity is every day more condemned to alienation, more drowned in the mad maelstrom of compulsive speed. Not only there is no longer leisure for growth in human values, moral greatness and spiritual aptitudes [but it has also] caused traditional moral values to decline and disappear.[12]

Similarly, Shariati saw movement away from the Islam of the Prophet (*islam e nabavi*) and the Islam of the Qur'an as the root cause of Muslims' manifold problems. Writing as an Iranian and as a Shi'a, Shariati also viewed the corruption of what he called Alid Shi'ism (*shi'a e alavi*) by the Safavids and their successors, thus turning it into what he called Safavid Shi'ism (*shi'a e safavi*), as the main cause of the crisis in Iranian Islam and society. According to Shariati, the most damaging aspect of this falling away from the Islam of the Prophet and the Qur'an has been

Islam's transformation from a religion of knowledge, activity, justice, and piety into one of ignorance, passivity, superstition, and tyranny.

Writing mainly for an Iranian audience, Shariati blamed this falling away from true Islam and true Shi'ism on the religious establishment, which he accused of having been in collusion with political power-holders since the time of the Safavids (1502–1736). Explaining his vision for the Islam of the future, he wrote: "Tomorrow's Islam will not be the Islam of the book of prayers. It will be the Islam of the Qur'an. Tomorrow's Shi'ism will not be the Shi'ism of Shah Sultan Husayn. It will be the Shi'ism of Husayn."[13]

Finally, these thinkers have seen the Muslim countries' continued political, economic, and cultural penetration by foreign powers as a new and insidious form of external threat that has replaced outright occupation and the colonialism of the past.[14] The Iranian intellectual Jalal al-Ahmad (1923–1969) described this new and hidden state of being dominated in graphic terms: "At the beginning, the Western man was sahib and his wife memsahib, but today he is a counselor and adviser or representative of UNESCO. And although he is not wearing his colonial hat, his mission is the same."[15]

According to al-Ahmad, the worst aspect of this new form of dependency has been the sapping of the capacity of what he calls the Eastern man for independent thinking, creating, and inventing, turning him into a mere consumer of Western man's products and ideas. This state of mental and cultural dependency, has eroded the foundations of Islamic morality, culture, and society, and ultimately has undermined the Faith itself.

Some key Muslim reformist thinkers today believe that the lack of fundamental reforms will perpetuate Muslims' problems and their scientific, technological, economic, military, and political weakness, and hence their dependent state. Even Islam itself may well become endangered. Unlike the above-noted intellectuals, however, adherents of this trend take a more critical view of their own intellectual and cultural traditions, including their Islamic heritage. In particular, like their nineteenth-century predecessors, they consider the gradual extinction of the rationalist discourse and rigorous and innovative *ijtihad* in the Muslim world to be a major cause of Muslims' past and current problems. Moreover, they are willing to accept their share of responsibility for these failures and not to blame others, notably the West, for their misfortunes. That said, they are not oblivious to the harmful consequences for Muslims of Western policies during the colonial era, the Cold War period, and even today.

In short, similar factors, namely external threats and internal crises—social, economic, political, moral, and cultural—have affected the thinking of Muslim reformers. However, because of both the different nature of today's threats and the experiences of Muslim societies during the late nineteenth and twentieth centuries, current thinkers' prescriptions for countering these threats and solving Muslims' problems differ in many respects from those of their predecessors.

Encounter with Modernity

The acceleration of European imperial expansion into Muslim lands in the last years of the eighteenth century posed a challenge of a magnitude that Muslims had never faced before. Prior to the European conquest of Muslim lands, foreign invaders such as the Mongols may have caused horrific material damage, but they had not been able either to undermine Muslim societies' cultural and religious foundations or to shake Muslims' belief in the superiority of their values and civilization. None of the earlier conquerors had been able to offer an alternative system of values and laws that could claim to be superior to those of Islam and hence capable of replacing those values and laws as the organizing principle of Muslim societies at both spiritual and material levels. On the contrary, in due course earlier invaders had accepted Islam as faith and civilization and had expanded it to new frontiers, as illustrated by the Mogul Empire in India and by the Ottoman Empire, which resurrected the caliphate and extended Islam's frontiers to Europe. Thus, in seeking to solve Muslims' problems, earlier renewers and reformers had only to advocate a return to what they considered to be the pure Islam of the time of the Prophet and to seek guidance only from the Qur'an and the *sunna* as they understood them.

The Western challenge was different. Unlike the earlier nomadic invaders, European conquerors represented an advanced and vibrant civilization, at a time when the Muslim world was at its weakest economically and militarily and at its least dynamic intellectually and scientifically. Because of this coincidence of Islamic decline and European ascent, the latter acquired an aura of invincibility that previous conquerors lacked. This aura also endowed the civilization underpinning European power with an inherent superiority for many Muslims, and, indeed, other conquered peoples. Moreover, the Europeans offered both a new intellectual framework for looking at the world and a new model for organizing society and governing it. In other words, they offered an alternative system of values and model of sociopolitical organization—modernity—to one based on Islam.

The basic ideas of modernity were progress, emancipation, and liberty, thus holding up the vision of a continuously improving human condition. If, for Muslims, the ideal society had already been realized at the time of the Prophet, for the adepts of modernity, utopia was yet to be achieved. In short, while Islam appeared stagnant, modernity appeared dynamic. Additionally, since Christianity is an important foundation of European civilization, many Muslims came to believe that somehow Islam, as a religion and as a cultural and civilizational construct, was less conducive to scientific, economic, social, and political progress.

In sum, faced with this new reality, for the first time in their history Muslims began to doubt the superiority of their own culture and values and the sociopolitical, legal, and ethical systems built upon them. This new found doubt, in turn, led them to ask difficult questions about the factors, including their religious and cultural values, that had led to their decline, and hence their domination by Western powers.

The contemporary Iranian Muslim reformist thinker Hujat al-Islam Muhsen Kadivar (b. 1959) has explained this phenomenon very well. According to him, before the encounter with modernity, Muslims were comfortable with their beliefs, ethics, and laws, and did not face any difficulty in dealing with different issues.[16] But after this encounter, Muslim certainties were shaken.

This erosion of Muslims' self confidence has had two important and still relevant consequences for the Islamic world. First, since their encounter with modernity, the main struggle in Muslim countries has been a tug of war between the need to accommodate modernity and the urge to maintain cultural authenticity and indigenous systems of value. Second, the dominant paradigm in their intellectual discourse has been modernity and how to deal with it. This fact has meant that all types of sociopolitical and cultural discourses in the Muslim world, whether secular or Islamic, including current Islamic reformist thinking, need to be examined in light of this overarching paradigm.

Modernity and Imperialism

Muslims' first encounter with modernity was a consequence of the European powers' imperial expansion into their lands, often following some form of military defeat at the hand of the Europeans. This coincidence between Europe's imperial expansion and the introduction of modernity to the Muslim world has profoundly affected Muslims' collective psychology and shaped their responses to modernity and its challenges. Muslim responses are explained by this fact rather than by any theory of Muslim cultural exceptionalism based on the idea that Islam and Muslims are especially impervious to the influence of modernity, despite the widespread popularity of this view among Western scholars since the nineteenth century. In reality, the nature and range of Muslim responses to modernity have been quite similar to those of other non-European, and even some late-modernizing European, countries.

The following have been the three most important consequences of this coincidence.

1. Modernization efforts by societies challenged by the West have had a defensive character. Muslims and other non-European peoples have tried to acquire the results of modernity, namely science and technology and the economic and military power that derives from them, in order to be able to resist European/Western encroachments on their territory and other interests, without wholeheartedly embracing the philosophical and moral underpinnings of modernity;
2. At least for significant numbers of non-Europeans, modernity has been identified with foreign domination. This has led many of them to see modernity as threatening to their indigenous cultures and identities; and
3. Many non-Europeans have experienced modernity not in its emancipatory function, but rather in its dominating, oppressive, and predatory dimension, thus eroding faith in its moral claims.

These realities have faced non-European, notably Muslim, societies with a major challenge, namely, how to benefit from the results of modernity without having to adopt its entire philosophy at the expense of their own cultural identity and indigenous values. Indeed, the history of the non-European world in the last two centuries can be summed up as efforts to achieve these two seemingly contradictory objectives.

Non-European Responses to Modernity

Three main responses to modernity can be observed among non-European societies—namely, total embrace, rejection, and synthesis, often pursued simultaneously by different segments of society. At times, experimentation with one alternative has led to the strengthening of the opposite impulse, in turn setting off a third reaction.

Generally speaking, early modernizing efforts, often directed from the top, have prompted reassertion of indigenous cultures and value systems, albeit in a different form, and often in the guise of new ideologies with authenticist impulses. For example, the early eighteenth century modernizing reforms of Peter the Great in Russia led to the emergence of the authenticist movement of Slavophilism.[17] Meiji Shintoism, varieties of Confucian revivalist movements, and Islamic and Hindu revivalist movements in the nineteenth and twentieth centuries are also manifestations of this reaction.[18]

In the Muslim world, revivalist movements of the last four decades have been responses to the modernizing efforts of the so-called modernizing dictators—Ataturk in Turkey, the Pahlavis in Iran, Bourghiba in Tunisia, Suharto in Indonesia, and their counterparts in other countries—and to the social and cultural consequences of their policies. These modernizers embraced the project of modernity in its outward manifestations and pursued economic, social, and cultural policies that led to a polarization of Muslim societies at every level between a narrow elite and the rest of the people. Moreover, the manner in which these reforms were implemented resulted in what Timothy McDaniel has called "a regimentizing modernization rather than a liberating modernity."[19] This particular experience of modernization eroded the appeal of the entire project of modernity for most Muslims, because they came to see it "as guise for other projects, including accumulation of power."[20]

The socialist-inspired models of modernization, as carried out by leaders such as Gamal Abdel Nasser of Egypt and Houari Boumedienne of Algeria, fared no better than their capitalist-inspired counterparts; they, too, failed to win Muslims over to the project of modernity.[21] The result, as noted above, was the emergence of revivalist movements and efforts by Muslim intellectuals to offer alternative models of socioeconomic and scientific and technological development based on Islamic precepts and indigenous cultural heritages. These alternative models reflect the basic traits of other authenticist responses to the challenges of modernity and the upheavals caused by the process of modernization.

This response to the tension caused by the challenge of modernity and the disruptions in the fabric of society triggered by the process of modernization seeks solace in an idealized and superior version of the indigenous culture rooted in the past, seeing in it the best and most appropriate solutions to contemporary problems.[22] Yet, while claiming to resurrect the idealized past, this reaction offers an ideological and highly distorted vision of the past.[23] Irrespective of the cultural milieu in which they appear, such authenticist reactions are not mere evocations of tradition but rather schematized responses to modernity.

In conformity with the general pattern, Islamic revivalist projects are based on an idealized and ideologized vision of the Islamic past and community, and their goal—the recreation of the *madinat al-nabi* (city of the Prophet)—is utopian. They look both backward and forward in an apotheosis of truth, and they are as much myth as history.[24]

Examples of synthesis between "what is regarded as the best in the indigenous culture and . . . the most positive features of modernity"[25] include religiocultural reformist movements such as Kang Youwei's attempt to modernize Confucianism in the early twentieth century, the early Meiji reform period in Japan when efforts were made to create a synthesis of Western progress and Japanese values, and the early Islamic reform movements. In fact, all religiocultural reform movements fall within the category of synthesis, although the relative weight of modernity and tradition varies for different movements, at different times and places, and among key thinkers and leaders.

The attraction of synthesis lies in the fact that "as the Chinese Cultural Revolution and Boris Yeltsin's attempts to repudiate the Russian past show, cultural iconoclasm is fraught with danger and history cannot be ignored, [yet] some form of modernity is an imperative."[26] Moreover, "modernization without modernity," especially if a democratic form of government and an emancipatory social and political ethics and practice are considered essential to a modern society, has not been limited to non-European societies. On the contrary, late-modernizing European countries—Germany, Italy, and some countries on the European periphery—have experienced modernization under non-democratic and even fascist governments.[27] Russia's modernization took place under Soviet communism.

Historically, most efforts at synthesis have failed, partly because they have tried to combine elements of native culture with manifestations of modernity rather than examining the native culture in light of modernity as a philosophical frame of reference. Moreover, the discourse of synthesis is complex and thus difficult to communicate at a mass level of comprehension and motivation. In particular, it lacks the ideological zeal of either committed modernizers or religious and cultural traditionalists and revivalists.

Additionally, the proponents of synthesis historically have been mistrusted and opposed by both traditionalists and modernists. Muslim reformist thinkers today, however, have sought a more nuanced approach to the relationship between modernity and indigenous cultures and systems of values. Their method is not merely picking and randomly combining elements of their own cultures and modernity. On the contrary, they do assess their own culture in light of modernity; but they also take a critical approach to modernity and its outcomes. In their critique of aspects of modernity, they draw heavily on the ideas of Western critics of modernity, or at least versions thereof, including those of postmodernists.[28]

That said, Muslim reformists still believe in the essentially positive nature of modernity, especially its emancipatory potential, while rejecting the view that all of its positive potential has been realized in present-day modern societies. Rather, like Jürgen Habermas, whose ideas have greatly influenced many reformist thinkers, they view modernity as "an unfinished project." All of its lofty potential has yet to be realized.[29]

In sum, the current reformists' form of synthesis aims to create nativized or homegrown versions of modernity as an alternative to the Western model. This trend has to be distinguished both from nativist reactions as reflected in religious revivalist movements or Slavophilism and from other random combinations of elements of tradition and modernity. Rather it is more inspired by ideas developed in the West, such as the notion of modernity as an unfinished project and the concept of multiple modernities.[30]

This new trend in synthesis is the result of a century and a half of Muslims' experimentation with all the above-noted responses to the challenge of modernity, along with the influence of philosophical and practical questioning of modernity in the West. The final judgment on the efficacy of efforts at synthesis and development of homegrown modernities, including its Islamic variants, should wait until Muslim societies fully absorb the impact of these developments.

Muslim Responses to Modernity: A Historical Perspective

Historically, Muslims' encounters with modernity most often began with military defeat at the hands of European powers, as exemplified by Napoleon Bonaparte's conquest of Egypt in 1798–1800; the defeat of the Mogul Empire in India and its incorporation into the British Empire in 1857; Iran's defeat in the Russo-Iranian wars (1804–1813 and 1824–1828); and successive Ottoman reverses in their encounters with Russia and other European powers. Following these military defeats, Muslims became painfully conscious of their scientific, technological, and military shortcomings compared to the Europeans. This sudden awareness led to deep soul-searching among Muslims regarding the causes of their decline and to a still continuing debate about how to reverse it.

Depending on their specific geopolitical, social, and political conditions and structures, individual Muslim societies reacted differently to this challenge. Nevertheless, there were significant similarities in the range of their responses. Muslims' first response was to try to obtain the know-how necessary to rectify the military imbalance with the European powers; hence the focus on military reform and instruction. The first modern educational institutions established in the Ottoman

Empire consisted of military schools (naval engineering school—1773; military engineering—1793; and military science—1834).

In Iran, the first students sent abroad by the reformist Crown Prince Abbas Mirza Qajar studied military sciences and engineering. In Egypt, Muhammad Ali's first attempts at reform were focused on transforming the Egyptian military according to the model of European armies. Reforms soon extended to educational, administrative, and legal spheres.[31]

Intellectually, all three types of reaction to modernity described above have been observable in Muslim societies since their earliest encounter with it until the present time.

The first reaction, total embrace of Western-style modernity, has been identified with the new and expanding elites educated in the West and later also in Western-style educational institutions. The total modernizers viewed Islam as practiced and implemented in the educational and judicial spheres of their respective countries as a major cause of Muslims' decline. However, during the first period of reform in the nineteenth century, sensitivity to the people's strong religious beliefs led most of them to portray their modernization agenda as compatible with Islam. For example, the Iranian secular modernizer Mirza Malkum Khan and his followers openly said that new ideas should be expressed in Islamic terms in order to gain popular acceptance.[32]

The second, rejectionist response was represented by the uneducated masses and the clerical establishments. From their perspective, the main cause of Muslims' decline had been the erosion of Islamic values and piety, and the failure to manage and govern society according to Islamic law. To reverse the process of decline and recapture their lost strength and vitality, Muslims should revive and observe Islamic rules and values.

The third reaction—in the context of this study the most important—has been that of synthesis. The adherents of this trend maintain that Islam is not a hindrance to scientific and other progress and have worked hard to validate their views. The most influential early representatives of this trend were Sayyid Jamal al-Din Assadabadi, known as al-Afghani, Sheikh Muhammad Abduh, and their followers. They advocated a kind of reform in Islam close to the second definition of the term noted earlier, namely the restoration of Islam's rationalist and scientific spirit and the interpretation of its basic tenets in ways more suited to Muslims' current conditions and needs.

To the list of the supporters of synthesis must be added a new generation of political figures with a modern education. As noted by Albert Hourani, they "set high value on the social morality of Islam, and tried to justify the introduction of Western institutions in Islamic terms, as being not the introduction of something new but a return to the true spirit of Islam."[33]

Afghani, Abduh, and the New Islamic Reformism

Sayyid Jamal al-Din Afghani (1838–1897) and Sheikh Muhammad Abduh (1849–1905) are rightly recognized as the originators of a new conception of reform in

Islam. Abduh is generally considered to be the father of Islamic modernism, while Afghani is indisputably the most ardent promoter of Islamic unity as a necessary element in any Islamic intellectual, economic, and political revival.[34]

The shock and the oppressive reality of European imperial domination of the Muslim world, a fact that Afghani viewed as a serious threat to Muslims, was the key motivation behind the development of his ideas. Thus, in his apprehension of the external threat, Afghani had much in common with earlier traditionalist reformers. For Afghani, reform was necessary because it was the only way for Muslims to reverse European domination. Afghani's Iranian origins, notwithstanding his name, and the fact that Iran was a battleground for Anglo-Russian rivalry, greatly contributed to his anti-imperialist views and shaped his project of reform.[35] For him, the multidimensional revitalization of Muslim countries and their unity was the only chance for regaining their independence, and he worked for both tirelessly, although not always successfully.[36]

To encourage the intellectual and scientific revitalization of Muslim societies, Afghani stressed the point that Islam and science were not only compatible, but that, of all religions, Islam was the friendliest to science. He acknowledged, however, that Muslims had lost their rationalist and scientific spirit—or more accurately, had passed it on to the Europeans. The level of their forgetfulness was so high that, when confronted with their own scientific legacy in European garb, they could not recognize it.[37]

Other Muslim reformers of the mid-nineteenth to early twentieth centuries subscribed to this vision. For example, the Tatar reformist Shihabeddin Marjani struggled to show that Islam, once rid of "the narrow dogmatism of traditional theology . . . was perfectly compatible with modern science."[38] On the Indian subcontinent, Sir Sayyid Ahmad Khan (1817–1898) was the principal proponent of this view.

Afghani's contributions went even further. Most important, he reintroduced a broad notion of rationalism to the interpretation of Islamic sources, including the Qur'an. He also emphasized the importance of striving. He called such activity Islam's essence and asked Muslims to fight against the spirit of passivity and fatalism that had gained a hold over their minds, souls, and societies. These ideas have motivated later generations of Muslim thinkers, including the major contemporary figures.

Sheikh Muhammad Abduh, a disciple of Afghani's, embraced a similar position, although his approach was less rationalist than Afghani's because he was influenced less by philosophy and more by traditional Islamic learning.[39] Nevertheless, he greatly contributed to the development of a reformist discourse in Islam and his ideas are still influential today. The cornerstone of Abduh's thought was the idea that the changes that had occurred in the Muslim world were irreversible and that more changes were likely on the way. Therefore, his main concern was preservation of society's moral fabric. To achieve this goal, Abduh concluded that it must be demonstrated that the changes that had taken place "were not only permitted by Islam, but were, indeed, its necessary implications if it were rightly understood."[40]

In Abduh's view, this approach did not mean that religious leaders should legitimize everything that was done in the name of change and modernization. On the contrary, he saw Islam as a principle of constraint that "would enable Muslims to distinguish between what was good and what was bad among all the suggested directions of change."[41] Methodologically, Abduh criticized *taqlid*, the practice of imitating earlier *ulema*, and instead emphasized *ijtihad* (independent interpretation) and reliance on fundamental sources—Qur'an and *sunna*.

The type of reform promoted by synthesizers was not pursued either systematically or for a sustained period. By the early twentieth century, the first type of reaction, manifested in the shape of a Westernizing trend, accelerated and became dominant by the 1920s, at least at the elite level. The masses, meanwhile, remained loyal to their religious and cultural beliefs and traditions.

This interruption of the trend toward a synthesis between Islam and modernity and the ascendance of modernizing regimes had far-reaching ramifications for the sociopolitical, economic, and cultural evolution of the Muslim world, and ultimately it spurred the rise of revivalist movements, some with radical tendencies.

Ascendance of the Modernizers: An Ephemeral Victory?

By the 1920s, the modernizers had gained the upper hand within the political systems of most Muslim countries. From the 1920s through the 1970s, they experimented with various versions of state-sponsored developmentalist projects; in other words, they pursued modernization without modernity.

Despite their many flaws, these policies expanded educational opportunities and made it possible for traditional, religious, and often financially disadvantaged segments of society to acquire a modern education. This development deeply affected the evolution of Islamic thinking in nearly every sphere of life, and it produced new types of Muslim reformers. These reformers espoused ideas that, at least on the surface, echoed the perspective of traditional reformers, including the restoration of a pure form of Islam and a return to an idealized past. However, they aimed to achieve these goals by using different analytical and methodological tools. They had acquired these tools through their access to modern education and the influence of the West's dominant ideologies, namely capitalism and socialism. The result was the development of alternative Islamic socioeconomic and political projects on the basis of an "ideologized" as well as idealized Islamic past.

The emergence of this trend in the late 1960s and the early 1970s surprised development experts. Yet, it was quite in line with traditional reactions to the first and often state-sponsored, modernizing efforts in other cultural milieus and other times, such as the post-Petrine Russia.

The Return of Islam: A Reaction to Modernization or Its Result?

In 1958, Walter Laqueur predicted that in coming decades Islam would play no role in the Middle Eastern countries' social, political, and cultural development.[42]

Laqueur was not alone in this view. His statement reflected the consensus among development experts and the principal theme of development theories dominant throughout the 1950s–1970s. These theories maintained that the process of economic and social development would inevitably eliminate traditional social, political, and cultural structures and systems of values and would lead to the secularization of society and hence the marginalization of religion as a sociopolitical force and key ingredient in a society's organization.

This widespread opinion among development experts regarding the evolutionary path of all non-industrialized countries is best captured in the title of Daniel Lerner's book, *The Passing of Traditional Society*.[43] This view is rooted in the post-Enlightenment belief in linear progress, with secularization in an increasingly differentiated public sphere as an important aspect. Thus, it is no wonder that Islam's political revival in the last several decades has surprised, and even shocked, development experts, scholars of religion and politics, and even specialists on the Muslim world. History has proven belief in a linear and uninterrupted progress from traditional to modern societies and the concomitant erosion of the role religion in society to be misplaced—and not only in the case of Muslim societies. This has led prominent scholars such as Peter L. Berger, once a proponent of the idea of an inexorable secularization, to change their opinions on this matter.

Against all expectations, development and modernization have not eliminated religion either as a spiritual or as a social, political, and cultural force. As Berger has observed, "the world today, with some exceptions . . . is as furiously religious as it ever was and in some places more so than ever."[44] Other scholars, including Pippa Norris and Ronald Inglehart, have noted that there has been "no worldwide decline of religiosity or of the role of religion in politics."[45] This has been especially true of the Muslim world where, since the end of the 1960s, Islam has reemerged as a potent sociopolitical force contesting the validity of the dominant paradigm of Western-inspired development and concomitant secularization, as well as the power of its custodians.

A combination of social and economic ills and external reverses were responsible for Islam's social and political revival. Internally, developmentalist projects and ideologies had failed to deliver on their promises, at least not adequately and not for a large enough number of people. In particular, most Muslim countries had failed to absorb all the newly educated population into full employment in either government or in private sector. Meanwhile, the skewed pattern of modernization had created a deep cultural divide within Muslim societies without any precedent. On one side were the more or less Westernized elites and, on the other, the uneducated masses as well as the newly educated but culturally adrift classes. This cultural rift had far-reaching implications for societal relations and in the competition for power and privilege among different segments of society. Because in all societies there is a close connection between the dominant cultural-ideological paradigm and the equation of power and privilege, these cultural differences became inextricably linked to issues of power—who wields it and who benefits from it.

Different versions of developmentalist ideologies served as justification for the existing power structures. In response, increasingly novel formulations of Islam became the overarching paradigm for those seeking to change the balance of power within Muslim societies and the social, economic, and political structures underpinning it. This is not to suggest that religious and moral issues did not play important roles in this context. They did. It is merely to emphasize that the element of power and control over its levers was also major, even if at times unconscious motivation in spearheading the process of Islamic revival.[46]

Externally, political and military reverses suffered by Muslims, notably Jerusalem's fall to Israel in the 1967 Arab-Israeli war, also contributed. These reverses discredited Muslim, especially Arab, regimes and their ideologies and created greater receptivity on the part of Muslims to new ideological frameworks based on Islam. Thus Islam's emergence as the dominant sociopolitical and cultural paradigm in Muslim countries has come about as a reaction to modernization and its disruptive effects on the part of those who either did not adequately benefit, or even suffered, from it. At the same time, this phenomenon has also been a product of the encounter with modernity and the process of modernization, as reflected in the works of key Muslim thinkers and activists of the 1960s and 1970s.

These thinkers considered Islam of the Prophet's time and the society based upon it (madinat al-nabi) as the only viable models for an alternative to existing ideologies and sociopolitical systems. Yet they were deeply influenced by modern ideologies and methodologies and were themselves the product of secular educational systems. Even those who were clerics were familiar with modern sciences and ideas.

Ali Shariati, the influential Iranian Islamic thinker, had a secular education and was a product of the Pahlavi modernization project. He benefited from the free state-run university system and went to study in France at government expense. None of these opportunities would have existed without the developmentalist strategy of the Pahlavi years. Indeed, Shariati's knowledge of Islamic sciences was limited and made him vulnerable to attacks by clerics, notably the reformist cleric Ayatullah Murtaza Mutahari, who doubted Shariati's commitment to Islam and resented his attacks on official clergy. Moreover, Shariati's interpretation of Islam and his Islamic blueprint, "Monotheistic System and Monotheistic Worldview,"[47] were deeply influenced by Marxist and neo-Marxist ideas even though he criticized Marxism.[48]

Even Ayatullah Mutahari, who had had a classical Islamic education, was somewhat familiar with Western philosophies and thinking, and he often quoted Western sources in support of his ideas.[49] This, too, was the result of modernization and the effort of the hawse (religious seminaries) to reform and equip themselves with modern sciences, in order to be able to compete more effectively with the new secular educational system, and to provide an alternative to the developmentalist and secularist discourse promoted by the government.

In Egypt, Sayyid Qutb was enrolled at a very young age in a secular rather than

Qur'anic school. In 1948 he was sent by the Egyptian government to the United States for specialized education. This early secular education and his firsthand experience of the West did not dilute his faith in and commitment to Islam. Rather, he became disillusioned with the West and embraced Islam with even greater fervor. Nevertheless, these early experiences helped to shape his views, his manner of interpreting Islamic concepts, and his entire philosophy.[50]

It is notable that both Shariati's definitions of such Islamic terms as *mustazafin* (the downtrodden) and *istikbar* (arrogance) and Qutb's definition of *jahiliyya* (the time of darkness and disbelief) are totally novel and indeed modern renditions. In fact, as noted by an Iranian author within the Iranian context, most ideas referred to as traditional or as a return to the source "are outcomes of modernity."[51]

Moreover, both Qutb and Shariati were reacting to different internal and external realities that were also largely the outcome of modernization. Earlier Muslim thinkers and reformers had been mainly concerned about the decline of Muslim societies, which they explained in terms of Islam's loss of its earlier scientific and rationalist spirit and its consequence, namely the colonial penetration of Muslim countries by European powers. Their principal goal was to arrest this decline and to end foreign domination. Their solution was that the Muslims should rediscover their scientific past and acquire the scientific and technological know-how necessary to free themselves from the colonial yoke.

At the time when Qutb and Shariati were writing, direct colonial rule was no longer an issue, because by then most Muslim countries had acquired their independence or were on the verge of doing so. Rather, they were more preoccupied with the continued indirect influence of foreign powers on the ruling elites of Muslim countries.

The nineteenth-century reformers had been concerned that the lack of acquaintance with Western science and technology was making it impossible for Muslims to free themselves from the bondage of colonialism. By the early 1960s, however, key Muslim countries had undergone several decades of educational, scientific, and economic development and significant social and cultural changes, notably the emergence of a new secularized class and a good deal of desacralization of the social and political spheres. Consequently, Muslim intellectuals of this period were less concerned about acquiring those Western ideas that were behind the West's superior knowledge and power and more concerned about addressing the erosion of their indigenous cultures and values under the influence of foreign ideas and cultures.

The Iranian intellectual Jalal al-Ahmad was one of the earliest and most effective articulators of this concern over the effects of foreign ideas on indigenous cultures. He was also highly critical of the imitative models of development, which in his view have perpetuated the economic and political dependence of the developing world, including Muslim countries, on the great powers, despite the legal end of colonialism.[52]

In short, the main preoccupation of this new generation of Muslim intellectuals was how to offer a different model of social and economic development based on indigenous cultures and value systems.[53] Because Islam is an important, and in many cases the most important component of Muslims' indigenous cultures, it is not surprising that the 1960s and 1970s witnessed the emergence of a variety of Islam-based ideas and frameworks for the organization of society and polity.

Unlike their nineteenth-century predecessors, Muslim intellectuals of the 1960s and 1970s focused on the "Islamization of knowledge" instead of demonstrating that Islam and science are compatible and urging Muslims to rediscover their rationalist and scientific traditions.[54] They tried to show that Islam contains all that is needed to meet the requirements of Muslims in the modern world while protecting them against the dehumanizing aspects of modernization.

These intellectual trends culminated in the emergence of groups and movements dedicated to the realization of the Islamic alternative. Such groups shared certain traits in common, most notably commitment to Islam as the foundation of their alternative model of societal organization. But they also reflected the peculiarities of their respective societies and countries and their unique historical experiences.

Muhammad Iqbal Lahori (1877–1938), the great Muslim poet and philosopher, forms a bridge between the nineteenth-century reformers and those of the 1960s and 1970s in that, while recognizing the achievements of the West, he warned against excessive infatuation with it and advocated the building of a socioeconomic and political system on the basis of a reconstructed Islamic thought. In sum, he offered a putative model of indigenous Islamic modernity. Because of this and other aspects of his thought, including his emphasis on activity versus a spirit of passivity as well as on social justice, Iqbal even today serves as inspiration to many reformist thinkers, especially in Iran and South Asia.

Contemporary Muslim Reformist Movements: Genesis and Ideas

By the late 1980s, a new breed of Islamic intellectuals emerged, advocating a different type of reformist Islam. This new notion of reform differed both from earlier understandings of the term and from that characteristic of the Islam-based ideologies of the 1960s and 1970s. This new type of reformism, which has its roots in the reformist movements of the nineteenth century, is characterized by a rationalist, historical, and contextual approach to the interpretation of Islamic sources, in order to make them more relevant to Muslims' needs in today's world and more compatible with new ethical standards of human rights. It aims to reconcile reason and spirituality, religion and freedom, and ultimately to develop a kind of nativized modernity anchored in Muslims' spiritual heritage while embracing all the emancipatory and liberating aspirations of Western modernity. It also embraces openness to other cultures and civilizations and aspires to a world where the logic of dialogue and tolerance rather than violence and dominance prevails.

Success and Disillusionment: The Case of Iran

Iran is the only country where the proponents of the Islamic alternative gained political power and established an Islamic state. However, Iran's Islamic experience has neither been a political or an economic success, and thus it has generated deep disillusionment with the entire Islamic project both in Iran and elsewhere in the Islamic world. In Iran, the poor record of the Islamic regime has generated the most intense, wide-ranging, and innovative debate within the country's intellectual and religious establishments. It has also led to the emergence of reformist thinkers both within the ranks of the clergy and among lay intellectuals well versed—to varying degrees—in Islamic sciences. Interestingly, nearly all of these reformist thinkers were engaged in the struggle against the Shah and held positions in post-revolutionary governments. Many of them are still actively involved in politics.

In addition to general disappointment with the economic and political performance of the Islamic government, two other factors have contributed to the development of reformist thinking in Iran.

First, as noted by the reformist thinker Mustafa Malekian, the experience of having to deal with external economic, social, and political realities has demonstrated the inadequacies of the regime's Islamic ideology in addressing such issues. This realization of the limits of their Islam-based ideology has forced them to find new interpretations for Islamic legal, economic, and other concepts more suited to dealing with external realities and problems.[55]

Second, the increased familiarity of religious students and scholars with modern disciplines and foreign languages, resulting from dramatic changes in the curricula of religious seminaries carried out over the years, has led to the emergence of a significant number of reform-minded clerics. Some of these clerics have been key figures within the reformist movement.

Failure and Its Consequences: Turkey and the Arab World

Unlike in Iran, in Turkey and in the Arab world it has been failure to gain power or to hold on to it that has spearheaded reformist thinking. A good example of this phenomenon is the transformation of Turkey's Islamic party following the ouster of the Erbekan government by the Turkish military in 1997 and the change in the ideological orientation of some of its key leaders, notably Recep Teyyip Erdogan.[56] This change in orientation and ideology propelled the newly formed Justice and Development Party (Adalet ve Kalkinma, known as the AK Party) to electoral success. Erdogan, the party's leader, became prime minister in 2003, and in 2007 a key member, Abdullah Gul, was elected to the presidency by the Turkish parliament.

Islamist movements in the Arab world did not make this kind of successful transition into mainstream politics and movement toward fundamental reform. This inability to reform was largely the result of the politically closed nature of Arab governments and the lack of a long democratic tradition such as Turkey's (albeit under the watchful eye of the military). In Algeria, the Islamists' bid for power through elections in 1991–92 was thwarted by the military, an act that plunged the country into a bloody and lengthy civil war, the effects of which are still felt. In Tunisia, the Islamist party al-Nahda was banned after doing well in the parliamentary elections of 1989, and its leader, Rashid Ghanoushi, was forced to go into exile in Britain.

The failure of these efforts to gain power, and in some cases the experience of exile, have contributed to the moderation of the Islamists' views and even to the embrace of a reformist discourse to varying degrees. Ghanoushi, whose views were never as radical as those of some members of the Algerian Islamic Salvation Front (FIS), has evolved even more in a reformist direction since his exile in Britain. After living in exile in Europe, some ex-members of the Algerian Islamic Armed Group (GIA) have greatly moderated their views upon their return to Algeria.[57] In Morocco, following a degree of political opening under Muhammad VI, the Justice and Development Party has moderated its Islamist views in order to compete for power. The party is openly modeling itself after the Turkish party of the same name.[58]

In Egypt, the main Islamist movement, the Muslim Brotherhood, remains banned from politics, although its members have been able to stand for election as independent candidates. This limited access to politics has encouraged a segment of the Brotherhood's membership to form a new party called al-Wasat (the Center party), with the goal of expanding their appeal beyond the brotherhood's loyalists by embracing a reformist agenda.[59] Some Egyptian militants have also undergone a change of heart after their acts of violence failed to produce political change. They are now espousing reformist discourse.

The Rise of Extremism and the Changing International System

The rise of extremist Islamist movements, notably the jihadists, and the changing international context following the collapse of the Soviet Union, have also contributed to the emergence of reformist discourse. The activities of the extremists, especially extensive and daring terrorist attacks such as that in the United States on September 11, 2001, in Spain in March 2004, and in London in July 2005, have subjected at least two Muslim countries—Afghanistan and Iraq—to retaliatory and preemptive military attacks led by the United States. They have generated strong anti-Muslim feelings in the West and in the non-Muslim countries of Asia and have sullied Islam's image.[60]

These developments have heightened awareness among Muslims that unless reformist voices in the Muslim world are able to spread their message both among the masses and internationally, extremist views may dominate debate and gain more influence, thereby effectively undermining Muslims' best interests. These concerns have helped to revitalize reformist forces, although not sufficiently, in all Muslim countries.

The Soviet Union's collapse and the end of the bipolar international system weakened the position of Muslim countries. For many Muslims, the new situation also rendered less relevant some varieties of the Islamic model as an alternative to both Western and socialist systems. The Soviet Union's ideological defeat made an impression on Muslim intellectuals who in the past had been greatly influenced by socialist thinking. Here, too, Iran provides the best example of how this transformation has taken place. Today in Iran, most reformist Muslim thinkers, including some from the ranks of the clerics, who in the past had been sympathetic to socialist ideas, have embraced the democratic model.[61] Thus, an important part of reformists' intellectual efforts have been devoted to finding ways of reconciling Islam and the new dominant discourse of democracy.[62]

The thesis of the clash of civilizations, with its implied assumption of the inevitability of a violent encounter between the West and all or parts of the Muslim world, has also acted as an impetus to check the growth of extremist ideas and to seek alternatives. The first of these ideas was that of the dialogue of civilizations advanced by the reformist ex-president of Iran, Muhammad Khatami. More recently, the Spanish and Turkish prime ministers have advanced the idea of an alliance of civilizations.

Islamic Reformist Thinking: Early Debates and Themes

Muslim reformist thinkers are often accused by their detractors of being innovators and under the influence of foreign ideas and therefore lacking in Islamic legitimacy. In reality, however, reformist Muslims also look to early Islam and its traditions to validate their views and positions. What separates current reformists from those who define reform as return to a literalist and restrictive interpretation of Islam, lies in their choice of various traditions of Islam's early history and its golden age and in their assessment of those traditions.

Indeed, many of the debates currently under way within reformist and traditionalist/literalist circles concerning issues such as the relative role of reason and context on the one hand, and tradition on the other hand, in the interpretation of Islamic scriptural and legal sources have precursors in the debates that characterized the early periods of the development of Islamic legal, theological, and philosophical systems. In those days, too, jurists and theologians hotly argued about the role and scope of reason in interpreting Islamic sources, and about how to balance the requirements of time and place and the safeguarding of Islam's fundamental and eternal essence. Therefore, it is necessary to review the arguments that took place during the early period of the formation of different schools of Islamic thought, along with the ebb and flow of their fortunes. This exercise will help place the current debate into the proper historical context, and contribute to an assessment of the prospects of today's reformist discourse in different Muslim countries.

Reason versus Tradition

After the death of the Prophet Muhammad, the Muslim community was faced with a conundrum: how to find answers to new legal and moral questions arising for Muslims and Muslim societies because of new developments and for which there was no clear guidance either in the Qur'an or in the *sunna*. What sources should be used in the search for answers?

One early division that emerged among Muslim religious scholars as they struggled to cope with new conditions and issues was that between the Ahl al-Hadith and the Ahl al-Ra'y. The first group maintained that the *hadith,* meaning reports of the behavior of the Prophet and his closest associates (*sahaba*) in similar matters, transmitted through trustworthy narrators, should be the main source for answering new questions. The second group maintained that the opinion of learned scholars based on common sense and reason (*ra'y*), should be the main source.[63]

An early proponent of the latter approach was the founder of the Hanafi school of law, Numan Ibn Thabit, known as Abu Hanifa (699–767), and a representative of the first approach was the Sufyan al-Thawri.[64] Ahmad Ibn Hanbal (780–855), the founder of the Hanbali school, was not born at the time when this split between the Ahl al-Hadith and Ahl al-Ra'y occurred. Yet he later became the best known, most prestigious, and most ardent representative of the Hadith school.

Initially, there was some degree of interaction between the two camps. However, their divisions became solidified in the mid-eighth century, and in the following three centuries pitted the proponents of the two camps against one another. A particularly intense and violent episode in the history of rivalry between these two tendencies was that between the Mu'tazilis—the most rationalist group—and the followers of Ibn Hanbal.

At times, ruling caliphs became engaged in these disputes, now favoring one group and later another. Thus the Abbasid Caliph al-Mamoun lent his support to the Mu'tazilis. However, since his support was accompanied by the persecution of those Muslims who did not adhere to this school and ushered in the period known as *mihna* (ordeal or inquisition), it ultimately proved detrimental to the position of the rationalists, and finally led to the Mu'tazilis' demise and eventual disappearance.

However, the Mu'tazilis' ideas continued to exert influence on Islamic jurisprudence and theology, especially within Shi'ism. Aspects of their thinking inspired some of the nineteenth-century reformist thinkers, and their ideas continue to exert influence on current reformist thinkers. In Iran, those who espouse "religious rationalism" (*aqlaniat e dini*), are partially inspired by the Mu'tazilis.[65] In addition to its rationalist bent, the Mu'tazili perspective is attractive to many reformist thinkers because of the important role it assigns to justice, at a time when there is widespread preoccupation in Muslim societies with the question of justice in its various social, economic, and political dimensions.

The excesses of the period of *mihna*, together with the staunch resistance of Ahmad Ibn Hanbal in defense of tradition, made him a hero and a martyr in the eyes of the Mu'tazilis' detractors, who considered their ideas blasphemous. By contrast, support from caliph al-Mutasim, who succeeded Mamoun, helped to establish the dominance of the traditionalists.

Another major contribution to the consolidation of traditionalism as the dominant school in Sunni Islam was the work of Abul Hassan al-Asha'ri (c. 874–935), although he used reason more than Ibn Hanbal, perhaps because of his early association with the Mu'tazilis. The victory of the traditionalists meant that, while the mainstream Islam that evolved allocated a role for reason in finding answers to various questions faced by Muslim communities, it did so within strict limits and mostly in relation to secondary issues of jurisprudence (*fiqh*).

Another reason for the victory of the traditionalists was that the rationalists were accused of having been unduly influenced by Greek philosophies, thus deviating from the true Islam. In a similar vein, many of today's Muslim reformist thinkers are accused by their opponents of being unduly influenced by foreign philosophies. Moreover, the traditionalists' victory forced the more rationalist schools of Islamic law, such as the Hanafi school, to incorporate many of the views and positions of the traditionalists, in order to become acceptable to more conservative Muslims.[66]

This turn of events had significant and wide-ranging ramifications for the development of Islamic law, theology, philosophy, science, and in general for the overall intellectual development of the Muslim world. The most negative consequence of this turn of events was that as early as the tenth century it led to a long period of stagnation and atrophy in all of these areas. Additionally, it provided the traditionalists with the weapon of excommunication (*takfir*) against those who did not agree with their views. In the last few decades, a new breed of extreme traditionalists has resurrected the practice of *takfir* against their opponents.

Literalism versus Contextualism

This early split between rationalists and traditionalists also extended to theology (*kalam*). Ironically, traditionalists used rational arguments in their disputations with the rationalists and tried to demonstrate the falsity of the latter's positions by using their own methods. Beyond this, however, they disagreed on many fundamental issues, notably the nature of God's attributes and how references to these attributes should be interpreted—literally or allegorically—and the question of predestination versus free will.[67] But the most important of their disputes related to the issue of the createdness or preexistence of the Qur'an. Ultimately, the Mu'tazili position that the Qur'an was created was one of the main reasons for their defeat in their confrontation with the traditionalists.[68]

Clearly, each of these theories has implications for the evolution of Islamic thinking. To advance a different interpretation of the Qur'an in response to new needs and circumstances becomes much more difficult if the Qur'an is considered the eternal, uncreated, and immutable word of God. However, it is not necessary to go as far as the Mu'tazilis and challenge the uncreatedness of the Qur'an in order to be able to adapt Qur'anic injunctions to new conditions by the use of rationalist and contextualist methods. This approach is justified by making the point that some of the Qur'anic verses were revealed for dealing with a specific issue at a particular time. This is known as the *shu'un al-nuzul* or *asbab al-nuzul*, meaning the circumstances of the revelation of certain verses of the Qur'an. Accordingly, in

Muslim population of the European countries and the reformist discourse there is quite advanced.

The concluding chapter brings together insights gained from the regional studies and identifies the factors that have promoted the emergence and evolution of reformist discourse and those that so far have hindered its strengthening. Based on these insights, it offers ideas on the outlook for success or failure of the current wave of reformist discourse, and it highlights those internal and external factors that could help or hinder the progress and ultimate success of the latest reformist current in Islam.

The length of chapters varies depending on the number of countries covered, as is the case with chapters dealing with the Arab world, or on the richness and diversity of discourse and the number of thinkers to be covered, as is the case with Iran. The basic methodology is descriptive, analytical, and comparative. The descriptive method has been adopted in order to make available to broader audiences an impressive body of work that is not well known beyond academic circles and in some cases is little known even within those circles. For example, the chapter on Iran includes the works of thinkers and religious figures that are not well known in the West. The chapter on the Maghreb makes a special contribution by introducing thinkers who write in French or Arabic and whose works are not well known to English-speaking publics.

The analytical methodology is used in order to demonstrate how the historical, socioeconomic, and political experiences of different countries have shaped the character of their present reformist discourse, as exemplified in the works of the most prominent contemporary reformist thinkers in the Muslim world, in Europe and the United States, as well as in the works of some earlier reformists whose ideas are still influential. In support of the comparative purposes of the study, all authors address a number of basic questions regarding the methodology of reformist thinkers and activists in different countries and regions, and their positions on important issues, such as democracy, human rights, and women's and minority rights.

The overarching conceptual framework of the volume is the ongoing debate in the Muslim world regarding the definition of what constitutes modernity—is it a single phenomenon or can there be multiple modernities?—and the relationship sbetween tradition and modernity and between modernity and religion. This choice, in addition to the continued relevance of the paradigm of modernity and tradition in the Islamic world, reflects the fact that the reformist discourse in its various shades is an effort to answer these questions and to provide a formula that could enable Muslim societies to find ways of mediating between the requirements and necessity of accommodating modernity and the pull of traditional, religious, and authenticist impulses.

The editor has tried to ensure that the volume is written in a clear and jargon-free style, in order to make it accessible and useful not only to academics and students but also to other interested persons, including journalists and those involved in policy making.

A Note on Spelling and Transliteration

Efforts have been made to achieve consistency in the spelling of names and terms. There are two exceptions to this rule: the first regards the names of Maghrebi authors and thinkers, which have been retained in their French spelling because the authors themselves write their names in this fashion; the second regards any quotations in which the author has used different spelling.

Throughout the text standard Arabic transliteration has been used for Arabic names and Islamic legal terms. Persian names and terms have to the extent possible been transliterated in the same fashion. The names of world leaders and political figures have been rendered according to the standard spelling of their names.

Notes

1. On the definition of these terms and their evolution, see John Voll, "Renewal and Reform in Islamic History: *Tajdid and Islah,*" in John L. Esposito, ed., *Voices of Resurgent Islam* (Oxford: Oxford University Press, 1983), pp. 32–47.

2. For example, many Sunnis saw the ideas of Abd ul Wahhab as innovation, whereas for others he is an archetypal renewer of the faith in the sense of return to the essentials of Islam and elimination of extraneous accretions.

3. The Shi'a also include the practices and sayings of the imams as sources of law.

4. The reformist movement of Jadidism in Russia and Central Asia was based on this new conception of *tajdid*. See Adeeb Khalid, *The Politics of Muslim Cultural Reform: Jadidism in Central Asia* (Berkeley, CA:: University of California Press, 1998).

5. The underlying belief of the first type of reformers and renewers is that the Qur'an and the *sunna* of the Prophet provide the normative standards for Muslims' individual and collective lives for all times, and that the community created by the Prophet of Islam is the perfect model of an Islamic society and polity. Thus, for these reformers the task, as put by John Voll, is one of "restoration and renewal" of the faith and efforts to approximate under new conditions the ideal model of society embodied in the Muslim community of the Prophet's time. The second perspective is reflected in the following item on the Web site of the Fars News Agency: "Javdanagi e Islam beh in ast ke pasokhguy e porseshhaye zamane bashad" (Islam's Eternality Depends on Its Ability to Provide Answers to Contemporary Problems) available at: http://www.farsnews.com/newstext.php?nn=8603130452.

6. Ibn Taymiyya believed that the Mongols had remained faithful to their tribal laws, the Yassa. See Nazih N. Ayubi, *Political Islam: Religion and Politics in the Arab World* (New York: Routledge, 1991), p. 127. This perception of the Mongols reflects a deep-rooted and still-persistent belief among Arab thinkers and ordinary people alike that the Muslim world's problems are the result of the contamination of the pure Islam of Arabia with Persian, Turkish, and other non-Arab traditions. Many non-Arab Muslims, including some reformist thinkers, consider the pre-Islamic practices of Arabia to be among the corrupting influences on Islam. For example, Rashid Rida blames the corrupting effect of mysticism on Islam on the influence of secret Zoroastrians who wanted to weaken Islam from within. Material on the corrupting influence of Sassanian culture on Islam is extensive, and even some Iranian Muslims subscribe to this thesis. See Albert Hourani, *Arabic Thought in the Liberal Age* (Cambridge: Cambridge University Press, 1962), p. 232.

7. Hamid Algar, *Wahhabism: A Critical Essay* (New York: Islamic Publications International, 2002), and Jalal Abualrub, *Biography and Mission of Muhammad Ibn Abdul Wahhab* (Orlando, FL: Medina Publishers and Distributors, 2003).

8. Sayyid Qutb, *Islam: The True Religion,* trans. Ravi Ahmad Fidai (Karachi, Pakistan: International Islamic Publishers, 1981), pp. 25–26.

9. Sayyid Qutb *Milestones,* trans. Ahmad Zaki Hammad (Indianapolis, IN: American Trust Publications, 1993).

10. Murtaza Mutahari *Fundamentals of Islamic Thought: God, Man, and the Universe,* trans. R. Campbell (Berkeley, CA: Mizan Press, 1985), pp. 36–46.

11. Ali Shariati, *On the Sociology of Islam,* trans. Hamid Algar (Berkeley, CA: Mizan Press, 1979).

12. Ali Shariati, *Marxism and Other Fallacies: An Islamic Critique* (Berkeley, CA: Mizan Press, 1980), p. 32.

13. Quoted in Laleh Bakhtiar, trans., *Shariati on Shariati and the Muslim Woman* (Chicago, IL: ABC Group International, Inc., 1996), p. xxxviii.

14. In the third world parlance of the 1960s and 1970s this new state was referred to as neocolonialism.

15. Jalal al-Ahmad, *Gharbzadeghi.* The work was published clandestinely in 1962. There have been several English translations: *Westoxication,* (Islamic Students' Association of Europe and the U.S. and Canada, 1979); *Plagued by the West* (Delmor, NY: Center for Iranian Studies, Columbia University, 1982); *Occidentosis: A Plague from the West* (Berkeley, CA: Mizan Press, 1983); and *Westruckness* (Costa Mesa, CA: Mazda, 1997).

16. Muhsen Kadivar, *From Historical Islam to Spiritual Islam,* available at http://www. Kadivar.com/Htm/Farsi/Papers/papers007.htm.

17. For a brief discussion of the origins and evolution of Slavophilism and bibliographic sources, see Shireen T. Hunter, *Islam in Russia: The Politics of Identity and Security* (Armonk, NY: M.E. Sharpe, 2004), pp. 166–67.

18. Timothy McDaniel, "Responses to Modernization," in *Modernization, Democracy, and Islam,* Shireen T. Hunter and Huma Malik, eds., (Westport, CT: Praeger, 2005), pp. 38–42.

19. Ibid., p. 42.

20. Ibid., p. 43.

21. The critics of modernity have seen in the development of fascism and totalitarian socialism the dark, totalizing, and dominating side of modernity as a master narrative with universalist claims.

22. This idealized past does not need to be necessarily Islamic. Various nationalist movements in Iran, Egypt, and post-Ottoman Turkey built ideologies on the basis of an idealized view of their pre-Islamic past.

23. McDaniel, "Responses to Modernization," p. 41.

24. Ibid., p. 42.

25. Ibid., p. 43.

26. Ibid.

27. On the impact of timing on the nature of modernization, see Alexander Gerschenkron, *Economic Backwardness in Historical Perspective* (New York: Praeger, 1965).

28. For examples, see David Held, *Introduction to Critical Theory* (Berkeley, CA: University of California Press, 1980); also Stephen Crook, *Modernist Radicalism and Its Aftermath: Foundationalism and Anti-Foundationalism in Radical Social Theory* (London and New York: Routledge, 1991).

29. Jürgen Habermas, *The Philosophical Discourse of Modernity* (Cambridge: MIT Press, 1991).

30. Schmuel N. Eisenstadt, ed., *Patterns of Modernity,* Vol. 2, *Beyond the West* (New York: New York University Press, 1987); idem, "The Reconstruction of Religious Arenas in the Framework of 'Multiple Modernities,'" *Millennium Journal of International Studies,* vol. 29, no. 3, 2000.

31. Ottoman reforms were known as *Tanzimat.*

32. Hamid Algar, *Mirza Malkum Khan: A Study in the History of Iranian Modernism* (Berkeley, CA: University of California Press, 1969), p. 127.

33. Hourani, *Arabic Thought in the Liberal Age,* p. 68.

34. On the anti-imperialist dimensions of Afghani's ideas and personality, see Nikkie R. Keddie, *Sayyid Jaml ad-Din "al Afghani": A Political Biography* (Berkeley, CA: University of California Press, 1972).

35. Today the Iranian birth of Afghani is accepted even by the Arabs. See ibid.

36. Ibid., see also Elie Kedourie, *Afghani and Abduh: An Essay on Religious Disbelief and Political Activism in Modern Islam* (London: Frank Cass, 1966).

37. Keddie, *Sayyid Jamal ad-Din "al Afghani,"* pp. 103–7.

38. Alexandre Bennigsen and Chantal Lemercier-Quelquejay, *Islam in the Soviet Union* (New York: Praeger, 1967, p. 35).

39. For example, according to Albert Hourani, Abduh was introduced to Avicenna by Afghani.

40. Hourani, *Arabic Thought in the Liberal Age,* p. 139.

41. Ibid.

42. Walter Z. Laqueur, ed., *The Middle East in Transition* (New York: Praeger, 1958).

43. Daniel Lerner, *The Passing of Traditional Society: Modernizing the Middle East* (Glencoe, IL.: Free Press, 1958).

44. Peter L. Berger, ed., *The Desecularization of the World* (Washington, DC: Ethics and Public Policy Center, 1999), p. 2.

45. Pippa Norris and Ronald Inglehart, *Sacred and Secular: Religion and Politics Worldwide* (New York: Cambridge University Press, 2004), p. 229.

46. See, among others, Shireen T. Hunter, ed., *The Politics of Islamic Revivalism: Diversity and Unity* (Bloomington, IN: Indiana University Press, 1988).

47. *Nizam e tawhidi va jahanbini e tawhidi* (Monotheistic System and Monotheistic Worldview). Some authors have translated *tawhid* in this context as "unicity." As will be explained in chapter 1, in Shariati's parlance a *tawhidi* system is one in which there are no social, economic, or cultural cleavages and contradictions.

48. Ali Shariati, *Marxism and Other Fallacies: An Islamic Critique* (Berkeley, CA: Mizan Press, 1980).

49. For examples, see Mutahari, *Fundamentals of Islamic Thought.*

50. Unlike their nineteenth- and early twentieth-century counterparts, some of these Muslims experienced less than ideal aspects of life in Europe and the United States. Rashid Ghanoushi, the Tunisian Islamist leader, for example, has talked of his experience in France's slums.

51. Cyrus Ali Nejad, "Tajadod va tajad khahi dar iran: Goft e ghouyé ba Dr. Mashallah Ajoudani" (Modernity in Iran: A Conversation with Dr. Mashallah Ajoudani), available at http://www.bbc.co.uk/persian/arts/story/2005/05/05013_pm-cy-ajoudani.shtml.

52. Al-Ahmad's most famous work in this area is *Gharbzadeghi,* or "Westoxication." See note 15.

53. For a survey of changing Muslim perceptions of the West, see John Voll, "Islamic Renewal and the 'Failure of the West,'" in Prasenjit Duara, ed., *Decolonization: Perspectives from Now and Then* (London & New York: Routledge, 2004), pp. 199–217.

54. Ismail al-Faruqi, a Palestinian political scientist and activist who lived and worked in the United States, was the originator of the concept of Islamization of science.

55. Mustafa Malekian, *Mushtaqi va mahjuri, goft e ghouhaie dar bareh farhang va seyasat* (Longing and Separation: A Talk About Politics and Culture), 2d ed. (Tehran: Nashr e Neghah e Muaser, 1386 [2007]).

56. In the late 1990s Erdogan, then mayor of Istanbul, was sent to prison for reciting a

poem by the Turkish nationalist Zia Gokalp that included lines such as "Mosques are our barracks." See "Askar Duasi" (Soldier's Prayer) in Zia Gokalp, *Kulliyati-i*, ed. F. A. Tansel (Istanbul, 1989).

57. For details see the chapter on the Maghreb.

58. See the chapter on the Maghreb.

59. See the chapter on the Arab East.

60. Anti-Muslim feelings were strong in Russia even before these events, because of the Chechen war and a series of terrorist acts against Russians.

61. See the chapter on Iran.

62. Whether the experience of the Iraq war, and the recent retreat of the West from promoting democracy in the Muslim world, coupled with new repressive measures by some Muslim countries, will erode the legitimacy and relevance of the "democracy" paradigm is yet to be seen.

63. Christopher Melchert, *The Formation of the Sunni Schools of Law, 9th–10th Centuries C.E.* (Leiden: Brill, 1996), p. 1.

64. Abu Hanifa was born in Kufa, Iraq, to Persian parents in 699. He was imprisoned by the Abbassid caliph al-Mansur and died in prison in 765.

65. For example, the Iranian reformist thinker Hassan Yussefi Eshkevari is one who sees in Mu'tazili thinking a historical precedent for religious rationalism. See Cyrus Ali Nejad's interview with him, "Tajadod khahi va roshanfekran e dini: Goft e ghouye ba Hassan Yussefi Eshkevari" (Modernism and Religious Intellectuals: A Conversation with Hassan Yussefi Eshkevari, available at http://www.bbc.co.uk/persian/arts/story/2005/08/050812_pm-cy-eshkevari.html. Many reformist thinkers in Indonesia, notably Harun Nasution, and those gathered within the organization known as Jarangan Islam (Liberal Islam), have also been inspired by the Mu'tazilis.

66. On the evolution of the Hanafi school under the influence of the traditionalists, see Melchert, *The Formation of Sunni Schools of Law*, pp. 32–38.

67. For example, the literalists, also called anthropomorphists, interpreted references to God's hands, feet, throne, and so forth in the Qur'an as denoting physical attributes. By contrast, the rationalists, notably the Mu'tazilis, interpreted these terms allegorically. For example, they maintained that references to God's throne meant his majesty, and his hand, his power, and so forth. For details, see Harry Austryn Wolfson, *The Philosophy of the Kalam* (Cambridge, MA: Harvard University Press, 1976), pp. 112–43.

68. With the exception of the Hanbalis, who maintained that not only the Qur'an itself is uncreated, but that its recitation and the paper on which it is written are also uncreated, other schools adopted an intermediary position, for example, that the Qur'an is uncreated but its recitation is created. Wolfson, *The Philosophy of the Kalam*, pp. 263–74.

1

Islamic Reformist Discourse in Iran

Proponents and Prospects

Shireen T. Hunter

Over the last two decades, a widespread and sophisticated reformist Islamic discourse has emerged in Iran. Those involved in this discourse include both lay intellectuals familiar with Islamic sciences and clerical figures of varying ranks, including senior ayatullahs. This vibrant discourse has produced a vast body of literature on issues ranging from the need to rethink the methodology of examining and interpreting Islamic sources to Islam's relationship with modernity, democracy, human rights and women's rights, religious pluralism, and tolerance.

Many of today's most prominent lay and clerical reformist figures were involved in the struggle against the Shah's regime. After the establishment of the Islamic Republic, many of them occupied government positions of varying degrees of importance, including the office of the presidency. Some are still active in the political arena, and in the last few years some of them, notably Ayatullah Mehdi Karrubi, have created political parties and participated in electoral politics. Others, either by choice or because of various government-imposed restrictions, have abandoned political activity and limited their contribution to the ongoing debate to writing books and articles and to commentary.

The ultimate goal of Islamic reformist thinkers and activists is the fundamental transformation of the Iranian society, polity, and political culture. They want to make Iran a law-based state within which the following principles prevail: individual freedoms and the rights of various religious and other minorities are respected; competition for political power is open and fair; there are no restrictions on free debate and the press; and popular will is the basis of political legitimacy. They oppose the cult of personality and hero-worship, and favor a system of reward based on merit and service to the common good rather than closeness to centers of power and influence.

In view of the ambitious agenda of Iranian reformists, their success or failure in gaining wide popular acceptance for their views, along with their ability to acquire and retain political power that would enable them to realize their program, will largely determine the trajectory of Iran's future social, cultural, and political evolution.

The prevalence of reformist interpretations of Islam over its more conservative readings would enable Iran successfully to mediate the requirements of modernity and preservation of the essence of its religious and cultural values and thus, as put by some reformist thinkers, to manage to "nativize modernity," notably one of its key manifestations, democracy.[1]

The success of Iran's reformist discourse and that of its proponents would deeply and positively influence the nature of its relations with the outside world, because Iranian reformists want to make Iran an active and constructive player in the international arena. The reformists believe that Iran has much to offer to ongoing debates regarding the myriad challenges facing the world, and that it could best accomplish this goal through dialogue and cooperation with others rather than through confrontation and self-righteous preaching. Iran's success in this endeavor might even have a positive impact on the spread of reformist thinking and practices in other Muslim countries.[2]

Yet despite the significance of the current debate for Iran's evolution and potentially that of other Muslim countries, beyond the narrow circle of specialists, the bulk of the work of Iranian reformist thinkers is unknown in the West and in the Islamic world. Certainly, there is no body of material that provides an accessible and relatively comprehensive review of the works of the most influential Iranian reformist thinkers.[3]

This chapter's principal goal, therefore, is to disseminate to a broader audience the ideas of Iran's key Muslim reformist thinkers. To that end, this chapter will: (1) examine the reformist literature and its authors; (2) analyze different Islamic reformist trends and identify their points of convergence and divergence; (3) draw some conclusions regarding the potential impact of this trend on Iran's social, cultural, and political evolution; and (4) assess the prospects for the success of Islamic reformism in Iran on the intellectual and political levels.

Despite its many new features, current reformist thinking in Iran is a product of the country's social, cultural, and religious evolution over the last century and a half in response to internal and external stimuli. The current discourse also builds on the works and ideas of earlier religious and lay reformist thinkers, as illustrated by the current reformists' frequent references to earlier works and thinkers. Therefore, analysis of the current thinkers' ideas and works will be preceded by a discussion of the history of Islamic reformism in Iran, including reasons for its emergence, its various strands, and its lack of success thus far. This discussion will provide a necessary backdrop against which to examine the current discourse. It will also indicate what factors are likely to help or hinder the success of this latest wave of Islamic reformism in Iran.

Tradition and Modernity: The Still-Relevant Paradigm

Hamid Dabashi has observed that the main philosophical and epistemological weakness in the work of Abdolkarim Soroush is his effort to reconcile two constructs—Islam and Western modernity—that no longer exist. Modernity has self-destructed, and globalization has rendered both Islam and the West irrelevant as cohesive geographical and civilizational constructs.[4] Irrespective of the validity of this opinion, the fact remains that in Iran the dominant intellectual paradigm is still modernity (*moderniteh*) and its relationship to tradition (*sunnat*). Even for those who criticize aspects of modernity, or even the entire project of modernity—often citing its Western critics—modernity remains a central paradigm. This reality is reflected in the large number of books and articles that have been written on this and related subjects in Iran in the last two decades.[5] In short, Iranian intellectualism, Islamic and otherwise, is still mainly preoccupied with the question of how to respond to the challenge of modernity. Islamic reformism is one of these responses. Therefore, the current manifestation of Islamic reformism is best understood within the historical context of Iran's encounter with modernity and Iranians' different responses to it.

Iranian Responses to Modernity: Historical Background

The conditions of Iran's encounter with modernity and its responses to the multidimensional challenges posed by this encounter have been similar to those of other non-European countries.

Iran's first timid efforts at modernization began in the early nineteenth century in response to its defeat in the Russo-Iranian wars (1804–1813 and 1824–1828).[6] These defeats opened the country to military, political, and economic penetration by Russia. Shortly thereafter, Britain and other European countries obtained trade and economic concessions and political privileges similar to those obtained by the Russians. Thus from the very beginning, Iran's reform efforts, like those of other non-European countries, were defensive in motivation and objectives.

In the following decades, too, the relative quickening of the pace of Iran's modernization was a response to the country's growing economic and political penetration by outside powers and their devastating economic and political consequences. Thus enlightened and reformist statesmen, notably Mirza Taqi Khan Amir Kabir and Mirza Hussein Khan Mushir al-Dawleh, who worked for reform in the face of internal opposition from the *ulema* and the court as well as foreign obstruction, were largely motivated by defensive impulses and the desire to retain Iran's independence.[7]

The modest steps undertaken to modernize Iran's educational system, coupled with the increasing number of Iranians who studied in Europe (notably France), acquainted a small but growing number of Iranians with the philosophical basis of modernity and ideas of the eighteenth-century Enlightenment, especially its French proponents. The emerging intellectuals of the nineteenth-century Iran were particularly influenced by the ideas of the French Revolution.[8]

Other strands of European political philosophies, notably socialism, also influenced the emerging class of Iranian intellectuals. Socialist ideas were transmitted to Iran by Caucasian intellectuals, who had become familiar with the ideology through contacts with Russia, and by the Iranian immigrant workers in the Caucasian oil fields in Baku.[9]

The introduction of various European sociopolitical ideas to the country gradually led to demands by Iranians for a representative form of government, an end to monarchical absolutism (*istibdad*), and establishment of the rule of law. Efforts to get the government to satisfy these demands culminated in the Constitutional Revolution of 1905–08, the adoption of the 1906 Constitution, based on the separation of the three branches of government and their independence, and the establishment of the first elected parliament.[10] However, Iranian constitutionalists faced formidable challenges from the clerical establishment, the conservative elements of the merchant community, and the religious masses who saw them and their agenda as threatening Islam's dominant position in Iranian society. It was the influence of these groups that forced the constititionalists to limit the extent of their political reforms, as reflected in the 1906 Constitution. This constitution was a compromise document combining elements of Western constitutionalism—in this case that of Belgium—with Islamic traditions. Article 2 of the Supplement to the Constitution best represents its compromise nature. The article provided for the presence of no less than five high-ranking clerics at the parliament in order to ensure that no legislation contradicted Islamic law.[11]

The 1906 Constitution is thus an example of the early type of synthesis between modernity and tradition, characterized by a haphazard mix of modern and traditional elements. It also demonstrates the existence in Iran of all three of the broad responses to modernity characteristic of non-Europeans, even in this early period.

Principal proponents in Iran of the first type of response—total embrace of modernity—included Mirza Agha Khan Kirmani and Fathali Akhundzadeh, later joined by Sayyid Hassan Taqizadeh. They advocated total modernization of Iran, which for them meant Europeanization of every sphere of thought and life.[12] This approach had a number of drawbacks. First, as the contemporary Iranian scholar Ali Mirsepassi has noted, it was purely imitative and made its proponents mere transmitters of European ideas and not producers of culture and ideas.[13] Second, the proponents of this approach lacked an adequate grasp of all the historical, social, and cultural developments that had given rise to modernity in Europe. Nor did they appreciate how much the manifestations of modernity, namely the process of modernization and its outcomes, varied in different European countries. They held a rather monolithic view of modernity, the factors behind its emergence, and the process of its unfolding in different European contexts. They tended to reduce the causes of European success in modernization to science and law, and concluded that if Iran could establish the rule of law and acquire scientific knowledge, then it, too, would become part of the modern world. Third, this approach underestimated the tenacity of historical and traditional patterns of behavior and their capacity to resist change, especially if it is imposed by force.

The rejectionist response was adopted by the clerical establishment, together with some members of the merchant community.[14] The rejectionists advocated a stricter observance of Islam and opposed the proposed political and other changes.[15] The most prominent representative of this position was Ayatullah Fazl allah Nouri, a staunch opponent of the Constitutional Revolution.

Most Iranian secular intellectuals and a few enlightened clerics adopted the third approach, namely that of synthesizing tradition and modernity. Secular intellectuals favored a more extensive introduction of principles and practices identified with modernity. The enlightened clerics, did accept the need for some changes, but they insisted on maintaining and applying Islamic principles, laws, and morality.

Some of those who opted for synthesis did so because they believed it was the best approach and most likely to succeed. Others, notably Mirza Malkum Khan, did so for a practical reason: they realized that, because of the religiosity of the masses, any type of modernization seen as contrary to Islam would fail. In his communication with the English poet and traveler Wilfred Blunt, Malkum admitted that, in order to make his ideas acceptable to the masses, he was "determined to clothe [his] material reformation in a garb which [his] people would understand, the garb of religion."[16]

Accordingly, the proponents of synthesis tried to demonstrate Islam's compatibility with modernization and modernity, which they defined as reliance on reason and rational thinking, but without the anti-religion dimensions of Western, especially French, secularism. The most prominent representative of this trend was Sayyid Jamal al-din Afghani, who argued that those "who forbid science and knowledge in the belief that they are safeguarding Islam" are Islam's true enemies.[17]

Some enlightened clerics, such as ayatullahs Sadiq Tabatabai, Seyyed Abdullah Behbahani, Muhammad Hussein Naini, and Akhund Mulla Kazem Khorasani, all of whom supported the constitutionalist movement, subscribed to aspects of this approach, especially in regard to governance.[18] They all tried to show that the fundamental principles of constitutionalism were compatible with Shi'a Islam.[19] However, none of them approached the issue of reconciling Islam and modernity, including democracy, in a systematic fashion, largely because they were not familiar with the ideas and philosophies that had given rise to modernity.

The Pahlavi Era: Modernization Without Modernity

The founding of the Pahlavi dynasty in 1925 was a landmark event in Iran's modern history. It heralded the end of the period of efforts at synthesis between the imperatives of modernization and the demands of tradition, whether out of conviction or for the sake of expediency, and it ushered in a period of conscious embrace of modernization, interpreted as Europeanization. However, neither the Pahlavi kings nor the elites associated with them had accepted and internalized the philosophy of modernity based on individual freedom and subjectivity. Rather, the Pahlavi project of modernization led to what Timothy McDaniel has called a "regimentizing modernization instead of a liberating modernity."[20]

The Pahlavis' modernization project, especially from the mid-1960s until the collapse of the dynasty in 1979 as a result of the Islamic Revolution, fundamentally altered Iranian society. It did so by spreading modern education, expanding communication networks, increasing urbanization and industrialization, and encouraging the growth of an entrepreneurial as opposed to a merchant class. During this period, both the spontaneous rise of Iranian nationalism and the propagation of a nationalist discourse by the government seemed to support the conclusion that Iranian nationalism could be a plausible alternative to Shi'a Islam as the basis of collective identity and political legitimacy.

Taken together, these developments altered the balance of power and influence between traditional centers of power, notably the clergy and the merchant community, and the new bureaucratic and economic elites that had emerged as a result of Pahlavi modernization. Interestingly, many members of the new elites came from traditional backgrounds and even from economically disadvantaged classes that had benefited from the opportunities for upward mobility provided by the Pahlavis' reforms.

These changes, meanwhile, deepened the cultural divide in Iran between the modernizing elites and two groups: (1) those whose social and economic positions had deteriorated as a result of modernization, such as the traditionally powerful clergy and elements of merchant community and other religious classes, and (2) those who had not benefited from the fruits of modernization such as the largely religious rural and urban poor. Thus, the cultural debate between the traditionalists and the modernizers became inextricably linked to questions of identity, power, and privilege.

From its very beginning, the Pahlavi modernization project was challenged by Islamic and leftist forces. The left, which had gained in influence partly because of economic and social changes produced by the Pahlavis' policies, notably the emergence of industrial workers and a larger intelligentsia, offered its own project of modernization without modernity, inspired by the Soviet model. For their part, Islamically oriented segments of society whose position had eroded first led a defensive struggle against the Pahlavis' project and later offered their own, Islam-based models of modernization without modernity.

Many factors contributed to the failure of the Pahlavi project, notably the difficulties inherent in any rapid process of modernization in an age of rising expectations. Iran's particular geopolitical conditions as an arena of first Russo-British and later Soviet-American rivalry did not help this process. However, a main cause of the failure of Pahlavi project was its lack of attention to social and political institution building and to developing popular support for its reform projects.[21]

Islamic Forces Under the Pahlavis

Islamic forces, of which the Shi'a *ulema* were the highest representatives, responded to the Pahlavis' modernization project in the following ways:

1. Resistance to its secularizing dimensions;
2. Periodic accommodation in the face of more serious challenges, such as foreign occupation and communism (1940s, 1950s);
3. Efforts to reform and renew Islam (1950s and 1960s); and
4. Active and, at times, violent opposition, culminating in the Islamic Revolution of 1979.

Resistance took various forms, including opposing significant changes in family law based on Islamic law; opposing the abolition of the veil and the granting of voting rights to women; and opposing land reform and efforts to give pre-Islamic Iranian culture a privileged position over that of Islam. Efforts directed at Islam's reform and renewal began as early as the 1940s under the Grand Ayatullah Sayyid Hussein Boroujerdi. They included reforming the educational system of religious seminaries; encouraging greater familiarity with modern sciences and foreign languages among the clergy and seminary students; sending clerics abroad; expanding contacts with other Islamic centers, notably al-Azhar in Cairo; working for reconciliation between the Shi'as and the Sunnis; and establishing Islamic centers in Europe.[22] More important, a number of clerics attended secular schools and universities, particularly in disciplines such as philosophy and theology (*daneshkedeh-e m'aqul va manqul*) at Tehran University. Ayatullah Muhammad Behesti, one of the key figures in the Islamic Revolution, had obtained a doctorate in philosophy from the Tehran University. Ayatullah Ali Akbar Khamenei, the current Supreme Leader, reportedly had attended secular primary and high school as well as religious school.[23]

The result of the efforts of the religious leadership, coupled with the broader educational developments in the country, was the emergence of a new breed of clerics familiar with non-religious subjects and Western ideas. Later, this trend was strengthened by the establishment of Islamically oriented private schools, known as "Alavi," plus the creation of centers for the propagation of Islam and publishing houses dedicated to printing Islamic materials.[24]

However, during this period there were other Islam-based intellectual trends and activities that did not involve the clergy. Many religious-minded lay activists and intellectuals played a significant role in establishment of Islamic centers and publications. The first of these centers was the Islamic Center (Kanoon e-Islam), founded in 1940. The center organized a series of lectures and published a magazine called *Student* (Danesh amouz). Some sources attribute the founding of the center to Mehdi Bazargan, an engineer educated in France and one of the most important contemporary Muslim intellectuals and reformists.[25] Other sources attribute the founding of the center to Ayatullah Mahmud Taleqani, a reform-minded and left-leaning cleric.[26] Since Bazargan and Taleqani were close friends, it is probable that both contributed to the center's establishment. Another center was that of the Society for the Propagation of Islamic Teachings (Anjoman-e-Tabliqat-e-Islami), founded by Dr. Mahmud Shahabi.[27] Muhammad Taqi Shariati (Mazinani),[28] the father of Ali Shariati, known as the ideologue of the Islamic Revolution, established the Center for the Propagation of Islamic Truth (Kanoon-e-Nashr e Haqayeq).[29] The center's goal was to confront not only Marxism and communism but also the traditionalists who had changed Islam "from a dynamic, moving, active religion of *jihad* into a religion of indifference in the face of what destiny supposedly had in store."[30] Ayatullah Ali Akbar Khamenei, frequented this center and later various literary circles in which Ali Shariati also took part.

Another group whose ideas were to prove very influential in the development of Islamic political and social thought in Iran, albeit under a different guise, was the Movement of Socialist Theists, or "God Worshiping Socialists" (*nehzat-e-khoda parastan-e-socialist*). Ali Shariati was among those deeply affected by this group's ideas. The movement was founded in 1944 by Jalal eddin Ashtiani and Muhammad Nakhashb, and it attracted university students with a religious inclination.[31]

Socialist Theists were critical of traditional approaches of the *ulema* to Islam. According to Jalal eddin Ashtiani, religious leaders had become too preoccupied with otherworldly matters and were ignoring people's social and economic problems. Consequently, many educated people had come to see religion as a barrier to progress. Socialist Theists were particularly critical of what they saw as the clerical establishment's support for capitalism. According to them, this support had enabled reactionary forces to use religion as a bulwark against progressive forces. Yet they recognized the importance of religion in human life and rejected Marxism's materialist interpretation of human history. In one of their writings they went as far as to state: "We [Socialist Theists] believe that materialists cannot be socialists, while every theist and believer in God is a true socialist."[32] The ultimate goal of the Socialist Theists was to create a synthesis between true religion and socialism as an economic and social system based on the belief in one God.

Socialist Theists did not believe in the separation of religion and politics since both were part of human life. In their political philosophy they rejected both dictatorship and liberalism and emphasized the Islamic notion of consultation (*shur'a*). Another important hallmark of the thinking of the Socialist Theists was a deep mistrust of both Western liberal powers and world communism. According to them, both the Western countries and the communist bloc, under the guise of promoting democracy and defending the world proletariat, respectively, were in fact expanding their domination over new markets and peripheral nations. To counter both ideologies, they attempted to develop a "middle school of thought" based on Islam, believing that only this way of thinking could bring about revolutionary change in the Middle East.[33] Their ideas in this respect were adopted by Iran's new leaders and were reflected in the Islamic regime's slogan "Neither East nor West, only Islam," albeit without any attribution to them.

The activities of the above-noted groups and centers were mostly limited to educating the public on Islam and propagating Islamic ideas, although the Socialist Theists formed various political parties or joined the existing parties.[34] Unlike these groups, the Society of the Fedaiyan-e-Islam was a militant organization whose members engaged in violent political activities, including assassination. They murdered the historian and critic of Shi'a clergy, Ahmad Kasravi, and in 1951 they assassinated Hadj Ali Razmara, Iran's prime minister.[35]

The group was founded in 1945 by Sayyid Mujtaba Navab Safavi, who claimed descent on his maternal side from the Safavid dynasty. He was educated at both religious and secular schools and attended the German Technical College in Tehran. After graduation, he worked in the British-dominated petroleum industry. After becoming involved in a workers' strike, he fled to Najaf in Iraq to pursue religious studies.[36]

The Fedaiyan, too, believed that the prevalent understanding of Islam at the time had become mixed with superstition and that some clergy were complicit in this. Like the Socialist Theists, they believed that at least some of the clergy had put religion at the service of the rich and the powerful, notably the rich merchants of the bazaar. Moreover, according to Navab and his disciples, the clergy had nurtured a sense of fatalism and inaction among the population by telling them "It is the duty of the Mahdi to come and change human life for the better forever."[37] They advanced a number of proposals for changing this situation by introducing reforms in the seminaries. Some of their ideas, such as making the clergy financially independent from the bazaar and other donors, were later picked up by the Ayatullah Murtaza Mutahari.

However, unlike the Socialist Theists or intellectuals such as Bazargan, the Fedaiyan were not seeking any synthesis of Islam and other ideologies and they advocated a government and economic system based on Islam. They failed fully to develop their ideas and to produce a blueprint for an Islamic political and economic system. However, they assigned a significant role to the clergy in a future Islamic government. According to Taghavi, surviving members of the group do not agree on what Navab had in mind regarding the nature and extent of the clerics' role. Some of them told him that Navab believed that the clergy should have a supervisory function, similar to the one envisaged in the 1906 Constitution, whereas others said that he favored a role similar to the *velayat-e faqih* (guardianship of the Islamic jurist).[38]

This may explain why conservative circles in Iran today see the Fedaiyan as the harbinger of the Islamic government that came to power in 1979, and on most issues they espouse positions similar to those of the Fedaiyan. Another reason may be that, after the official dismantling of the group in 1955 and Navab's execution, many of its members and sympathizers joined the conservative group Heyathay-e-Mutalefeh-e-Islamic (the Coalition of Islamic Groups), which still is one of the influential conservative groups in Iran.[39]

Aspects of the Pahlavis' modernization policies contributed to Islam's renewal and revival. These included the expansion of education to disadvantaged and highly religious classes; the establishment of free university education; the offering of government grants for students to study abroad and the establishment of Islamic studies courses in state universities which attracted many ex-clerics. They generated a new generation of Islamically oriented intellectuals and a new Islamic discourse attractive to a younger generation of Iranians.

However, as is often the case with early reactions to modernization, those who had benefited from the new opportunities turned against the Pahlavis. The newly educated classes, with roots in traditional and economically less advantaged classes, had either forgotten or had no experience of the chaos and the extremely underdeveloped state of pre-Pahlavi Iran, nor did they recognize that they owed their new conditions to Pahlavi reforms. Key intellectual figures such as Mehdi Bazargan and Ali Shariati would never have been able to afford a European education without the Pahlavis' policy of sending gifted students abroad for further studies at government expense. Nevertheless, they focused entirely on the shortcomings of the Pahlavi modernization project, notably the lack of adequate civil and political freedoms.

Islam's intellectual revival also benefited from many Iranians' disappointment with secular leftist alternatives. During the 1960s and the 1970s, it was Islamically oriented lay intellectuals such as Ali Shariati, who offered the most novel and seemingly most cohesive Islam-based discourse, challenging both the secular nationalist and leftist discourses, although Shariati borrowed heavily from the latter.

Islamo-leftist intellectuals (the Mujahedin e Khalq) and Islamo-liberal intellectuals (the Islamic wing of the National Front and later the Freedom Movement) also directed anti-Pahlavi activities.[40] The Mujahedin engaged in guerrilla operations in Iran, while members of the Freedom Movement organized Islamic associations, garnered support for anti-regime activities among Iranian students abroad, and lobbied Arab governments opposed to the Shah, receiving considerable help from them. After Ayatullah Rouhullah Khomeini's move to France, such intellectuals worked to convince Western governments of his democratic intentions.[41] Meanwhile, the clerics effectively used the extensive network of mosques to garner opposition to the Shah.

The above-noted developments intensified interaction between religiously minded lay intellectuals and the clerical establishment, especially its reform-oriented and activist wing. The main center of this encounter was the Husseinieh-e-Irshad, a religious institute founded in Tehran. According to one author, there was "a synthesis of traditional and modern" in the Husseinieh-e-Irshad that enabled students, university professors, intellectuals engaged in professions and the potentially intellectual forces, such as high school students, clergy, and young students of religious seminaries [*tulab*] to gather together."[42]

Islamic Reformist Thinking Before the Revolution: Revivers and Intellectuals

Muslim reformist thinkers of the 1960s and 1970s, whose line of thinking is still present in Iran, wanted to revive religion as a social and political force and to reconcile it with modernity—a synthesis, even if many of them did not use such terminology. However, they differed in their understanding of what reform meant, its extent, the balance between religion and modernity, and the relative importance of intellectual activity versus political action.

These thinkers may be roughly divided between "revivers" (*ahyageran*) of Islam and religious intellectuals, based on the relative roles of Islam and modernity in their thinking.

Revivers of Islam

The first group, the revivers of Islam,

> while being familiar with modernity and accepting the necessities of modern world [wanted] to establish religion's presence with its traditional roles in society as a transcendental paradigm. The revivers [relied] on tradition and [looked] at the modern. They [gave] a religious gloss to the modern world and created a new social structure based on religious foundation in the modern world. They opposed the separation of tradition and modernity. While believing in the connection between the two, they assigned an important role to tradition. This trend still tries to give a reading of modernity that is compatible with religion and tradition.[43]

This analysis ignores one important dimension of the perspective of revivers, namely the centrality of Islam and its ethical system as the underpinning of individual and collective life. The late Ayatullah Murtaza Mutahari best represented this trend.

Ayatullah Murtaza Mutahari

Ayatullah Murtaza Mutahari believed that reform should begin from within religion and not through the instrumentalization of religion. His criticism of Ali Shariati, for example, was based on the belief that Shariati had used religion as an instrument to achieve other ideological and political goals.[44] Mutahari promoted what he called a moderate Islam (*islam-e-motadel*), which opposes ignorance (*jahl*), superstitions (*khurafat*) that had gained influence among the people, and stagnation (*jomoud*). Mutahari criticized both those who were against any form of new thinking and reform in religion and those who wanted "to confine Islam to the archives of history." Instead, he favored an internally generated reform in Islam, which, by making it more responsive to contemporary needs, would counteract the influence of government-imposed secular reforms and the appeals of materialistic ideologies such as socialism.

According to Mutahari, an important component of this internally generated reform of religion was the restructuring of the existing clerical establishment and its intellectual renewal and reinvigoration. He bemoaned the fact that the clergy often followed popular religious beliefs rather than correcting false beliefs and guiding the people in the right direction. He called this phenomenon "populist infection"

(*awam zadegi*). His other concern was the clergy's financial dependence on popular contributions. He elaborated his ideas regarding the fundamental problems of
the clerical establishment and ways to resolve them in a book titled *Fundamental
Problems of the Clerical Establishment.*[45]

Methodologically, Mutahari emphasized the importance of reason in interpreting
religious texts, albeit within limits. He maintained that the application of reason
to analysis and interpretation of religious sources has its own laws, and that not
every opinion can be justified under the guise of reasoning.[46] He gave preference
to the Qur'an against *hadith* because of the unreliability of many *hadith* and the
existence of forged *hadith*. He made a distinction between the immutable (*sabit*)
laws of Islam and those that are subject to change (*mutaqayer*), and he argued
that the latter should be adjusted according to the times. Indeed, he first popularized the terms that are now common currency in reformist discourse, namely the
importance of context and the requirements of time and space, which he called
muqtaziat-e-zaman va makan.

On political matters, he favored modern forms of administration and a popularly
elected legislature, provided that no legislation was against the fundamentals of
Islam.[47] However, his ideas on more specific issues related to the nature of an
elected government and individual rights and freedoms were not well developed.
According to one author, when, immediately after the revolution he was asked
about what kind of government the Islamic republic should be and the extent of
people's rights and freedoms, Mutahari's response was in the form of "hasty, general
remarks" to the effect that "freedom, the rights of individuals and democracy were
all inherent in Islamic government."[48]

Mutahari's writings and speeches indicate that, while he believed in the supremacy of Islam, he did not advocate either its forced inculcation in people nor
limits on the freedom of expression in the name of protecting Islam. He emphasized
the Qur'anic injunction that there is no compulsion in faith, accepted the principle
of freedom of thought and conscience, and advised that Islamic teachings should
be propagated in a peaceful and nonconfrontational manner.

Some present-day reformist thinkers do not consider Mutahari an innovative
or even a reformist thinker. For example, Mustafa Malekian categorically states
that Mutahari did not have any original ideas, and he certainly did not develop
a new theology; he "only gave a more rationalist rendition of the views of his
masters."[49] This may be so, but it does not negate the fact that Mutahari was a
pioneer in promoting a rationalist and contextual Islam, while remaining within
the religious mainstream.

Mutahari's intellectual grounding in *fiqh* (jurisprudence), philosophy, and other
Islamic sciences, coupled with his familiarity with contemporary issues and ideas,
bestowed on him a degree of legitimacy and credibility that some of today's reformists lack due to the shallowness of their Islamic learning. Some of his ideas
were, at the time, progressive and highly controversial. For example, he ruled that
women did not have to cover their faces, for which he was severely criticized. He

also ruled that the importance of saving the life of a woman at childbirth, or any other time, overrules any prohibition regarding contact with the opposite sex.[50]

Moreover, in his book titled *The System of Women's Rights in Islam*,[51] he criticized the abuse of some Islamic rules related to women. However, he offered no concrete recommendation on how to prevent such abuse, nor did he propose changing the rules. Even worse, he tried to justify practices such as polygamy, although he did say that monogamy is preferable. This attitude on his part may be attributable to the conditions of the time.

Shortly after the success of the Islamic Revolution, Ayatullah Mutahari was assassinated by a member of Furghan, an Islamo-leftist militia whose members were devotees of Shariati. Based on his writings, it seems likely that, had he lived, he would have offered more progressive readings of tradition better suited to new circumstances. Moreover, because of his very close relations with Ayatullah Khomeini, he might have curbed some of the excesses of the Islamic government and gradually advanced a more reformist discourse.

Ayatullah Muhammad Husseini Beheshti

Ayatullah Beheshti is mostly known as a political activist, a shrewd politician, and an important figure in the unfolding of the Islamic Revolution. It is perhaps because of his pivotal role during the immediate aftermath of the revolution that he was assassinated, together with a number of other high officials, in a June 1981 bombing incident attributed to the Mujahedin-e-Khalq.[52]

Beheshti's reputation as a thinker is not very high and, indeed, his intellectual output in terms of books and articles is fairly limited. Yet he had attended secular educational institutions in addition to religious seminary and obtained a doctorate in philosophy from the Tehran University. For some years, he had lived in Hamburg as the director of the Islamic Center. In recent years there has been an effort to emphasize his intellectual contributions to Islam's multidimensional revival in Iran and to the emergence of the Islamic movement, which culminated in the 1979 revolution. For this purpose, a foundation has been set up for the study of his ideas.

Irrespective of the extent of his intellectual and scholarly merits, Beheshti definitely was a key figure among the revivers and did much to educate the clergy in modern disciplines and foreign languages, in order to enable them to reach younger generations and to acquaint them with Islamic values and political notions. Beheshti was relatively reformist in his approach to the study of *fiqh*. He favored the interpretation of *fiqh* in ways more relevant to contemporary concerns and needs, especially socioeconomic issues, and hence more appealing to the younger generation. His approach to the interpretation of the Qur'an, however, was only marginally contextualist. He did not believe that Qur'anic verses apply only to particular conditions of their revelation, and he considered them valid for all times.[53] However, notwithstanding his methodological conservatism, his views on many issues were fairly progressive. For example, he maintained that there is no clear prohibition in Islam against music unless it is an accompaniment to other vices. Similarly, he called Islam a religion of joyfulness (*neshat*) and criticized those who equated being a good Muslim with being morose. Similarly, he considered activism a central feature of Islam.[54]

Beheshti opposed superstitious beliefs and stagnant thinking. However, while advocating the use of reason in all domains, he emphasized that reason by itself was not sufficient to guide people in their individual and collective lives and that human beings also need revelation. This view led him to reject liberal interpretations of individual rights and freedoms and to argue that, in an Islamic society people's freedom is not absolute but is restricted by divine prohibitions. Yet according to all accounts, he was tolerant of different views. For example, he defended Shariati against his clerical attackers while disagreeing with most of his views, especially those regarding the clergy.[55]

Beheshti was also unique among his contemporaries in believing strongly in the importance of social and political institution building, and in particular the establishment of viable political parties. This is why he created the Islamic Republican Party. He also emphasized social justice and equity and said that any Islamic society lacking these elements was "a false Muslim society" (*islam-e-qolabi*).[56] His departure from the Iranian political and intellectual scene, together with ayatullahs Mutahari and Taleqani, intellectually impoverished the clerical establishment, weakened the trend toward an inner reform of Iranian Islam, and contributed to Iran's postrevolutionary political fragmentation, factionalism, and neglect of institution building, with highly negative consequences for the country.

Ayatullah Mahmud Taleqani: Reviver and Intellectual

Another important religious figure in Iran during the fateful years between the end of the Second World War and the Islamic Revolution was Ayatullah Mahmud Taleqani. He falls between the revivers and the intellectuals. Ayatullah Taleqani (b. 1910 or 1911) was much older than other religious figures who contributed to Islam's politicization in Iran and to the Islamic Revolution. He was also politically active early in his career, although mostly in a clandestine fashion. He had close ties with Navab Safavi, the founder of the Fedaiyan-e-Islam. This fact indicates that he was not averse to resorting to violence in pursuit of his goals.[57]

Taleqani was a reviver in the sense that he wanted to restore Islam's central role in Iranian society, which he deemed had been eroded by the Pahlavis' modernization project. He was an intellectual in that he wanted to offer a version of Islam more suited to Iran's new socioeconomic realities, and in the process he contributed to Islam's ideologization. In terms of both generating an Islamic consciousness (*aghahi*) and developing a social theory based on Islam, he was ahead of other revivers and intellectuals, including Shariati.[58]

The main impetus behind Taleqani's efforts was his concern about the inroads made by leftist forces in Iran, notably the Tudeh Party. He realized that without the

development of an Islamic socioeconomic theory that addressed issues of ownership, income distribution, and an equitable social and economic environment, Islam
would lose its appeal to youth.[59]

This concern inspired him to write his treatise, *Islam and Ownership*.[60] His views
are close to socialist ideas. He recognized the right to private ownership, but he also
said that a person's labor is the source of his right to ownership. In reference to the
exploitation and development of resources, he maintained that these rights exist
in Islam as long as individual activities do not harm the public interest—in which
case the government has the power to limit such activities. He opposed excessive
accumulation of wealth and sought to prevent it through the proper collection of
Islamic taxes and prevention of wasteful consumption. Finally, he concluded that
an Islamic economic system is based on *tawhid*. This means that the world and all
that is in it belongs to God, and that human beings, as God's vice-regents, must
use it not in the interests of particular classes or for individual aggrandizement,
but for the welfare of all.[61]

Taleqani believed not only in justice in social and economic relations but also
in equity. According to him, an equitable society is one in which everyone has an
equal opportunity to develop his/her potential.[62] Taleqani had an activist view of
Islam. In a speech on Struggle and Martyrdom (*Jihad va Shihadat*), he defined
jihad as an essentially defensive act principally for the purpose of protecting Islam
and Muslims. He unequivocally stated that struggling in the way of God (*fi sabil
allah*) does not mean "to conquer or plunder," but to fight against despotism and
injustice.[63]

Ayatullah Taleqani's political ideas were less well developed than his socioeconomic philosophy. Nevertheless, there is enough in his sayings and writings
to enable one to sketch the basic contours of his political views. First, he believed
that universal sovereignty belongs to God. Second, at the earthly level, this divine
authority is vested in the Prophet and the imams, and, in their absence, in the just
ulema and just believers. The upshot of this view is that any monarchical system,
which he believed is inherently despotic, is illegitimate.

However, Taleqani was vague about the mechanism through which the *ulema* and
just believers should manage the affairs of the people. Some of his writings, notably
his introduction to Ayatullah Naini's famous treatise *Admonition of the People and
Refinement of the Nation*,[64] in which Naini supported the constitutionalists during the 1905–08 revolution, give the impression that he favored a constitutional
government. Taleqani also argued in favor of a more consultative religious body,
instead of having a single (*marj'a e taqlid*) source of emulation. However, as noted
by Hamid Dabashi, although Taleqani used Naini's work, he tried "to breathe new
revolutionary zest into his words perhaps beyond the author's intention." This
implies that for Taleqani a constitutional government was not sufficient to prevent
despotism.[65] Taleqani was passionately opposed to any form of dictatorship, political or religious, and the concentration of power in one individual. Had he lived,
Taleqani would have disapproved of the institution of a supreme religious leader.

Based on his writings and some accounts that in 1979 he supported a "Democratic Islamic Republic" as opposed to Khomeini's "Islamic Republic," it is prudent to assume that he favored a conditional democracy under clerical supervision, but not what has come to amount to a religious semi-dictatorship.[66]

Moreover, Taleqani's emphasis on individual freedom in matters of faith, his belief that faith not based on true awareness and chosen freely is worthless, his reminding people that in Islam there is no compulsion in faith and that no one can make believers of people by force, indicate a basically tolerant approach to diverse views.

Unlike Ayatullah Mutahari, Taleqani did not write or comment on the issue of women's rights in Islam. But if the account is to be credited in Elaine Sciolino's book *Persian Mirrors*,[67] in which she recounts that Taleqani's daughter Azam told her that, during her youth, and before the quickening of political struggle against the Shah, she abandoned wearing the veil and her father did not object, then it indicates that he had progressive ideas in this respect.

In terms of methodology of interpreting Islamic sources, Taleqani favored a contextualist and goal-oriented approach. He opposed a merely ritualistic Islam and stressed the point that Muslims should be conscious of the ultimate objective of Islam, which is the creation of a just society.

Religious Intellectuals

Religious intellectuals (*rowshanfekran e dini*) also refuted a basic rupture between modernity and tradition. But unlike the revivers, they believed that "only by undergoing renovation (*nowsazi*) and reconstruction (*bazsazi*) can tradition become present in the modern world."[68]

In the prerevolutionary era, religious intellectuals fell into two categories. The first were religious liberal nationalists. They used scientific methods to reconcile religion with science, democracy, and popular rule, offered a politically liberal and mildly nationalistic reading of Islam, and favored evolutionary change. Mehdi Bazargan, one of the founders of the Iran Freedom Movement, was the best representative of this type of religious intellectual.

Mehdi Bazargan and the Scientific Reading of Islam

Mehdi Bazargan is rightly credited as being the first intellectual to reintroduce Islam to a younger and more educated generation of Iranians as an important moral, intellectual, social, and political force. Indeed, many of the themes that he introduced nearly fifty years ago are now hallmarks of reformist thinking in Iran.

Several fundamental beliefs regarding the nature and potential role of religion in general, and Islam in particular, constitute the underpinnings of Bazargan's reformist philosophy. First, Bazargan believed that religion functioned both as an instrument for improving people's lot and as a tool in their oppression. If misused, religion can lead to stagnation, corruption, and eventually even disbelief. Used properly, it can be a source of value and social activism. Second, he distinguished between religiosity, or ostentatious piety, and true religion, and was highly critical of the former. Third, Bazargan believed in an active, socially engaged, and life-affirming religion, in this case Islam. He criticized Iranian Muslims for being preoccupied with ritualistic aspects of their religion and not its social and moral dimensions. He partly blamed the clergy for this. Fourth, he sincerely believed that Islam was in no way incompatible with modern sciences, and he spent a good part of his intellectual life to prove the correctness of Islamic precepts through mathematical and other scientific methods. Fifth, he believed that becoming modern did not mean abandoning one's religious beliefs. Studying in 1930s France, he was pleasantly surprised by the high rate of church attendance in France, despite the country's official secularist ideology.[69]

Bazargan initially believed that religion and politics are not separate, and that both are part of society's fabric.[70] Moreover, because Bazargan believed that despotism is an affront to God, he viewed religion, especially Islam, as the best barrier against despotism. In this belief he seems to have been influenced by the ideas of Ayatullah Naini. However, given his educational background and other influences to which he had been subjected, it is safe to say that he saw the role of religion in politics as a spiritual and cultural referent emphasizing the importance of justice, equity, and freedom and not as a justification for political rule by the clergy. Moreover, Bazargan opposed any form of despotism and considered religious despotism the worst type; thus he opposed the concept of *velayat-e faqih*. The experience of the Islamic Republic drastically changed his mind about the role of religion in politics and prompted him to write against mixing the two. In economic matters, he believed in free enterprise with a social conscience. This attitude partly reflected his family background in the well-off merchant class, whereas the Socialist Theists and others favoring a socialist economic and social system came from poor working-class backgrounds, as did Islamic revolutionaries.

Bazargan also maintained that Islam is against all forms of discrimination based on race, ethnicity, or gender, and he claimed that long before the French Revolution, Islam had advocated freedom, equality, and brotherhood.[71] Ultimately, however, Bazargan was a secular and nationalist intellectual, and his Islamism reflects more his religious family background, authenticist tendencies, and reaction against imitative modernization rather than a commitment to developing an Islamic socioeconomic and political ideology. This is why the true Islamists never trusted him, and after his brief premiership (February–November 1979), he was excluded from active participation in politics.

The second category of religious intellectuals includes revolutionary ideologues, best represented by Ali Shariati and his followers. They wanted to transform religion into a revolutionary ideology and to create an ideal society run by a just and pious vanguard.[72] Following the revolution, Shariati's disciples lost out to the clerical elements and their supporters. However, many of them joined the government and exerted influence behind the scenes, while his devotees remained loyal to him and his vision. This is the reason why, in Iran today, there is a renewed interest in Shariati and his ideas, although in a revised form. This newfound interest has given rise to a school of thought within the reformist intellectual trend that may be aptly characterized as neo-Shariatism. Because of Shariati's relevance to contemporary reformist discourse, his ideas and how they are currently being reinterpreted will be discussed here.

Ali Shariati: The Ideologue of the Islamic Revolution?

Ali Shariati is one of the most controversial figures of Iran's recent intellectual history. He has passionate followers and defenders, and equally passionate detractors. For example, Taqi Rahmani, a contemporary Iranian intellectual and author of books on religious intellectualism and reason, calls Shariati the peak of Iranian thought (*shah beit-e andisheh-e-irani*).[73] Others view him as someone with only a superficial knowledge of Islam and modern sociopolitical disciplines and lacking a coherent ideology.

Similarly, the question of Shariati's true ideological leanings and his approach to religion is still hotly debated. Iranian intellectuals still ask themselves whether Shariati was a Marxist who cynically used Islam to make his message appealing to religious masses. Or was he an innovative thinker who developed a new sociopolitical theory based on Islam? Was he a totalitarian ideologue who despised popular democracy, or a democrat with egalitarian impulses? Was he against clericism and, as some of his statements indicate,[74] an early proponent of "Islamic Protestantism,"[75] with his theory of "religious government minus the clergy"? Or did he mastermind the theory of *velayat-e faqih*, by promoting the idea of the role of pious clergy as the vanguard in the establishment of his ideal society based on the concept of *tawhid*, in works such as *The Community and the Spiritual Leadership* (Ummat va imamat)?[76] Was he rabidly anti-West (*gharb setiz*) or merely a critic of Western policies such as colonialism?

These questions cannot be easily answered. What accounts for this difficulty are Shariati's contradictory statements and writings, most of which are passionate outpourings of feelings rather than rationally argued theories and positions or guidelines for action. He also shifted positions during various stages of his intellectual development.[77] It was the emotional and incoherent aspects of Shariati's writings that led Ayatullah Mutahari to remark that his Islamology (*islam shenassi*) was more Islamic poetry or storytelling than a scientific study.[78] Moreover, on many issues such as women's rights, Shariati did not take clear positions. In his works on women, Shariati called on them to follow the examples of Fatima and Zaynab, the Prophet's daughter and granddaughter, which are those of piety, self-sacrifice, and courage. But he was silent on such critical issues as veiling and on the equality of men and women in respect to family law and economic, political, and judicial rights.[79]

Therefore, any judgment on Shariati will to some extent depend on which aspects of his work are emphasized. Nevertheless, if viewed through the eyes of a neutral analyst rather than a passionate disciple or an implacable antagonist, Shariati's work provides a fair description of his positions on various socioeconomic and political issues. It also allows an assessment of his role in promoting revolutionary action, if not in providing the blueprint for the Islamic Revolution and the system of government that followed.

Shariati's Vision of Islam. For Shariati, the true Islam is that of the time of the Prophet Muhammad. Islam was then a revolutionary movement and ideology. Its goal was to destroy the existing system and replace it with one based on justice. In the course of its consolidation and expansion, this revolutionary ideology and movement was transformed into political, economic, and cultural institutions, and it morphed into a culture (*farhang*). Shariati does not feel any affinity with this type of Islam or its religious, cultural, and especially political representatives, as reflected in the following statement:

> The time of the emergence of ideology and revolution was the time of the Prophet's anointment [*be'that*]. When this ideology and revolution enters the realm of history, historical tradition, culture, civilization, and sciences develop, but the ideology and revolution disappears. Abu Ali Sina [Avicenna], the man of science and culture, emerges but Abu Zar—who is the symbol of ideology and revolution—disappears.[80]

Here, it is important to note Shariati's fascination with Abu Zar Ghafari, one of the Prophet's companions and a harsh critic of the unjust rule of Caliph Othman. In fact, Shariati modeled himself after Othman in his disregard for caution or power disparities in the pursuit of justice and in preferring revolutionary action to lengthy arguments and gradual change, as reflected in the following statement:

> I am obliged to emulate my beloved Abu Zar Ghafari, who when in Medina and Syria raised his voice and committed imprudent acts, instead of following the manner of people of science, research, and critics. They [the cultured] explain in a slow and polite manner certain realities for the elite and learned people. But Abu Zar took a camel's bone and went straight to the Commander of the Faithful and cried: O Othman, you have made the poor poor and the wealthy wealthy.[81]

In the Sunni context, Shariati defines the true and revolutionary Islam as the Prophetic Islam (*islam e nabavi*) upheld by the likes of Abu Zar. The antithesis of prophetic Islam is that promoted by Mu'aviya and other corrupt Umayyad caliphs. Shariati has the same view regarding Shi'a Islam. According to him, for 800 years, Shi'ism was a revolutionary ideology defending justice. This type of Shi'ism is that of Ali, Alid Shi'ism (*shi'a-e-alavi*), which was corrupted by the Safavids and turned from a revolutionary ideology into an institution and a culture, and hence an instrument of oppression. Shariati also made a distinction between what he called Red Shi'ism, which is a creed that fights against injustice, corrupt rulers, and foreign invaders such as the Mongols, and Black Shi'ism, which is based on a culture of mourning and hence passivity.[82] According to Shariati, Prophetic Islam (read Sunni Islam) and Alid Shi'ism are one and the same, while Sunni–Shi'a disagreement and strife are the consequence of the corruption of both versions of true Islam. This perception of Islam informed Shariati's social, political, and religious philosophy. It also reflected his ideological, utopian, and activist character. For Shariati, ideology was essential for human life at both the individual and the collective levels, because it is ideology that determines "the direction of the social, class, and national life of peoples. It defines its value systems, social order, and the ideal type of life for the individual and the society in all of its dimensions. It answers the questions of: How is one? What is one doing? What should one do? And, what should one be?"[83]

For Shariati, "religion is an ideology based on a particular worldview, a particular understanding of human beings and their relations to the world, a system of values, and a collection of laws that are inspired by this worldview." And, since Islam is a religion, it is also an ideology, whose goal is humankind's salvation.[84] Shariati also considered that his own and his followers' greatest achievement had been "Islam's transformation from a culture to an ideology."[85]

Both in his thinking and in his personality, Shariati demonstrated a penchant for revolutionary action and impatience with polite criticism and slow reform. This tendency is reflected in his response to a comment that it might have been better if he had refrained from sharp and satirical criticisms of religious traditions and their representatives, and had confined himself to analysis and criticism as is the manner of impartial scholars.

> I am not a scientific scholar. I am weighed down by the burden of centuries of torture and history. Now that I have taken refuge in Fatima's abandoned mud hut, which has been my hope for freedom from 5,000 years of enslavement to ignorance and injustice, I see that some people have turned this, too, into a fortress of ignorance and injustice. Now you are telling me that I should engage in slow and polite scientific research. The logic of Shi'as like me is not the logic of Abu Ali Sina and Ghazzali, scholar or Orientalist. It is the logic of Abu Zar.[86]

Shariati and Marxism. In his book *Marxism and Other Western Fallacies*, Shariati criticizes Marxism for its purely materialistic view of the world and human history.[87] Nevertheless, Shariati's ideological bent, his perception of religion as an ideology, and his search for Utopia wherein all human contradictions are resolved, attracted him to the Marxist analysis of world history and the human condition. Shariati's own interpretation of human history, although expressed in Islamic terminology, was heavily influenced by Marx's view of the predominance of economic factors, notably the conflict between labor and capital, in determining the nature of human history and the trajectory of its evolution.

Shariati's utopian vision of an ideal Islamic society was reflected in his theory of *tawhid* (monotheism–unicity). A society based on *tawhid* is an egalitarian and class-less society, where there are no divisions or contradictions and everyone is united in Islam. According to Shariati, in a *tawhidi* system there is "no contradiction between man and nature, spirit and body, this world and the hereafter, matter and meaning. Nor can *tawhid* accept legal, class, social, political, racial, national territorial, genetic or even economic contradictions."[88] In other words, Shariati's ideal society based on *tawhid* is an Islamic Utopia that bears close resemblance to the Marxist Utopia of a classless society where all differences and contradictions—religious, ethnic, gender, and so on—are dissolved in a global brotherhood of the proletariat.

The opposite of a system based on *tawhid* is the one based on *shirk* (polytheism), wherein economic, class, racial, and other divisions and contradictions prevail. According to Shariati, "Tawhid sees the world as an empire and Shirk as a feudal system."[89] In Shariati's view, the capitalist system is the modern representation of *shirk*. Moreover, this conflict between monotheistic and polytheistic orders dates back to the time of Cain and Abel. Abel represents the communitarian, pastoral society, whereas Cain represents the feudal system of land ownership.

Shariati did not subscribe to Marx's view of religion as the opiate of the masses and a phenomenon that will disappear because of historical necessity. He was criti-cal of Marx for viewing class as the main factor of self and group identification and the single cause of social differences. He saw religion as another element in individual and collective identification and hence a factor in social divisions. He called this "belief class." He did, however, view the official clergy as representa-tives of a system based on *shirk*. It was Shariati's famous triangle of "Gold, Sword, and Worry Bead" (*zar, tigh va tasbih*), modeled after Marx's triangle of "govern-ment, capital, and religion" as the people's enemies, that led Ayatullah Mutahari to criticize him harshly.

Mutahari also criticized Shariati's interpretation of history. Mutahari maintained that Shariati's view of history was materialist and pointed out that his conception of monotheism was against Islam's view of this concept. Mutahari noted that Islam's conception of monotheism is universal and self-contained and does not need inputs from Marxism or Existentialism. Mutahari went so far as to accuse Shariati of giv-ing "an Islamic cover" to his Marxist and existentialist ideas.[90]

Mutahari's criticism of Shariati may be too harsh. But there is no doubt that Shariati was deeply influenced by Marxist ideology. He viewed capitalism as Is-lam's real enemy, while considering Marxism merely a rival.[91] It was Marxism that informed Shariati's interpretation of Islam and not the other way around, especially since—as he himself was aware, and as Mutahari pointedly stressed—his grounding in Islamic sciences was most superficial. However, Shariati's Marxism was very eclectic and his grasp of Marxist theory was less than perfect. This deficiency led the secular left to criticize the shallowness of his analysis.[92]

Shariati's present-day followers try to distance him from Marxism. Some of them, like Reza Alijani, claim that a prominent characteristic of Shariati was his lack of subservience to the dominant discourse (*ghofteman-e ghaleb*) of the time, which was Marxism, and they point to the left's rejection of Shariati as a full-fledged Marxist.[93] They acknowledge that he was influenced by dialectical thinking, which is associated with Marxism and its derivatives, but they note that dialectics was not invented by Marx and has roots in Iran's own culture. Moreover, Shariati believed that the Iranian mind has always been attracted to ideas of social activism for the sake of justice, a belief that is also often identified with leftist movements. In support of this view, staunch supporters note his interest in Mazdak, the pre-Islamic Prophet who preached a communalist creed and whose influence led to large-scale social upheaval followed by repression.[94]

Islam, Government, and Revolution. Despite some ambiguity and inconsistency in his positions, ultimately Shariati believed in revolutionary action and did not have much faith in the success of evolutionary and democratic change. He justified this view in light of the fact that most people have a low level of education and economic conditions, which renders them vulnerable to manipulation by the powerful. Given this reality, privileged classes would retain their power even within an outwardly democratic system, and, consequently no real change would take place. Moreover, because of their ignorance, most people would likely make a wrong choice with similar results.

On these grounds, Shariati emphasized the role of a revolutionary vanguard to guide the people until the elimination of socioeconomic disparities. Because of such views, today some of Shariati's detractors accuse him of ideological rigidity or, worse, totalitarian tendencies. Abdolkarim Soroush, for example, views Shariati as an ideologue and ultimately undemocratic. According to Soroush, this undemocratic characteristic derives from the very nature of ideology, which is based on certain axioms and which aims at molding societies, peoples, and relationships according to its own view of an ideal state of being. In this context, differing views have no place and legitimacy, whereas that is a necessary prerequisite for a democratic system.[95] The Iranian journalist and dissident Akbar Ganji, in a speech in Paris in the summer of 2006, reportedly accused Shariati of having said: "my program is to eliminate democracy and freedom. I want a government that controls the people from above and that the people should be brainwashed."[96] The noted Iranian intellectual Ehsan Naraghi, also in the summer of 2006, stated: "in Shariati's work, there is no sign of democracy and freedom." He added that, from his perspective, "Shariati and communism are neighbors."[97]

Shariati's supporters dispute this perception. But they admit that Shariati believed in a "guided democracy" or, as he called it, a "committed democracy" (*democracy e moteahed*), for a transitional period after revolutions, in order to pass from a democracy of leaders to a democracy of votes (*az democracy e-ra'sha beh democracy-e-ra'yha*). However, other Shariati devotees, such as Hashem Aghajari, maintain that he wanted a "populist democracy," which has connotations of the Marxist-Leninist definition of democracy as the "dictatorship of the proletariat" and calls to mind various undemocratic regimes with the name "People's Democratic Republic of . . ."[98] Yussefi Eshkevari argues that, despite certain accusations, "one can never consider such a free-spirited, freedom-seeking and democratic person as Shariati an opponent of democracy."[99] However, he offers no concrete evidence as to Shariati's democratic convictions. It is interesting to note that, following the election of Mahmoud Ahmadinejad to the Iranian presidency in 2005, largely as a result of the votes of the economically deprived, Shariati's ideas about electoral democracy as an inadequate tool of reform have gained a new currency among Iranian youth.[100]

Shariati also clearly advocated the idea of an Islamic state similar to what existed during the time of the Prophet and the first few of his successors. But he was silent on what form this Islamic state should take, although he dismissed Islamic empires, such as that of the Ottomans, as representative of true Islamic governments. In *The Community and the Spiritual Leadership*, Shariati declared that there is no separation between the Prophet's spiritual leadership and political leadership, and hence there is no separation between religion and politics in Islam. Such views clearly helped popularize the idea of an Islamic state in Iran, as opposed to any other form of government.[101] In other writings, such as *Shi'ism, the Perfect Party* (Tashayo, hezb e tamam), Shariati demonstrated his dislike for party politics, a necessary ingredient of democratic systems of government.

All of Shariati's writings on Shi'ism offer an activist and revolutionary interpretation of Shi'a concepts, notably the epic of Karbela and the concept of *intizar* (waiting for the arrival of the Mahdi). In other writings, such as *Hussein and Mahbouba*, he exalted sacrifice and coined the famous phrase "if you cannot kill, die." Given the guerrilla activities in Iran in the early 1970s, many at the time interpreted this statement as indicating Shariati's support for guerrilla movements. But Sussan Shariati, his daughter, now argues that this was an emotional outburst of a teacher who had seen two of his students killed in a skirmish with security forces, and therefore cannot be interpreted as support for guerrilla action.[102]

This discussion demonstrates that different groups choose different aspects of Shariati's thought and hence they come up with different interpretations of his overall vision. However, despite all the efforts of the present-day neo-Shariatis and Shariati's descendants to portray him as a democrat, believing first and foremost in the cultural transformation of society, he was a leftist intellectual who believed in revolutionary action and assigned an important role for a revolutionary vanguard in creating the new society after having dismantled the old system.

His use of Islam as the cornerstone of his ideology and worldview (*jahan bini*) largely stemmed from his religious family background, his own religious, mystical, and spiritual inclinations, and his authenticist tendencies, which had been sharpened by his becoming acquainted with similar ideas developed by Third World intellectuals, most notably Frantz Fanon.[103] Additionally, like other leftists in Iran who in the late 1960s and 1970s adopted an Islamic veneer and vocabulary, Shariati, too, had seen that the complex discourse of variants of Marxist ideology were not capable of reaching the uneducated and religious masses, and therefore he set out to ideologize Islam.

It would be a gross oversimplification to attribute the Islamic Revolution to the influence of one individual, Shariati, as some people have done. But there is no denying that he played a significant role in promoting a revolutionary discourse of Islam as opposed to Bazargan's evolutionary approach. He also contributed to the radicalization of the clergy, since they did not want to concede the ideological and political field to him and his followers. His theories using Islamic terminology won large numbers of Iranian youth to the idea of Islamic revolution. Ehsan Naraghi's words that *"he made people fall in love with revolution"* are an apt description of Shariati's role.[104] After the revolution, most of his supporters were sidelined and some joined the Islamic regime. Many of the regime's current critics and proponents of a reformist Islamic discourse, especially on the left, are in reality neo-Shariatis.[105]

Today, even Shariati's most ardent disciples, such as Yussefi Eshkevari, a reformist ex-cleric, believe that some of his views are no longer relevant to Iran's current conditions and that some others need reinterpretation in order to offer solutions to contemporary problems. Meanwhile, a new generation, frustrated with the experience of gradual reform under former president Muhammad Khatami and a regressive trend under President Mahmoud Ahmadinejad, are again looking to Shariati's revolutionary ideas for guidance for action.

Islamic Revolution: Impact on Islamic Reformist Thinking

During the first decade (1979–89) of the revolution, the revivers of Islam triumphed and eliminated liberal and leftist religious intellectuals from the political scene. Some of the left-leaning figures joined the revivers and occupied high offices in the government. Mir Hussein Mussavi, who was prime minister for nearly a decade, and Behzad Nabavi, an ex-member of the Communist Tudeh Party, Mussavi's minister of heavy industries, are prominent representatives of this group. This period witnessed many excesses, ranging from the extremely harsh treatment of even passive opponents of the regime, including execution, to the expropriation of property owners and large-scale purification campaigns in various ministries, universities, and the army.

Many of today's reformist thinkers and new religious intellectuals were engaged in these acts to varying degrees. Said Hajjarian, the so-called intellectual architect of the reformist movement that led to Hujat al-Islam Muhammad Khatami's victory in the presidential election of 1997, was a high-ranking intelligence officer. Abdolkarim Soroush was a member of the committee charged with the purification of universities, although he now claims that his goal was to facilitate the reopening of the universities.

The second period (1988–97), which saw the end of the Iran-Iraq war and the death of Ayatullah Khomeini, was a period of introspection and self-criticism by the regime and of growing popular disenchantment with the system. A major cause of this disenchantment was Iran's virtual defeat by Iraq after heroic resistance and immeasurable material and human sacrifice. This experience dealt a serious blow to the system's ideological foundations and hence the basis of its legitimacy.

During his presidency (1989–97), Ali Akabar Hashemi Rafsanjani tried to reform Iran's statist economy, a legacy of the leftist-Islamist governments of the first decade, to rebuild war-damaged areas, to ease social and political constraints, and to improve Iran's external relations. However, the reforms were doomed by fundamental contradictions of Iran's economic and political systems, the obstruction of hard-line conservatives and leftists, and the rampant corruption of the era of reconstruction. Consequently, the conditions of the people did not improve, although a minority, including Rafsanjani's family, enriched itself, leading to the deepening of socioeconomic disparities and growing popular frustration. Early in his presidency, Rafsanjani admitted to mistakes committed by the regime, including in foreign policy. However, the regime's self-criticism did not extend to questioning the entire system's (*nizam*) ideological foundations. This task was performed by religious intellectuals, who also submitted to critical analysis their own role in the establishment of an ideological and utopian society.[106] Abdolkarim Soroush, Hujat al-Islam Muhsen Kadivar, and ex-ayatullah Muhammad Shabestari were among the pioneers of this trend. Some others, like Said Hajjarian, went beyond analysis and engaged in political activism, thus acquiring the label of "activist intellectuals."[107]

The nearly decade-long exclusion of key figures of the current reformist movement from power also greatly contributed to their intellectual evolution from left-leaning hardliners to reformists, thus reflecting the impact of power relationships and political considerations in the emergence of reformist discourse.

The election of Muhammad Khatami to the presidency in May 1997 marked the beginning of the third period in the evolution of reformist thinking in postrevolutionary Iran. During this period, the government itself championed reform and provided a more open atmosphere for debate. However, given the character of Iran's political system, especially the executive branch's limited power, reformist thinkers and activists and even members of the cabinet, such as Ayatullah Muhajerani, were repressed by the judiciary, which was dominated by conservative forces.[108]

Mahmoud Ahmadinejad's upset victory in the presidential election of June 2005 marked the fourth period in the evolution of the Islamic system, characterized by a reversal of the political fortunes of the reformists. However, this has not meant the elimination, or even the diminishing, of reformist discourse in Iran. It has led to soul-searching among reformist thinkers, and more so activists, about the causes of their defeat, and it has resulted in a redefining of future strategies, including greater, although not sufficient, willingness to collaborate with other moderate forces.[109] Meanwhile the more moderate conservatives have tried to appropriate some of the reformists' discourse as their own.

Typology of Reformist Thinkers

Muslim reformist thinkers in Iran can be classified on the basis of three criteria: profession; methodology; and degree of reformism, with overlaps among the three. Professionally, reformist thinkers include those who either belong to, or have belonged to, the clerical establishment, and others who are mostly engaged in teaching, research, journalism, and politics. The latter define themselves as "religious intellectuals" or "religious new thinkers." Methodologically, they are broadly divided between those who use traditional Islamic methodology and those who use modern methodologies, such as hermeneutics (*marafat shenassi*), phenomenology (*padideh shenassi*), and historicism. Some of the most reform-minded clerics use a combination of both traditional and modern methodologies. There are also varying degrees of reformism within both groups.

Reformist Clerics

Before discussing the methodologies and views of key reformist clerics in Iran, it is important to note that the practice of *ijtihad* and the use of reason in interpreting Islamic sources have been strong in Shi'a traditions. Similarly, Mu'tazili influences, albeit of the more moderate type, have continued within Shi'a Islam. Furthermore, in the last two centuries, the Usuli school of *fiqh*—which, unlike the Akhabaris, who stress *hadith* (*naql*), emphasizes reason (*aql*)—has been dominant within Iran's clerical establishment.

Because of these traditions, the Ayatullah Khomeini himself stressed the importance of taking into account the requirement of time and space in the interpretation of Islamic sources and favored a contextualist approach. He warned against the dangers of stagnation, superstition, and ostentatious displays of piety. During his lifetime, through the exercise of *ijtihad*, he issued a number of *fatwas* on certain prohibitions in Islam, such as music and chess playing, and declared that they are permissible provided that they are not used for corrupt purposes.

Today, many reformist clerics use Ayatullah Khomeini's example to justify their own positions. In a speech on the anniversary of his death in 2007, the reformist Ayatullah Yussef Saanei noted that Khomeini had been against stagnation (*tajarud*) and superstition (*khurafat*) and that he favored a rationalist and contextualist approach to the interpretation of Islamic sources.[110] Saanei added that in his own choice of methodology he had been inspired by Khomeini. In short, the traditions of Shi'a Islam in general, and in Iran in particular, have been conducive to the emergence of reformist clerics.

Reformist clerics in Iran can be broadly divided into those who use traditional methodology based on *usul al-fiqh* to offer a reformist reading of Islamic sources; and those who use modern methodologies or a combination of both to achieve a similar purpose. The ayatullahs Hussein Ali Muntazeri, Yussef Saanei, and Seyyed

Muhammad Moussavi Bojnourdi are the most important representatives of the first category. They advance reformist views on human rights, women's rights, and democracy, albeit to varying degrees.

In addition, there are other important clerical figures, some of them active in politics, who also espouse reformist positions on many issues, especially in regard to political participation, human and gender rights, and the need to tolerate diverging views. Among the better-known figures in this category are Ayatullah Hashemi Rafsanjani and Hujat al-Islam Mehdi Karrubi. However, they have not systematically developed their ideas and hence their views will not be discussed here, although, when appropriate, reference may be made to them.

Hujat al-Islam Muhammad Khatami

Before discussing the views of other reformist clerics, the ideas of Iran's former reformist president Seyyed Muhammad Khatami should be noted. In terms of religious knowledge and rank, Khatami is not comparable to the senior reformist clerics discussed here, nor is he as theoretically sophisticated as some of the other key clerical and lay reformist thinkers. Yet he has played a much more significant role in popularizing the Islamic reformist discourse than more learned ayatullahs. In his capacity as Iran's president, Khatami fundamentally altered the content and expanse of public debate in Iran by adopting a reformist discourse, emphasizing the rights of the citizenry and not just their duties, and, most important, stressing the significance of open questioning and critical reasoning in the construction and maintenance of civilizations.

Khatami does not concern himself too much with detailed religious issues, such as whether the Islamic penal code should be applied or not, or the nature of *ijtihad* and the most suitable methodology for the interpretation of Islamic sources. His main concerns are more of a political and social nature, such as the relationship between religion and freedom, religious democracy (*mardomsalari e dini*), challenges posed by modernity to Muslim societies, the extent of permissible borrowing from the West, and civilizational dialogue.

Nevertheless, Khatami's views on these subjects are informed by a particular conception of the relationship between God and humankind and the rights and responsibilities that flow from this particular understanding of this relationship. Khatami's view of humans is that they are God's vice-regents on earth, endowed with power, consciousness, and free will. However, all these human attributes are contingent on God's will.[111] This particular understanding of the relationship between humankind and God is very much in the Shi'a tradition, with its belief in free will as opposed to predestination. It also reflects the greater emphasis put on reason in Shi'a tradition. According to Khatami, God congratulated himself because, after creating man, he conferred reason on him.[112] Another important underpinning of traditional Shi'ism, which also informs Khatami's overall philosophy, is the emphasis on justice.[113]

In short, in Khatami's view rationality and justice should be the guides for all human thought and action, including in efforts to interpret religious sources. Thus, in his methodology, Khatami belongs to the rationalist school and calls for a rationalist Islam (*islam e aqlani*). However, Khatami also believes that human reason and free will should be tempered by spirituality and be used at the service of God and his creation. According to him, religion without reason degenerates into superstition, and reason without religion and spirituality leads to dehumanization and becomes the source of many injustices.[114] To achieve individual and collective happiness, humans need both reason and spirituality.

Khatami has a similar view regarding the relationship between freedom and religion. He believes that religion without freedom results in what was experienced during the Middle Ages and prevents intellectual growth. Freedom without religion leads to excessive materialism and individualism and many social ills.[115] He has said that Iran's salvation lies in "combining religion and freedom."[116] More specifically, Khatami has made the exercise of certain freedoms contingent on their not threatening Islam's foundations. But at the same time, he has warned that Islam should not be defined so narrowly that any disagreement with the dominant view held by the government or society could be interpreted as undermining its foundations.[117] Khatami is particularly critical of those who accuse anyone who defends the people's fundamental rights and their right to determine their own destiny as being anti-religion and liberal. In defending his positions against his accusers, he has said that Islam totally rejects fascism while it offers a critique of liberalism.[118]

In general, Khatami is a great advocate of both self-questioning and criticism and the questioning of others' ideas and philosophies. The important thing for him is the free process of questioning with an open mind and without prejudice. He maintains that without such questioning, cultures become stagnant.

This basic attitude favoring questioning and constructive criticism informs Khatami's approach to Western civilization and modernity. He opposes both the attitude of infatuation (*shiftegi*) on the part of Iranians (and Muslims in general) toward Western civilization, which leads to the trampling of all aspects of indigenous culture, and that of hatred and rejection (*nefrat*), which leads to self-destructive thinking and action.[119] Khatami is also critical of the despiritualizing dimensions of modernity and holds them responsible for phenomena such as colonialism and oppressive ideologies.[120]

This fundamental belief in human subjectivity, albeit one contingent on the Divine subjectivity,[121] and commitment to justice, have led Khatami to support a system of government based on popular participation, the accountability of government to the people, recognition of the fact that people have rights as well as duties, and hence support for human rights for all Iranian citizens irrespective of religion, ethnicity, or gender.

Yet Khatami has not openly challenged the institution of the supreme leader, which many reformist thinkers regard as incompatible with a people-based (*mardom salar*) government. He has, however, spoken against using religion as an instrument for achieving political and other interests (*istefadeh e abzari az din*) and has said that questioning the institution of the supreme leader is permissible. Khatami has also refrained from expressing clear opinions on issues of concern to women, such as the reform of family law or the veil. Nor has he addressed the controversial issue of Islamic punishments, even after leaving office. Nevertheless, given his basic philosophy, his positions on these issues are presumably close to those of other reformist clerics.

Khatami is a champion of dialogue among civilizations, including between Islamic and Western civilizations. However, he has also been critical of what he sees to be the objectification of Muslims and Islamic civilization by Western Orientalists. He argues that, for a dialogue between the West and the Islamic world to be successful—a dialogue that he maintains is necessary to avoid war and conflict—Westerners should look at Muslims and Islam as equal partners and not mere objects of study and conversion.[122] He also blames what he calls "the logic of force" for global divisions and conflicts and recommends that it be replaced with the logic of dialogue.[123]

Ayatullah Hussein Ali Muntazeri

Ayatullah Hussein Ali Muntazeri operates within the confines of traditional Shi'a jurisprudence and applies *ijtihad* only to secondary issues (*forou*) of Islamic tradition and not its foundational aspects (*usul*). However, he pushes the limits of traditional *ijtihad* and offers liberal readings that are more responsive to Muslims' new needs and challenges they are facing in the modern world. Methodologically, he relies more on reason than on *hadith* in reaching his decisions, especially if there are only one or two *hadith* regarding a particular problem and they appear to contradict the spirit of Qur'anic verses. He emphasizes the importance of time and space (*zaman va makan*) in the interpretation of Islamic rules, and he is a proponent of "searching *fiqh*" (*fiqh e puya*).[124] This methodology endeavors to find the most suitable answers, from existing rules, to questions facing Muslims.

From the perspective of religious intellectuals, who want more fundamental reforms such as Ali Reza Alavitabar, this approach is not sufficient because it does not scrutinize the foundations of the faith. Nevertheless, they admit that Ayatullah Muntazeri has helped combat stagnation (*jomoud*) and fundamentalism (*bonyadgaraie*) within religious seminaries, and has encouraged new thinking in *fiqh*.[125]

Ayatullah Muntazeri has made liberal rulings regarding apostasy (*irtad*), rejecting the death penalty.[126] He has ruled that if a Muslim converted to another religion after thorough research, this would not amount to apostasy. More important, he has said that in the Qur'an there is no mention of the death penalty for apostasy.[127] He has also ruled that while veiling (*hijab*) is necessary in Islam, its exact form is not clear, thus allowing for a less restrictive form of veiling. Moreover, if a woman's work and livelihood were at stake and she could not migrate to a place where veiling was allowed, she would be exempt from this duty.[128]

Ayatullah Muntazeri has an interpretation of the purpose of the Islamic penal code (*hudud*) and the conditions under which penalties could be applied that in reality make their application impossible. Muntazeri, like such prominent Shi'a scholars as Sheikh Tusi and Allameh Helli, believes that punishments should not contradict the reasoning (*aqlaniat*) of the society and the requirements of human dignity (*karamat-e-insani*). According to Muntazeri, punishments are for safeguarding the interests of the individual and society and for securing divine and human rights. Since attacking human dignity is viewed with disfavor by the legislator (God), any act that is against human dignity cannot secure either the rules of the *shari'a* or divine and human rights.[129] Further, Muntazeri believes that the question of what is insulting or degrading to human dignity is bound by time and space. Consequently, changing times and social and cultural attitudes justify reconsidering the application of Islamic punishments.[130] Difficulties in meeting all the requirements, such as the number of witnesses and their reliability, also argue against the application of the *hudud*.[131]

Muntazeri holds progressive views on issues of governance and democracy. He is the only one among the senior clerics associated with the Islamic Revolution who has openly said that the Islamic regime has failed to realize the revolution's objectives. He has criticized the revolution's excesses and, referring to Qur'anic verses, has argued that the injunction to uphold justice applies also to those who hold different religious and political views.[132]

Furthermore, he is opposed to *velayat mutlaqeh* (absolute guardianship)[133] and believes that government should be run by experts while the *ulema* should have only a supervisory role.[134] He maintains that, in the contemporary world, the Islamic injunction to enjoin the good and warn from evil (*amr bel maru'f va nay e min al-munkar*) requires the formation of political parties.[135]

On the question of human rights, Muntazeri believes that, by virtue of their humanity, human beings have been granted dignity by God, and that any act that infringes on this dignity is condemned by the Qur'an. Part of this dignity is the right of all to equal citizenship and the rights deriving from it, irrespective of their religion.[136] These rights include freedom of conscience, opinion, and expression. He has said that "at the time of the Prophet and the Commander of the Faithful [Ali] there were no political prisoners and nobody was tried and jailed for holding certain opinions and for expressing them."[137] Ayatullah Muntazeri has been a spiritual leader for younger reformist clerics, including his students.

Ayatullah Yussef Saanei

Ayatullah Yussef Saanei, too, uses traditional methods of *ijtihad* to issue liberal *fatwas* on a wide range of issues, notably the following: the type of retaliation for killing Muslims and non-Muslims and men and women (*qessas*) and monetary compensation (*diyeh*) for such crimes; the age of adulthood for females (*bolooq*); and the necessary conditions for the application of the Islamic penal code.

Referring to the views of such prominent Shi'a religious scholars as Mirza Qumi (early nineteenth century) and Ayatullah Sayyid Ahmad Ansari, Saanei has stated that Islamic punishments can be applied only after the return of the Hidden Imam.[138] He has emphasized the difficulties involved in getting adequate proofs for certain crimes, such as adultery, which further argue against their application.[139] In 2006 he openly called for a total revision of this code.

Saanei considers any confession obtained in prison or under duress to be invalid.[140] He has also ruled that the punishment and compensation for killing of Muslims and non-Muslims and men and women should be equal.[141] Saanei has a generally progressive view regarding women's rights and on several occasions has emphasized the equality of men and women. He has been in the forefront of efforts to make the monetary compensation paid to the survivors of someone who has been killed (*diyeh*) equal for men and women.[142]

Saanei has strongly supported women's right to compete for the highest political office, including the presidency and even as supreme leader (*velayat-e-faqih*).[143] He has said that "being a man is not an honor according to the book [Qur'an], the Sunna of the Prophet, and reason." He has noted that all *hadith* regarding *velayat-e-faqih* refer to knowledge as the basis of qualification and not gender. This fact proves that Islam recognizes the equality of men and women.[144] Yet Saanei does not consider disparity in inheritance of males and females as being against the principle of gender equality. He supports the traditional position that, because men are breadwinners, they should have double the inheritance of women—although this position does not reflect the current socioeconomic conditions of Iranian women.[145]

Saanei has liberal views on politics and governance. He supports democracy and believes in the centrality of the people's role in legitimizing power by expressing their will through fair elections. He emphasizes the importance of freedom of opinion and expression, especially "freedom after expression," meaning that nobody should be punished after expressing an opinion.[146] Ayatullah Saanei's liberal views have made him a target of criticism by lay and clerical conservatives.

Ayatullah Muhammad Moussavi Bojnourdi

Ayatullah Muhammad Moussavi Bojnourdi is the head of the Imam Khomeini Center for Islamic Studies and of the Islamic Human Rights Commission. He is one of the most reform-minded senior clerics. He favors a rationalist and contextualist approach to the interpretation of Islamic sources, and believes that, in interpreting these rules, Islam's core values of justice and mercy should be kept in mind.

He graciously answered the following questions that this author put to him in writing:

Q: What is your eminence's understanding of religious new thinking and reformist Islam?

A: Our understanding of religious new thinking is based on the following considerations.

First Islam is a universal and eternal religion. Therefore, it should be able to answer questions that inevitably arise from societies' development and to provide solutions to emerging problems. Therefore, we believe that in our religious thinking and *ijtihad* we should take into account the requirements of time and space and adjust our interpretations of religious rules to society's developments and needs.

Second, Islam is a universal religion, and after the return of the *Mahdi* it will spread throughout the world. Therefore, its rules should be applicable globally. In order to realize this goal Islam should encourage new thinking (*now andishi*) and move in the direction of reform and renewal. For my part, I boldly declare that *my view of Islam is reformist and favors new thinking* [emphasis added].

Q: Your eminence has said that we should have democracy in a religious society and not a religious democracy. What do you mean by this statement?

A: Democracy means the rule of the people (*mardom salari*), in the sense that people take part in governing and decide their own destiny. Now, let us examine the question of whether we have two kinds of democracy, secular and religious, or rather that democracy is a single notion and construct. Sometimes democracy and the rule of the people are realized in a secular society and sometimes in a religious society.

In a religious society, because people believe in religious principle in their practice of democracy, they do not go beyond the limits set by their religious beliefs. Yet because the people participate in governing and deciding their own destiny, there is democracy in a religious society.

However, to qualify democracy as religious will not be a correct interpretation of the term. This is so because one cannot have two kinds of democracy, secular and religious. Just as one cannot have religious and secular physics or religious and secular economics, one cannot have two kinds of democracy, secular and religious. Therefore, when I said democracy in a religious society and not democracy conditioned by religion, I was expressing the view that democracy cannot have two meanings. Rather, religion can be a container for democracy, but not a condition. We cannot put a religious condition on democracy, and people's rule in a religious and Islamic society requires that the society be governed according to democratic principles and with people's direct participation in governance.

Q: What are your eminence's views regarding the revision of the Islamic penal code, and women's rights regarding judgeship, witness, and the guardianship of their children?

A: The purpose of Islamic legislation regarding punishments is to reform people and not to exact revenge. Some of these punishments are based on preexisting customs that were quite widespread at the time of Revelation, but lack legitimacy today. For instance, in my opinion, today stoning has no legitimacy because it is considered torture by all enlightened people.

Moreover, the safeguarding of Islam's prestige and good name is of utmost importance. Therefore, we should define Islam in such a way that does not undermine its global standing. If today some issues damage Islam's prestige we should interpret them in a way that does not harm Islam's standing.

Imam Khomeini himself favored this approach as reflected in the following example. In the year 1360 [1980], the issue of stoning (*rajm*) became a problem. I went to Imam and told him that today this punishment is a cause of shame for Islam, and asked him to institute another punishment. He told me to instruct the courts not to order this punishment and instead "guide them [the guilty] to repentance."

Regarding apostasy, because there is freedom of conscience in Islam, I do not believe in the death penalty. Moreover, one cannot force someone to become a true believer. Regarding women's testimony, the interpretation of the Qur'anic rule that two women's testimony is equal to that of one man as a sign of women's mental inadequacy is incorrect. The Qur'an was trying to establish the principle of sufficiency of testimony, rather than setting a general standard. Therefore, this Qur'anic rule does not mean that the testimony of two women is always equal to that of any man. [After this interview, Ayatullah Bojnourdi, in a speech in July 2006 at a gathering on women's right at Tehran University, openly stated that the testimony of women is equal to that of men.][147]

Regarding women judges, my opinion is that women can be judges and that there is no limitation in this regard in Islam. In Islam, the measure of judgeship is justice and not gender. All *hadith* regarding the inability of women to be judges, both in terms of their reasoning and sources are weak. In short, maleness is not one of the conditions of judgeship.

Regarding the guardianship of children, I have written that the mother should have the guardianship of both male and female children until the age of puberty. After that, it should be up to the child to decide which parent he or she wants to be his or her guardian, and nobody can order the child. Following my recommendation, the parliament passed a law that gives the guardianship of male and female children to the mother until the age of seven. This law was finally approved by the Guardian Council.

Q: Should non-Muslims have equal rights with Muslim citizens?

A: According to Islam, if the ruler considers it to be in the society's interest, law-abiding non-Muslims should be equal with Muslims. In Iran, all citizens are equal according to the public law, and religious minorities observe their own religious rules and laws only in matters of personal status.

Later, in the speech referred to earlier, Ayatullah Bojnourdi went beyond this qualified endorsement of equality between Muslims and non-Muslims. He stated that the Qur'an has eliminated all forms of racial, religious, and gender discrimination by emphasizing the basic dignity of human beings. Therefore, there is no difference between men and women in terms of their human dignity and hence rights. It follows from this reasoning that in his view non-Muslim Iranian citizens should have equal rights with Muslims.

Hujat al-Islam Muhsen Kadivar

Hujat al-Islam Muhsen Kadivar is one of the most outspoken and prolific reformist figures in Iran. Methodologically, Kadivar remains within the classical Shi'a tradition, albeit its most rationalist and contextualist form. According to Kadivar, in Sunni Islam, Ash'ari traditionalism defeated the Mu'tazilis' rationalism. But in Shi'ism the founders of the Shi'a *fiqh*, such as Sheikh Mufid, Sheikh Tusi, and Allameh Helli, moderated Mu'tazili rationalism and thus retained an important role for reason in Shi'a jurisprudence. However, Kadivar does not believe in the self-sufficiency of reason, and he maintains that humankind needs revelation in order to awaken its innate reason. He likens this reason to an "inner Prophet."[148] Moreover, like Muslim philosophers, especially Avicenna, and his inspiration, Sheikh Mufid, Kadivar believes that reason and revelation are never in conflict.[149]

In his methodology, in addition to reason Kadivar emphasizes the importance of context and historical analysis of religious sources. He also allocates an important role to justice in the understanding and interpretation of Islamic rules, and their application to contemporary conditions. This aspect of his methodology, too, reflects his Shi'a intellectual foundations.

Based on his particular approach to the understanding and interpretation of Islamic law and jurisprudence, Kadivar believes that Islamic rules should always meet the following three criteria: compatibility with reason; compatibility with the requirements of justice, since "justice is the measure of religion and not religion the measure of justice"; and compatibility with the requirements of time and the people's preferences.[150]

According to Kadivar, Islamic regulations of the Prophet's epoch met all these requirements. They were superior to the existing laws and traditions (*urf*) of the Arabian Peninsula in terms of both reason and justice, and they were approved by the community. Today, many of those laws relating to women, religious minorities, and the penal code do not meet the requirements of rationality, justice, and compatibility with existing conditions.[151] This line of reasoning leads Kadivar to identify two different types of Islam, namely "historical Islam" (*islam e tarikhy*), and "spiritual Islam" (*islam e manavi*).[152]

Historical Islam considers

> the dominant culture and the temporal and spatial conditions of the Prophet's time as Islam's sacred, unchanging, desirable and ideal forms and concepts . . . and [believes that] as one gets further away from that sacred past and grows distant from those historic conditions one becomes distant from authentic Islam. [For the proponents of historical Islam] Islam's revival only means the recreation of the conditions of those early days.[153]

By contrast, spiritual Islam,

> after considering the temporal and spatial conditions of the period of the formation of the religion [Islam], views religiosity [*dindari*] as the knowledge and realization of religion's spirit and its ultimate goal.[154]

Muslims' encounter with modernity constitutes a "critical juncture" or a "point of departure" (*nogteh e atf*) for them in the process of transition from historical Islam to spiritual Islam. The reason for this situation is that the process of modernization posed a significant challenge for Muslims in terms of reconciling some of their religious principles with the discourses and standards of modernity. This challenge became more serious when many aspects of modernity were transformed into the "tradition of the time" (*urf e zamaneh*) or the "contemporary rationality" and conflicted with some religious principles.[155]

According to Kadivar, Muslim responses to the challenge of modernity—

whether total rejection or total embrace—have failed to resolve Islam's and Muslims' fundamental problems in the context of this encounter.[156] Kadivar suggests that only the paradigm of "spiritual and goal-oriented Islam" (*islam e manavi va qayatmadar*) can solve these problems. The fundamental characteristics of this Islam are:

1. In every epoch the validity of *shari'a* rules depends on their justness and compatibility with the requirements of reason;

2. All religious rules of the period of Revelation that no longer meet these requirements are part of the temporary (*muvaqat*) and not eternal and unchanging (*sabet*) rules of religion;

3. The only lawgiver (*shar'e*) is God and the Prophet, and no one except the sinless infallibles (*ma'sum*) can establish religious rules;

4. Those religious rules that, because of lack justice or rationality, fall out of the purview of religious rules (*howzeh e ahkam e sharei*) are not replaced by other religious rules. Instead, in these circumstances "rational laws" (*qavanin e uqalai*) without reference to religious rules become the basis of action; and

5. The purview of *fiqh* and *shari'a* (Islamic jurisprudence and Islamic law) becomes narrower, but the purview of religion grows and becomes deeper.[157]

Kadivar's views on issues ranging from human and women's rights to democracy derive from this particular conception of religion and *shari'a*. Kadivar believes that, current Islamic rules regarding women's rights, in many respects, do not meet the criteria of either justice or rationality and therefore they should be changed. He asks how it is that a fourteen-year-old boy is considered a child, while a nine-year-old girl is considered an adult and can be subject to criminal prosecution and punishment. He then asks, "is it not better to make eighteen the age of adulthood both for girls and boys?" He applies the same logic in support of equal rights for men and women in other areas.[158]

Kadivar considers veiling obligatory in Islam, but opposes its imposition by force. In general, for the following reasons he believes that no religious principle should be imposed by force:

1. Islam has declared that there is no compulsion in faith (*la ikraha fi din*);

2. Islam is a religion based on persuasion and not coercion (*eqnai na ejbari*); and any coercion in religious matters leads to hypocrisy and corruption and erodes true faith (*iman*).[159]

Following this logic, he also supports equal rights for Muslims and non-Muslims[160] and opposes the death penalty for apostasy. Regarding the issue of Islam's compatibility with democracy, Kadivar says that a certain interpretation of Islam—traditionalist/literalist—is incompatible with what he calls maximalist or liberal democracy, because such democracy completely relegates religion to the private domain. By contrast, the reformist reading of Islam is compatible with deliberative democracy (*democrasieh rayzananeh*) because, according to reformist Islam, "all members of society have equal rights in terms of participation in the [society's] political life and the determination of its destiny irrespective of their race, religion, gender, and opinion."[161]

Kadivar believes that democracy is the best system of government for today's conditions. He is highly critical of Iran's present political system based on the guardianship of the *faqih* and believes that this theory has no basis in Shi'a *fiqh*. He has tried to substantiate his views by citing various Shi'a theorists on the subject.[162]

Kadivar' s interpretation of Islamic rules and his prescriptive writings regarding how they should be applied in effect leads to a version of a secular model of society. However, in this version, religion is not aggressively eliminated from the public square and there is no discrimination against religious people.

Sheikh Abdullah Nouri

Another reformist cleric worthy of note is Sheikh Abdullah Nouri. He was publisher of the reformist daily *Khordad* and he was tried on charges of publishing materials incompatible with Islamic principles and insulting Ayatullah Khomeini and his views. Nouri's approach to the study of religious law and his views on individual freedoms and people-centered governance are similar to those of personalities discussed above. These views are explained in his defense against accusations against him published in the book *Hemlock of Reform*.[163]

There are a number of other senior clerics who espouse reformist views, especially on political issues and the relative roles of the people and the Supreme Leader in deciding major issues facing the country. One of them is the late Ayatullah Reza Tavasoli, who died in early 2008, and was known as the cleric of the reformists.[164]

Ex-Clerics

Muhammad Mujtahed Shabestari

The former ayatullah Muhammad Mujtahed Shabestari is viewed as the pioneer of new Islamic theology (*kalam e jadid*) in Iran.[165] He spent a long time in Germany at the Islamic Center, and is fluent in German, and is well versed in Western philosophical and theological concepts, notably religious hermeneutics. His views and writings clearly show the impact of these ideas.

The following concepts form the cornerstone of Mujtahed Shabestari's system of thinking:

1. Any interpretation of religious or other sources is deeply affected by the interpreter's preferences, preconceptions, and prejudgments;[166]

2. The impact of these factors in various interpretations intensifies as the time elapsed between the production of the original source and its interpretation lengthens. This happens because in every cycle of interpretation the preconceptions (*pish fahmha*) of the later interpreters are added to those of earlier ones.

According to Shabestari, "The understanding of a text (*matn*) does not occur at once and without any prelude, or without passing from one stage to the next and without completing the understanding of the first stage with the next. On the contrary, there always exists a pre-understanding of a given text that becomes more extensive and constitutes the prelude for its later understandings. This process is especially necessary for the understanding of difficult texts, and this is the reason why such texts are subject to frequent study and analysis. During each of these cycles of study, the pre-understandings are different and the analyst constantly moves from one cycle to the next."[167] Shabestari call this process the "hermeneutical cycle" (*dor e hermeneutic*), thus indicating his preferred methodology for the analysis of religious texts and sources.[168]

Shabestari believes that the cycle of interpretation never ends, and therefore there can be no final interpretation of sacred texts and other sources that is valid for all times. Nor can there be a single valid reading of religious texts and sources. He further maintains that the main cause of diverging views among religious scholars is the difference in their preconceptions and prior understandings of religious texts. Every interpreter approaches the text with desires and purposes that differ from those of previous interpreters and most probably from those of the original authors of various texts. Shabestari admonishes all interpreters to be conscious of the baggage that they bring to their interpretations.[169]

Shabestari notes that the act of interpretation is not a mere linguistic exercise; it is the interpretation of lived experiences within different historical contexts. A contemporary interpreter of the Qur'an and the Prophet's *sunna* approaches them from the vantage point of his or her experience and seeks answers for questions that were not posed at the time of the Prophetic Revelation and leadership.[170]

In Shabestari's view, what bridges this wide gap in time and experience is the fact that people today and past generations "share a common humanity and lasting experiences that relate to the essence and foundation of humanity."[171] This is why today's Muslims can recognize their own questions in the past generations' questions, and can relate their own answers to those provided by earlier interpreters.

In this way, they realize that the connection between present and past generations is both possible and meaningful.

Preconceptions of Fuqaha *and the Limits of* Fiqh. This philosophical and methodological outlook leads Shabestari to have a narrow interpretation of the purview of *fiqh* and a contextualist, historicist, and critical approach to it. This approach results in constant "reconstruction of religion" (*bazsazi e dini*), which he considers necessary if religion is to remain relevant to people's lives and avoid intellectual ossification.

In advancing this view, Shabestari is largely reacting to realities of life in the Islamic Republic, especially religion's instrumentalization by competing groups to acquire and retain power and to exclude others. Shabestari argues that *fiqh* has no constitutive function; its function is interpretive. According to him the science of *fiqh* emerged when, after the Prophet's death and Islam's expansion, Muslims encountered new conditions, experienced new events, and faced new questions for which no obvious answers could be found either in the Qur'an or in the *sunna*. The Muslims' search for answers to these questions was the beginning of *fiqh* and *ijtihad*. As proof of the limited nature of *fiqh*, Shabestari says:

> Muslims' laws, political systems, administrative, economic, and social organizations, and criminal laws were not created by *fiqh*. Some were reflective of the social life of Arabs of Mecca and Medina, and others belonged to the countries that Islam conquered. In fact, most of Islamic contractual and criminal laws either existed among Arabs or in other societies conquered by Islam . . . Thus the idea that the book [Qur'an] and the *sunna* are the source of all sociopolitical systems, administrative organizations, and contractual exchanges among Muslims does not correspond to reality.[172]

Shabestari further notes that the Qur'an has neither proscribed nor prescribed a particular form of government. The Qur'an's main concern is value-related (*arzeshi*). This means that the Qur'an wants to ensure that governments, whatever their form, are based on justice. This concern with justice is the eternal and unchangeable variable and not the form of government.[173] The inescapable conclusion of this line of argument is that, at any time, a people's type of government should be determined by the people, based on the criteria of justice and nothing else.

Two other important conclusions flow from this argument:

1. Because of the complexity of contemporary Muslims' social, political, and economic life they require a diverse range of knowledge, which is outside the purview of *fiqh* and hence outside the grasp of the jurists (*fuqaha*);
2. There is non-exclusivity of opinion regarding values and general divine injunctions (*ahkam*).

The implication of these conclusions is that *ijtihad* is a form of human knowledge rather than a "sacred gift" bestowed on a particular individual or group. This view has significant implications for the clerical establishment's role both as interpreters of the *shari'a* and as spiritual guides for believers. It also implies that the *ulema* are not the successors of the Prophet and the imams and hence do not possess a God-given right to lead, much less to rule society.

Governance, Democracy, and Human Rights. Shabestari expounds his views regarding these issues in his book *A Critique of the Official Reading of Religion*,[174] in which he criticizes what he considers the distortion of the original ideological foundations of the Islamic Revolution and the Islamic Republic's Constitution. The book's underlying premise is that fundamental economic, social, and technological changes in Muslim countries in the last 150 years have created new living conditions and new popular aspirations. Dealing with these new conditions and responding to these new aspirations requires new skills and new methods and structures that do not exist in *fiqh* and are not possessed by the *fuqaha*.

He argues that the Islamic Revolution and the Islamic government's constitution were both rational (*uqalai*) phenomena. The development of the Islamic Republic's constitution and system of government were legal and political exercises. They were not inspired by the holy book (Qur'an) and *sunna*. Nor were they informed by the sciences of *fiqh* or *kalam* (theology). Similarly, political values enshrined in the constitution are essentially the products of modernity rather than inspired by the Qur'an and the *sunna*.[175] Shabestari argues that, over the course of two decades, this rationalist reading of Islam was replaced with a *fiqh*-based reading of Islam (*islam e feqahati*) that became the official reading of Islam.

Shabestari identifies the basic components of this reading as follows:

1. Islam has eternal economic, social, and political systems;
2. The type of government is derived from the Qur'an and the *sunna* and is not subject to reasoning;
3. The purpose of Islamic government is to ensure the implementation of Islamic rules.[176]

The outcome of the preponderance of this view within the Islamic system has been that people's political rights enshrined in the constitution have become limited on the basis of the "traditional *fiqh*" (*fiqh e sunati*); and the form and duties of the government and the people's rights have been determined by religious edicts (*fatvahaye e fiqhi*).[177]

According to Shabestari, this development has led to repression, disregard of people's constitutional rights, and religion's abuse for individual and group advantage. Moreover, instead of strengthening people's religious beliefs, this reading, and the practices following from it, have eroded people's religious belief.[178]

This experience under the Islamic Republic informs Shabestari's thinking on governance and people's rights. Shabestari maintains that democracy is the only viable system of government for present times. He defines democracy as a "method of governance" (*ravash e hukumat*) that is the opposite of dictatorship because the former is based on two basic principles of freedom and equality. He adds that one either accepts democracy or not, and that democracy cannot be qualified as, for example, "Islamic democracy." He admits, however, that one can speak of a democracy of Muslims (*democracy e muslmanan*), which would be influenced by Islamic values as long as Muslims remain faithful to them.[179] He adds that one cannot ensure people's loyalty to religious beliefs by repression.[180]

Shabestari believes that human rights, as currently understood, are a product of modernity and not, as their opponents claim, a product of Western culture. He maintains that it is fruitless to try to find their equivalents in Islam or in other premodern cultures. Therefore, efforts to develop Islamic human rights and juxtapose them to Western human rights are futile.[181] Rather, human rights are of concern in all societies that to a greater or lesser degree have been touched by modernity.

After noting that human rights are non-religious (*qeir e dini*) and not anti-religion (*zed e dini*), he asks how Muslims should determine their position in regard to these rights. He answers the question by recommending that Muslims separate the inherent (*bel zat*) characteristics of the Prophetic message from its incidental (*bel araz*) aspects, which were determined by the conditions prevailing in Hijaz at the time of the Prophetic mission. He then suggests that Muslims ask themselves whether Islam's fundamental message, which is monotheistic behavior (*suluk e tawhidi*) and the safeguard of people's faith, would not be best preserved within a democratic system and by observing human rights. He answers this question in the affirmative and recommends that Muslims accept human rights. This fundamental position leads Shabestari to support equal rights for all citizens without distinction of race, religion, and gender, and to favor a revision of Islamic penal codes.[182]

Shabestari's particular reading of Islam, and the practical conclusions that he draws, result in a kind of nondogmatic secularism, within which religion has a place in the public sphere, but neither aspires to the domination of public discourse on what is permissible nor interferes in the conduct of society's economic and political life.

Hassan Yussefi Eshkevari and Seyyed Muhsen Saidzadeh, the next two ex-clerics, are among the most outspoken proponents of reformist Islam in Iran and critics of the current political system, especially the institution of *velayat-e faqih*. Because of their political and other reformist views, they both were imprisoned and were stripped of their clerical position and dress. This has led Saidzadeh, who among reformist thinkers is the most ardent champion of women's rights, to withdraw from the public scene.

In their methodology, Eshkevari and Saidzadeh are close to Kadivar and

Shabestari and, like them, they advocate a rationalist and historicist approach to the analysis and interpretation of Islamic sources. Eshkevari's thinking is also influenced more directly by the ideas of the Mu'tazilis, by Muhammad Iqbal, especially his concept of the total restructuring of Islamic thought and changing the understanding of what it means to be a Muslim, and by Shariati and his notion of a kind of Islamic Protestantism.

Muhsen Saidzadeh

Muhsen Saidzadeh has elaborated his views regarding the nature and purview of *fiqh* and the rules and method of interpreting religious sources, including the role of reason in this process, in his book *Women in Civil Society: What Is Their Share?*[183]

The following are Saidzadeh's basic views on these issues:
1. *Fiqh* is a branch of human knowledge. Everyone can become a *faqih* (jurist) because understanding religion belongs to all Muslims;
2. The method and logic of understanding is rational and hence is not limited to a particular group or profession;
3. Edicts issued by the *fuqaha* (jurists) do not have general validity. They are only binding on the individual who has asked a question; and
4. The purview of *fiqh* is limited to discovering the secondary rules of the *shari'a* and to determining practical duties based on interpretive evidence. Therefore, the following areas are outside the purview of *fiqh*:
    a. Non-religious matters (*umur e urfi*), namely, the accepted norms of behavior and speech of people at any given time and place. Thus *fuqaha* cannot determine what the *urf* was that the Qur'an had in mind;
    b. Non-religious traditions and modes of behavior ratified by religion (*umuur e emzai*). These include those Islamic rules that are essentially the ratification of practices that existed among Arabs in the era of the Prophetic mission. Thus, a *faqih* cannot endow these rules with divine character;
    c. Rational and theoretical matters. This is so because *fiqh* is based on the transmission of texts (Qur'an and *sunna*);
    d. All scientific, technical, and other human knowledge, including theology (*kalam*);
    e. Constitutional rights, whether or not accepted by the *shari'a*, because irrespective of whether the *faqih* accepts it or not, human beings have the right to life and possess inherent dignity and the freedom to choose their own destiny. Therefore, any ruling on such issues, especially those related to government and the method of governance, requires the peoples' acquiescence in order to be legitimate; and
    f. Empirical matters.[184]

Saidzadeh, like Kadivar, distinguishes between religion and religiosity. He defines religion as divine and metaphysical, and religiosity as terrestrial and human. Religion is abstract (*mujarad*) and non-material. Religiosity is a social phenomenon bound by time and space. According to Saidzadeh,

> Religiosity is influenced both by religion and by the world. It is colored both by obedience to religion and by reason. . . . Religious people, in addition to obeying religion, utilize their reason, knowledge, and experience. When religion spreads among the people and acquires operational dimensions, it also acquires popular coloring. Thus Iranian religion becomes different from Iraqi religion, and Saudi religion from that of Jordan. . . . This means that one cannot give human affairs divine aspects. Nor can one look for answers to all human questions in religious revelation. Separating the spheres of religion and religiosity also means distinguishing reason from revelation.[185]

According to Saidzadeh, most of what is permitted by religion and what is prohibited (*maruf va munkar*) are for purposes of guidance (*ahkam e ershadi*). Therefore, they are influenced by time and space. Based on this reasoning, Saidzadeh reaches the following conclusions:

1. Neither the *faqih* nor the government can force people to observe rules intended as guidance, or even devotional rules (*ahkam e ebadi*) such as prayer and fasting, because judgment, punishment, and reward on these matters belong to God;
2. All acts of government, including those related to war and peace (*jihad*), are subject to popular acceptance. The Prophet's *sunna*, which sought Muslims' *baya'a* (pledge of allegiance) in Medina before setting up a government and waging *jihad*, supports this view. There is no historical evidence that the Prophet forced anyone to wage *jihad* or declared those who refused to do so apostates;
3. All administrative and political matters are human affairs and hence not subject to religious rules; and
4. All issues related to civil society, including women's participation and rules regarding their dress and behavior, are not the subject of religious law (*shari'a*) but are part of "guiding rules."[186]

In Islam, according to Saidzadeh, women's rights fall into two categories:

1. What the Prophet said as the messenger of God. All Qur'anic verses that fall in this category consider women equal to men in rights and duties;[187]
2. What the Prophet said as a political leader.

The latter rulings are influenced by the traditions of Arabia, which considered men and women unequal.[188] Although Saidzadeh does not say so clearly, the latter rulings fall under the category of the so-called ratifying rules (*umur e emzaei*) and therefore may be changed. He then argues that the Prophet's own behavior, such as his giving the right of divorce to his wives, attests to the equality of men and women and he concludes that, everything considered, in Islam the balance is in favor of gender equality.

In a broader context, Saidzadeh maintains that the Universal Declaration of Human Rights and other international conventions should now be considered as part of "world tradition and rationality" (*seyreh e uqala va urf e mardom e dunya*), and therefore should be given religious validity.[189] As evidence of the appropriateness of this approach, he notes Khomeini's changing attitude toward women's rights between 1962–64 and 1979. Before 1979, Khomeini opposed gender equality and voting rights for women, but in 1979 he supported equal rights for women and their participation in politics.[190]

Yussefi Eshkevari

Yussefi Eshkevari, too, distinguishes between Islam as faith (*iman*), which transcends time and space, and Islam as culture (*farhang*), which is bound by time and space and is diverse.[191] This division is similar to Kadivar's distinction between historical and spiritual Islam. He also subscribes to the idea of the possibility of multiple interpretations of religion.[192] Eshkevari is first and foremost what was earlier described as a neo-Shariati. He reinterprets some of Shariati's views, notably regarding democracy and Islamic government, and considers others irrelevant to present conditions. Eshkevari adds, however, that they may become highly relevant again in the future.

Nevertheless, he remains faithful to Shariati's fundamental message, namely that the initial spirit of Islam, which gave it vibrancy and made it a religion of justice and liberation, has been buried under layers of formalistic rituals and preexisting customs. Eshkevari believes that Iran today has neither a functioning Islamic nor an Iranian civilization. Moreover, it faces the daunting problem of underdevelopment and historic and chronic decadence. He then defines the goal of Islamic reformists as nothing short of creating an indigenous modernity based on what he calls "a guiding, dynamic, and faith-inspiring Islam," just as Hellenic culture became the foundation of the Renaissance and gave birth to European modernity. He mentions the Protestant Reformation as the other important contributory factor in this development.[193] To achieve these goals, Eshkevari believes that it is necessary to take a critical approach to both indigenous traditions and the Western discourse of modernity and to avoid blind imitation of either, but instead to combine the best of both to create a new civilization.[194]

Part of his critique of tradition relates to the structure of religious leadership. Here Eshkevari favors a sort of Islamic Protestantism, which implies a sharp erosion of the clergy's position, thus showing his faithfulness to Shariati's notion of religion minus the clergy. According to Eshkevari, because the discriminatory aspects of religious laws were determined by time and space and have become the foundation of an unjust system, they are no longer valid. He maintains that, if Islam is understood to be historical Islam, then it would be very difficult to eliminate discrimination and create a democratic (*mardom salari*) political system.[195] However, reformist Islam, or what he calls "religious intellectualism" (*rowshanfekri e dini*) can accommodate democracy, by focusing on Islam's core values, such as justice and respect for human dignity, and by utilizing a rationalist method of interpretation of sources.

Eshkevari has not written much on women's rights. But he gave an indication of his position in this regard at a conference in Berlin in April 2000 in response to a question from the audience. He stated that most of the rulings about women in Islam are in the category of the changeable rules and therefore may be adjusted according to circumstances. However, he confessed that this change could not come about easily or rapidly.[196]

Eshkevari believes that religious new thinking, religious enlightenment, or religious intellectualism, is the only way for Muslim societies to "nativize modernity."[197] Only by doing so can Muslim societies enter the modern world. He argues that only religious new thinkers can reach the religious masses, because, as experience has shown, secular intellectuals' discourse is discounted on account of their absolute privatization of religion.[198]

Ahmad Qabel

Another reformist ex-cleric who has been highly critical of the Islamic system and especially the behavior of the Ayatullah Khamenei is Ahmad Qabel.[199] Ahmad Qabel studied under Ayatullah Muntazeri and philosophically and methodologically subscribes to the principle of judging what has been related (*naql*) according to each era's standard of reason (*aql*). In fact, his official Web site is called "Shari'at e aqlani" (rationalist *shari'a*).

Qabel maintains that various interpretations of related texts should be judged in light of necessary conditions (*shurut e lazem*) and the standards of human reason (*meyar e aql e bashari*) of each era. Like many other reformist thinkers, Qabel distinguishes between *din* (religion) and *shari'a* (religious law), and he maintains that the latter should be subjected to rational and critical analysis. He holds the lack of such a critical approach to *shari'a* largely responsible for the inadequate level of Muslims' scientific and socioeconomic development.[200] Qabel believes that some of the texts and interpretations that were too progressive according to the customs of the times have been ignored by most *faqihs*. He suggests that these interpretations should be reconsidered according to reason and those of their aspects that are compatible with current knowledge should be accepted. He also recommends that contradictory or conflicting interpretations of religious texts and rules should not be accepted. Moreover, early reliable texts should be examined in a holistic (*negah e majmouei*) rather than piecemeal fashion. All these measures are necessary to develop a new reading of the *shari'a*.[201]

Qabel also believes that it is possible to develop a "rights-based" (*haq mehvari*) as opposed to a duty-based *shari'a*, because the Qur'an, the sayings of the Imams, and the views of many *ulema* prove that Islam recognizes certain "inherent rights" (*huquq e fetri*) for human beings. He cites evidence that people's rights (*haqh al-nass*) are more important than God's rights (*haq al-allah*). Such an interpretation of rights in Islam makes the observance of internationally accepted human rights possible.[202]

Qabel has argued that there is no justification in the Qur'an for punishment by death for apostasy, nor any prohibition against qualified women leading prayers.[203] He has been critical of the persistence of discrimination against women and religious minorities in Muslim countries, and he has attributed this to the lack of a rational and critical approach to the *shari'a*.[204]

Qabel has criticized the institution of the Council of Guardians (*shuray e negahban*) and in general has opposed the clergy's involvement in politics. He is reported to have said that the Islamic Republic's experience has shown the Iranian people that "an ideal society cannot be achieved with political Islam. This experience is hugely valuable. It is, if you like, the real achievement of the Islamic Revolution."[205]

Qabel is one of the more well-known and activist members of a younger generation of clerics with reformist ideas, largely gathered within the Association of Qum Theological Teachers.

Lay Religious Reformists

Another important group of reformist thinkers consists of lay intellectuals with varying levels of expertise in Islamic sciences. Some of these intellectuals are also active in politics and within various nongovernmental organizations, some of which they themselves have set up.

Abdolkarim Soroush

The most prominent representative of this group is Abdolkarim Soroush, whose real name is Hussein Hajifaraj Dabagh. He is a typical product of the Pahlavi modernization project and the Islamic reaction to it. He is also the perfect example of Iranian intellectuals' disillusionment with the Islamic government that they helped bring to power. Soroush attended an Alavi school and, while studying pharmacology at Tehran University, he sought instruction in Islamic philosophy from Ayatullah Mutahari, who referred him to one of his students. He also experimented with different Islamic groups. He briefly joined the conservative Hujatieh Society and later, while studying in England, he became interested in Shariati's ideas, although nowadays Soroush is one of Shariati's harshest critics.[206] Finally, he joined the forces supporting Ayatullah Khomeini and served in the commission overseeing the purification of universities and the rewriting of school texts.

While in England, Soroush became interested in the philosophy of religion, particularly in the question of why and how scholars and thinkers draw different conclusions and interpretations from the same texts.[207] This interest led him to develop his theories of religion, knowledge of religion, spiritual and temporal dimensions of religion, and the appropriate domain of religion.

The main components of Soroush's thinking are as follows:

1. The essence of religion is different from human understanding and knowledge of religion. While the essence of religion is constant, human understanding of it is changeable. It evolves as human knowledge and experience of religion expands along with other fields of science. According to Soroush, "just as no understanding of nature is ever complete and is enriched by new scientific works and the arrival of competing views and historical developments, so are understandings of religion. This applies both to jurisprudential (*fiqhi*) views and to fundamental beliefs (*nazariat e itiqadi va usuli*)."[208]

2. Human understanding of religion, like that of other spheres, is defective and is influenced by individual and collective pre-understandings and prejudgments. Therefore, there is not a single reading of religion that is valid; rather, the validity of various readings is relative. This perspective leads Soroush to subscribe both to plural readings of Islam and to the view that there is more than one route to religious truth, and hence to belief in "religious plurality." Soroush expands his views on the subject of religious pluralism in his book *Straight Paths*.[209]

3. Religion, which according to believers is "a sacred, divine, and mysterious truth," is transformed into an earthly and human enterprise once it acquires "a visible and external existence."[210] Soroush explains this process as what could be called the "profanation of the sacred" and its consequences in the following words:

When revelation (*vahy*) and sacred truth acquires visible and earthly reality, in essence the heavens come to earth and God's holy and beloved servants, who are the carriers of his trust (*amanat*), come into contact with people on earth in the shape of divine prophets and engage in intellectual and other-worldly (*maeishati*) exchanges with people. As a result, religion acquires external existence and history. It creates societies and cities and brings people under its influence. In the history of this actualized religion, many wars, peace, agreements, disagreements, negligence, and decline occur. Cultures and civilizations develop; sects, religious leaders, and establishments emerge. Books are written and conflicts develop. Later, falsifications occur. Conquests are made in the name of religion, and religion acquires the imprint of different ethnic, intellectual, and philosophical influences. The institution of religion enters into exchanges with other institutions. It influences them and is influenced by them and itself becomes a sociohistorical force, and like other forces leads to desired and unwanted consequences. *In short, religion becomes a human and earthly institution and like all other human organizations and institutions becomes an instrument for all kinds of abuse and injustices.*[211]

In these two respects, Soroush's views are similar to those of other thinkers discussed earlier, notably Kadivar, who makes a distinction between Islam's spiritual and historical dimensions. However, Soroush applies this principle to all religions and elaborates this aspect of his perspective within the context of his theory of "the theoretical expansion and contraction of the *shari'a*" (*gabz va bast e theoric e shariat*).[212] According to this theory, because of changes in other branches of knowledge, the nature of religiosity and religious knowledge changes in different historical epochs; in other words it is subject to "contraction and expansion."

Soroush extends this aspect of religion even to the unfolding of the Prophetic mission itself in his book *The Expansion of the Prophetic Mission*.[213] He maintains that the Prophetic experience takes shape and expands within history as the message of revelation evolves over time in response to situations, historical incidents, and questions that arise.

4. The distinction between the intrinsic and the contingent (*zati va arazi*) dimensions of religion. According to Soroush, the greatest part of what is understood as religion is of the "contingent" type and as such is not the main goal of the Prophetic mission. According to Soroush, the contingent aspects of religion are those aspects that could have been different from what they are now, including language, social and cultural contexts, and legal aspects. In this respect Soroush's view is similar to that of those scholars, notably Shabestari, who distinguish between the transcendent aspects of religion and those that are bound by time and space. Soroush maintains that the measure of one's commitment to religion is commitment to its intrinsic rather than contingent dimensions.[214]

5. Religious knowledge is a branch of general human knowledge. Therefore, just as other thinkers and scientists cannot judiciously expound on religion, religious scholars are not qualified to deal with other disciplines. Nor can other disciplines be endowed with religious attributes. Therefore, just as there can be no Islamic thermodynamics or chemistry, so too there cannot be Islamic management or politics. The upshot of this view is that the clergy should not interfere in government and administration because, first, they lack the necessary skills, and second, because as a group who earn their living in their capacity as the "carriers and interpreters" of religion they cannot be objective in these matters.[215] Yet Soroush does not believe that the establishment of a democratic form of government requires an a priori de-religionization of society. In his theory of "religious democracy," he argues that the two are compatible, provided that two conditions prevail: tolerance of diversity of opinion, including religious; and a rational approach to the study and interpretation of religion.[216]

Soroush opposes religion's ideologization, as was done by Shariati, for the following reasons: first, religion is timeless whereas ideologies are the products of particular historical circumstances; second, ideology is only concerned with specific and out-wardly accessible issues, whereas religion deals with the mysteries of life and creation. He therefore concludes that the "ideologization of religion eliminates its ability to create wonder, depth, and wisdom." He likens this process to translating poetry into prose, which makes it soulless, one-dimensional, and depressing. Thus, if poetry is more substantial than prose, so religion is more substantial than ideology.[217]

Soroush's initial goal in making these distinctions between religion, which is eternal and unchanging, and religious knowledge, which is contingent and change-able, was to make it possible to revive Islam and to reconcile it with modernity by, as he put it, reconciling "tradition and change, the 'earth' and the 'heavens,' and 'reason' and 'revelation.'"[218]

In the last few years, however, Soroush has evolved into a secular thinker and has relegated religion to the private sphere. In Soroush's present outlook, religion is a personal understanding of spirituality, a perspective that is in line with his mysti-cal proclivities. He has also become a critic of Shi'ism, or at least what he calls its extreme form (shi'a qali). He has even challenged some of its basic principles as being incompatible with the principle of the end of the cycle of Prophecy with Muhammad (khatamiat).[219] In a June 2005 speech at the Sorbonne, titled "Shi'ism and the Challenge of Democracy," Soroush stated that Shi'ism, with its belief in the infallibility of imams and its messianism, is not conducive to democracy. This statement elicited critical responses from even lay intellectuals, including one of the translators of Soroush's works, Mahmoud Sadri, who challenged this interpretation in a letter. Sadri noted that Christianity, despite its messianism, has not hindered democracy, while Sunni Islam's lack of a messianic dimension has not encouraged democracy's flourishing in the Sunni world.[220]

Soroush created even more controversy when, in an interview with a Dutch journalist in early 2008, he essentially said that the Qur'an was the product of Muhammad's thoughts and feelings rather than revelation from God. As evidence of this view, he pointed out that one can see the impact of the Prophet's emotional state in various Qur'anic verses. Moreover, he likened revelation (vahy) to poetic or mystical inspiration.[221] The main response to this interview came in a letter from Ayatullah Ja'ffar Subhani addressed to Soroush in which he attacked his positions. Soroush replied to Subhani's letter and received another response from him.[222]

Notwithstanding recent controversies generated by some of Soroush's opinions, his role in pioneering the Islamic reformist discourse in Iran cannot be exaggerated. It could even be said that, without Soroush, there might not have been an Islamic reformist discourse in Iran. Yet in light of Soroush's new positions, it is increas-ingly difficult to consider him an Islamic reformist thinker. Rather he is more of a secular intellectual with spiritual and mystical inclinations.

Mustafa Malekian

In the last decade, Mustafa Malekian has emerged as an important proponent not so much of reconciling Islam and modernity, but rather of finding a way for people to have a spiritual life while embracing fundamental values of modernity and liberalism. Malekian has not elaborated a coherent framework for his ideas in a book or a series of successive and logically interconnected articles. His book *A Way to Freedom: Reflections on Rationalism and Spirituality*[223] is a collection of articles that together set out an overall conceptual framework, but without an introduction. His other book, *Longing and Separation: A Talk About Culture and Politics* (Mushtaqi va mahjuri: goft e ghouhaie dar bareh farhang va siasat), is a collection of interviews on various subjects. However, his basic thesis can be gleaned through these works and especially in the preface to *A Way to Freedom*, titled "A Talk with the Reader." In it Malekian explains his thesis by saying, "I earnestly and sincerely believe that if there is a way to freedom it is only through a synthesis (*talfiq*) of rationalism and spirituality (*aqlaniat va manaviat*) and respect for the right of each of these great virtues."

Malekian believes in the limitations of a totally rationalist system of thought and worldview and considers the most serious shortcoming of modernity to be its scientism (*elmzadeghi*). He explains this phenomenon as the "effort to construct a worldview that encompasses the whole of existence, passes judgment on it, and makes observation and experimentation, which are only different ways of getting to know the universe, the only way." This scientism, he says, leads to materialism and thus deprives modern man of "a full and varied spiritual life."[224] He adds, however, that having a spiritual life does not mean "belonging to one of the historical religions. Rather, it means having an outlook on life and humanity that results in serenity, joy, and hope."[225]

Malekian believes that return to a traditional way of life, including one based on a traditionalist interpretation of religion, is neither possible nor desirable. The best solution is to rectify modernity's shortcomings by adopting a critical attitude toward both tradition and modernity, and by refusing to accept any assertion that is not supported by reasoning; in short by upholding free thinking (*azadandishi*) and rationalism (*estedlal geraei*).[226] He considers this rationalism to be against ideology, superstition, wishful thinking, prejudice, and stagnation.[227]

Malekian's views on other issues, such as the methodology of interpreting religious texts, governance, human rights, and women's rights, follow from these two basic principles. Most of Malekian's writings are explanatory rather than prescriptive. Nevertheless, his views can be gleaned through the way he posits and explains issues. Malekian favors a rationalist approach to the interpretation of religious sources and believes in the contingent rather than intrinsic nature of most aspects of the *shari'a*.[228] He clearly supports a democratic form of government and believes that what he defines as "modernist Islam" (*islam e tajadudgerayaneh*) is compatible with modernity, liberalism, and human rights as expressed in the Universal Declaration of Human Rights.[229]

On women's rights, Malekian believes in providing equal opportunities for women even if their roles in society may differ. He agrees with the feminist assertion that historically most issues have been viewed from the perspective of men and that it is time that the feminine perspective is given a chance. He then adds that if everything can be looked at from women's perspective, it should also be possible to have a reading and interpretation of the Qur'an from women's perspective. This he believes would eliminate discriminatory practices against them.[230]

Ali Reza Alavitabar

Ali Reza Alavitabar is a self-described leftist religious intellectual.[231] His views have many points in common with other Muslim reformist thinkers. For example:

1. He subscribes to a contextual interpretation of religious sources, a method that he calls "modern" interpretation of religion;[232]
2. He advocates an understanding of religion compatible with the contemporary body of knowledge and understandings (*maaref*), and that can answer practical needs of the time;[233]
3. He denies that the clergy have an exclusive right to interpret the Qur'an and other religious sources; and
4. He rejects the practice of basing all legislation on religious principles, even if most people do not agree with them.

Alavitabar has focused on issues that have not received adequate attention from other reformist thinkers or at least have not been as clearly articulated by them. For example, he has spoken against polarizing the debate in Iran between modernity and tradition and he has offered a third way—religious intellectualism—as a way to reconcile the two. This third way is distinguished by its critical analysis of both modernity and tradition.[234]

Alavitabar believes that, on many issues, religious intellectuals can find common ground with traditionalists concerned about the excessive identification of religion and the clergy with government. This, he believes could encourage democratic reform. Alavitabar also subscribes to the thesis of multiple modernities. Noting that externally induced (*borounza*) modernities have failed, he argues that Iran should develop its own homegrown (*darounza*) version of modernity. He maintains that reformist religious thinking will facilitate the process of the construction of a homegrown modernity. In this view, Alavitabar echoes Eshkevari's notion of "nativization of modernity" (*boumi kardan*).[235]

Alavitabar favors a democratic form of government, but is also critical of aspects of Western liberal democracies because he believes that, given the wide disparities of wealth in Western societies, equality among people is more apparent than real. He adds that, "from the perspective of a leftist democrat, it is possible to offer legitimate and fundamental criticism of liberal democracies. These are neither old nor do they have any link to traditional or Leninist interpretations of Marxism. Therefore, it is too early for us to join Mrs. Thatcher in declaring that there is no other choice [except liberal democracy]."[236]

Emmad Eddin Baqi

Emmad Eddin Baqi is another prominent lay reformist thinker. He is also a journalist and human rights activist and heads the Society for the Protection of Political Prisoners. He comes from a modest and religious background. As a youth, he joined various Islamic groups and became engaged in anti-Shah activities. After the Revolution, he taught at a high school and also joined the Revolutionary Guards, although he did not see active service in the Iran-Iraq War. He joined the reformist forces that brought Khatami to power. In 1998, he was imprisoned after giving an interview while visiting Said Hajjarian in the hospital following an assassination attempt on Hajjarian's life.[237]

Baqi's philosophy is best understood by analyzing his writings on human rights, religion, and secularism. In a speech titled "Religion, Secularism, Human Rights" (*din, secularism, hquq e bashar*), Baqi first describes the three main intellectual trends in Iran regarding these issues:

1. Human rights are based on humanism and can only be realized within a secular system;
2. All human rights exist in the Qur'an and in the Islamic *fiqh*. There are variations within this school; some believe that *fiqh* is only a human construct and as such it has many points that clash with human rights, while there is no conflict between the Qur'an and human rights. Moreover, since some of the Qur'an's verses do not have specific subjects and some are subject to change (*mutaqayer*), any discrepancies between the two can be smoothed out in light of other verses; and
3. There is no inherent incompatibility between religion and human rights, and it is possible to reconcile religion and human rights and religion and secularism.

Baqi then declares that he belongs to the third trend. He states that it is much easier to find common points between Qur'anic injunctions and the writings of Imam Ali, especially his sermons (*nahj al-blaqah*) and principles of human rights than between the latter and *fiqh*. In support of this view, Baqi notes that Qur'anic injunctions and Ali's teachings regarding prisoners of war and their treatment and other issues are similar to the provisions of the Geneva Conventions of 1949.[238]

Baqi, too, considers *fiqh* a human construct dealing with worldly matters of daily life and shaped by historic conditions and events. He also believes that ninety—or according to some, 99 percent—of Qur'anic injunctions are of the ratifying (*emzaei*) type. He says if the Prophet were to come back, he would rectify those aspects of Islamic law that are defective today, as he corrected laws of Arabia 1,400 years ago.[239] Baqi's conclusion is that, although many aspects of "historical Islam" are incompatible with present-day human rights standards, the process of the shaping of historical Islam does not warrant the view of their intrinsic incompatibility. Rather, by using "the logic of historical Islam, but not its outcomes, a new Islam can be developed."[240]

For Baqi, the main tool for creating this new Islam is *ijtihad* in the very foundations of *fiqh*.[241] Baqi further argues that, as recently as fifty years ago in secular societies, human rights were also not understood in their present sense. He faults secularists for comparing certain Islamic principles with present-day standards rather than with their antecedents in the same societies. Baqi also faults secularists for dismissing the entire religion for shortcomings in some of its regulations, and he points out that secularism too has its weak points. Baqi believes that governments' legitimacy is contingent on popular consent, and he argues that a government that lacks popular legitimacy also lacks religious legitimacy. He justifies this view by pointing out that, when the Prophet created the government in Medina, it was with the people's approval.[242]

Conclusions

The origins of Islamic reformist thinking in Iran date back to the late nineteenth century and are a direct result of Iran's encounter with modernity and its carriers, the European powers. It also reflects one of the main responses—synthesis—of non-European cultures and countries to the challenge of both modernity and European power. However, certain traditions of Shi'ism have made Iranian Islam more receptive to reformist discourses. These are the openness of "the gates of *ijtihad*" in Shi'ism; the emphasis in Shi'ism on justice; and the lingering rationalist (Mu'tazili) influences.

One strand of Islamic reformist thinking in Iran has also been deeply influenced by socialist ideology. Even today, it is not absolutely clear whether some reformist thinkers are more socialist or Islamic. Are they using religion as an instrument to get their message across to the still-religious masses? Or are they truly trying to create the intellectual, religious, and cultural foundations of an Islamic reformation, renaissance, and eventually modernity? What is clear is that because of the experience of the Islamic Revolution and government, along with the erosion of the credibility of socialist economic and political systems (if not the egalitarian aspirations of socialism) following the collapse of the Soviet Union, present-day reformists are less utopian in their goals and less totalitarian in their methods as compared to earlier reformers inspired by socialism, such as Ali Shariati.

The course of the evolution of Islamic reformist thinking has also been closely linked with the process of Iran's socioeconomic and, to a lesser extent, political modernization and the resulting implications for the balance of power and privilege between traditional classes and structures and those classes that emerged as a result of modernization. For example, despite the very limited and episodic nature of Iranian parliamentarism in the twentieth century, it is undeniable that the Constitutional Revolution altered Iran's political culture.

Since the Constitutional Revolution, the basis of legitimacy has been the will of the people and not the divine right of kings, or the *faqih*, even though the kings and the *faqihs* have not submitted to the people's will. The Pahlavi kings, especially Muhammad Reza Shah, had to legitimize their policies and rule through holding referenda, even if they were fully orchestrated to yield the desired results. Ayatullah Khomeini, too, had to get the people's seal of approval for his Islamic Republic through referendum. Without these experiences, Islamic reformists could not talk of "religious democracy." Moreover, both the prerevolutionary and postrevolutionary reformist thinkers and intellectuals have been the product of an essentially secular modernization project, notably in the educational field, and a religious reaction to it.

It is important to note that, without these modernizing efforts, individuals such as Ali Shariati and others would not have had the opportunity to pursue higher education in the West and to develop the intellectual skills with which to challenge the system and its brand of modernization. Even the Islamic government has pursued a developmentalist policy, in many respects out of necessity, but also because of its ambitions to become an example for the rest of the Muslim world. Thus, it, too, has expanded essentially secular education despite its religious trappings, built communications networks, and encouraged contacts with the outside world. In short, the Islamic government has become an agent of modernization, even if unwittingly.

These factors, plus disenchantment with the Islamic government, have played significant roles in the evolution of the young supporters of the revolution and now a younger generation of Iranians who no longer believe in the regime's ethos and see in the reformist discourse a possible way out of the current situation. Iran's experience in many ways proves the thesis that early stages of modernization result in a rise of religious sentiments, which are then used to mobilize those who have suffered by this process, only to fade away later.[243]

Intellectual debate in Iran, especially the Islamic reformist discourse, has also been affected by philosophical trends in the Western world. Especially important have been Western criticism of modernity and its consequences, including colonialism and imperialism, with all their subjugating rather than emancipatory dimensions, of which Muslim societies have been principal victims. The continued resilience of religion in the West and elsewhere, which has undermined the long-held developmentalist/modernization thesis of an inexorable march toward absolute secularization, has also contributed to the rise of Islamic reformist discourse.

The emergence of reformist discourse is also related to power. Most Muslim reformists in Iran had been part of the revolution and were later sidelined. They know that in a purely secular society they would not have any special claim to leadership and hence power. But within a reformed Islamic system, they would enjoy at least comparative advantage over both secularists and traditional Muslims.

Like other responses to the challenge of modernity, current religious reformist thinking in Iran in many ways continues to be a defensive reflex. It reflects Muslim religious intellectuals' belief that, without fundamental reforms, the Muslim world will never escape from the trap of underdevelopment, tyranny, and foreign domination. Religious reformist thinking is also a response to recognition of the fact that Iranian society, like other Muslim societies, still remains fundamentally religious. And thus the only way to popularize reformist notions and to loosen the hold of tradition is through religious discourse.

Will religious reformism succeed this time?

The answer to this question requires a prior answer to the question why earlier reformist discourses did not succeed. Part of this failure in the Iranian context was due to the following factors: the complexity of the discourse, which made reaching large audiences difficult; the lack of an adequate number of reformist clergy and the limited conception of reform by the reformist clerics; the strong anti-clericism of Iran's newly educated classes; the extraordinary dimensions of Iran's development problems, which seemed to argue for swift action rather than lengthy consensus-building; and, finally, the fascination of the educated classes with European ideologies, both liberal and socialist.

External circumstances also negatively affected the course of Iran's political evolution and limited opportunities for the flourishing of an Islamic reformist discourse and agenda. For example, World War I interrupted Iran's parliamentary experiment and contributed to the rise of the Pahlavis with British assistance. It is conceivable that, had the 1906 Constitution been fully applied, gradual and longer-lasting religious and judicial reform, with the participation and approval of the senior clergy, might have been possible. If so, it would have forestalled the religious-secular dichotomy that emerged in Iran and still persists. The Cold War also had negative consequences for Iran's democratic development, as reflected in the turbulent years that culminated in the Anglo-American removal of the popular government of Muhammad Mussadeq.

Some of these obstacles have now disappeared. As was shown here, a significant number of reformists are clerics of various ranks. Moreover, Iranian intellectuals have a more critical attitude toward all ideas, and the desire to develop an indigenous type of modernity without, however, plunging into nativist way of thinking, is much stronger now than before.

Other obstacles, including external challenges, still remain. Most important is that reformist thinkers, especially the lay intellectuals, are seen by the more religious-minded masses—still the main audience to be won over—as lacking in religious commitment and knowledge. Some are seen as secularists at heart who are using religion to gain acceptance and eventually power. Additionally, their discourse still remains complex and inaccessible to less well-educated groups. Meanwhile, they are opposed both by traditional religious groups and by secularists who do not believe in their democratic commitment. Moreover, reformist thinkers are divided among themselves on the intellectual and practical levels. Thus they are incapable of offering a coherent and unified message, a fact that puts them at a disadvantage in regard to both secular and traditionalist thinkers.

Externally, tensions between Iran and the West, especially the United States, have not helped reformist thinkers, who are at times accused of being pro-Western. In this context, the role of reformist clergy, who operate within the bounds of traditional methods of interpretation of Islamic sources but offer a progressive interpretation of them, could ultimately be more important in producing long-lasting reform with broad popular acceptance than the role of lay intellectuals with questionable Islamic credentials. Religious reformist thinking in Iran has the potential to reconcile faith and reason, to mediate between tradition and modernity, and to develop homegrown modernities.

The problem, in addition to those mentioned above, is that, so far, reformist thinkers have been deprived of the ability to translate their ideas into concrete reforms. However, given the inability of conservatives to resolve Iran's manifold problems, along with the lack of an adequate audience for secular purists, in the long run, religious reformers offer the best chance for nonviolent and evolutionary change in Iran in the direction of a more innovative rather than imitative model of socioeconomic development and homegrown democracy.

Notes

1. Of course, democracy is a characteristic of an emancipatory modernity and not its dominating and oppressive perversion.

2. Because of different dynamics of various cultures and societies, however, developments in one country do not necessarily affect developments in others, even if a group of countries shares common cultural values, as is the case with Muslim societies. Thus the triumph of Islamic reformism in Iran would not necessarily affect the course of cultural and intellectual developments in other Muslim countries; for example, the Islamic Revolution in Iran, despite earlier fears, was not replicated in other Muslim countries.

3. An exception is Abdolkarim Soroush, about whom more has been written. But even most of his books have not been translated into European languages.

4. Hamid Dabashi, "Blindness and Insight: The Predicament of a Muslim Intellectual," in *Iran: Between Tradition and Modernity*, ed. Ramin Jahanbegloo (Lanham, MD: Lexington Books, 2004).

5. It is impossible to provide a comprehensive list of these writings. However, the Web sites of Melli Mazhabi, No Andish, and Mehr News, among others, carry lists of the latest publications on this subject, available at www.gooya.com.

6. On the Russo-Iranian wars, see R.K. Ramazani, *The Foreign Policy of Iran: A Developing Nation in World Affairs, 1500–1941* (Charlottesville: University of Virginia Press, 1966). Abbas Mirza, the only Qajar prince truly committed to reform, sent the first group of Iranian students to study in Europe.

7. See Fereydoun Adamiyat, *Amir kabir va iran* (Amir Kabir and Iran) (Tehran: Chapkhaneh e Payam, 1944–45).

8. According to Mokhber al-Dowleh Hedayat, the historian of Qajar Iran, all young Iranian intellectuals and nationalists had books about the French Revolution and were full of fiery words.

9. Ferydoun Adamiyat, *Fekr e democracy e ejtemaie dar nehzat mashrutiat e iran* (The Idea of Social Democracy in Iran's Constitutional Movement) (Tehran: Payam, 1345 [1975]).

10. On developments that led to the Constitutional Revolution, see Feridoun Adamiyat Fakr, *Azadi va nehzat e mashrutiat* (The Idea of Freedom and the Constitutional Revolution) (Tehran: Entesharat e so khan, 1340 [1962]).

11. Davood Feirahi, *Ijtihad va siasat dar doreh e mashrouteh* (Ijtihad and Politics in the Era of Constitutionalism), available at http://emruz.info/print.aspx?ID=4428.

12. Ferydoun Adamiyat, *Andisheha ye mirza aga khan kirmani* (The Ideas of Mirza Agha Khan Kirmani) (Tehran: Chapkhaneh Pirouz, 1346 [1967]). Also see Ali Gheissari, *Iranian Intellectuals in the Twentieth Century* (Austin: University of Texas Press, 1998), p. 41.

13. Ali Mirsepassi, *Intellectual Discourses and the Politics of Modernization: Negotiating Modernity in Iran* (Cambridge: Cambridge University Press, 2000), p. 62.

14. A large portion of the merchant community, particularly the most prosperous elements, supported the Constitutional Movement.

15. See Feirahi, *Ijtihad va siasat.* On Khorasani, see the critique of the book *The Political Ideas of Khorasani,* published in *Kherad nameh, hamshahri,* no. 10, Dey 1385 (December 2005), available at www.kadivar.com/Index. asp?DocId=1639&AC=1&A1&ASB=1&AGM=1&AL=1.

16. Hamid Algar, *Mirza Malkum Khan: A Study in the History of Iranian Modernism* (Berkeley: University of California Press, 1969).

17. Nikkie R. Keddie, *An Islamic Response to Imperialism: Political and Religious Writings of Sayyid Jamalal-Din al-Afghani* (Berkeley, CA: University of California Press, 1983), pp. 103–7. For more on Afghani see the Introduction to this volume.

18. Secular Iranian historians such as Adamiyat and Ahmad Kasravi have maintained that they were not in favor of these ideas and only supported the Constitutionalists in order to prevent further damage to the country by the incompetent Qajar kings. However, this appears to be too harsh a judgment and reflects the authors' anti-clerical tendencies.

19. Ali Gheissari claims that these clerics "tried to develop a Constitutional theory in accordance with a new approach to Islamic and, more importantly, Shi'a principles" (*Iranian Intellectuals in the Twentieth Century,* pp. 26–27). However, he is silent on what was this new approach.

20. Timothy McDaniel, "Responses to Modernization: Muslim Experience in a Comparative Perspective," in Shireen T. Hunter and Huma Malik, eds., *Modernization, Democracy and Islam* (Westport, CT: Praeger, 2005), p. 42.

21. However, the process of Iran's transformation since the mid-nineteenth century and its failures cannot be understood properly if the external context of Iran's developments is not taken into account. Any analysis of Iran's modernization trajectory that does not consider the impact of Russo-British rivalry and later the Cold War is bound to be inadequate.

22. Emad Eddin Baghi, *Do faghih: moroury bar didehgahay e ayatullh boroujerdi va imam khomeini* (Two Faghihs: A Look at the Perspectives of Ayatullah Boroujerdi and Imam Khomeini), available at www.emrouz.info/archives/print/2006/04/029307.php.

23. *Zendeghinameh* (Life Story), available at the official Web site of the leadership at http://www.wilayah.net/langs/fa/index.php?p=bio.

24. Other scholars have characterized the Pahlavi project as pseudo-modernization. See Huma Katouzian, *The Political Economy of Modern Iran: Despotism and Pseudo-Modernism, 1926–1979* (New York: New York University Press, 1981).

25. See Abbass Kazemi, *Jameeh-e-shenasi rowshanfekr-e-dini dar Iran* (The Sociology of Religious Intellectualism in Iran) (Tehran: Entesharat-e Tarh Now, 1383 [2005]).

26. See Seyed Mohammad Ali Taghavi, *The Flourishing of Islamic Reformism in Iran: Political Islamic Groups in Iran (1941–61)* (London/New York: RoutledgeCurzon, 2005), p. 61.

27. Ibid.

28. His surname refers to his birthplace, Mazinan, in the northeastern province of Khurasan.

29. For a discussion of these organizations, see Kazemi, *Jameeh-e-shenasi rowshanfekr-e-dini dar Iran.*

30. See *Shariati on Shariati and the Muslim Woman,* trans. Laleh Bakhtiar (Chicago: ABC International Group, 1996), p. xiv.

31. For details on the ideas and backgrounds of the founders of this group, see

Taghavi, *The Flourishing of Islamic Reformism*, pp. 14–57; also Ali Rahnema, *An Islamic Utopian: A Political Biography of Ali Shariati* (London and New York: I.B. Tauris, 1998), pp. 24–30.

32. Quoted in Taghavi, *The Flourishing of Islamic Reformism*, p. 29.

33. Ibid., p. 45.

34. See ibid.

35. See Sohrab Behdad, "Utopia of Assassins: Navvab Safavi and the Fadaian-e-Islam," in *Iran: Between Tradition and Modernity*, Jahanbegloo, ed., pp. 71–94.

36. For details, see ibid., p. 115. According to this source, the reason for the strike was the beating of an Iranian worker by his British employer.

37. Quoted in ibid., p. 122.

38. Ibid., p.124.

39. The interview with Hojat al-Islam Hadi Khosrowshahi on the fifty-second anniversary of Navab's death is available at http://www.roozna.com/Negaresh_FullStory/?Id=53878 December 2007.

40. In 1975 a wing of the Mujahedin rejected Islam and adopted Marxism-Leninism as its ideology. After the victory of the Islamic Revolution the Marxist wing renamed itself *Peykar* (Struggle).

41. Ibrahim Yazdi, a member of Bazargan's Freedom Movement, has admitted to doing so in his memoirs. See his interview, "We were so preoccupied with ousting the Shah that we did not think about the outcome." Fars News, available at Fars News Archives at www.farsnews.com.

42. Kazemi, *Jameeh-e-shenasi rowshanfekri-e-dini dar Iran,* p. 77.

43. Ibid.

44. See *Ostad motahari va rowshanfekran* (The Learned Teacher Motahari and the Intellectuals), available at www.motahari.org.

45. Murteza Mutahari, *Mushkelat e assasi dar sazeman e ruhaniat* (Tehran: Entesharat e–Sadra, n.d.).

46. For an elaboration of these points, see Murtaza Mutahari, *Islam va moqtaziat-e-zaman* (Islam and the Requirements of the Time) (Tehran: Entesharat e Sadra, 1373 [1994]).

47. Ibid.

48. Forough Jahanbakhsh, *Islam, Democracy and Religious Modernism in Iran (1953–2000)* (Leiden: Brill, 2001), p. 128.

49. Mustafa Malekian, *Mushtaqi va mahjuri, goft e ghouhaie dar bareh farhang va seyasat* (Longing and Separation: A Talk About Politics and Culture) 2d ed. (Tehran: Nashr e Neghah e Muaser 1386 [2007]), pp. 200–201.

50. This might not appear as significant to Western audiences, but considering that in many Muslim countries, women, especially the poor and uneducated, die because of such prohibitions, the importance of such opinions in advancing a more progressive interpretation of Islam becomes evident.

51. Murtaza Mutahari, *Nizam e huquq e zan dar islam* (Qum: Sadra, 1353 [1979]).

52. Some have speculated that rival clerics, notably Ayatullah Hashemi Rafsanjani, may have been responsible for his death. They point to the fact that Rafsanjani left the gathering only thirty minutes before the explosion took place.

53. See the text of an interview with Beheshti on his approach to the study of the Qur'an available at http://www.beheshti.org/maghalat/bardasht.asp.

54. See Beheshti comments in answer to a query on these matters, available at http://www.beheshti.org/maghalat/mosighi.asp.

55. See a critique of some of Beheshti's works, available at http://www.beheshti.org/naghdeassar/bayadhanabayadha.asp.

56. Ibid.

57. *Society and Economics in Islam: Writings and Declarations of Ayatullah Sayyid*

Mahmud Taleqani, trans. R. Cambell, with annotations and introduction by Hamid Algar (Berkeley, CA: Mizan Press, 1982), p. 12.

58. Seyed Javad Meynagh, "Reflections on the Significance of Taleghani's Social Theory," published by London Academy of Iranian Studies, available at http://www.iranianstudies.org/lectures/Taleghani.htm.

59. Concern over communist inroads among Iraq's impoverished Shi'as was the main reason that Ayatullah Muhammad Baqir Sadr developed his ideas on Islamic economics and politics.

60. Mahmoud Taleqani, *Islam va malekiat* (Islam and Ownership) (Tehran: n.p., n.d.

61. Ibid., pp. 25–59.

62. See Meynagh, "Reflections on the Significance of Taleghani's Social Theory."

63. Taleqani, *Islam va malekiat*, pp. 75–96.

64. Mirza Muhammad Hussein Naini, *Tanbih al-umma va tanzih al-milla*, with an introduction by Taleqani (Tehran: n.p., 1334 [1955]).

65. Hamid Dabashi, *The Theology of Discontent: The Ideological Foundations of the Islamic Revolution in Iran* (New York: New York University Press, 1993), p. 233.

66. Said Amir Arjomand maintains that Taleqani favored a Democratic Islamic Republic. See his *The Turban for the Crown* (New York: Oxford University Press, 1988), p. 102.

67. Elaine Sciolino, *Persian Mirrors: The Elusive Face of Iran* (New York: Free Press, 2000), p. 110.

68. Kazemi, *Jameeh e shenassi e rowshanfekri e dini*, p. 80.

69. See Taghavi, *The Flourishing of Islamic Reformism in Iran*, pp. 62–111.

70. See Qulam Reza Khajeh Sarvi, *Rabeteh e din va siasat az didgah e muhandes bazargan* (The Relationship Between Religion and Politics from the Perspective of Engineer Bazargan), available at http://www.tiknews.net/display/?ID=49954&page=1.

71. For more details, see Jahanbakhsh, *Islam, Democracy and Religious Modernism in Iran*, pp. 106–7.

72. Kazemi, *Jameeh e shenassi e rowshanfekri e dini*, p. 99.

73. Muhammad Milani, "Shariati, shah beit andisheh-e-irani: gofto ghou ba taghi rahmani" (Shariati, the Peak of Iranian Thought: A Conversation with Taghi Rahmani), *Nameh*, no. 50, 1385 (2006), available at nashrieh-nameh.com/article.php?articleID=821.

74. In his "Where Shall We Begin," Shariati says, "The intelligentsia [*ruhsanfekran*] should begin by an 'Islamic Protestantism' similar to that of Christianity in the Middle Ages, by destroying all the degenerating factors which, in the name of Islam, have stymied and stupefied the process of thinking and the fate of the society," available at www.shariati.com/begin/begin7.thml.

75. One of Shariati's most ardent supporters today who calls for Islamic Protestantism is the dissident intellectual Hashem Aghajari. However, his definition of Protestantism bears little resemblance to the original movement. Rather, he uses the term as meaning "a progressive religion rather than a traditional religion that tramples people."

76. Ali Shariati, *Ummat va imamat* (Tehran: Husseinieh e Irshad, 1353 [1973]). *Imamat* is belief in the successorship of Ali and his children from Fatima and their spiritual and political leadership over the Shi'a believers. Since the occultation of the twelfth Imam the Shi'a community is without a leader. According to some opinion, in the absence of the Imam the clergy have the responsibility to guide the community both in spiritual and political matters.

77. For an excellent account of Shariati's shifting positions, notably his advocacy of revolutionary action at one point and a more evolutionary attitude at another, see Rahnema, *An Islamic Utopian*.

78. See *Ostad motaheri va rowshanfekran*.

79. This is evident from reading Shariati's main lectures on women. See *Shariati on Shariati and the Muslim Woman*.

80. Ali Shariati, *Collected Works* (Majmouh e-asar), Vol. 26 (Tehran: n.p., n.d.) pp. 255–56 (author's translation).

81. Ibid., Vol. 22, p. 300.

82. Ali Shariati, *Red Shi'ism: Religion of Martyrdom, Black Shi'ism: Religion of Mourning, available* at www.shariati.net/redblack html.

83. Shariati, *Collected Works,* Vol. 16, pp. 28–29.

84. Quoted in Khalil Movahed, *Shariati va ideology* (Shariati and Ideology), available at www.mellimazhabi.org/news/08news2006/0508khalil.htm.

85. Ibid.

86. Ibid.

87. Ali Shariati, *Marxism and Other Western Fallacies,* trans. R. Campbell (Berkeley, CA: Mizan Press, 1980).

88. Ali Shariati, "The World View of Tawhid," in *On the Sociology of Islam: Lectures by Ali Shariati,* trans. Hamid Algar (Berkeley, CA: Mizan Press, 1979), p. 86.

89. Ibid., p. 83.

90. *Ostad motaheri va rowshanfekran.*

91. See Hashem Barouti, *Shariati va marxism: goftgoui ba reza alijani, maghloub e goftman ghaleb naboud* (Shariati and Marxism: A Conversation with Reza Alijani), available at www.sharghnewspaper.com/850331/html/v2.htm.

92. For an account of the left's criticism of Shariati see Rahnema, *An Islamic Utopian,* pp. 201–6.

93. For a more detailed analysis of the impact of Marxism on Shariati's thinking and analytical methodology, see Barouti, *Shariati va marxism.*

94. Ibid.

95. For a criticism of Shariati's ideological vision, see Abdolkarim Soroush, *Farbahtar az ideology* (More Substantive Than Ideology) (Tehran: Moassesseh eye Farhangi-e-Sarat, 1373 [1990]), pp. 94–142.

96. Quoted in the speech of Hassan Yussefi Eshkevari, a disciple of Shariati, at the Kanoon Tawhid, London, titled "Ma va miras e Shariati" (Us and Shariati's Legacy), available at www.mellimazhabi.org/news/072006news/2607eshgavari.htm.

97. "Ehsan naraghi, takid kard, zarourat bazghasht eslahtalaban beh shiveh e khatami" (Ehsan Naraghi Emphasizes the Necessity of the Reformists' Return to Khatami's Approach), available at http://emrouz.info/print.aspx?ID=306.

98. For the text of Aghajari's comments, see www.isna ir/Main?NewsViews. aspx?ID=News-738461&Lang=p.

99. Eshkevari, "Ma va miras e Shariati."

100. Ibid.; and Ahmad Zaiabadi, *Dr shariati va nakaramadi entekhabat dar jameeh e no-motavazen* (Dr. Shariati and the Inefficacy of Election in an Unbalanced Society), available at www.bbc.co.uk/Persian/iran/story/2006/06/060619_mj-z-shariati-30years-on.shtml.

101. Shariati, *Ummat va imamat.*

102. "Ali shariati dar goftegou ba Sussan Shariati: vazeyat e doghaneh" (Shariati in a Conversation with Sussan Shariati: A Dualistic Situation), available at www.sharghnewspaper.com/850331/html/v2.htm.

103. Shariati's father was the founder of the Society of Socialists Believing in God.

104. Emphasis added. See the account cited in note 97.

105. One bastion of neo-Shariatis is the cultural-political organization Melli-Mazhabi.

106. Mahmoud Alinejad, "Coming to Terms with Modernity: Iranian Intellectuals and the Emerging Public Sphere," available at www.iranchamber.com/podium/society/050526_coming_to _terms_with_modernity2.

107. Kazemi, *Sociology of Religious Intellectualism in Iran,* p. 100.

108. Attaullah Muhajerani now lives in England and has abandoned his clerical garb and even his beard. Abdullah Nouri's defense during his trial, published under the title *Showkaran e eslah* (The Leaders of Reform) (Tehran: Entesharat e Tarh e Now, 1378 [1999]), is an excellent guide to his thinking.

109. By the time of the completion of this work (Summer 2008), there had been a rap-prochement among Rafsanjani, Khatami, and Mehdi Karrubi, each representing different shades and wings of the reformist spectrum, both intellectually and politically.

110. Ayatullah Saanei's speech, "Imam khomeini va raz e ehyaye ijtihad dar asr e hazer" (Imam Khomeini and the Secret of Reviving Ijtihidad in the Present Time), available at www.saanei.org/page.php?pg=showpayam&id=37&lang=fa.

111. Khatami has expressed such views mostly in the context of speeches delivered on particular occasions. See *Ghozideh-ye-sokhanranihaye rais jomhour dar bareh-ye-ttoeseh-ye-siasi, toseeh-ye-eqtesadi va amniat* (A Selection of President's Speeches on Economic and Political Development and Security) (Tehran: Entesharat-e–Tarh-e-Now, 1379 [2000]), p. 270.

112. Khatami elaborates on these issues in his *Islam, ruhaniat va enqlab e Islami* (Islam, the Clergy and the Islamic Revolution) (Tehran: Entesharat-e–Tarh-e-Now, 1379 [2000]).

113. In Shi'ism, justice (*'adl*) is one of the pillars of faith, together with the oneness of God (*tawhid*), Muhammad's prophecy (*nubuva*), the successorship of Ali and his descendants from Fatima (*imamat*), and the Judgment Day (*maad*).

114. For an elaboration of Khatami's views on this topic, see Mohammad Khatami, *Islam, Liberty and Development,* trans. Hossein Kamaly (Binghamton, NY: Institute of Global Strategic Studies, 1998), pp. 39–49. Idem, "Moderniteh akharin halgheh efrat va tafrit ast" (Modernity Is the Last Link in the Chain of Excess), available at www.farsnews.com/newstext. php?nn=8506150462. Here Khatami observes that belief in the self-sufficiency of reason led Western countries to try to absorb other civilizations within their own.

115. See Seyyed Muhammad Khatami, *Mardom salari* (The People's Rule/Democracy) (Tehran: Entesharat-e–Tarh-e-Now, 1380 [2001]), various chapters.

116. Ibid., p. 29.

117. Khatami, *Islam, the Clergy, and the Islamic Revolution*, p. 143.

118. Muhammad Khatami, *Islam liberalism ra naqd va fashism ra rad mikond* (Islam Rejects Fascism, and Offers a Critique of Liberalism), Mehr News, available at www.mehrnews.com/fa/NewsDetail.aspx?NewsID==5121519/.

119. He elaborated on these themes at a lecture in New York in 1999 that the author attended.

120. See Seyyed Muhammad Khatami's speech at the Washington Cathedral, September 2006, available at www.khatami.ir.

121. Farzin Vahdat, a scholar of Iranian descent, has written on the issue of the dilemma of human subjectivity and how to reconcile it with divine omnipotence for Iran's Islamic intellectuals, including Shariati. See his "Post-Revolutionary Islamic Discourses on Modernity in Iran: Expansion and Contraction of Human Subjectivity," *International Journal of Middle East Studies,* vol. 35 (2003), pp. 599–631.

122. Mohammad Khatami, *Islam, Dialogue and Civil Society* (Canberra: Centre for Arab and Islamic Studies, The Australian National University, 2000), pp. 1–14.

123. See Seyyed Muhammad Khatami, speech at the University of Virginia, Charlottesville, September 2006, available at www.mehrrnews.co/fa/NewsDetail.aspx?NewsID=377558.

124. Ayatullah Khomeini in the last years of his life recommended this approach.

125. Ali Reza Alavitabar is one of these intellectuals. See the news Web site Mahdis, available at mahdis.com/tablu/modules.php?name=News&file=articles&sid=6184.

126. Ayatullah Montazeri, "Har tagyir e mazhab irtad nist" (Not Every Change of Religion Is Apostasy), available at mehdis.com/tablu/modules.php?name=news7file=article&sid=18112.

127. Ibid.

128. Ibid.

129. "Pasokh beh soalhaei piramoun e mojazat e islami" (Answer to Questions Regarding Islamic Punishments), available at www.amontazeri.com/Farsi/Payamha/52.htm.

130. Ibid.

131. Ibid.

132. See *Pasokhhay e ayatullah e ozma montazer beh soalat e site e rouz* (The Answers of the Grand Ayatullah Muntazeri to the Questions of Rouz Site), available at www.montazeri. com/Farsi/Payamha/83.HTM.

133. See Muntazeri's statement during a visit by the youth branch of the reformist group *Jebehe e mosharekat* (The Participation Front), available at mehdis.com/tabula/modules.s ph?name=News&file=article&sid=15280, May 2004.

134. Ibid.

135. See *Zamamdari, modiriyat va sharayet e an az didgah e ayatullah montazeri* (Governing, Management, and Their Qualifications from the Perspective of Ayatullah Montazeri), available at www.amontazeri.com/Farsi/vageeat/html/0004.htm.

136. *Hoghough e bashar ya hoghough e momenan: taghrirat dars fegh e hazrat ayatullah montazeri piramoun e hormat e insan* (Human Rights or Rights of the Faithful: Ayatullah Montazeri's Teachings on Human Dignity), available at www.amontazeri.o/Farsi/Baya-niye/26.HTM.

137. See *Pasokhhay e ayatullah e ozma montazer beh soalat e site e rouz.*

138. See the interview with the Italian journalist Giorgio Fornoni, available at saanei.org/ fa/page.php?pg=showdialog&id=79 (in Persian).

139. Ibid.

140. Ibid.

141. See Ayatullah Yussef Saanei, interview by Bruno Philip (*Le Monde*), available at saanei.org/fa page.php?pg=showdialog&id=35.

142. This is a burning issue now in Iran, and women activists are working hard to get the Parliament to pass a law to make the *diyeh* for men and women equal. Figures such as Rafsanjani have indicated that this law and other laws discriminatory to women should be changed.

143. See Ayatullah Yussef Saanei, interview by Brian Murphy (Associated Press), at www. saanei.org/fa/page.php?pg=showdialog&id=76.

144. Meeting with Professor Gilles Keppel, available at www.saanei.org/fa/page.php?pg =showmeeting&id=42&query=.

145. Ibid.

146. See Ayatullah Yussef Saanei, interview by the *Chicago Tribune*, at saanei.org/fa/page. php?pg=showdialog&id=75. Also see interview with ISNA (Iranian Students News Agency), available at www.saanei.org/page.php?=showdialog&id=60&lang=fa.

147. "Ayatullah moussavi bojnourdi: shahadat e zan ba mard barabar ast" (Ayatullah Moussavi Bojnourdi: Woman's Testimony Is Equal to That of a Man), available at www. Entekhab.Ir, 6 Mordad 1385. July 27, 2006.

148. Ayatullah Mutahari has said the same thing before.

149. Muhsen Kadivar, *Daftar-er-aql: majmoueheye maqalat-e-falsafi alami* (The Book of Reason: A Collection of Philosophical and Theological Articles) (Tehran: Entesharat-e-Etteleet, 1376 [1998]).

150. See his *Nowandishi e dini va hoghough e zanan* (Religious Reformism and Women's Rights), available at www.Kadivar.com/Htm/Farsi/Speeches/speech820601.htm.

151. Ibid.

152. See Kadivar's *Az islam e tarikhy beh islam e manavi* (From Historical Islam to Spiritual Islam), available at www.Kadivar.com/htm/Farsi/Papers/Paper007.htm.

153. Ibid.

154. Ibid.

155. Ibid.

156. Kadivar reviews efforts by some clerics to resolve some of these dichotomies, including Ayatullah Khomeini's idea of what he called "the *fiqhi* government" (*hokumat e fiqhi*), and finds them all inadequate. Ibid.

157. Ibid.

158. See Hujat al-Islam Muhsen Kadivar's speech, "Women's Rights in Contemporary Islam from a Different Angle" (Hoqough e zanan dar islam e moaser az zavehi digar), at www.Kadivar.com/htm/Farsi/Speeches/Speech820615.htm.

159. Kadivar, "Az islam tarikhy beh islam manavit."

160. See Hujat al-Islam Muhsen Kadivar, "Compatibility of Islam and Human Rights" (Sazeghari e islam va hoqough e bashr), interview with Behnam Bavandpour (Deutche Welle), available at www.Kadivar.com/htm/Farsi/Interviews/Interview-840600.htm.

161. See *Sazeghari e islam va democracy: kodam islam? kodam democracy?* (Compatibility of Islam and Democracy: Which Islam? Which Democracy?), available at www. Kadivar.com/htm/Farsi/Papers/Paper-830912.htm.

162. He elaborates his views in this regard in two books: *Hermeneutic e ketab va sonat* (Hermeneutics of the Book and the Sunna) (Tehran: Entesharat-e-Tarh-e-Now, 1379 [1997]), and *Naqdi bar qaraat e rasmi az din* (A Critique of the Official Reading of Religion) (Tehran: Entesharat-e-Tarh-e-Now, 1379 [2000]). Also see his *Tamulati dar Qarat e Insani Az Din* (Reflections on Human Reading of Religion) (Teharan: Entesharat-e-Tarh-e-Now, 1383 [2003]).

163. For Nouri's views and his defense against charges brought against Ayatillah Rez a Tacasili, see his "Shawkaran e islah" (The Hemlock of Reform) (Tehran: Entesharat-e-Tarh-e-Now, 1378 [1999]).

164. For examples of his political views see the interview of *Noandish* with Aya tullah Reza Tavasoli available at http://www.noandish.com/com.php?id=13897.

165. Shabestari abandoned his clerical profession in recent years.

166. For an elaboration of this thesis, see *Hermeuneutic e ketab va sonat.*

167. Ibid., p. 21.

168. Ibid., p. 20.

169. Ibid., pp. 23–24.

170. Ibid., p. 23.

171. Ibid., p. 32.

172. Ibid, pp. 57–60.

173. Ibid., p. 60.

174. See *Naghdi az Qaraat e rasmi az din* (Tehran: Entesharat e Tarh e Now, 1379 [1997]), pp. 13–15.

175. Ibid., pp. 21–27.

176. Ibid., p. 30.

177. Ibid.

178. Ibid., pp. 31–34.

179. For an extensive discussion of these issues see ibid., pp. 106–51.

180. Ibid., pp. 111–12.

181. Ibid., pp. 191–206.

182. Ibid., pp. 223–80.

183. Seyyed Muhsen Saidzade, *Zanan dar jameeh e madani: ta cheh andazeh sahm darand* (Tehran: Nashr e Ghatreh, 1377 [1998]).

184. Ibid., pp. 11–22.

185. Ibid., pp. 46–47.

186. Ibid., pp. 55–58.

187. He lists the *ayat* of various Suras regarding these issues. Ibid., pp. 100–101.

188. Ibid., pp. 101–3.

189. Ibid., p. 108.

190. Ibid., pp. 108–17.

191. Hassan Yussefi Eshkevari *Shariati va naqd-e-sonnat* (Shariati and the Critic of Tradition) (Tehran: Chap-e-Yadavaran, 1378 [1998]), pp. 125–26.

192. Ibid.

193. Ibid., p. 129.

194. Ibid., pp. 129–30.

195. See his *Islam, azadi va moderniteh* (Islam, Freedom, and Modernity), *Aftab*, no. 9, Aban 1380 (October–November 2001) and *Mardom salari e dini* (Religious Democracy), *Aftab*, Issue no. 23, Bahman 1381 (January–February 2002).

196. For the text of the speech see Ziba Mir-Hosseini and Richard Tapper, *Islam and Democracy in Iran: Eshkevari and the Quest for Reform* (London: I.B. Tauris, 2006), pp. 163–70.

197. Iranian reformist thinkers often use these terms interchangeably, although subtle distinctions exist among them.

198. See the interview of Cyrus Nejadi with Eshkevari, *Tajad khahi va rowshanfekri e dini; goftgu ba hassan yussefi eshkevari* (Desire for Modernity and Religious Intellectuals), available at www.bbc.com.uk/persian/arts/story/2005/08/050812_pm-cy-eshkevari.shtml.

199. Qabel detailed his criticism of Khamenei in an open letter to him. For the text, see "Nameh e ahamd ghabel beh rahbar jomhuri e islam e iran" (The Letter of Ahmad Qabel to the Leader of the Islamic Republic of Iran), published on the BBC Persian Web site at www.bbc.com.uk/persian/iran/story/2005/06/050601.

200. Qabel addresses this issue in the context of Shi'a historiography. See Ahmad Qabel, "Sokhanrani e Ahmad Ghabel dar husseinieh e ershad" (Speech at Husseinieh e Ershad), available at www.advarnews.us/article/3908.aspx.

201. Ahmad Qabel discusses these issues in a series of articles on his Web site called "Shariat e aghlani" (The Rational Shari'a), available at ghabel.persianblog.com/1384_3_ghabel_archive.html.

202. Ahmad Qabel "Haq mehvari" (Right Centeredness), MIZANNEWS, available at www.mizannews.com/archives//000848.html.

203. See his "Ertad" (Apostasy), available at ghabel.persianblog. co/1384_3-ghabel_archive. html.

204. See Ahmad Qabel, "Sokhanrani e Ahmad Ghabel dar husseinieh e ershad."

205. Quoted in Ali Sadrzadeh, "The Shattered Illusions of the Revolution," in *Qantara: Dialogue with the Islamic World*, available at www.qantara.de/webcom/show_article.pup-476/_nr-83/i.html.

206. For details, see Mahmoud Sadri and Ahmad Sadri, eds. and trans., *Reason, Freedom, and Democracy: Essential Writings of Abdolkarim Soroush* (Oxford and New York: Oxford University Press, 2000), pp. 3–23.

207. Ibid., p. 14.

208. Abdolkarim Soroush, *Gabz va bast e teorik e shariat* (The Theoretical Contraction and Expansion of the Shari'a) (Tehran: Sarat, 1379 [1991]), pp. 214–15.

209. Abdolkarim Soroush, *Sarathay e mostaghim* (Straight Paths) (Tehran: Moassesseh e Farfangi e Sarat, 1378 [1999]).

210. Abdolkarim Soroush, "Shariati va jameeh e shanassi e din" (Shariati and the Sociology of Religion), *Kian*, no. 13, 1372 (1993) (author's translation).

211. Ibid., emphasis added.

212. Soroush, *Gabz va bast e teorik e shariat*.

213. Abdolkarim Soroush, *Bast e tajrobeh e nabavi* (The Expansion of Prophetic Experience) (Tehran: Sarat, 1999).

214. Abdolkarim Soroush, *Zati va arazi dar din* (Intrinsic and Contingent in Religion) 1377 (1998). Also see Jalal Tavakolian, "Tavaroghi dar daftar ayam e soroush" (A Review of Soroush's Life), on the occasion of his sixtieth birthday, available at www.dsoroush.com/Persian/On_DrSoroush/p-CMO-13840929-jalal.Tavakolian.html.

215. Soroush elaborates these ideas in the following articles: *Horiat va rouhaniat* (Freedom and the Clergy), 1372 (1993) and *Saghf e maeishat bar sotun e shariat* (The Ceiling of Livelihood on the Column of Shariat), 1374 (1995).

216. Sadri and Sadri, *Reason, Freedom, and Democracy in Islam*, pp. 122–54.

217. Soroush, *Farbahtar az ideolog*, pp. 126–29.

218. Soroush, *Gabz va bast e teorik e shariat*, p. 45.

219. Soroush was criticized for this view by Hudjat al-Islam Bahmanpour. For Soroush's response to Bahmanpour's criticism, see "Payravi az foqahay e sonnat ra mojaz midanm" (I Consider It Permissible to follow Sunni faqihs), available at Baztabat, www.baztab.ir/news/29757.php.

220. Mahmoud Sadri, *Taamoli dar bab e nasazegari e mardomsalari e modern ba velayat va mahdaviyat dar tashaio* (A Reflection on the Incompatibility of Modern Democracy and Guardianship and Messianism in Shi'ism) 1384 (2005), available at www.dsoroush.com/Persian/On_DrSoroush/p-CMO-13840529-MahmoudSadri.html.

221. The text of the interview is available at http://www/drsoroush.com/Persian/Interviews/p-CMO-kalameMohammad.html.

222. For Ayatullah Subhani's response, see http://www.drsoroush.com/Persian/On_DrSoroush/p-CMO-Sobhani2.html.

223. Mostafa Malekian, *Rahi beh rahaei: goftarhaei dar bab e aghlaniat va manaviat* (A Way to Freedom: Reflections on Rationalism and Spirituality) (Tehran: Nashr e Negah e Moaser, 1380 [2001]).

224. Ibid., pp. 375–76.

225. Ibid., p. 376.

226. Ibid., pp. 376–77.

227. See Mustafa Malekian, "The Precondition of Reformism Is Tolerance," interview with *Emrous*, available at www.emrouz.info/archives/print/2006/01/00457.php.

228. The articles in Malekian, *Rahi beh rahaei*, pp. 251–312.

229. Ibid., 93–106.

230. "Religious New Thinking and the Question of Women: Woman Man, Which Image? A Conversation with Mustafa Malekian," available at manaviat.blogfa.com/post-25.aspx. Muatafa Malekian, "Feminist Approach to the Interpretation of the Qur'an," interview with *Emrous,* available at emruz.info/print.aspx?ID=1658.

231. See Ali Reza Alavitabar, "Democracy Does Not Mean Following the People. I Am Religious, Leftist, Democrat, Reformist and a Product of the Movement of the Imam's Line," available at www.mehrenews.com/fa/NewsDetail.aspx?NewsID=343322.

232. See Ali Reza Alavitabar, "Sunnat va moderniteh dar rowshanfekri e dini: ghoftogouyi ba alireza alavitabar" (Tradition and Modernity in Religious Intellectualism: A Conversation with Ali Reza Alavitabar), interview by Syrus Alinejad (BBC), available at www.bbc.co uk/persian/arts/story/2005/11/051102_pm-cy-alavitabar-4. shtml.

233. Ali Reza Alavitabar, "Vazifeh e ma entebagh e mafahim e dini ba moderniteh e hakem bar jahan e feeli ast" (Our Duty Is to Adapt Religious Concepts to the Modernity That Is Dominant in Today's World), available at www.emrouz.info/archives/print/2006/02/005138. php.

234. Of course, the first person to speak about religious intellectualism was Soroush. However, he did not do so explicitly in the context of avoiding polarization between modernity and tradition.

235. See Ali Reza Alavitabar, "Sunnat va moderniteh dar rowshanfekri e dini: ghoftoghouyi ba alireza alavitabar." Here it is important to note that many secular intellectuals in Iran also believe in this view.

236. Ali Reza Alavitabar, *Liberalism va democracy* (Liberalism and Democracy), available at www.emrouz.info/archives/print/2006/06/030986.php.

237. See Fatemeh Kamali Ahmadsaraei, "Zendeginameh emmad eddin baghi" (The Biography of Emmad Eddin Baghi), available at www.emadbaghi.com/archives/000370.php.

238. Emmad Eddin Baghi's speech at Kanoon e Towhid is available at www.emadbaghi.com/archives/000119php.

239. Ibid. He attributes this opinion to Ayatullah Allameh Tabatabaei, Mutahari, and Montazeri.

240. Ibid.

241. Emmad Eddin Baqi, "Huquq e bashar ya huquq e momenan" (Human Rights or the Right of the Believers), available at www.emadbaghi.com/archives/000119.php.

242. Emmad Eddin Baqi, "Mashroiyat e dini va rowshanfekri e dini" (Religious Legitimacy and Religious Intellectualism) (speech, extracts), available at www.emadbaghi.com/archives/000522.php.

243. Donald Eugene Smith, "Religion and Political Modernization in Comparative Perspective," in Donald Eugene Smith, ed., *Religion and Political Modernization* (New Haven, CT: Yale University Press, 1974), p. 17.

2

Reformist and Moderate Voices of Islam in the Arab East

Hassan Hanafi

During the last four decades, the discourse on Islam in the Arab world has been dominated by various extremist and fundamentalist or literalist interpretations of the faith.
Two sets of factors have been responsible for this state of affairs. The first relates to
the Arab countries' internal developments and includes the following: (1) the triumph
of secular developmentalist authoritarianism in post-independence Arab countries; (2)
Arab governments' manipulation of religion for political ends, including the undermining of their secular political opponents, especially those on the left, as was done by
Anwar al Sadat in Egypt; (3) the bureaucratization of religious establishments; and (4)
the co-optation of conservative Islam in exchange for political quietism.[1] The second
set of factors concerns external developments, including major regional and international events, with the following being the most important: (1) the Arab defeat in the
1967 Arab-Israeli war and the fall of Jerusalem to Israel; (2) the continued Arab-Israeli
conflict and the worsening plight of the Palestinians; (3) the 1979 Islamic Revolution
in Iran; (4) the Soviet-Afghan War, followed by a bloody Afghan Civil War; and (4)
the Bosnian and Chechen wars during the 1990s and early 2000s.

During the Soviet-Afghan war (1979–1989), the United States and its regional
allies instrumentalized Islam by characterizing the war waged by the Afghan resistance groups against the Soviets as *jihad*, glorifying the *mujahedin* and using them
as counters to the combined Soviet and communist threat. These policies greatly
contributed to the rise of extremist and jihadist discourse and groups among Arab and
non-Arab Muslims, many of whom joined the resistance forces in Afghanistan.[2]

Yet even during these turbulent decades, fundamentalist and radical readings
of Islam have not gained mass appeal in the Arab world, and most Arab Muslims
have never committed a violent act inspired by radical Islam. Throughout this period, the mainstream Islam to which most Arabs adhere has remained religiously
conservative and politically moderate, even quietist.

This research was conducted with the oral help of Heba Raouf and Dr. Diaa Rashwan
and with oral and written help from Hossam Tammam.

Moreover, despite the seeming ascendancy of fundamentalist and radical interpretations of Islam, a number of Arab scholars have engaged in more modernist
readings of Islam, using nontraditional methodologies derived from the social
sciences, history, literary criticism, and semiotics. This author, for example, undertook a major project on "tradition and modernism." The project's goal was to
reconstruct disciplines such as theology, philosophy, jurisprudence, mysticism,
and scriptural sciences, in light of the challenges faced by contemporary Muslims,
including colonialism, both old and new; poverty; socioeconomic and political oppression; state disintegration; mass lethargy; economic and political dependence
on outside powers; and excessive Westernization. Another Egyptian scholar, Nasr
Hamed Abu Zayd, has applied linguistic and hermeneutical methods to the study
of the Qur'an.[3] Others such as Said al-Ashmawi and Jamal al-Banna also helped
advance the reformist discourse.[4]

The work of these scholars was a continuation of the endeavors of earlier Arab
reformist thinkers, such as Muhammad Abduh and Ali Abd al-Raziq, although they
were operating within different sociopolitical conditions, responding to a different
set of challenges, and using different methodologies. What links the more recent
reformists with earlier generations is their ultimate objective, namely, to solve the
Arabs' and Muslims' many problems and to make Islam more relevant to Muslims'
new conditions and needs.

In the last fifteen years, Islam's moderate and reformist voices have become
more numerous. This resurgence has been stimulated by long-standing concerns
that inspired earlier reformers, by a process of learning and reassessment undergone by some Muslim radicals, and by a general sense of disenchantment with
long-established Muslim organizations, such as the Muslim Brotherhood, and their
modes of operation.

This increase in the number of Islam's moderate and reformist voices reflects
the desire of Muslim intellectuals, professionals, and activists to play a more
significant political role in their respective countries. By advancing moderate and
reformist discourse, they hope to overcome the existing governments' resistance
to their participation in the political process, although so far without much success. Moreover, they are contesting the domination of the field of debate by both
radical and politically quiescent, conservative Muslims. They combine a reformist
discourse with social and political action.

These new moderate and reformist voices, especially their younger representatives, are the focus of this study. Because of Egypt's importance as the Arab world's
intellectual center, the influence of trends developed in Egypt on the rest of the
Arab-Muslim world, and the diversity and richness of its moderate and reformist
discourses, the Egyptian case will be treated in detail. The Arabian Peninsula and
the Gulf region will also receive considerable attention, partly because Arabia is
the birthplace of Wahhabism, and so the emergence of reformist voices there is of
particular interest and significance. Reformist voices in Syria, Jordan, Yemen, and
among Shi'a Arabs will be treated more briefly.

The Range and Characteristics of Reformist and
Moderate Discourses

The new Islamic discourse in the Eastern reaches of the Arab world can best be characterized as "post-fundamentalist." It covers a wide spectrum of Islamic thinking and praxis—pluralistic, open, rational, realistic, civil, parliamentary, liberal, intermediary (*wasati*), cultural, modernist, reformist, and social, although not quite socialist. As is the case with other social and political intellectual discourses, various tendencies, ranging from left to right and center, are observable within this post-fundamentalist discourse. Most of these new readings originated in established Islamic organizations, particularly the Muslim Brotherhood, partly as a result of some of their members' reaction to these organizations' prevailing views and modes of operation. Other reformist voices developed independently from such long-established institutions. Most of the reformist and moderate proponents are in their forties and fifties. Others, such as the members of the "Repentant" group, al-Ta'ibun, are even younger. Some of them belong or once belonged to larger organizations such as the Muslim Brotherhood, while others act independently. They also differ in the manner in which they express their views. One notable development has been the emergence of a new type of preachers (*du'ah al-judud*) who spread their ideas orally. The representatives of reformist and moderate discourse are inspired and influenced by a variety of intellectual sources, including the ideas of the Muslim Brothers, mysticism, Shi'ism, and secular political ideologies such as Marxism and Arab nationalism.

In this study, however, the ideas of the representatives of these new voices, rather than their organizational affiliations, will be the main criteria used to compare their perspectives against those of the extremists of the relatively recent past, and to assess the degree of continuity or discontinuity between these new discourses and traditional Islam, especially in the long term.

Intermediary Islam and the Muslim Brotherhood

The Muslim Brotherhood is the main wellspring of reformist and moderate Islamic voices in Egypt, Jordan, and Syria. In Egypt, the Wasat (Center) Party, founded by Abu al-'Ela Madi, an engineer in his forties, best represents this discourse. Madi is part of the 1970s generation among the Muslim Brothers' membership. In the 1970s he took part in student Islamic activities and later joined the Islamic group al-Jama'a al-Islamiyya and became its emir in Assiut. He and other leaders of the group later joined the Brotherhood. Madi became one of the Brotherhood's most visible young leaders and the youngest member of its *shur'a* (consultative council).

Madi gradually became disenchanted with the organization's secretive culture and its autocratic structure. The Brotherhood's leadership had encouraged him to form a political party, then later withdrew its support on the grounds that the party's philosophy was closer to secularism than to Islam. This reversal on the part of the Brotherhood's leadership led him to leave the organization.[5]

The Wasat Party is not based on religious affiliation. Initially its membership included Christian Copts. Because of this fact, and because the Egyptian government thought that the party might become a counterweight to the Muslim Brotherhood, the government initially did not oppose its formation. However, the government, too, later changed its attitude. It pressured Wasat's Coptic members to withdraw their support, thus enabling the government to characterize Wasat as a religion-based party, something that is prohibited by the Constitution.

The Wasat Party is a timid effort to embody a tendency toward ideological and political openness within the Muslim Brotherhood that is known as the "public action" trend. Its membership is open to all Egyptian citizens, including non-Muslims, provided that they accept Islam's cultural as opposed to dogmatic role in Egyptian society. The party also reflects the political ideas of independent Muslim thinkers from various generations, such as al-'Awa and al-Bishri 'Emara. They support their ideas by legal opinions from sources placed somewhere between the Muslim Brothers and independent thinkers such as Yuseuf al-Qaradawi.

As Wasat's leader, Madi supports a modern state with an Islamic referent, and not a religious state based on the concept of *hakimiyya* (rule of God). In Madi's view, the Islamic political system is civil and democratic, based on principles of political pluralism, national coalition, and human rights.

Another prominent member of the Wasat and one of its cofounders is Salah Abd al-Karim. He is an aviation engineer, a professor of aviation technology at Cairo University, and an active member of the Engineers Union. He, too, favors a cultural, nondogmatic, nonritualistic, and future-oriented Islam. Although the general frame of his thought is cultural, his legal view is deduced from Islamic law. He stresses the importance of civil work, independence of religious institutions and endowments, and reform and revision of personal status and family laws. He attributes Egypt's cultural crisis to the destruction of the traditional value system, structural violence, corruption, and the disparity between rich and poor. He also stresses the importance of education, science, environment, technical development, and tourism. His views on foreign policy and international relations are defined by concern for Egyptian and Arab national security.[6]

The Wasat party's underlying principles are:
1. The nation (*umma*) is the origin of power and civil society is the cornerstone of the state;
2. The rights of the nation have priority over its duties;
3. All segments of society are entitled to social cohesion and to public welfare;
4. The process of decolonization of the Arab and Muslim worlds, especially in Palestine, must continue; and
5. Violence should be rejected as an instrument for change.

These underlying principles inform the party's program, which has the following dimensions:

1. The political dimension deals with issues of public freedom and political reform.
2. The economic and social dimensions deal with issues of how to encourage investment; the respective roles of the private and public sectors in the economy; how to implement social and educational reforms, especially how to eliminate illiteracy and to create a knowledge-based society; how to deal with poverty and; and how to establish social justice and medical care.
3. The cultural dimension deals with the following issues: how to encourages creativity in culture, art, and science; how to include ethical factors in policies designed to reform the educational system and the mass media; and how to modernize religious discourse and patterns of cultural behavior.
4. The section on foreign policy and international relations emphasizes the importance of creating and maintaining regional and international balances of power; the centrality of the Palestinian problem; the importance of intra-Arab relations; and the need for a dialogue of cultures.[7]

The party's program as described above is informed by its cultural vision of Islam. It emphasizes rights over duties; encourages dialogue among various social and political groups; favors the formation of a national coalition and front; and wants to bridge polar extremes such as secularism and Salafism, traditionalism and modernism, conservatism and progress, rationalism and fideism, realism and idealism, the right and the left.

New Reformist Projects

The new moderate and reformist voices that have emerged from within the Muslim Brothers have greatly influenced their old guard and have prompted them to develop their own reformist projects in Egypt, Syria, and elsewhere.[8] Positions outlined in these projects regarding the Islamic penal code and *shari'a* rulings on women's rights are not as progressive as those of more reformist voices. Nevertheless, these projects represent an important evolution in the Muslim Brothers' positions, especially regarding socioeconomic and political issues.[9]

The Syrian Reform Project

Of all the reform projects developed by the Muslim Brotherhood in various Arab countries, the project produced by the Syrian Muslim Brothers (outlined in Figure 2.1) is articulated in the best fashion. The project is divided into theoretical and operational parts. The theoretical section explains the project's underlying prin-

Figure 2.1 **The Syrian Reform Project**

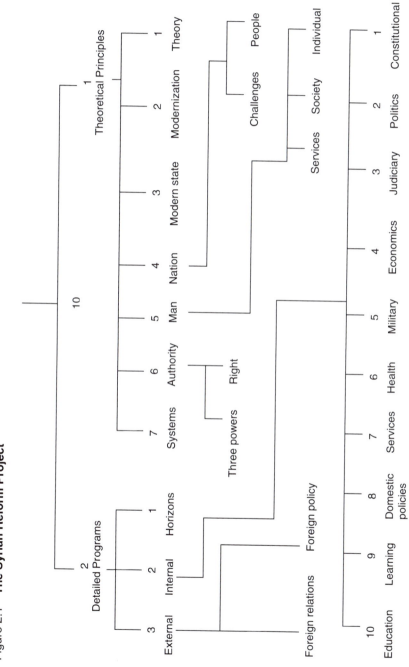

ciples, which remain largely religious. However, these principles express an Islamic worldview that is not directly related to politics.

The project does not address the question of methodology and instead talks about the project's "intellectual [*fikriyya*] and theoretical points of departure." These include unity of creator and dignity of creature; vice-regency of man on earth; human freedom; justice for all; the need for diversity, in order to encourage dialogue and mutual knowledge; and a view of the world as a space to implement the divine call. It also refers to the foundations of the modern state, *murtakazat*. Another term used in this context is *nuzum;* it refers to constitutional reform and the rule of law.

According to this project, the Islamic state is neither religious nor theocratic. Rather, it is a civil, contractual, representative, pluralist, institutional, and legal state and is based on the principles of peaceful transfer of power and equal citizenship.

In this project, *hakimiyya* is defined not as direct rule by God, but as the exercise of his rule through the people's representatives. This definition implies that states' political authority derives from the popular will as expressed through elections. The main responsibility of the state is to implement the constitution and to establish the rule of law. The political system is based on the separation and independence of legislative, executive, and judicial powers. The judiciary is responsible for the management of customary law. The state is responsible for defending the country against foreign aggression and for maintaining internal stability. The project favors a mixed system that combines elements of liberal and state-based economic systems and is in accordance with Islamic ethical guidelines.

At the same time, the system envisaged in the project has an Islamic referent and is based on the following Islamic principles: (1) *tawhid* (monotheism and the vice-regency of man); (2) *istikhlaf* (plurality in opinion); and (3) *shur'a* (consultation). *Tawhid* is not simply a creed based on the belief in one God. Rather it is a unitarian vision of man, society, and nation, and its goals are security, equality, justice, and freedom. The state is the political embodiment of the nation and the homeland (*al-watan*), and it reflects its historical, cultural, political, economic, internal, and external dimensions.

The project's detailed political program sets the following goals: maintaining freedom; finding common ground among people; and generating a national renaissance. Its economic program emphasizes increase in production, justice in distribution, and rationalization in consumption. The Palestinian issue is at the center of foreign policy concerns; it is considered as a national cause, and it has priority over Arab, Islamic, and international concerns.

According to the project, the individual—male and female—is the society's cornerstone. Society should preserve the family, reject rote imitation of foreign models of social and individual behavior, strengthen religious awareness, and revolt against injustice.

This project views the *shari'a* as being more than just the penal code (*hudud*).

In application of the *hudud*, it recommends the exercise of leniency, graduation, and the balancing of benefits and costs. The project's position on gender equality is somewhere between those of the reformists and the conservatives. It views men and women as human (*insan*); they have been created from the same soul and are legally equal. It grants women considerable political rights, including the right fully to participate in public life, to vote, to be to be elected to political office (except as head of state), to become judges, to preach, and to issue legal opinions. However, on issues dealing with family and inheritance, it follows traditional Islamic principles and laws, which are based on the notion of complementarity rather than equality of men and women.

The Egyptian Reform Project

The reform project of the Muslim Brothers in Egypt is similar to that of Syria. It is divided into three parts: theoretical principles; the foundations of the modern state; and systems and methods (Figure 2.2).

Reformist elements in the Egyptian Brotherhood and in the Wasat Party use the term *minhaj* (pl. *menahij*), which may be loosely interpreted as "methodology." It means road, way, or behavior. In the project's context it refers to "methods of change" and the Brothers' views on issues such as: coup d'état, popular revolt, constitutional parliamentary action, and civil society institutions and movements. It also encompasses systems and concepts, policies and measures. It is different from *manhaj*, which means method of reasoning, research, and discovery. The Egyptian Brothers' project also uses the terms *murtakazat* (foundations), *raka'iz* (basis), *muntalakat* (points of departure), *mafahim* (concepts), *ru'ia* (vision), and *ru'ia shamila* (global vision). The last term refers to an Islamic worldview.

The Egyptian reform project's "foundations" and "points of departure" reference Islam, including the divine law (*shari'a*); *fiqh*, however, is considered as a purely human construct. It considers the basis of Islamic law to be Islam's five universal intentions, namely life, reason, justice, freedom, equality, human dignity, and public welfare. The advocates of the reform project believe that the laws that are intended to achieve these basic objectives should be interpreted in a fairly broad, rather than restrictive, fashion. They justify this position on the ground that that "the gates of *ijtihad* are open."

The principal concepts and visions included in the project are moderation; rejection of violence; distinction between faith and changing socioreligious practices; finding solutions for problems by taking into account changing conditions (the contextual approach); dealing with other political forces on an equal basis; taking advantage of others' experiences; equal rights of citizenship irrespective of religion (only the head of state need be Muslim); recognition of the other; *jihad* as self-defense; and respect for human rights. Their position on women's rights is almost identical to that of the Syrian Brothers.

According to this project, too, the Islamic state is neither religious nor theocratic.

Figure 2.2 **The Egyptian Reform Project**

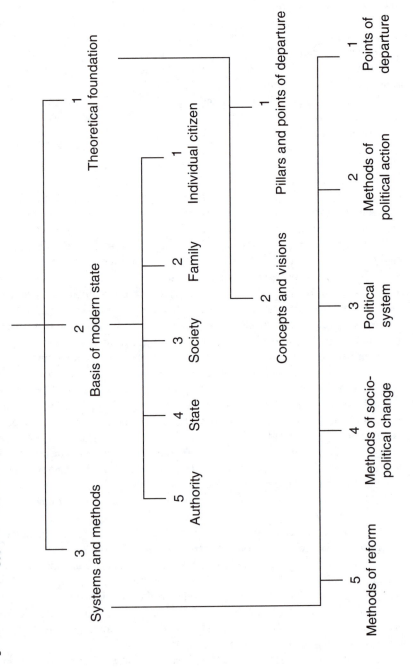

It is a civil, institutional, legal, contractual, and representative state with Islamic referents. In this state, political power is obtained through popular elections and is transferable through the same process.

In economic matters, the project emphasizes sustainable development.

Other Reform Projects

The electoral programs of Jordan's Islamic Action Party and Lebanon's Islamic Pact are similar to the Syrian and Egyptian reform projects. In regard to a number of issues, including women's rights, these projects fall short of the positions of the more reformist groups and thinkers in some other Muslim countries. In other respects, however, notably regarding political matters, they are nearly semi-secular. For example, the new generation of Muslim Brothers no longer subscribes to such concepts as *hakamiyya* (rule of God), popularized by Abul A'la al-Mawdudi and Sayyid Qutb, and it rejects theocracy. They are mainly concerned with problems of this world and not the other world.

Enlightened Islam

This trend is similar to the Wasat Party's perspective and is represented by another Muslim Brother, 'Abd el-Mun'im Abu al-Futuh. In the 1970s he was the emir of the Islamic group at Cairo University, and he still maintains an on-again off-again relationship with the mother organization. He represents the center-right within the moderate Islamic trend, while Abu al-'Ela Madi represents the center-left. His basic ideas can be gleaned from his book *Modernizers, Not Destroyers*.[10] In this book, he stresses Islam's importance as a cultural and not a political worldview, based on the following principles: servitude to God; submission of the self to God; good intentions; long-term vision; world-affirmation and commitment to life; endogenous creativity; universal humanism; and freedom of thought and citizenship.

He pursues the Muslim Brothers' traditional line of thinking and links himself to the classical reformism of Afghani, Muhammad Abduh, and Rashid Rida, with some inspiration from al-Ghazali's and Abdul Qadir Jilani's mysticism. He considers moral education to be the prerequisite of political change. He still opposes Nasserism and the exaggerated role of charismatic leadership. He believes in the importance of achieving national unity by emphasizing citizenship and discouraging religiously based identities (confessionalism). Palestine is still at the heart of his thinking.

Islamic Left

No viable Islamic left has emerged in the last two decades that could continue Qutb's socialist phase.[11] However, an older generation has kept alive the tradition of a left-leaning Islam with strong concern for social justice. This generation includes the Islamic left (Hassan Hanafi); Islamic socialism (Adel Hussein, Ahmed Abbas

Salih); and the Labor Party and its weekly, *al-Sha'b*. The Islamic left seems to be losing ground to the "consumerist Islam" of new preachers (*al-du'ah al-judud*) such as 'Amr Khaled.

Democracy and Muslim Moderates

The new moderate voices that have emerged from the Brotherhood emphasize democracy's importance and call themselves Democratic Muslim Brothers. Their concept of democracy is founded on a people-centered political and civil process and is not merely a modern interpretation of the concept of *shur'a*. This was the older generation's position within the Brothers because their notion of democracy was very limited. The new voices recognize that there is only one democracy, although its specific manifestations may vary in different cultural contexts. It is based on populism and not on theocracy or monocracy.[12] They maintain that the caliphate, the leadership of Muslim community, is a political issue and is not related to Islamic law. This view, which is shared by most secularists, is similar to that of an earlier reformist thinker, Ali Abd al-Raziq (1888–1966), as explained in his famous book *Islam and the Principles of Government*.[13] They assert that democracy does not need any religious justification and that the traditional concept of *ahl al-hall wa al-'aqd* (people who are qualified to bind and dissolve) is subjective and does not exist in reality. Today, people directly choose their representatives.

The new democratic voices consider the peaceful transfer of power to be a natural process since no one can rule a country forever. They believe that democratic parties should be national in character, not international (like the international Muslim Brothers organization, as well as international communism or socialism), and that the main criteria in elections should be parties' political programs, not confession or sectarianism. They favor equal citizenship and equality before the law for all irrespective of religion, sect, ethnicity, or class, and they assert that a just non-Muslim head of state is better than an unjust Muslim. They believe in the judiciary's independence from the executive branch.

Despite some important changes in the Muslim Brothers' positions, these democratic principles are absent from their projects. This is the reason that the old guard opposes the new reformist and moderate voices that have emerged from within its ranks.

The Brotherhood's largely middle-class old guard is still more influential among Egyptian Muslims, who are mostly conservative. However, a new and well-educated generation, with roots in Egypt's lower classes, is challenging their views and leadership.

Muslim Reformist Activists

Some former members of the Muslim Brothers, disillusioned by the failure of ideologies, the demise of historical and social mega-narratives, and the erosion of certitude have chosen social activism.[14] They are mostly professionals with secular education—medical doctors, engineers, business executives—rather than al-Azhar graduates, albeit within an Islamic framework. They are not thinkers interested in developing theories. They are Muslim activists concerned with operational issues and are more interested in the media than in scholarship. They interpret Islam in order to find answers to practical questions, such as whether Islam permits music.

They are more influential among the masses (horizontally) than among scholars (vertically).[15] They developed their ideas at the end of the 1980s, largely because they were concerned about the Brothers' future, despite their electoral victories in the parliamentary elections of 1987. The most prominent representatives of this trend are discussed below.[16]

Hisham Ga'far

Hisham Ga'far is in his early forties and is a graduate of Cairo University's political science department. He was very active in the political section of the Brothers but had reservations about some aspects of their thinking, especially regarding political issues. This concern is reflected in his master's degree thesis on "Political Dimensions of the Concept of *Hakimiyya*," which was a central concept in the Islamic discourse of the 1970s. In his thesis, he concluded that the concept of *hakimiyya* (rule of God) is not enough to form a political project. He is a major contributor to the ideas of the Wasat Party.

After leaving the Brothers and becoming disengaged from direct political action, he became the chief editor of the IslamOnline network and has been largely responsible for the network's success in developing an Islamic political consciousness. In a paper titled "Islamic Movement and Post-Politics,"[17] he gives a definition of politics that is closer to culture than to religion. According to this definition, the Brothers have become more like a pressure group than a political party. In the paper he argues that the ineffectiveness of the Egyptian state and the weakness of its institutions are due to the supremacy of the state over society and the state's refusal to allow more space for independent societal movements. This situation has resulted in the intellectual and operational stagnation of the civil society, including the Brothers.

Meanwhile, the Brothers' belief that a global Islamic ideology requires a global Islamic organization has prevented its evolution into a social movement. In developing this view, Hisham may have been influenced by the ideas of the Tunisian Islamic thinker Rashid al-Ghanoushi, who has argued that that the idea of a supranational Islamic organization is a replica of the post-independence totalitarian Arab state. According to Hisham, as the totalitarian Arab state has failed the global Islamic organization has also become irrelevant and should be replaced with a multilayered structure. Hisham also stresses the priority of cultural activity over direct political action, believing that cultural change is the most important change in society. In this he reflects Hassan Al Banna's notion of the Islamic project.

Mohammad Mus'ad

Mohammad Mus'ad founded the Nama' (Development) Center within the Brothers, in order to enhance intellectual consciousness and the administrative capacities of Muslim leaders. The center became independent and reached its peak in the 1990s. Later, together with Hisham Ga'far and others, he founded South Group Research (SGR), the first forum for this generation, reflecting the generational transformation in Egypt's modernization movement.

Ahmad Abdullah

Ahmad Abdullah is in his mid-forties and has a degree in medicine from Cairo University. He was active in the Muslim Brothers' student movement and later pursued a political career using the Socialist Labor Party as a legal cover. But he soon became disenchanted both with politics and with the Brothers, and he concluded that democracy has to be built from the bottom up by educating the people to become more active participants in the game of power. He also lost his belief in any mega-Islamic narrative and instead focused his attention on issues such as dialogue with other religions, openness toward the other, human rights, and the struggle against globalization.

Magdi Sa'id

Magdi Sa'id, in his mid-forties, is a medical doctor. He, too, became disenchanted with the Brothers and the utopian Islamic project. He turned his attention to relief work and traveled to Chechnya, Daghestan, Albania, England, and Europe. He has worked on the media and in the Internet and has written articles for Islam Online on topics ranging from sustainable development to the feminist movement to the struggle against globalization.

'Amr Abu Khalil

'Amr Abu Khalil, in his mid-forties, is another ex-Brothers activist. He, too, became disenchanted with Islamic political action and turned to social activism. He founded the first specialized psychological center in his hometown of Alexandria. In cooperation with Ahmad Abdallah, he created an Islam Online site on "youth problems and their solution."

Ahmad Muhammad and Muhammad abd al-Gawwad

Both Ahmad Muhammad and Muhammad abd al-Gawwad are ex-members of the Brothers and both are experts in business administration. After becoming disillusioned with politics and with the Brothers, they turned their attention to self-management and human development. Abdul Gawwad founded a center called The Future. In his writings, he combines administrative sciences with Islamic culture.

The reformist activists described above have the following points in common:

1. They have a pragmatic approach to Islam and want to make it relevant to people's everyday lives. In other words, theirs is an "operational" rather than theoretical Islam;
2. They have a non-ideological, non-dogmatic, and flexible approach to issues such as the role of *shari'a,* the penal code, and human rights. What is important for them is how various positions on these issues can help resolve people's concrete problems in ways that will improve their daily lives. For this reason, Islam Online has become an important source of opinion and information for common citizens, especially the youth who have questions or look for solutions to their problems, but also want to retain their Islamic consciousness; and
3. Methodologically, their approach to the interpretation of Islamic law and other sources is "circumstantial." In other words, they are concerned with the question of what kind of interpretation will best help people in particular circumstances and in a practical manner.

Peaceful Islam: The "Repentants" (al-Ta'ibun)

The "Repentant" group is made up of ex-jihadis who, after the assassination of President Anwar al-Sadat in 1981, spent years, even decades, in prison, mostly without trial. In prison they reassessed their views and deeds. The group began issuing booklets under the title "The Correction of Concepts Series." One of them deals with the subject of "Islam and the Challenges of the 21st Century." The booklets are written and reviewed by a group of ten people.[18] The following titles and themes explain the group's basic philosophy.

1. "An Initiative for Cessation of Violence: A Legal View and a Realistic Vision."[19] In this work, issued in July1997, the group announces its decision to abandon violence and accepts to live in civil society.[20] They explain this decision in light of five principles: (1) the traditional idea of public welfare (*al-masalih al-'amma*), a legal concept in *fiqh* (*'ilm al-quwa'id al-fiqhiyya*); (2) the traditional concept of limiting damage (*la dharar wa la dhirar*); (3) the concept of hindrance or obstacle (*al-mani'*), which means factors that prevent the application of Islamic law; (4) the concept of *qudra,* meaning capacity and feasibility; and (5) the modern concept of realism as explained in Qutb's "Islamic Worldview, Features and Components." The upshot of this reasoning is that, in recognizing Muslims' current problems, they opt for accommodation with others.

2. "The Renewal of Religious Discourse."[21] This work is a response to 9/11's negative consequences for Muslims. The authors assert that renewal must come from Islam's roots—the Qur'an and the *sunna*. They note that because it is difficult to establish the *sunna*'s historical authenticity, in the process of renewal people's demands and issues that are not dealt with in written sources should receive more attention.

Methodologically, within the dialectics of permanence and change, they stress change over permanence. They combine sociopolitical analysis with scriptural arguments. They maintain that the discourse of renewal should address relations between Muslims and the West, and they advise Muslims to reject both conspiracy theories and self-flagellation. In order to renew Islam, they favor the changing of religion's ritualistic and formalistic aspects (*'ibada*), and advise that religion (*din*) should become connected with the world (*dunya*) and more concerned with issues such as democracy and women's rights, because, they say, preaching God means preaching life. They believe that sociopolitical issues and concerns should have priority over religious discourse. Nationalism is an important element in their discourse, reflecting a return to the early stands of Muslim Brothers before the crisis of 1954.

3. "The Legal Prohibition of Religious Extremism and Declaring Muslims Apostate." This manuscript strongly condemns religious extremism by analyzing its causes, manifestations, and wisdom. It uses textual arguments that Muslim governments and religious institutions had used historically to condemn the Kharijites and other Islamic groups. These arguments were based on the selective use of Islamic sources, their misinterpretation, and even invention of new *hadith*. Historically, such practices were politically motivated and were used against political opposition.[22]

The ex-jihadi and ex-takfiri groups' rejection of religious extremism has resulted from a process of self-questioning and criticism. Questions asked by the writers include: What crimes did we commit to deserve prison and torture? Can those who torture prisoners be considered Muslims? If they are not Muslims, are they apostates? Are those who obey them and execute their orders also apostates? Their conclusion was that religious extremism is in itself repugnant, shortsighted, and unjust. It appears as fanatical, oppressive, rigid, harsh, and utopian.

They also reflect on the causes of religious extremism and attribute it to the following factors: ignorance of the essence of religion and a literalist reading of religious sources; emphasizing secondary rather than main issues; exaggerating what is prohibited; emphasizing textual ambiguities and ignoring textual clarities; being ignorant teachers and educators; and being ignorant of the realities of Muslims' life and history. They conclude that these shortcomings have caused Muslims to become caught between the two extremes of negligence and extremism in their belief and practice. Muslims lost Andalusia, Palestine, and Jerusalem because of their negligence, and in their dismay over these setbacks they turned to extremism. Once Muslims return to a state of equilibrium, to the middle (*wasat*), both negligence and extremism will dissipate. Extremism is also reflected in the anathematization of sinners as was done by the Khawarij. Much harm results from this attitude: an emphasis on punishment—including the death penalty—over mercy, a lack of justice, and social and legal anarchy.

They maintain that, once someone has declared the *shahada*, he or she becomes a Muslim and cannot be labeled apostate because of his bad deeds. They argue that Islam as a religion is distinct from faith (*iman*). Islam is religion's external (*zahir*) and *iman* its internal (*batin*) manifestation. A Muslim is judged according to external and not internal criteria. A sinner is not an apostate (*kafir*) or a polytheist (*mushrik*). Moreover, in Islam the doors of mercy are wide open through repentance, forgiveness, and expiation by good deeds. Ignorant Muslims cannot be declared apostate. Dependence (*muwalat*) on non-Muslims is not a reason for apostasy in an interdependent world.

They take a tolerant and pluralistic attitude toward non-Muslims and declare that there is nothing wrong with visiting non-Muslim sick persons, congratulating them on occasions such as marriage or the birth of a child, or giving them financial help and cooperating with them in charitable work.

4. "Fatwa al-Tatar of Sheikh ul-Islam Ibn Taymiyya: An Analytical Study." In this paper, Ibn Taymiyya's *fatwa* is reviewed, analyzed, and corrected.[23] This *fatwa* is used by the takfiris to declare Muslim societies *kafir*. The Repentants maintain that all legal opinions and rules should be directed toward achieving the universal intentions of the law, namely public welfare, *maslaha*. The understanding of this concept changes according to time, space, and different communities, thus inevitably leading to changes in legal opinions such as those that prohibit speaking French or wearing a hat.

Based on this perspective, they maintain that Ibn Taymiyya's *fatwa* declaring the Mongols apostates should be interpreted according to its historical context. There can be no analogy between the Mongols and the current Muslim states. Muslims need unity not apostasy. Military confrontation against legal governments cannot solve Muslims' problems. They also maintain that, given human nature and the identity between revelation, reason, and reality, not all human legislation is wrong. Islamic thinking is divine, ethical, realistic, humanistic, harmonious, and universal. Public welfare now requires obeying the laws of states.

5. "Shedding Light on the Misunderstanding of Jihad" and "An Appeal for Reconciliation with Society." The first paper aims to correct old stereotyped legal opinions on the subject of *jihad*.[24] According to Repentants, *jihad* is a means, not an end. It does not permit self-destruction. It does not legitimize killing civilians, tourists, or other innocent people. They now favor national reconciliation.

The second paper is essentially about the recognition of the principle of nationalism and its compatibility with Islam.[25] The authors maintain that the essence of nationalism and Islam is the same; that Muslims and non-Muslims share the same values of love of country and of fellow countrymen. No contradiction exists between Islam and society, for there is a distinction between contradiction and difference of view. Contradiction is opposition and mutual exclusiveness, while difference of view does not need to lead to exclusion and lack of cooperation among different segments of society. They also argue that Islam commands that people should be guided toward good and not be cursed. Therefore, preachers are spiritual guides and not judges, as noted by Muhammad al-Mamoun al-Hudeibi in his famous book, *Guides Not Judges*.

In this paper, Islam is defined as good behavior and the absence of hypocrisy and opportunism. Poems are used to support scriptural arguments and political analysis is linked to textual analysis. The religious discourse in the work is not merely abstract and analytical; it is addressed to the beloved reader. The paper also emphasizes Egyptian nationalism and bonds of citizenship among all Egyptians, irrespective of their religion, thus denoting a tolerant and pluralistic view of Islam.

6. *"The Guidance of People Between Ends and Means."* This paper is the most theoretical of the series. It is based mainly on sociopolitical and historical analysis and is a call for a peaceful and non-violent Islam.[26] It maintains that Islam chooses the most realistic means to achieve its goals. This peaceful discourse is a legal accommodation between duty and reality. Predication is similar to prophecy and both are equal to sincerity, honesty, and success. The new discourse shares people's joys and sorrows and does not oppose those of their customs and manners that are not in direct opposition to Islam, but articulate their needs.

To find the best means to achieve Islam's goals is the role of *hisba* (ensuring the proper application of Islamic law), which is the main function of Islamic government. Evildoers may become means of realizing Islam's ideals, and negative actions could have positive outcomes. For example, social opposition could result in social coalition. The unity of the community is better than its divisiveness. Reconciliation can be achieved by finding an accommodation between the rights of God and the rights of people and among different class interests.

In support of this view, they argue that, historically at many sensitive times, reconciliation has prevented bloodshed. Islam prefers peaceful coexistence to cold war, dialogue of cultures to clash of civilizations. Dialectics, which Islam recognizes as *tadafu'*, can be solved peacefully. They argue that Islam favors gradual social change, as evidenced by the principle of the abrogation of one verse by another (*naskh*) and also by the fact that Islam considers patience a virtue. They also maintain that solitude and isolation are not Islamic practices because they prevent social interaction and lead to antagonistic and hateful relations between certain individuals or groups and the rest of society. Seclusion is only justified at times of turmoil and instability (*fitna*). They consider *jihad* only one means among others for achieving Islam's goals. It is part of Islam, but it does not define it in its entirety, because the famous Qur'anic verse of the sword is abrogated by another verse "There is no coercion in religion."

7. *"Advice and Clarification to Correct Concepts of Those Who Assume Responsibility for Society."* This paper aims to correct the notion of *ihtisab*, which means the social responsibility of individuals and groups to check the functioning of the system of accountability.[27] This effort is partly motivated by the fact that the jihadis use the concept of *hisba* in order to impose their authority on people by ordering them to do good and desist from evil, according to their particular definition of what is good and what is evil. According to this booklet, the exercise of accountability (*hisba*) requires sincerity not opportunism, certainty not conjecture, direct testimony not espionage or secrecy, preventing damage, respecting freedom of belief and behavior, and showing sympathy and respect for others. It should be done peacefully, not forcibly, and without causing more damage. This new interpretation of *hisba* frees Muslims from the responsibility of implementing it through coercive measures.

8. *"Perspectives on the Truth of the Dignity of Faith."* This paper defines dignity (*isti'la*) as meaning self-sufficiency, a concept that was part of Sayyid Qutb's Islamic worldview. The jihadi groups used it to justify their sense of superiority over other Muslims, hence their right to check and correct others' actions and even to condemn them.[28] In the definition of the Repentants, however, self-sufficiency means self-independence or what philosophers called *cogito*. It does not mean violence, aggression, arrogance, feelings of superiority, or the power to violate the rights of others. Nor does it mean neglecting causality, total dependence on God, and forgetting one's own capacities. They reach this conclusion by defining dignity of faith as transcendence and faith as the self or the subject. They maintain that misinterpretation of this concept could lead to totalitarian and extremist ideologies, such those of the Nazis and al-Qaeda. This work represents a major effort in Islamic thought and a move away from the more literalist Ash'ari to the more rationalist and contextualist Mu'tazili tradition.

9. *"The Necessity of Confrontation and the Understanding of Its Consequences."* This paper recognizes the error of believing in the necessity of violence.[29] It argues that judgments, being the product of human thought, can be erroneous. Errors in judgments on Islam do not mean errors in Islam itself; revelation is completely correct, but human understanding of revelation may be right or wrong. This is at the core of the difference between *shari'a* (Islamic path and foundational law) and *fiqh* (Islamic jurisprudence). "Necessity" is not a cosmic phenomenon or a natural law, but a human judgment, meaning a probability. The justice of a cause does not mean that it should be achieved through confrontation; confrontation negates human reason. Rather, a just cause can be defended by other means. The first Islamic state in Medina was established without recourse to force; by contrast, Islamic groups in Egypt and Algeria have tried to establish Islamic states through violence. In choosing the means to achieve a goal, Muslims should consider the consequences of their actions. Wisdom suggests that Islamic struggle first needs study to weigh its potential results.

10. "The Application of the Law Is the Privilege of the Rulers: The Penal Code, the Declaration of War, and the Tribute."[30] This paper argues that the application of the penal code (*hudud*) is in the purview of rulers, not individuals. Declaration of war, too, is a national decision which should be taken by the ruler. It defines *al-jizia*—generally translated as a tax on non-Muslims—as a moral contract between the non-Muslims and the Muslim ruler concerning the equal rights and duties of the latter. This tax may be abolished in the name of equal citizenship and through the participation of non-Muslims in external defense and internal security of Muslim-majority countries. The Repentants recognize the authority of the state and the right of the ruler to perform his sociopolitical and economic functions. In support of their positions, they use rational, social, political, and historical rather than scriptural arguments.

11. "Al-Hakimiyya, a Legal Theory and a Realistic Vision." This work represents a semi-final rupture with the famous concept of *hakimiyya*, developed by Mawdudi, which means the rule of God. It was also a central theme in Qutb's "Signposts on the Road."[31] The work is a research project rather than a simple confession. It is addressed to the nation's youth. The main points of this work are the following:

1. No one is outside the faith even if he is a thief or a adulterer;
2. Predication (preaching, often meaning enjoining the good and warning against evil) is good guidance, not judgments on or an evaluation of the deeds of others;
3. Divine mercy is absolute;
4. Small sins are nothing (*lamam*);
5. Behavior of others should be judged according to appearances because only God can know the reality;
6. Commitment to religion does not legitimize declaring others apostates;
7. To assume wrongly that someone is a Muslim is better than to view him as an apostate;
8. No one can be anathemized without proof;
9. Differences of opinion are allowed, not prohibited;
10. Love of non-Muslims is not dependence;
11. The rule of the Creator does not mean the apostasy of creatures;
12. The criteria of belief are the intentions and meanings, not terms and syntax;
13. Creed is common between the ruler and the ruled;
14. Declaring rulers apostates is more dangerous than declaring the people apostates;
15. Political regimes cannot be labeled as believers or non-believers;
16. Islam is a whole lifestyle, not only a penal code;
17. God exercises rulership through man; and
18. Comparing current Muslim regimes with Mongol rule is wrong.

The paper further argues that Egyptian civil law does not necessarily contradict Islamic law, and that objective analysis of scriptural arguments relating to *hakimiyya* shows that Islamic groups extrapolated them out of context. They point out that scriptural texts in this regard refer to the Jews' not applying the Torah on purpose but considering their rabbis as God by obeying their orders. This misinterpretation, the paper argues, is the result of not knowing the context and reasons of the verses' revelation (*asbab ul-nuzul*). Knowing the context places these texts in their natural proportion. More generally, they maintain that given human nature (*fitra*), the rule of God and the rule of man are identical and that human beings have the right to promulgate laws. In this respect, the concept of "public welfare" (*maslaha*) should be the main guide. They also consider that disobeying political rulers and revolting against them is illegal. They justify this judgment partly on pragmatic grounds and historical experience. They point out that historical analysis of all the revolts against the Umayyad shows that they were unsuccessful, useless, and bloody.[32] They conclude that the status quo is better than mere hope. What exists is realpolitik.

This line of argument provides an insight into their methodology, which appears to be a contextual rather that literal interpretation of Islamic sources. Moreover, they maintain that revelation, reason, and reality are the same, a view that indicates a rationalist dimension in their thought and method.

12. "The Struggle and the Bombings of al-Qaeda, Errors and Dangers." This work is a break with al-Qaeda's notion of *jihad*.[33] According to this work, al-Qaeda's strategy is a shortsighted understanding of and an erroneous reading of reality. For example, the United States is not engaged in a crusade against Islam; it has policies with religious dimensions, promoted by neoconservatives. Moreover, al-Qaeda's philosophy is closer to fanaticism than to ideology and policy making and it has had negative consequences for Muslims, including Afghanistan's destruction; injuries caused to Muslim minorities in the West; setting up Islam as the new enemy of the West after the fall of communism, leading to a closer American-Israeli alliance against Arabs and Muslims and to rapprochement between the United States and Europe; deepening Islam's negative image as both religion and culture; and intensifying anti-Muslim sentiments in the West and many other non-Muslim countries.

At the theoretical level, the work argues that al-Qaeda's definition of *jihad* is wrong. *Jihad* is a defensive war and is justified only when Muslims are attacked. It is, in effect, similar to national self-defense as stipulated in the United Nations Charter. It is a means among many to realize the Islamic value-system. It is based on sacrifice, altruism, and public welfare. It is justice, mercy, and forgiveness. Its goal is to implement universal intentions of Islamic law, which are to preserve life, reason, objective truth, national dignity and wealth, and individual and collective human rights. It declares al-Qaeda bombings to be illegal, and all *fatwas* issued to justify the killing of innocent people as wrong, because in Islam civilians are protected in time of war. It refutes the idea of suicide bombers as martyrs and condemns killing of tourists, because this is against the security treaty signed between them and the state when it gave them entry visas. It stresses that relations between Muslims and others are based on freedom, equality, and justice. These relations are codified by peace treaties, truces, and good neighborly relations.

These conceptual corrections are made on the basis of a selective use of textual arguments, the Qur'an, and *hadith*, more than on rational and sociopolitical analysis. They are also based on the works of traditional authors. These arguments had existed before, but in the past they had not received much attention from the jihadi groups.

Gamal Sultan and *al-Manar al-Jadid*

The review *al-Manar al-Jadid* represents another reaction to the takfiri way of thinking and links itself to the old *al-Manar* of Rashid Rida. Gamal Sultan, the editor of the review, was a member of a jihadi Islamic group, accused of being part of a secret organization that wanted to carry out a coup d'état. His writings indicate a tendency against apostasy and in favor of secularism, religious reformism, modernism, rationalism, nationalism, and Marxism. He is also in favor of cultural as opposed to political Islam. Most of his writings reject the extremists' positions, except very few that support the Repentants' positions.[34] His review reflects the same spirit.

Liberal Islam

A liberal version of the moderate and reformist voice of Islam has emerged on the Arabian Peninsula, especially in Saudi Arabia, the cradle of Wahhabism. It is called by different names by various movements, such as the reformist movement Haraket al-Islah, and the legal human rights movement Haraket Huquq al-Insan al-Shar'yya. Nevertheless, they all fall under the overall rubric of Muslim liberals or centrists (*wasat*), and include both Sunni and Shi'a groups.

These voices have emerged as a result of a new reading of official Wahhabism. Additionally, the following factors have contributed to this trend:

1. Liberalization of the media and political discourse in 1999. This development generated new forums, such as the daily, *al-Watan*, for the dissemination of reformist and moderate ideas, as did the salons that were formed around this time. Examples of the latter include the Wasatiyya salon of Muhsen al-Awaji, established in 2000, which represents moderate Muslims; and Tuwa, established in 2002, which serves as a forum for free thinkers.

2. The events of September 11, 2001, and their fallout gave greater urgency to the articulation of moderate and reformist discourses. This led moderate

and reformist thinkers and activists to publish many booklets, present many complaints, and issue many declarations. These activities have mostly been positively received, even by some members of the royal family.

These new voices criticize traditional Wahhabism, call for democratic political reform, and link religious reform—Sunni and Shi'a—to political reform. They created a national democratic political forum in 2003. They characterize themselves as centrist, enlightened, rationalist, and reformist. Abd el-Aziz al-Kasim is their leader. The best known of their writings is the plea ('arida) presented to then–crown prince Abdullah in January 2003. In response, Abdullah ordered the formation of a commission for national dialogue and the holding of partial municipal elections. The following are the group's most prominent figures.

Abd el-Aziz al-Kasim

Abd el-Aziz al-Kasim is known as the Democratic Sheikh. He was born in the early 1960s and became active in Islamic resurgence movements in the early nineties. Then he joined the group of fifty-two ulema to formulate an "Address of Demands" (khitab al-matalib) to King Fahd in 1991. He became an active member of the Commission for the Defense of Legal Rights, founded by the Islamic political opposition in 1993. He was arrested and later released in 1997. He is now a freelance legal counselor. Political issues and concerns are a central focus of his thinking. He is critical of those who totally reject any sociopolitical system inspired by Western models or theories. He argues that Muslims need a system of thought that can combine freedom and justice through ijtihad, and democracy is the best system to achieve this goal. The content of democracy can vary; it does not necessarily mean secularism or Westernization.

Abd el-Aziz al-Kasim favors the development of a strong civil society and argues that Islam endeavors to create such a society through the system of accountability (hisba), which enjoins the good and warns against evil. He suggests that hisba implies independence of the judiciary from the executive branch. He further argues that nationalism—in this case Saudi—does not contradict Islam. To support his idea, Abd el-Aziz al-Kasim notes that the notion of homeland (watan) exists in the Qur'an and that longing for one's homeland is a natural feeling; even the Prophet expressed such feeling upon leaving Mecca. However, his liberalism does not extend to social issues and, in particular, to women's rights, and hence is of a limited nature. He is also silent on the rights of minorities; in traditional societies like Saudi Arabia, this issue is in the realm of political management rather than that of religious analysis.

Abdallah al-Hamid

Abdallah al-Hamid, known as the Modernizer (al-mujaddid), was born in 1958. He studied at the Imam Muhammad bin Saud University in Riyadh and at Al-Azhar, where he received his Ph.D. in 1977. After returning to Saudi Arabia, he was appointed professor of literature at Imam Saud University. In 1993, he cofounded the Commission for the Defense of Legal Rights, an act that led to his dismissal from the university and his imprisonment in 1994–95.

The focus of his thinking is more religious than political. An important foundation of his thought is that the Qur'an should be the main source of reference for Muslims. He justifies this position on the ground that Islamic political theory formed under the Abbassid caliphs was negatively influenced by other sources and ideas besides the Qur'an. He maintains that Ahmad Ibn Hanbal was the first and the real founder of Wahhabism. Ibn Hanbal's ideas were later renewed by Ibn Taymiyya according to the particular conditions of his time, hence his reputation as a modernizer. But Ibn Taymiyya's followers merely imitated him and did not renew his ideas according to new conditions.

Abdallah al-Hamid distinguishes between two types of Salafism, modernizing and conservative, and notes that the Saudi establishment has adopted the conservative version. He then concludes that it is now time to renew Salafism. This requires social and spiritual development and connection to everyday life, he says, and he faults the clergy for dissociating religion from life. He also maintains that progress can come about only through respect for human rights, the establishment of civil society, and the institutionalization of *shur'a* which, he argues, is a better term than democracy even if their meanings are the same.

Hassan al-Malki

Hassan al-Malki, known for rebelling against Salafism and Wahhabism, was born in 1970 in Geezan, near Yemen. He began as a conservative Salafi, distributed cassettes of the Wahhabi Sheikh Ben Baz's sermons, spent time in Afghanistan, and finally studied mass communications at Imam Saud University. After graduation in 1992, he was shocked by the rigid atmosphere around him, a feeling that encouraged him to pursue his intellectual activities with a more open mind. He began work at the Ministry of Education and wrote articles that led to his imprisonment in 1996. He has written several books, including one after September 11 criticizing the Saudi educational system.

Hassan al-Malki's goal is to alter the Salafi historiography of Islam and its educational methods. He even questions the soundness of Wahhabism. In his book, *For Saving Islamic History,* he criticizes the Salafi concept of Islamic historiography as being immune from criticism, sacred and divine. He argues that political and religious personalities in Islam, and those who have written about them, were simple human beings, subject to human passions, desires, and conflicting interests. They were as imperfect as Mu'awiyya, the despotic Umayyad caliph, and Ibn Taymiyya, the rigid literalist who declared those who opposed his views apostates.

Hassan al-Malki's view of Islamic historiography as being basically subjective leads him to conclude that the reform of Saudi society must begin with a rereading of Islamic history and learning from the past and not merely by imitating it. In his books, *Methods of Education: A Critical Reading to Tawhid Curriculum in General Education* and *Refutation of Revealing Ambiguities,* which is a critique of Ibn abd ul-Wahhab's book *Revealing Ambiguities,* he has criticized the Wahhabi concept of divine unity (*tawhid*) and rejected the notion that Wahhabism is an absolute and eternal doctrine. He has refused to mock non-Wahhabi Muslims, label them as apostates, make *jihad* against them, and exclude them from the *umma*. Because of these views, he has been attacked by conservative clergy, including Salih al-Lahidan and Salih al-Fazan, and has been accused of deviant Murji'ite and Shi'a tendencies.

Mansour al-Nogaidan

Mansour al-Nogaidan (the Repentant), born in 1970, initially followed an extreme version of Salafism. He destroyed musical tapes, burned a shop selling videos and contemporary literary books, and even threw away his watch and used the sun to keep time. He was imprisoned and in Jeddah prison underwent a real conversion. Upon his release, he began to read the works of modernist Islamic thinkers. In 1999 he was appointed imam of one of the mosques in Riyadh. In February 1999 he wrote his first article in *al-Hayat*, titled "Was Ibn Abi Daoud Treated Unjustly?" In it, he argues that positive aspects of Ibn Hanbal's life—such as his resistance to pressures from Caliph Mamoun and the Mu'tazili sheikhs, who, because of his rejection of their ideas, anathematized him—were due to political conditions rather than to his personality or thinking.

Sheikh Hammouda al-Shar'aibi condemned this new reading of history and answered Mansour al-Nogaidan. This led to the latter's dismissal from the mosque. After that, he turned to journalism and in September 2000 was appointed editor of the religious section of the daily newspaper *al-Watan*. After being dismissed from that job, too, he now works as a freelancer. In January 2003, the jihadists, including Ali al-Khadair and Ahmad al-Khalidi, declared him to be an apostate and deserving of the death penalty. He has completely abandoned Wahhabism and Salafism in all its forms and has called on others to do the same. He has also called for the revival of the concept of *irja'* (leaving judging humans to God).

According to al-Nogaidan, Muslims today need an enlightened understanding of the Qur'an and of Islam's universal intentions. He argues that this new reading should take into account developments and changes that have taken place in the Islamic world and globally, as well as the requirements of public interest and popular needs. This is the way religious concepts and texts should be understood. He maintains that the Qur'an is an open and multifaceted book. He quotes the Fourth Caliph, Ali ibn Abu Talib, who said that the Qur'an is a written book, which does not speak except through human understanding. Enlightened *ijtihad* is capable of spelling it out in order to awaken the nation and bring about reform.

Al-Nogaidan is the most liberal of Saudi reformist thinkers and has shocked many by saying that Islam needs a Luther-like reform. He combines liberalism and humanism. In his article "The Legal Status of Identity Card," he defends women's right to have an identification document. He criticizes the morality police for ordering good and preventing evil. He calls this practice an innovation (*bid'a*) and calls for its abandonment. He has also attributed terrorist actions in Saudi Arabia to the practice of *takfir*. This led to the attacks noted above. He responded in an article titled "My View on Apostasy Declarations."

Muhammad Sa'id Tayyeb

Muhammad Sa'id Tayyeb (the Liberal) was born in 1939 in Mecca. In the 1950s, he became a Nasserite and was imprisoned. During the 1980s he withdrew from politics, but he became engaged again after the first Gulf War. In 1992 he published "Intellectuals and Prince . . . al-Shura and the Open-Door Policy," which is seen as the blueprint of the liberal reformist movement, calling for democracy and freedom of expression.

Since the relative liberalization of mass media in 1999, he has expressed his views in the press and in his Tuesday salon, frequented by almost 800 intellectuals. In these forums he discusses issues related to politics, such as democracy, freedom of expression, and human rights. In his writings and statements, he stresses Islam's centrality. Religion is a red line that cannot be crossed. He maintains that women's rights should be based on the Qur'an and *sunna*, not on Western standards. His ultimate goal is to achieve a minimum degree of national consensus through dialogue among various groups and thus peace.

'A'id al-Quirni

'A'id al-Quirni presents an apolitical, peaceful, spiritual, and ethical Islam. His focus is to improve people's state of mind by encouraging individual and even mystical religious experiences. His work is mostly literary and deals with mundane religious issues. Because of this trait, his contribution to a reformist reading of Islam that could lead to fundamental reforms has been minimal.

Practical Objectives of Saudi Reformist Discourse

The following are the principal goals of Saudi reformist discourse:

1. Formulation of a unified political discourse, based on Islam and Saudi nationalism, that is capable of bridging the divide both between Sunnis and Shi'as and between conservative and reformist/liberal Muslims;
2. Development of an intellectual basis for dialogue with the West. A declaration titled "On What Basis Can We Co-Exist?" was a response to the open letter signed by sixty American thinkers, including Samuel P. Huntington

and Francis Fukuyama, to justify morally the American invasion of Iraq. An example of efforts at dialogue, it was signed by 150 Saudis. Sheikh Abd al-'Aziz al-Kasim even succeeded in getting the endorsement of non-liberal Muslims, such as Salman al-'Uda and Sifr al-Hawalli;

3. To develop a vision of the Saudi nation's present situation and future outlook. This was elaborated in the so-called Reformist Covenant. It was developed by a group of liberal intellectuals—Sunni and Shi'a—and issued as a declaration in August 2000 titled "A Vision for the Present and the Future of the Country," addressed to the then–crown prince Abdullah.

"A Vision for the Present and the Future of the Country" deals with Saudi Arabia's domestic problems and calls for social, political, and economic reforms, including separation of powers; the rule of law; equal rights of all citizens irrespective of regional, tribal, and sectarian differences; freedom of expression; the establishment of elected regional and national councils (*shur'a*); development of a strong civil society; just distribution of national wealth; fighting corruption and waste; and limiting consumption. On a purely religious level, the document is harshly critical of traditional Wahhabism, which rejects political and doctrinal pluralism. It also criticizes the principle of *sadd al-dharai'* (prevention of harm) in Wahhabism, which is used to justify all kinds of prohibitions; for example, based on this principle women are prevented from driving in order to prevent seduction (*fitna*). The declaration builds on an earlier document, titled "The Advice" (al-Nasiha), signed by 107 religious scholars and activists, including liberals such as Abdallah al-Hamid, Hamad al-Salneneg, and Solaiman al-Rashudi, and presented to King Fahd in 1992. The document's language was not religious, but Islamic law is the system of reference and the framework for all reforms.

The August 2000 declaration ignored sensitive issues such as the reform of educational methods and women's role in society, thus indicating the limits of Saudi tolerance for reformist and liberal ideas. Official reaction to the declaration and the Covenant was positive, especially on the part of Abdullah. He agreed to the demands and said only that he needed more time to implement them. He also organized a conference for national dialogue in June 2003, with the assistance of thirty scholars from all sectarian trends in the Kingdom—Sunni, Shi'a, Salafi, non-Salafi, Sufi, and Isma'ili Shi'as. No one from the official Wahhabi establishment was invited, indicating a desire to marginalize them, and not all members of the royal family agreed with the crown prince in his support for the reformist document.

The appearance of a middle ground between Islam and democracy is a big step forward in the life of Saudi Arabia. Liberal Islam concentrates on political reform while others give priority to religious reform, but both trends share the same goals. The difference is only in the pace of reform, which is faster in the political arena and slower in the religious sphere.

The reformist movement in Saudi Arabia faces an uncertain future, however. It is not clear whether it will continue to evolve and dare to address sensitive subjects, such as educational methods and women's rights. Nor is it yet clear whether it is the result of a temporary alliance between Islam and liberalism against Wahhabism and the doctrinal state, or represents an organic unity between the two concepts. Equally uncertain is the attitude of the Saudi leadership. Will King Abdullah continue to support it? Will he continue to protect the royal family, or will he align himself with the reformist trend? Will Wahhabi doctrine continue to dominate the state? Or will the state free itself from this doctrine as the reformists hope? And will the basis of political legitimacy ever change from lineage and Wahhabi doctrine to popular agreement through democratic means?*

The New Preachers (al-Du'ah al-Judud)

The "new preachers" represent one of the most influential elements among Islam's new moderate and reformist voices. They first emerged in Egypt, but have now sprung up in other Arab countries. They are an urban phenomenon and their culture is a combination of Islamic tradition and aspects of contemporary life, with a few borrowings from Western thought such as the concept of human development. They represent a new kind of religiosity, expressing the Islam of the 1990s bourgeoisie.[35] They reflect the ebbing of religiously motivated violence; the emergence of a moderate, intermediary Islamic discourse; and erosion of the influence of official Islam as represented by Al Azhar. The new preachers share some common traits with artists returning to religion, the preachers in bourgeois "Islamic salons," musical groups, and independent Muslim intellectuals. They belong to privileged classes and combine secular education with Islamic culture. They try to harmonize different paradigms with an Islamic reference, while dissociating themselves from official Islam. They give priority to praxis over logos. They are not interested in theoretical formulations on religion or the modernization of religious thought; they are interested in recruiting the youth and Islamizing society.

The new preachers are influenced by the Gulf region's Bedouin Islam, which considers religion and politics as totally separate. Their discourse deals with issues such as youth, sex, love, marriage, happiness, ethics, human behavior, good conduct, unemployment, and value systems.[36] Frankness is considered better than taboos.[37] Individual ethical themes prevail over collective themes. Jihad is rarely mentioned, nor is common action. They combine a call for individual values, such as hijab (veiling), with "la dolce vita"–style consumerism.[38] Their discourse is free of obsession with identity. It endorses globalization and its achievements and accommodation to the laws of the market, such as advertising Islamic products in English and French.[39]

---

*Editor's Note: The Iraq war and rising Sunni–Shi'a tensions in the region have led to a hardening of the position of Saudi authorities toward any kind of dissent, thus making the future of reformist trend in Saudi Arabia very precarious.

The new preachers combine music and wellness programs, such as yoga, with lectures and sermons on Islam. A female representative of this trend is Magda 'Amr, who combines instruction on yoga, organic vitality, meditative practices, and alternative medicine with lectures on Islam in the Abu Bakr Mosque to the upper-class female residents of the affluent neighborhood of Heliopolis.

'Amr Khalid is the male prototype of the same phenomenon. He is in his forties and comes from a bourgeois family. Placing himself outside the ongoing competition between political Islam and official institutional Islam, he offers a third type of Islam, which emphasizes the needs and aspirations of the individual, especially the youth, including religious and spiritual aspirations. He does not wear clerical garb and presents a modern image. He speaks in dialect rather than classical Arabic, as a way of getting closer to the masses. His ideas are based on the principle of reconciling religion and life and he holds that religiosity is not opposed to good living. He emphasizes the virtues of individual ambition, wealth, success, perseverance in work, and efficiency, and he sees wealth as a gift from Heaven to the faithful and ambition in individuals as a sign of God's love.

In Sudan, where Sufism and Wahhabism are the two main Islamic trends, Sheikh al-Amin 'Omar al-Amin, the spiritual leader of the Sufi Zawia al-Mukashifiyya al-Quadiriyya, represents this phenomenon, which is known as the "New Look." He preaches in the upper-class neighborhoods of Um Dorman.

Al Amin is in his thirties and was appointed the sheikh of the order in 1992. He lacks a systematic Islamic education and studied business administration at King Abd el-'Aziz University. He is a businessman with investments in Dubai and large interests in Sudan. His approach toward his disciples is direct and devoid of arrogance. He speaks in the Sudanese dialect and uses popular proverbs and local folklore. Nevertheless, he is still the master to be obeyed and directs the *dhikr* (devotional chanting) circle. He calls on his disciples to observe religious rules and choose the mystic path. However, he also offers them a path away from traditional asceticism, a path that emphasizes the importance of this world and the mastery of its causal laws, provided that no transgression of religious prohibitions is committed. He reconciles religion with wealth and good living in a way akin to Protestant ethics.[40]

Some other new preachers tackle social issues such as human and social development, education, and administration, plus subjects such as human rights, religious dialogue, civil society, and Islamic psychology.[41] They address some political subjects indirectly.

The Message (al-Risala), published by Tareq Suweidan, and *Iqra'*, published by Gassem al-Muttawwe', represent this more socially conscious trend among the new preachers. In their arguments, they use Qur'anic verses and prophetic tradition in a selective manner and without theoretical analysis of the reasons behind legal prescriptions and proscriptions. The discourse is very clear, without dogmatic complexities or metaphysical and eschatological discussions; rather, it appeals to the emotions of the listeners, especially the youth.[42] Indeed, the new preachers have attracted the Arab youth more successfully than political parties or traditional and political Islamic groups. They have made a positive contribution by offering a vision of religion that is open to life and modernity, emphasizes a joyful rather than somber view of life, and fills a spiritual vacuum.

However, their views have had negative consequences for the intellectual development of Arab youth. These include their conservative religious positions, especially regarding women, the penal code, and family law; their lack of intellectual rigor and disregard for theoretical issues; their emphasis on permanence rather than change in the interpretation of religious sources, and on faith combined with a good deal of superstition; the disconnect between faith and social action; and the lack of any effort to develop an Islamic worldview. These detract from the development of a truly reformist discourse capable of answering Muslims' questions and dilemmas as they try to mediate between their Islamic faith and the requirements of living in a globalizing world.

The new preachers are encouraged by Arab states, because they preach a non-political, non-violent, and individualistic version of religion. However, when one of them acquires too much of a following, the state turns against him.

Shi'a Moderate and Reformist Thinking

A Shi'a reformist and moderate trend exists today in those Arab countries with Shi'a majorities—Iraq and Bahrain—as well as those with a substantial Shi'a minority as in Lebanon, Yemen, Saudi Arabia, and the Gulf states, and to a much smaller degree in Egypt. It has emerged under more-or-less similar circumstances as Sunni reformism and it shares many points in common with it. Some of the prominent representatives of this trend are discussed below.

Abd al-Jabbar al-Rifa'i is a thinker from Iraq who returned to his country after living abroad (including Iran) during Saddam Hussein's presidency. He publishes the review *Contemporary Islamic Issues* (Mjallet quadaya islamiyya mu'asira) and is also the director of the collection *The New Theology* (Al-kalam al-jadid). The review represents one of the latest efforts to modernize Islamic thinking. In addition to articles on issues of specific concern to the Shi'as, it publishes articles on philosophy, religion, and new theology. In these series, issues are discussed such as the dialectics of tradition and modernity, authenticity and contemporaneity, historicism of religious knowledge, text and reality, comparative religion, pluralism, differences and tolerance, coexistence between cultures and religions, sociology of religion and other similar subjects.[43]

Al-Rifa'i was born in 1954 and studied in Najaf. He was first influenced by the Islamic left in Egypt and by Ali Shariati in Iran. He then turned to political Islam and later embraced Abdolkarim Soroush's notion of Islamic reformism, but he is now a reformist and modernizer of the classical type of Muhammad Abduh.[44] In addition to Al Rifa'i, Qabel Hassan al Shabander, who now lives in Sweden, and Majed Al Qarbawi, espouse reformist thinking.

In Lebanon, the Grand Ayatullah Muhammad Hassan Fadl Ullah is the most important and influential representative of the reformist trend in religious matters. His theological and religious views, including regarding women's rights are quite advanced, although not as liberal as those of some other reformists.[45]*

Hani Fahs is also considered a reformist thinker. He is a member of the Shi'a Council in Lebanon and also writes commentary in various newspapers, including *Al Hayat* in London. He supports both Sunni–Shi'a dialogue and dialogue between Muslims and Christians.[46] In the early 1980s, he was known for his support for Ayatullah Khomeini, but now he opposes the concept of the guardianship of the Islamic jurist, *velayat-e faqih*,[47] and he has expressed some unconventional views regarding the Hidden Imam Mahdi.**

In Bahrain, Muslim reformist thinkers are at the extreme pole of reformism, which raises the question whether they should even be considered Islamic reformers or rather should be seen as secular Muslim intellectuals. The following thinkers represent Bahraini Shi'a reformism: Ali al Dayri, Hassan Al Mahrous, and Nader Kazem.

In Saudi Arabia, Muhammad Mahfouz, Ga'afar al-Shayeb, and Zaki Milad represent the Shi'a reformist trend in the Eastern Province and the city of Katif. They had left the Kingdom in the 1980s and returned in the 1990s, following the agreement between the government and the Shi'a opposition. Initially, they were attracted to the Iranian Revolution and Ayatullah Khomeini's ideas, but now they embrace political pluralism and democracy and find common ground with the West on issues of human rights and civil society.

This Shi'a reformist trend is part of liberal and reformist Islam, as is clearly indicated by Muhammad Mahfouz's book *Islam and the Gamble of Democracy*. Saudi nationalism is another important component of this trend. Like its Sunni counterpart, Shi'a reformist thinking was allowed to flourish after the relative political opening of 1999 and in cooperation with Sunni reformers who were trying to find common ground with religious minorities. The Tuesday Club in Katif, under the supervision of Ga'afar al-Shayeb, played an important role in this connection. Shayeb hosted in this salon some representatives of Sunni liberal Islam, such as Abdallah al Hamid. Their forum is the quarterly *Word* (al-Kalima), devoted to Islamic thought, contemporary issues, and cultural modernization. It first appeared in 1993 in Beirut. Its advisory board includes Sunni as well as Shi'a scholars.

---

*Editor's Note: Fadl Ullah's political views, especially concerning Western policies in the Muslim world, are confrontational.

**Editor's Note: These unconventional views have undermined his credibility among the Shi'a. In general, he has increasingly become a media and political personality rather than a serious theologian and *faqih*.

In Egypt, Salih al-Wardani is both a theoretical thinker and an activist. He combines a modernist approach to the interpretation of *fiqh* with a socially and politically active reading of Islam. He is against sectarianism and advocates common action based on an objective analysis of external realities. Ahmad Rasim al-Nafis is an intellectual who writes for the state-sponsored cultural newspaper *Al-Quahira*. He is very critical of the entire Islamic movement, betraying a degree of criticism of Sunni Islam in general.

Conclusions

The rise of Islam's new reformist and moderate voices in the countries of the Arab East represent a reaction against Islam's politicization, the global organization of Muslims, and the intellectual and operational bankruptcy of both violent jihadists and the classical Islamic tradition. They also reflect the discrediting of post-independence developmentalist and authoritarian ideologies and states, as well as the continued importance of Islam as a religious, spiritual, and cultural frame of reference for Muslims.

These voices embrace different degrees of reformism, with some groups still retaining traditional positions on issues such as women's rights. Nevertheless, they all represent, albeit to varying degrees, an Islam that is life-affirming, recognizes the importance of the individual, is open to self-criticism and self-correction, believes in a dynamic, contextual, rational, socially relevant, and more democratic reading of religious sources, and is willing to engage in dialogue with the West.

The future of these reformist and moderate trends remains uncertain. Their progress at home is hampered by repressive governments, ultraconservative religious leaders, jihadi extremists, and those who have totally embraced the West and its cultural framework. Meanwhile, their discourse of intercultural dialogue and coexistence is being undermined by attacks on Islam in the Western media and the hegemonic policies of Western powers.

In order further to develop and expand, to be able to confront the forces of conservatism and extremism, and to develop a modernist discourse rooted in people's native cultures and values, reformist and moderate voices need greater political openness at home and more nuanced policies from the West toward Muslims and the Islamic world.

Notes

1. For Anwar al Sadat's use of Islam to counter both Nasserites and the Communists, see Raymond A. Hinnebusch, Jr., *Egyptian Politics Under Sadat* (Cambridge: Cambridge University Press, 1985), pp. 87–222.

2. All of these factors have been analyzed by Arab and Western scholars. See, among others, Ali E. Hilal Dessouki, ed., *Islamic Resurgence in the Arab World* (New York: Praeger, 1982); Shireen T. Hunter, ed., *The Politics of Islamic Revivalism: Unity and Diversity* (Bloomington, IN: Indiana University Press, 1988); Francois Burgat, *L'islamisme en face*

(Paris: Edition de la Decouverte, 1995); Nazih Ayubi, *Political Islam: Religion and Politics in the Arab World* (New York: Routledge, 1991).

3. Abu Zaid was accused of apostasy and had to leave Egypt. He lives in the Netherlands and is a professor at the University of Leiden. See his memoirs written with Esther R. Nelson, *Voice of an Exile* (Westport, CT: Praeger, 2004).

4. Carolyn Fluehr-Lobban, ed., *Against Islamic Extremism: The Writings of Muhammad Said Al-Ashmawi* (Gainesville: University Press of Florida, 2002).

5. The organization's leaders had encouraged him to set up the party because the government was continuing the ban on the Brotherhood's political activities imposed in 1954.

6. Dr. Salah abd al-Karim, *Egyptian Wasat Party Papers* (Cairo: International Shorouk, 1988).

7. *Wasat Party Papers*, with an introduction by Abd el-Wahab al-Messiry (Cairo: International Shorouk, 2004).

8. "Political Project for the Future of Syria." "Global Vision Project of Muslim Brothers for Reform in Egypt," 2006. "Initiative of General Guide Murshid of Muslim Brothers about General Principles of Reform in Egypt," "View on Muslim Brothers in Egypt," July 1996. "Electoral Program of the Islamic Action Front in Jordan," 2003. "Political Project of Islamic Group Jama'at in Lebanon," "Islamic Alliance in Lebanon," December 2003. "Electoral Program of Yemeni Assembly Tajammu' for Reform." A similar project was developed in Algeria, titled "General Policies of Muslim Society Movement in Algeria."

9. "Shura and the Multiparty System," "Participation in Governing," "Muslim Woman in Muslim Society," "The Brothers and American Policy," "Declaration for the People," April 1994. "Islam Is the Solution."

10. 'Abd el-Mun'im Abu al-Futuh, *Mujaddidun la mubaddidun* (Cairo: Bar Press, 2005).

11. Hassan Hanafi's project on "Tradition and Modernism," with its popular forum the "Islamic Left," may represent the left. This project is inspired by the ideas of Sayyid Qutb in his socialist phase, when he wrote "Social Justice in Islam," "The Struggle Between Islam and Capitalism," "The Future for This Religion," and before developing his rejectionist ideas in "Signposts on the Road."

12. The term *monocracy* was coined by Abul Ala Mawdudi and refers to a government based on *shari'a*.

13. Ali Abd al-Raziq, *Al-islam wa usul al-hukm* (Cairo: Misr Press, 1925).

14. Mohammed Hafez Diab, *Al-islamiyyun al-mustaquillun, al-huwiyya wa al-su'al* (Cairo: Merit, n.d.); Olivier Roy, *Tagribat al-islam al-siyasi* (London: Dar al-Saqui, 2005).

15. Mohammed Mus'ad Abd al-Aziz, "New Islamic Discourse in Egypt," M.A. Thesis, American University of Cairo, Egypt.

16. The material in this section draws from Hossam Tammam's paper, "New Islamic Voices . . . Defeat of Ideology and Retreat of Certainty," Cairo, August 16, 2006.

17. Hisham Ga'far, "Al-haraka al-islamiyya wa ma ba'd al-siyasa," IslamOnline.

18. They include Karam Mohammad Zuhdi, Ali Mohammad al-Sherif, Nagih Ibrahim Abdallah, Mohammad Essam al-Din Derbalah, Fu'ad Mahmoud al-Dawalibi, Hamdy abd al-Rahman abd al-Azim, and 'Asem abd al-Magid Mohammad.

19. Osama Ibrahim Hafez and 'Asem abd al-Magid Mohammad, *Mubadarat waqf al-'onf*.

20. The initiative was first made public during the trials of al-Jama'a al-Islamiyya's members, and was then formally issued in the name of the group's imprisoned leaders.

21. Najih Ibrahim Abdallah, *Tajdid al-khitab al-dini* (Riyadh: Ubaikan, 2004).

22. Osama Ibrahim Hafez and 'Asem abd al-Magid Mohammad, *Hurmat al-ghuluw fi al-din wa takfir al-muslimin* (Riyadh: Ubaidekan, 2004).

23. Najih Ibrahim Abdallah, *Fatwa al-tatar sheikh al-islam ibn taymia* (Riyadh: Ubaikan, 2004).

24. Osama Ibrahim Hafez and 'Asem abd al-Magid Mohammad, *Taslit al-adwa' 'ala ma waqu'a fi al-jihad min akhta'* (Riyadh: Ubaikan, 2004).

25. Najih Ibrahim Abdallah, *Da'wa li al-tasaluh ma'a al-mujtama* (Riyadh: Ubaikan, 2004).

26. Najih Ibrahim Abdallah, *Hidayat al-khala'iq bayn al-ghayat wa al-wasa'il* (Riyadh: Ubaikan, 2004).

27. Osama Ibrahim Hafez, 'Asem abd al-Magid Mohammad, *Al-nuskh wa al-tabiyn fi tashih mafahim al-muhtasibin* (Riyadh: Ubaikan: 2004).

28. Najih Ibrahim Abdallah, *Natharat fi hakikat al-isti'la' bi al-iman* (Riyadh: Ubaikan, 2004).

29. Najih Ibrahim Abdallah, *Hatmiyyat al-muwajaha wa fiqh al-nata'ij* (Riyadh: Ubaikan, 2004).

30. Najih Ibrahim Abdallah, *Tatbiq al-ahkam min ikhtisas al-hukkam* (n.p., 2004).

31. Najih Ibrahim Abdallah, *Al-hakimiyya, nathariyya shar'iyya wa ru'ya waqui'iyya* (Riyadh: Ubaikan, 2004), p. 430.

32. Examples include the revolts of al-Hussein, the al-Hurra Army, the Repentants' Army, Ibn al-Zubair, Ibn al-Ash'ath.

33. Karam Mohammad Zuhdi, Najih Ibrahim Abdallah, Hamdi Abd al-Rahman abd al-'Azim, Fou'ad Mohmoud al-Dawalibi, 'Asem abd al-Majid Mohammad, Mohammad Esam al-Din Derbalah (Riyadh: Ubaikan, 2005).

34. Gamal Sultan has written nineteen booklets: *Raid from Inside; Understanding (Fiqh) the Movement; Understanding the Difference; In Defense of Our Culture; The Crisis of Religious Dialogue; Roots of Alienation in Modern Islamic Thought; Revisionism Literature, The Story of Modern Arabic Poetry; Our Cultural Struggle; Culture of Harm (Dirar); Modernization of Islamic Thought; My Word to the Intellectuals; Islam and the Crisis of Nationalistic Thought; Islamic Resurgence and Its Impact on Thought and Society; The Crisis of Intellectuals in The Muslim World; Raid on Islamic Tradition; Introductions for Our Cultural Project; Modernization of Islamic Resurgence; Reviews of Islamic Movements Papers in Egypt;* and *Understanding Culture.*

35. Hossam Tammam, "Islam of the Bourgeoisie in Egypt" (obtained by the author through personal communication).

36. Walid Abdallah, *Love from Another Perspective: A New Outlook on Love* (introduction by Hind Ahmed). Dr. Hind Ahmed, Let Us Love, Dedicated to Every Heart Eager to Love, Dreams Chevalier, Youthful Hearts, Joy, Sentimental Problems" (Cairo: Lu'lu'a, 2004). Ahmed Zein, *Love in Islam, Desire Is Your Road to Paradise (The Double Error of Sensibility and Meta-Sensibility); How to Deal with Desire?* (Cairo: 1-Raya Production, n.d.); Yasser Nasr, *Woman's Liberation, Woman, Suspicions and Responses; Choosing One's Life Partner; Marriage in Islam* (Cairo: Arij, 2004).

37. Mohammad Gibril and Khalid al-Gindi, *The Medicine of Heavens* (Cairo: Al-Raya Production, n.d.); Hazem abd al-Rahman, *Who Constructs This Building? The Company of Goodness; Youth Is Power; The Course of a Drop.*

38. Tammam, "Islam of the Bourgeoisie in Egypt."

39. For example, at the al-Salam shopping center, Flash, L'amour.

40. Hossam Tammam, "Mysticism of New Look in Sudan" (unpublished paper).

41. Ragheb al-Sirganni, *Together We Build the Best Nation; A Message to the Youth of the Nation; We are Not in the Time of Abraham; Reading Is a Way of Life; Who Buys Paradise?; "Aren't You Supporting Him?" Torture in Prisons of Freedom* (Cairo: Iqra' Foundation, 2005). Mohammad Said Mursi, *How Can We Make Education a Pleasure? Problems of Family and School.*

42. Rghib al-Sergani, *Reading Is a Life-Style* (Cairo: Iqra' Foundation). Muhammad Gibril and Khalid el-Gindi, *Doubt, Oblivion and Hesitation; Hallucination, Sadness and Anguish; Insomnia, Despair and Obsession; Alienation, Frustration and Indifference; Seclusion, Fear, and Personality Weakness* (Cairo: Al-Raya Production, n.d.).

43. The series have articles by both Iranian reformists such as Soroush and Mustafa Malekian, as well as by Rifa' himself and other Arab thinkers.

44. However, the influence of Iranian Muslim reformists such as Ayatullah Muhammad Shabestari is observable in his work, notably in regard to the "New Kalam," of which Shabestari was an early proponent.

45. For views of Sheikh Sayyid Muhammad Hussein Fadallah, see his Web site, http://english.bayanat.org.Ibjurisprudence/Issues?htm.

46. "Scholar Urges More Understanding," available at http://archive.gulfnews.co/indepth/ramadan/more_stories/10071078.html.

47. See Mehdi Khalaji, "Iran's Shadow Government in Lebanon Policy Watch," *Peace Watch*, July 19, 2006, available at http://washingtoninstitute.org/templateC05.php?CID=2489.

3

Reformist Islamic Thinkers in the Maghreb

Toward an Islamic Age of Enlightenment?

Yahia H. Zoubir

During the last three decades, Western literature on Islam and on socioeconomic and political developments in the Arab and Islamic worlds has been dominated by two themes: Islamic radicalism, and Islam's incapacity to modernize and democratize. These shortcomings of Muslim countries are attributed to Islam's peculiarities, particularly its fusion of religion and politics and to its alleged lack of a rationalist spirit.[1] This literature overlooks any evidence contradicting these assumptions[2] and ignores the impact of noncultural factors on the Muslim world's current situation, notably those deriving from the nature of the international political system and great-power policies.[3]

This tendency in Western scholarship mainly derives from two factors: the continuing and pervasive influence of Orientalism and the exaggerated idea of an Islamic threat to Western civilization.[4] Consequently, Western scholars have paid more attention to radical discourses on Islam than to more moderate and reformist trends. According to the Algerian-born scholar of Islam, Mohammed Arkoun, the result of this attitude has been a "poverty of conceptual and theoretical frameworks" for the study of Islam and Muslim societies and their relations with the West.[5]

Nevertheless, despite their deep differences, both neo-Orientalists and Muslims—whether reformist, traditionalist, or radical—agree on one point: the Arab and Islamic worlds have been declining for nearly three centuries and today are stagnant. Indeed, the main preoccupation of Muslim intellectuals for the past two centuries has been to discover the causes of this decline and to find ways to reverse it. In this context, the central issues have been modernity and its role in the rise of European powers and how Muslims should respond to it.

The dynamics of challenge and response to modernity in the Maghreb countries have been similar to those in other Muslim societies. Thus the Maghreb, too, experienced the emergence of Islamic reformist movements in the late nineteenth and early twentieth centuries and, as in other Muslim countries, this reformist discourse came to be overshadowed by secularist and radical Islamist discourses in post-independence Maghreb.

In the last fifteen years, however, the failures and repressions of secular governments, along with the challenge of radical Islamists, have led to a revival of reformist thinking in the Maghreb. Most of this discourse is produced by lay intellectuals who reside abroad, largely because they cannot put their ideas into practice at home, although some of them have held ministerial positions at different times. Increasingly, reformist ideas are also being produced inside the Maghreb countries, especially in Tunisia. One impetus has been the desire of Islamic political parties to gain power.

The more progressive reformist thinkers still face difficulties in reaching wide audiences as well as fierce competition both from extremist and conservative Muslims and from the pure secularists. Nevertheless, together with moderate Islamic political parties, they and their ideas are becoming important elements of the Maghreb's intellectual and political landscape.

Islamic Reformist Thinking in the Maghreb: A Brief History

By the mid-nineteenth century, reform movements in the Maghreb were concerned with the same fundamental questions as were other Muslims, namely, why had Muslim countries weakened to the point of becoming colonies of European powers, and how could they stop and reverse this decline? In trying to determine the causes of Muslim decline, Maghrebi thinkers offered two basic explanations: the moving away from pure Islam and the loss of rationalist and scientific thinking.

Some reformist thinkers in the Maghreb, following the example of reformers like Muhammad Abduh (1849–1905), Jamal al-Din al Afghani (1838–1899), Muhammad Rashid Rida (1865–1935),[6] and Chakib Arslan (1869–1946), sought to restore Islam's rationalist spirit through *ijtihad*, the independent interpretation of Islamic scriptural and legal sources, and to eliminate those factors they considered responsible for Muslim decline. According to the Algerian Islamic thinker Malek Bennabi (1905–1973), these factors had caused the Muslims' domination by Europeans by putting them in a state of "colonizability."[7]

The reformers set out to establish movements and organizations to propagate their ideas and promote reform. Thus, in the aftermath of World War I, the Algerian traditionalist reformer Abdelhamid Ben Badis (1889–1940) initiated an Islamic reform movement, Nahda (Awakening), based on the first interpretation of the causes of Muslims' decline.[8] Ben Badis sought to reconstruct Algeria's Arab-Islamic identity, to combat superstitious beliefs and practices (which he believed were chiefly responsible for Muslims' decline),[9] and to restore the pure Islam of the Prophet and his first successors. However, his views regarding the characteristics of early Islam were closer to those of reformists like Muhammad Abduh. In fact, Ben Badis and his collaborators in the Association of *Ulema*, which he founded in 1931, were inspired by Abduh's *Islah* movement. They, too, believed that Islam is not an impediment to scientific and technological progress and that it is open to borrowing from Western ideas in order to revive itself. The association did remarkable educational and cultural work, revived the notion of an independent Arab and Muslim Algerian nation, and helped shape the modernizing efforts of the authorities. On religious and social issues, however, it remained conservative.

Other Algerian *ulema* contributed to this emerging reformist discourse. Benali Fekar and Tayeb al-Oqbi searched for innovative solutions to issues such as usury, interest, and secularism, which they interpreted as meaning the separation of politics and religion, by applying a historicist methodology to the interpretation of Islamic sources. Fekar held narrow traditionalist religious leaders to be mainly responsible for Muslims' decline.[10] For his part, Sheikh Tayeb al-Oqbi (1888–1960) tried to encourage positive change by referring in his sermons to the Qur'anic verse (XIII, 11), "God will not change the condition of a people as long as they do not change their state themselves." He initiated interfaith dialogue and called for separation of religion from politics.[11]

In Tunisia, Tahar Haddad (1899–1936), a professor at the religious university al-Zaituna and an active member of the nationalist Destur Party, in 1930 published *Our Women in the Shari'a and in Society*. In this book, he called for women's emancipation and used an innovative interpretation of Islamic sources to justify his views. The *ulema* launched bitter attacks against him, expelled him from al-Zaituna, and nullified his diploma.[12]

In Morocco, the best-known reformist figure was Allal al-Fassi (1910–1974). In his book *The Goals of the Shari'a* (Maqasid ash-shari'a), he defended political liberty and identified those Islamic precepts that can be adapted to modern conditions and form the basis of modernization, especially in the political sphere. Al-Fassi maintained that primeval sovereignty belongs to God alone, while "ordinary" sovereignty is founded on the will of the people. He argued that the "foundations of power in Islam are the will of Muslim peoples supported by a written constitution, which is the Qur'an."[13]

These thinkers pioneered reformist discourse in the Maghreb, and they still inspire the new generations of reformist thinkers.

Post-Independence Nation Building: Impact on the Evolution of Islamic Discourse

Despite differences in their colonial experiences, mode of acquiring independence, and political systems, after independence all Maghreb countries underwent a process of nation building and top-down modernization, based on developmentalist strategies—inspired by either socialism or capitalism—that were popular in the 1960s and 1970s.

This type of nation building and modernization was characterized by a lack of participatory and consensual politics; a belief that democratization should wait until a sufficient degree of economic and social progress was achieved; and a conception of the state as the main agent of progress. Nevertheless, even paternalistic regimes needed some basis for popular legitimacy. Because Islam has always been an important element of the Maghreb countries' social fabric, a core component of their peoples' identity and nationalism, and a major factor in the crystallization of their anticolonial identity and quest for independence, in order to gain popular legitimacy, Maghreb governments instrumentalized Islam in support of their political goals.

In Algeria, for example, as part of their plan to build a modern identity and society and to gain legitimacy, successive governments tried to integrate a modern type of Islam into their revolutionary perspectives, while simultaneously undermining independent Islamic organizations and bringing religious affairs under state control. They declared Islam to be the state religion in the constitutions of 1963, 1976, 1989, and 1996; they made Islam the foundation of collective identity; they promoted Islamic values; and they made Islam, together with modernization, the ideological underpinnings of the regime's developmentalist strategy. This took place within a framework characterized by a French sociologist as *laïcité islamique* (Islamic secularism).[14]

In secular Tunisia, too, including under Habib Bourguiba, the state has used Islam to justify its policies while keeping it under close state supervision.[15] Even President Zein Abidine Ben Ali, in office since November 1987, has made religious references in his speeches, launched a campaign to institute good morality based on Islamic precepts, and restored the preeminence of al-Zaituna.[16]

In Morocco, the relationship between the state and religion is even more complex.[17] The monarchy is constitutionally entrusted with the "protection" of Islam, and the king is the *Amir al-mu'minin* (Commander of the Faithful). Yet he does not have the authority and qualifications to interpret Islamic sources. In order to be able to use Islam as an instrument of political legitimacy and, at the same time, to prevent it from becoming a political rival, the state, especially the king, has tried to bring religion under its control. It has done so by co-opting the *ulema* class and by fragmenting it through means such as the creation of parallel religious institutions, like the ministry of religious affairs and appointed religious councils. Consequently, as observed by Malika Zeghal, the monarchy, along with the religious intermediaries implanted in society, emerged as the true religious institution.[18]

In Libya, after seizing power in 1969 Colonel Muammar al-Gaddafi advanced a new ideology, combining elements of Islam and socialism, and expounded it in his Green Book.[19] This strategy of instrumentalizing Islam for the purpose of serving state and regime interests, coupled with the failure of developmentalist projects and the lack of participatory politics, unwittingly enhanced the influence of conservative clergy, undermined reformist Islamic trends, and contributed to the emergence of radical Islamic discourse.

Maghreb's Muslim Reformist Thinkers: Who Are They?

Despite the unfavorable conditions noted above, reformist Islamic discourse survived in the Maghreb countries and in the last decade or so has gained new momentum with the emergence of new reformist thinkers. The reformist thinkers who are the main focus of this study have remained faithful to Islam, consider themselves part of the Islamic *umma*, and have developed new approaches to the study and interpretation of Islamic sources. Some reformists have gone as far as to become almost secularist, and their Islamic credentials are challenged by more mainstream Muslims and even other reformists. Nevertheless, since they consider themselves to be Muslims and describe their goal as reforming the understanding of Islam in order to improve the conditions of Muslims, their views will be noted here.

The most prominent Maghrebi thinkers discussed here are:

- the Franco-Algerian **Mohammed Arkoun**,[20]
- the Algerian anthropologist and prolific writer **Malek Chebel**,[21]
- the physicist and philosopher/theologian **Ghaleb Bencheikh**,[22] and his brother,
- the theologian **Soheib Bencheikh**,[23]
- the Tunisian historian **Mohamed Talbi**[24] (of Algerian origin),[25]
- the historian, sociologist, and professor emeritus at the Faculty of Literature of the University of Manouba in Tunis, **Abdelmadjid Charfi**,[26]
- the lawyer **Mohamed Charfi** [d. June 2008],[27]
- the anthropologist **Youssef Seddik**,[28]
- the political activist **Salah Eddin al-Jourshi**, cofounder of the Progressive Islamic Tendency Movement (Al-ittihaj al-islami al-taqaddumi) and president of the Tunisian League of Human Rights,[29]
- the man of letters **Abdelwahab Meddeb**,[30]
- the U.K.-based Moroccan political scientist **Abdou Filali-Ansary**,[31]
- the professor of philosophy and Islamic thought **Mohamed Abed al-Jabri**,[32] and
- the young Franco-Moroccan scholar **Rachid Benzine**,[33] who teaches hermeneutics and religion at the University of Aix-en-Provence in southern France.

In addition, there will be brief discussion of the work of Libyan reformist thinkers Al-Sadiq Nayhum (1937–1994) and Muhammad Abdul Mutalib Al Houni, who resides in Italy, and the works of a number of other religious leaders and political activists who advocate moderate or reformist Islamic discourse. The latter include the Spiritual Guide of the Algerian Alawi (Sufi) Brotherhood Sheikh Khaled Bentounes,[34] and one of the few female reformist thinkers, the Tunisian scholar of linguistics and applied Islamology Olfa Youssef. She is the author of *The Multiplication of Meaning in the Qur'an* (La multiplication du sens dans le Coran).

The Philosophy of Reformist Thinkers

Despite differences in the extent of these thinkers' reformism, the principles underlying their philosophical outlook are that, first, "Islam is a series of interpretations of Islam";[35] and second, it is the understanding of Islam that should be scrutinized and, when appropriate, reformed. These thinkers do not want to reform Islam itself, because, as put by Benzine, "'reform' implies mending, as though we [Muslims] had strayed from some original [understanding of] Islam and [now] wish to revive it."[36] Some reformist thinkers, notably Mohamed Talbi, do not even like to be characterized as reformist, "because all reformists followed a path which consisted in returning to the 'Pious Elders' [salaf] in Islam and imitating them. I [Talbi] can't see how we can progress in regressing."[37]

These thinkers want to achieve the goal of reforming the understanding of Islam by applying to the study of Islamic sources scientific methodologies derived from various Islamic and secular disciplines.[38] They consider the Qur'an the Word of God, but their approach to its analysis departs from that of traditional *ulema*. Their objective, according to Benzine, is:

to reexamine the modes through which Islam has been constructed historically; to "revisit" the successive interpretations and the ways the Qur'anic message and other founding texts (*hadith, sunna*, the corpus of the great juridical schools . . .) have been utilized, and to submit them to thorough scrutiny; and to submit all aspects of Islam's lived reality to the methods of scientific research and to the questioning of human sciences.

Benzine adds that their goal is *not*

to contribute to Islam's depreciation or demolition, as some might fear. It is to allow every Muslim, and every honest person, to better apprehend Islam's true message, far from ideological manipulations, and to knowingly accept it as his/her own.[39]

They agree that the clerics' theological work has been detrimental to Islam because it has remained frozen for centuries. Traditional *ulema* have not rigorously and diligently questioned the founding texts as they relate to the social and political order, and they have not removed the aura of sacredness given to these texts by their predecessors' interpretations.

To undo this damage, reformist thinkers seek to interpret Islam through a direct rational process, without the interpretative intercession of clerical commentators because, as put by Ghaleb Bencheikh, the Franco-Algerian theologian, the clerics' readings of the texts are "human extrapolations through successive, always approximate, interpretations, no matter how sophisticated. And, although those past interpretations belong to Islam's heritage, they are now outdated." Moreover, because "theological and doctrinal production is a mere human undertaking with its greatness and decadence, we [Muslims] need not slavishly restart what men of genius for their epoch might have produced. Cannot we be their worthy successors?"[40]

Youssef Seddik, meanwhile, maintains that the Qur'an is known only "under the cloak of a religious and exegetic tradition belatedly manufactured by clerics bound to official 'Islams' and closely controlled by political authority, from the time of the first caliphs until today."[41] Al-Jabri argues that Islamic legislation was mostly the ratification of existing realities, notably those of power, and was not based on either the Qur'an or Islam's spirit.[42] Seddik further maintains that the Qur'an is no longer the closed domain of erudite person, or contending legal schools. In his view, because of the closure of the "gates of *ijtihad*" by princes and imams, by the tenth century, Qur'anic exegesis ceased to produce sense. Seddik wants to reopen the gates in his book by discussing sixty percent of the Qur'an in French, "through a reading that is distanced from the exegetic dogma."[43] According to Seddik, the Qur'an has freed its recipients from recourse to mediators. As Nayhum observes, in Islam there is no "mediator" (*wasta*) between God and man.

Methodologies of Reformist Thinkers

Reformists believe that the Muslim world needs its own "Age of Enlightenment" (*al-islam al-munawwar* or *al-islam al-munir*).[44] They justify their position on the basis of Qur'anic Sura XXIV, verse 35, which they interpret as God commanding Muslims to seek knowledge.[45] They each have their preferred methodology, but most use the modern methods of the social sciences. They defend their approach on the grounds that dogmatic closure, "Islamic orthodoxy," or what Arkoun calls the "theological-political reason" and "the closed official corpus" instituted by the theological (and political) systems of the last eight centuries, has prevented Muslims from having an open understanding of their religion. Moreover, he maintains that "forces of perversion, manipulation, and mechanization of the 'faith' have multiplied in the postcolonial nationalist contexts."[46]

Arkoun uses the "order of reasons," according to which the philological historian combines linguistic, psycholinguistic, semiotic, ethno-sociological, and anthropological tools. Arkoun sees himself as a product of modernity, which in his view is "the intellectual attitude that characterizes Arab humanism of the tenth century."[47] Arkoun wishes to transcend Islam's theological treatment, and uncover what theologians and states have stifled and concealed. He does not reject theological and philosophical contributions but wants to enrich them "through the inclusion of the concrete historical and social conditions in which Islam has always been practiced."[48]

Arkoun sees Revelation as a consensual alliance between man and God. Following the ninth century Mu'tazalis, he considers the Qur'an as being created,* as manifested in a human language—Arabic—and historical; thus, human beings have the duty to understand and interpret it. Arkoun distinguishes between the "Qur'anic phenomenon" (Revelation) and the "Islamic phenomenon" (system of beliefs). The Islamic fact has been regularly exploited to defend and legitimize the interests of particular groups. In short, he believes, orthodoxy has usurped the Qur'an's message and has diffused its own version of Islam.[49]

---

*Editor's note: This view makes Arkoun's discourse unacceptable to even some mainstream reformists.

The Tunisian scholar Youssef Seddik, in *The Qur'an, Another Reading, Another Interpretation* (Le Coran, autre lecture, autre traduction), advances a similar view. He claims that, despite the fact that the Qur'an does not confer the right of interpretation on anybody, since the end of the tenth century traditional Islamic exegesis has appropriated the meaning of the divine message. Like Arkoun, Seddik blames the religious and political establishments for having hindered any rational and critical thinking about Islam because they wanted to apply their own reading to present conditions, and in so doing prevented reform.

Given this situation, he concludes that "it becomes necessary, within democratically conducted debate, to give the right of interpretation back to any citizen equipped with the same common sense and the same passion for listening that was kindled by the prophet Muhammad" in ordinary people, who "thanks to the Qur'anic word were elevated to the rank of God's interlocutors."[50] The significance of God's injunction, *iqra* (read), was not addressed solely to Muhammad but "to any reader," whether religious scholar, king, shepherd, or the most refined thinker.[51] This idea is similar to Talbi's view that "God does not talk only to the dead. He also speaks to the living."

Talbi's methodology is predominantly historicist, and he believes that the Qur'an should be read by each generation according to its own conditions. If the *hadith* "Read the Qur'an as if it was revealed to you personally" is correct, Talbi says, then "when God speaks, I must listen to him with today's mind, in my actual situation."[52] Talbi also believes that since "God has endowed man with free will,"[53] a person may have a different reading than that of orthodoxy, a point similar to the one that Chebel makes.[54]

Al-Jabri, too, advocates a rationalist and historicist reading of Islamic sources, meaning that both the circumstances of Revelation (*asbab al-nuzul*) and present conditions should be taken into account in interpreting these sources. Al-Jabri, like the fourteenth-century Andalusian theologian al-Shatibi, emphasizes the ultimate objectives (*maqasid*) of the *shari'a*, which are justice and the welfare of society rather than the letter of the law, and he advocates a reexamination of existing rules in light of these ultimate goals.[55]

Abdelmadjid Charfi favors a historicist approach and argues that: "God talks to man in the language that he understands. Otherwise his inspiration would be useless. This would also mean that the Prophet is compelled to utilize what is available to him, that which is common and known in his environment."[56] Charfi reconciles faith and science; characterizes Muhammad's prophecy as an experience in which man is involved according to social and natural laws; and analyzes Qur'anic discourse within its social and cultural environment.[57] He maintains that a distinction must be made between those rules that apply to specific situations and those that entail an enduring educational and moral objective. Islam's enduring principles are freedom; equality between men and women; abolition of all practices degrading to human dignity, including physical mutilations; promotion of justice; and good deeds. Finally he admonishes Muslims to focus on the objectives and functions underlying Islamic prescriptions.[58]

Charfi maintains that Revelation does not speak of *shari'a* as divine law or a juridical system but as *a path to follow*. Revelation does not consider *shari'a* the source of divine injunctions as it later became in Arab-Islamic societies. In this sense he subscribes to Talbi's "vector method," according to which God created man, delineated the path for him, endowed him with reason, and enjoined him to advance in that direction. He explains that this means that "God does not require that humans submit blindly but rather think rationally and infer the sense of the vector and accomplish new steps in that direction."[59] This view echoes Nayhum's vision of absolute freedom rather than absolute obedience as the beating heart of a Qur'an-based Islam.[60]

Abdelmadjid Charfi has also interpreted the notion of Muhammad as the Seal of the Prophets as meaning "closure from the exterior." He adds that "the fact of sealing sets a limit for man to base his knowledge and his behavior on an external norm." It means that man has achieved enough maturity not to need a guide or a tutor for every detail of his existence.[61] This closure also liberates humans from superstitions and everything that could prevent their autonomy.

According to Abdou Filali-Ansary, this understanding of the Seal of Prophecy opens the possibility for the development of universal ethics, and the overcoming of traditional theories on the role of Revelation and religion in directing human life.[62] Salah Eddin al-Jourshi and the members of the Progressive Islamic Tendency Movement, also subscribe to a rationalist and historicist methodology.[63]

Rachid Benzine uses an essentially historicist methodology. He believes that Muslims can consider the Qur'an as sacred and still be receptive to its rational criticism, because rational thinking reinforces faith by equipping it with a solid foundation and freeing it from superstition, ideology, and accumulated false interpretations. Benzine differentiates between the Qur'an, which is sacred, and its interpretations, which are not, because they are of human origin. He quotes the saying of Caliph Ali Ibn Abu Talib, that "the Qur'an is in the *mushaf*. It does not talk by itself: human beings are the ones who express it." The reading of the text, Benzine adds, must be accompanied by the understanding of the historical circumstances of its production.[64]

The Libyan Sadiq Nahyum employs, in addition to the symbolic dimensions of the Qur'anic text,[65] historicist and sociological methodologies to uncover what he considers distortions of Islam and its message. Nayhum traced the beginning of this distortion back to the Ummayad Caliph Mu'awiyya, because he took the power of legislation and administration away from the people, as prescribed by the Qur'an, and placed it in the hands of the clergy. Nayhum explained the evolution of world history in terms of a battle between feudalism and the people and accuses Mu'awiyya of having transformed Islam into a legalistic creed based on *fiqh* (Islamic jurisprudence), by which means power was transferred from the people to feudal interests.[66]

Al-Saddiq Nayhum believes that "Islam does not recognize the legitimacy of religious intermediaries. . . . Nor does it require that certain individuals or groups, such as political parties, represent anyone."[67] Muslims commune directly with God and represent themselves. Accordingly, he rejects the power of the *ulema* and says: "Arabs were not liberated from the power of ignorance and backwardness" through divine revelation of the Qur'an only to be delivered to the power of an obscurantist religious class who snatched the right of interpreting the Qur'an from the people.[68] Nayhum accuses the *ulema* of having usurped the power to legislate from the majority through their alliance with Arab rulers.[69]

Another Libyan, Mohamed al-Houni, blames the *fuqaha* (jurists) for the archaic interpretation of Islam. He distinguishes "between the Islamic holy texts that are the foundation of the Muslim religion and the explanations, interpretations, and inferences of the texts made by [medieval] religious legists, who lived in different times and under different personal and societal conditions."[70] For him, the major problem facing contemporary Muslims is that the (medieval) legists' interpretations have been hallowed and are treated as part of the Qur'an. Noting that many Qur'anic verses were responses to particular historical conditions, he says that the "Holy Qur'an itself is not above history." He considers many verses and *hadith* obsolete and believes that they should be abandoned. Al-Houni assails the Islamists' belief that "Islamic law, which consists of answers provided by legists and meant for their own epochs, is valid for all times and places."[71] He (and other reformists) also accuse the Islamists of "fabricating" Islamic history rather than studying it and of turning Islam into an ideology in order to serve their political interests.

In short, methodologically, the Maghrebi reformist thinkers favor a "dynamic reading [of religious sources], which must be substituted for the stagnant, conservative, immovable reading that kills the Word of God." Notwithstanding their different methodologies (hermeneutics, historicism, symbolism, and linguistics), they agree on the following points:

- orthodoxy has equated the *mushaf* (collection of written texts of the Revelation) with the transcendental Word of God, while ignoring the successive processes of oral transmission and their transformation into a written text. Hence, the historical context has been totally overlooked;
- rejection of Muslim orthodoxy constructed by traditional scholars, while remaining faithful to the main principles of Islam's message;
- emphasis on historical dimensions of the Islamic phenomenon; and
- every Muslim's right to personal *ijtihad*.

Reformist Muslim Thinkers and the State of the Arab-Islamic World

Like their pioneering predecessors and their counterparts in the Arab East and in the rest of the Islamic world, Maghreb's reformist thinkers are concerned about the crisis facing the Arab and Muslim worlds. Indeed, finding ways of resolving this crisis is a major motivation behind their intellectual efforts. They have a depressing view of the state of the Arab-Islamic world, which they see as facing a multidimensional crisis, largely attributable to the failure of authoritarian rulers, in complicity with domesticated *ulema*, to implement fundamental reforms. They bemoan the lack of technological and scientific progress; the persistence of outdated patterns of societal and gender relations;[72] and the monopolization of religious studies by a minority of clerics incapable of applying scientific methods to the study of the religious phenomenon.

Ghaleb Bencheikh is particularly critical of the official clergy, whom he holds responsible for distorting Islam by subjugating it to politics and using it to confer popular legitimacy on governmental policies.[73] Soheib Bencheikh, meanwhile, also blames Salafi groups who "wish to imitate, in every aspect, the example of Prophet Muhammad. But the prophet was so tied to his century, and anchored in the culture and the way of life of his time, that it is impossible to believe that he wished to impose his example for the coming centuries."[74]

Like other reformists, Abdelwahab Meddeb is critical of Wahhabism and considers Muhammad Ibn Abdul Wahhab as lacking in originality.[75] He is also critical of Saudi Arabia for spreading Wahhabism.[76] Sheikh Bentounes goes further and blames Wahhabi Islam for the rise of Islamist extremism.[77]

Mohamed Charfi, like Meddeb, held colonialism partly responsible for Muslims' current predicament. But, again like Meddeb, he conceded that Muslims were colonized because they were "colonizable."[78] They were "colonizable" because they had failed to become aware of their cumulative decline since the fifteenth century and had done little to remedy it. Most important, according to Charfi, they had failed to "evolve [their] philosophical conceptions and culture through *ijtihad*, which would have allowed [them] to adapt to modern times while remaining true to themselves."[79]

In a similar vein, Talbi attributes the decline of the Arab-Islamic world to the persecution of Ibn Rushd (Averroës), which culminated in the victory of conservative religious forces which believed that they had "reached the pinnacle of knowable and civilization; thus, any further evolution can only be decline." In support of this view he cites Ibn Khaldun, who complained that rational sciences had fallen under the strict surveillance of the *ulema*. As Khaldun said, "these sciences have migrated to the northern shore and I have learned that they are the object of great infatuation."[80] Malek Chebel, too, blames conservative *ulema* for engendering a spirit of inertia among peaceful Muslims and radicalism among the more activist.[81] Those who truly love Islam, he says, must try "to unite Islam with its time."[82] Meanwhile, Abed al-Jabri sees as counterproductive, and detrimental to Arab progress the current polarization of Arab thought between an imported modernism that discounts Arab tradition and a fundamentalism that would reenact the present day in the image of an idealized past. Reformist thinkers maintain that there is nothing shameful about emulating others' scientific achievements, reminding their audiences that the European Renaissance was made possible by their borrowing from the works of Muslim scientists and philosophers.

Reformist Scholars and Contemporary Political and Social Issues

The issues of secularism, democracy, human rights, freedom of conscience, and gender equality are some of the most controversial issues addressed by reformist thinkers.

Secularism and Democracy

Reformist thinkers believe that the lack of an official clergy makes Islam the religion most compatible with secularism, interpreted as the separation of religion from government. According to Ghaleb Bencheikh, "the absence of a central clerical structure in Islam makes it de facto secular in the etymological and theological sense."[83] They differ, however, in their interpretations of secularism. Many take a view similar to that of the Egyptian reformist thinker Sheikh Ali Abdul Raziq (1888–1966)[84] in his book *Islam and the Foundations of Power.*[85] In this book, Abdul Raziq emphasized the separation between religion and politics; matters of faith and matters of governance; the sacred and the profane. Islam provides the ethical basis of society, while governance is based on rational premises. Thus, there is no need for the caliphate as a model for the exercise of power.

Jabri maintains that secularism does not suit Muslim societies because it is based on the separation of church and state. Since there is no church in Islam, there is no need for any separation. Moreover, Jabri argues that concepts such as democracy, protection of minority rights, and rational conduct of politics "lose their justification and necessity when they are expressed through ambiguous slogans like that of secularism (*'ilmaniya*)."[86] He believes that Muslim societies need to maintain Islam as an ethical reference and a divinely inspired law, freed from its historic expressions. This would provide society and the state with ethical foundations "while rules and practices would be submitted to rational considerations and to what human experience has reached and shown as the best solutions."[87]

Because of the special connotations of secularism in Muslim countries, Mohamed Charfi, also advised that in these countries democracy should not mean "separation of Islam and the state, but the separation within the state of religious occupations from political functions"[88] To achieve this goal, Charfi proposed the creation of a religious authority that would be an essentially "moral authority" independent of other branches of government. Once the distinction between the law and religion is clearly established and recognized by all, muftis and imams would have to act within the law.[89] Charfi suggested that the members of this authority should be elected by popular vote. Filali-Ansary supports Charfi's idea but fears that the election of imams could again politicize religion.[90]

In general, for Muslim reformist thinkers secularism is not the French type of antireligious secularism but simply means the institutionalization of a political system that does not rest on theological foundations. They also agree that the Qur'an has not provided a particular model of the state. Ghaleb Bencheikh views the caliphate as an accidental event in Islam's political history since "nothing essential in the caliphate draws its raison d'être from the Qur'an or its justification from the *sunna*."[91] Rather, as noted by Jabri, it has merely laid down the ethical foundations of the state. In his book *Secularism from the Perspective of the Qur'an* (La laïcité au regard du Coran), Ghaleb Bencheikh challenges the view that Islam is "the depository of a global political system embracing all facets of life."[92] He refutes the notion of an Islamic state that might have existed during the Prophet's time or afterwards. He quotes several Qur'anic verses in support of his argument that "Islam has entrusted the people with the running of their affairs on the basis of consultation and without domination."[93]

He further argues that people do not need reference to Qur'anic verses in order to establish the principle of the separation of temporal and spiritual realms, because politics and Revelation are on different "epistemological levels." "The formal and technical aspect of the organization of the polis is neutral and exclusively human. Thus, with or without the presence of the Qur'an, it will always remain logically 'profane,'"[94] On the question of the separation of politics from religion, the Qur'an's position, according to Bencheikh, is that of "secular neutrality"[95] Accordingly, "politics must acquire its autonomy, thus saving religion from being politicized."[96] According to Bencheikh and the other reformist thinkers, only secularization in the above sense will allow the emergence of a modern society that will be able to extirpate from the religious discourse its "fundamentalist germs" and eliminate the "totalitarian counterfeit that has confiscated the Qur'an."[97]

Implicitly replying to both Islamists and neo-Orientalists, Ghaleb Bencheikh insists that "the precepts of the Qur'an and its moral commandments are of a general order and do not ascertain any political norm, much less a theory of state."[98] Sheikh Khaled Bentounes shares this view, stating that "Islam has not instituted a 'political model.' It has granted humans the freedom to choose the type of their society and political system."[99] Mohamed Charfi believed that, not only are Islam and secularism not irreconcilable, but they correspond to a faithful reading of Islamic religion and history.[100] Thus he refuted the idea that Islamic secularism is a contradiction in terms.

In sum, the reformist thinkers discussed here accept a minimum and qualified kind of secularism. Mohamed Talbi says: "I personally have nothing against secularism, as long as it is not used as an antireligious ideology. For it to be accepted in our societies, we need to explain to the people what it is, and to eliminate the perception of secularism as an insidious way to de-Islamize Muslims . . . as was done in Stalin's USSR."[101] Abdelmadjid Charfi shares this opinion and says: "*Laïcité* [secularism] not *laicism* [secularity] is the conquest over the instrumentalization of the religious by the political. Well understood, secularism is in the interest of religion as well as politics."[102]

All reformist thinkers believe in the democratic spirit of Islam, attribute the lack of democracy in Muslim countries to historical factors rather than to Islam, and believe in the possibility of using Islamic concepts such as *shura* to build democratic political systems. Jabri believes that the concept of *shura*, to the extent that it stresses consultation and understanding among members of Muslim communities, can be mobilized and referred to as legitimizing democracy. He adds that "believing in the oneness of God is the founding principle in our religious creed [Islam] and we should adhere firmly to it. However, we should believe that everything below God is plural and is founded on the principle of plurality. Especially, human governance (*hakimiyya*) should be strictly denied the character of unity."[103]

Others like Mohamed Talbi, however, believe that the only system available today to avoid arbitrary rule is Western-style democracy because "there has never really been any democracy in Islamic civilization."[104]

Freedom of Conscience, Human Rights, Individual Liberties

Reformist thinkers bemoan the absence of respect for human rights and individual liberties in Muslim countries, especially freedom of conscience. Abdelwahab Meddeb regrets that even in the most secular Arab country, Tunisia, Islam is declared official religion. This means that "the citizen is not free to choose his creed (or his non-belief), which should be the same as that of the prince."[105]

Mohamed Charfi and other reformist thinkers attribute present conditions in this regard to historical factors and not to Islam or the Qur'an. Charfi argued that, in order to generate positive change, "Muslims need to reread their history, in order to recover their religion in its purity."[106] He added that *shari'a* was written according to conditions of a particular time and place. The Islamic penal code, for instance, suited a nomadic society. Moreover, Islamic laws were mostly written by humans and are not sacred. Even those that were clearly Commandments from the Text can be changed. Charfi cited the example of Caliph Omar, who "never interpreted the Qur'an as a code. For him, the verses defined as juridical were mere recommendations tied to circumstances and which mu t change under different circumstances."[107] Therefore, Mohamed Charfi recommended that Muslims stop the unproductive debate over given verses and their meaning, and separate law from religion.[108] The harsh and absolute Islamic laws held and taught (*Islam enseigné*) by traditionalists are disconnected from the "lived Islam" (*Islam vécu*) of Muslims.[109] Charfi's conclusion is important:

> A Qur'anic verse is not an article in a code; it is not law. It is God addressing men, speaking to them in a language they understand, and providing them with a general recommendation. It behooves the legislator of every country to find for every epoch the law that best executes that recommendation. In the world we live in today, this would be the task of the state, which must itself be the expression of universal suffrage.[110]

If accepted, this view would mean the abolishing of Islamic *hudud*. Mohamed Talbi goes even further, and calls for abolishing of the death penalty because God desires life rather than death. He adds: "Abolishing the death penalty is in accordance with the Qur'an's intention. The 'vector reading' (*lecture vectorielle*) that I advocate points in that direction . . . The Qur'an tells me what to do today, not what was done in the past."[111]

Soheib Bencheikh, too, believes that "to use Islamic law, which is the product of patriarchal societies, as a universal law valid at all times amounts to a self-limitation of the evolution of Muslim societies. Justice in one century becomes injustice in another."[112] Unlike Talbi, Mohamed Charfi rejected replacing one religious law by another, because "religious laws are often considered immutable laws."[113]

Reformist thinkers have been particularly preoccupied with the question of the death penalty for apostasy. They have demonstrated that "death for apostasy" (under *hukm al-ridha*) does not exist in Islam. They challenge anyone to find any reference to it in the Qur'an; there is only one unreliable *hadith* that refers to it. Nayhum categorically rejected death for apostasy. And like other reformists, he believed that it comes from the Old Testament and is "an early Jewish introduction into the study of *hadith* and *sunna*."[114] Talbi asserts emphatically that the *hadith* concerning apostasy is "false"[115] and adds: "We condemn it as being non-Islamic and having no basis in the Qur'an, which affirms very clearly freedom of conscience."[116] In support of their position regarding apostasy, most reformists refer to *Sura* 2, Al-Baqara, which says, "There is no compulsion in religion. Verily, the Right Path has become distinct from the wrong path."[117]

Ghaleb Bencheikh subscribes to Talbi's and Nahyum's view in this respect. Soheib Bencheikh also uses the above verse and refers to another that is equally explicit: "The truth is from your Lord. Then whoever wills let him believe; and whoever wills, let him disbelieve."[118] Both Bencheikhs cite numerous verses in support of their belief that the Prophet's responsibility was one of transmission of the Message only, the task of dealing with those who do not believe is God's. Mohamed Charfi, for his part, considers the death penalty for apostasy as "the most disastrous idea that the *ulema* fabricated, [and] their most horrible invention . . . without any Qur'anic basis."[119] Talbi insists that the Prophet himself lacked the authority to punish any apostate because everyone is responsible before God. Talbi even refutes the term *mulhid* (atheist), or one who has gone astray, because it has become a pejorative appellation. He says one needs "to accept the other as he is and whatever he wants to be, without prejudice."[120] Talbi speaks not of tolerance, which he finds degrading, but of "recognition of the other." This is the only way that humans can be truly equal in everything.

The issue of apostasy is very sensitive for reformist thinkers because Islamists and most *ulema* use it to punish "heretics" and because it concerns freedom of conscience, which is a prerequisite of a democratic order. Nayhum argued that to inculcate in children the present repressive interpretation of the Qur'an is "the biggest brain-washing operation in history."[121]

Talbi's views on other rights derive from his basic notion that: "God endowed man with the possibility to choose—which is unique. . . . Not only has God created man free, but man too has chosen to be free at the ontological level [when he touched the tree despite God's order not to do so], and assumed the consequences. This is why Adam could touch the tree without, however, sinning."[122] Thus, it is by disobeying that man has experienced freedom. Talbi is a strong supporter of freedom of speech and even defends the rights of Islamists when persecuted for their ideas.[123]

Malek Chebel, too, is a strong advocate of freedom of conscience and human rights, as well as the elimination of *fatwas* calling for death, genital mutilation, and similar practices. He supports the rights of religious minorities in Muslim countries.[124] This view is similar to that of Al-Houni, who supports equal rights for religious minorities and believes that this is the Qur'an's intention.[125]

Women's Rights

Reformist thinkers oppose the patriarchal notions of women's rights espoused by both Islamists and traditionalists. They often cite those Qur'anic verses most favorable to women. But they do not entirely rely on the Qur'an because it also has unfavorable verses on women's rights. In justification of their position they point to changed socioeconomic conditions since the time of Revelation, and stress the need for a rationalist interpretation of Islamic sources. Chebel recommends the modernization of "the understanding of the texts. . . . Through this work of interpretation of the Qur'an, Islam needs to be adapted to modernity."[126]

To support their position on changing the rules detrimental to women's rights, reformists refer to Qur'anic verses on slavery, which nobody today applies. Al-Houni maintains that the reason Muslims changed their view on slavery was because as human societies evolve certain practices become unacceptable and are changed through secular legislation.[127] Reformists support complete gender equality in all areas, including the abolition of polygamy. Talbi says that he is "absolutely convinced that this was Islam's profound intention."[128]

Ghaleb Bencheikh has devoted almost half of his book[129] to the issue of women's rights, including the question of the veil. He writes:

> From an ontological perspective, there is no difference between men and women. I don't understand why hateful, rigorist, chauvinistic, and misogynous jurists continue to enslave, in anachronistic visions, a human being who is, like a man, God's icon on earth. I am not favorable to the veiling of women . . . there is no reason why the expression of faith should be through a headscarf. In fact, it's a recommendation that does not include any form of coercion.[130]

Abdelmadjid Charfi argues that: "One cannot be for progress and accept the inferior condition of women. That of Muslim women, in particular, needs urgent and radical improvement."[131] Sheikh Bentounes, too, believes that the issue of women's status needs urgent attention. He criticizes those Arab countries that still lapidate women, prohibit them from driving cars, and debate whether they should vote.[132] In essays that appeared in the Moroccan publication *Tel Quel* and using exegetic analysis based on linguistics, the Tunisian Olfa Youssef has demonstrated that the exegetes do not agree on the significance of the verses related to veiling. Certainly, they do not support the position of the more strict Islamists. Furthermore, using the same methodology plus a more contextualist approach, she argues that polygamy should no longer be practiced, and points out that the Qur'an also grants women the right to ask for divorce, a right that is not respected in most Muslim societies.[133]

All reformists believe that only a secular and democratic order in which religion and politics are separate will ensure the human rights of all, including those of women and religious minorities. To that end Ghaleb Bencheikh recommends that "Muslims provide an intellectual foundation for the development of a secular matrix based on the ideals of goodness and divine mercy enshrined in the Qur'anic revelation."[134] In his book *Manifest for an Islam of Enlightenment*, Malek Chebel enumerates what is needed to achieve such an Islam, which includes a rationalist and historicist interpretation of the text and fundamental reform of Islamic penal and family laws, plus expansion of education.[135]

Moderate Islamist Parties

Moderate Islamist parties, willing to operate within existing political systems and to use peaceful means to gain power, are becoming a major part of the political landscape in some Maghreb countries, notably Morocco. This situation is largely the result of the policies of some Maghreb countries to integrate moderate Islamic groups into the political process, in order to counter the influence of more radical forces. Yet this phenomenon is not totally new. In Algeria, during the civil conflict in the 1990s,[136] some moderate Islamist parties, such as the Movement for a Peaceful Society (MSP) and, to a lesser degree, the An Nahda (Awakening) party, were active in politics. They condemned violence and participated in various political actions aimed at building a semblance of stability.

The MSP and its leader, the late Mahfoud Nahnah, strongly opposed the Islamic Salvation Front (FIS) and advocated a reformist Islam based on *ijtihad* and adaptation of religious sources to modern conditions. He argued in favor of an Islamic polity, *shuraqratiyya*, a form of government combining an Islamic conception of democracy, based on consultation, and opposed to despotism and concentration of power in an individual or a narrow elite, with modern notions of democracy. Nahnah and the MSP endorsed the concept of pluralism. In 1991 Nahnah said, "Even God sought to have an opposition. He created Satan to that purpose."[137] Nahnah believed that secular and Islamist parties can coexist and on 3 June 1997 told the author in Algiers that he would collaborate with anyone, including atheist parties, if that could save the country.

The MSP's program states that any constitution must be inspired by Islamic principle, but it also insists that an Islamic system would guarantee civil and political liberties "provided that these liberties are not exploited to destabilize the bases of society, to plot against the nation, or to spread immorality among its members."[138] Nahnah often repeated that "Islam must be freely chosen by the people and that they would always be able to vote for a non-Islamic party in the future."[139]

The MSP maintains that, according to the *shari'a*, women are equal to men "in struggle and at work, in education, in the building of civilization, and in the elaboration of universal thought whose distinction is equity and a sense of moderation."[140] And because they are created equal to men, women have the right to "organize their lives, run their property, and assume part of the responsibility in the economic, political, and social spheres."[141] The party claims that it strives to "liberate women from ancient traditions not related to Islam" and to encourage them to "accomplish their mission side by side with men."[142] However, there are limits to the MSP's championing of women's rights. In 2003 its new leader, Boudjerra Sultani, opposed the abolition of the *shari'a*-based 1984 Family Code, arguing that "those who call for the pure and simple abolition of this text in reality fight against Islam."[143]

Meanwhile, the small intellectualist Algerian Party for Renewal (PRA), led by Nourredine Boukrouh, expressed ideas similar to those of reformist thinkers. In fact, the PRA's program states that "the best in Islam can only be the best in modernity."[144] The program also asserts that "everything in the world that is done in the name of reason and intelligence, and that has proved positive and useful for humankind is in itself a carrier of the *Islamic message*."[145] The party's position on the *shari'a* is that it "does not interpret it . . . as a sum of repressive commandments aimed at restricting human beings in general, and women in particular, but as a historical and circumstantial response open to adaptation and enrichment when confronted with new situations."

Like most parties, the PRA has avoided discussing the question of secularism. However, it attacked the FIS leaders for conferring upon themselves the role of deciders on what is licit and illicit in religious matters, and Boukrouh claimed that, once in power, Islamists would use Islam to establish a totalitarian order.[146] Partly because of the polarized state of politics in Algeria in the 1990s, the party did not succeed with voters.

In Morocco, the most reformist Islamic political party is Al Badil Al Hadari (Civilizational Alternative), led by the reformist thinker Moustafa Moâtassim. It was created in 1995 and legalized in June 2005.* Moâtassim expresses ideas similar to those of reformist thinkers. Regarding Islamic law, Moâtassim argues that "the problem is not in the texts of the *shari'a* but in the way some people interpret

---

*Editor's Note: The party was banned in February 2008 and its leader arrested on charges of having links with terrorism and plotting to kill army officers and government officials, thus raising questions about the party's and its leadership's commitment to reformist Islam. Government officials claimed that the party had a public, reformist face and a real, extremist face, and played a double game.

them,"[147] which often leads to extremism because some Muslims "accept as truths the thoughts of *ulema* and *fuqaha* of obsolete times and turn their theses into a sacred religious text."[148] Moâtassim and his party reject violence, intolerance, and extremism. They advocate dialogue between Islamists and secularists as the basis of understanding. According to Moâtassim, secular intellectuals should open up to Islam and understand it before condemning it, while Islamist elites should exercise *ijtihad*, show interest in the new fields of knowledge, and address the issues of human, women's, and minority rights as well as individual and political liberties. The party is willing to cooperate with like-minded parties,[149] but it and Moâtassim believe that "democracy as practiced in the West remains the best system that man has conceived and developed hitherto. In the absence of a democratic Islamic system, which should embody the application of *shura*, wisdom dictates that believers choose what might be in their best interests."[150]

By far the most significant moderate Islamic party in Morocco is the Justice and Development Party (PJD), whose leader is Saaededine al Othmani and whose origins can be traced to the 1960s. The party became important in the 1980s after Hassan II adopted a policy to integrate some Islamists into the political process as part of his dual strategy of repression and co-optation of Islamist groups.[151] Since becoming successful in politics, the PJD, which held conservative views on many issues, notably women's rights, has adopted more liberal positions. In 2006, it changed its attitude toward family law and its leaders even claimed that they were the ones who initially had called for the change of the family code.[152] The PJD has indicated that it wants to emulate the Turkish party of the same name led by Recep Teyyip Erdogan, which should lead it to adopt more progressive positions.

However, the Algerian MSP and the Moroccan PJD remain attached to the goal of the Islamization of society and the implementation of the *shari'a* and oppose secularization. The question is what kind of Islam and what reading of the *shari'a* they want to implement. If they accept the reformist reading, will they be able to disseminate those ideas among believers and counter the more radical interpretations of Islam? They do not as of yet seem to have arrived at that point. Nevertheless, given the serious challenge of the more radical Islamic discourses and the inaccessibility of secularist, and even advanced reformist, discourses to the religious masses, they may prove very useful as a bridge to a more reformist Islam in the Maghreb.

Experience indicates that Islamists of varying shades of radicalism change their thinking as a result of engagement in democratic politics and under other influences. For instance, the Tunisian Islamist Rashid Ghanoushi became far more moderate after his years of exile in England. Similarly, Rabah Kebir, a prominent member of the Islamic Salvation Front (FIS) who returned to Algeria in September 2006 after fourteen years in Germany, made his *mea culpa* in an interview in late September 2006. He admitted that the FIS's policy of defiance (*muqa'laba*) was wrong and should be replaced with peaceful contestation (*muta'laba,* claiming). He said that he and his colleagues reached this conclusion through serious *ijtihad* and admitted that the experience of living in democratic systems taught them that they should compete for power through legal means.[153]

Conclusions

The Maghreb's reformist thinkers are part of a new breed of Muslim scholars. They are products of both the recent history of nation building in the Maghreb and the region's Islamic character and history, including reform movements of the nineteenth and early twentieth centuries. They are committed to Islam and most of them are practicing Muslims. Their objective is not to reform Islam but to reform the understanding that Muslims have of Islam. For them, the Qur'an remains the Revealed Word of God; however, the interpretation is human, therefore imperfect and inexorably pluralistic. Reformist thinkers argue that through rational *ijtihad* one discovers that all the elements of modernity are in no way incompatible with Islam's precepts. In their view, Islam, properly understood, promotes collective and individual rights and dignity, tolerance, restrained government, freedom of conscience, pluralism, and gender equality.

In sum, one can be truly Muslim and truly democratic. They all agree that orthodoxy and various ideological interpretations of Islam have distorted its true nature. They condemn both the Arab-Islamic regimes that have instrumentalized religion to serve their political purposes, and the Islamists who have ideologized it for having undermined Islam and contributed to Muslim societies' stagnation.

Reformist thinkers are fully aware that their ideas run counter to the Islam practiced in Arab-Islamic societies and that they are suspected of being part of a Western plot to undermine the Islamic world. However, they believe that these problems can be overcome if the Maghreb's educational systems are fundamentally reformed and reformist views of Islam are propagated.

Because of governmental repression and opposition from conservative and radical Islamic forces, their views are not currently accessible to many people.[154] Nevertheless, gradually their ideas are getting around and are published in Maghrebi newspapers, and heated debates have been arranged. Reformist thinkers have made suggestions for making new studies of the sacred texts and for propagating the ideas of past and present reformist thinkers. Mohamed Talbi, for example, has urged the creation of centers for the study of Islam using hermeneutics and other scientific disciplines.

The best chance for these views to reach wider audiences is their adoption by moderate Islamist parties with strong anchoring in the Maghreb countries' social fabric. For this to happen, however, political systems must be liberalized and religion freed from state tutelage. Any plans sponsored by governments, such as the Moroccan government's organization of meetings between reformist thinkers Rachid Benzine and Olfa Youssef and members of *ulema* committees, are unlikely to succeed and may even backfire. Interaction needs to be more spontaneous in order to be successful; it should be the work of civil society. Reformist thinkers, for their part, must develop more concrete plans for solving people's social and economic problems. They must also be open to debate with traditional *ulema* on the basis of intellectual equality, and accept the questioning of their ideas and methods as they do those of the *ulema*.

Notes

1. Some of the following works illustrate those arguments: Samuel Huntington, "Will More Countries Become Democratic?" *Political Science Quarterly* 99 (Summer 1984): 216; Elie Kedourie, *Democracy and Arab Political Culture* (Washington, DC: Washington Institute for Near East Policy, 1992), pp. 1, 5. See also Bernard Lewis, "Islam and Liberal Democracy," *Atlantic Monthly* (February 1993); Amos Perlmutter, "Islam and Democracy Simply Aren't Compatible," *International Herald Tribune* (January 21, 1992).

2. Nazih Ayubi, in his book *Political Islam: Religion and Politics in the Arab World* (New York: Routledge, 1991), clearly shows that historically, in Islam, the domains of politics and religion were effectively separate.

3. For a more balanced analysis of the causes of the Muslim world's poor record in modernization and democratization, see Shireen T. Hunter and Huma Malik, eds., *Modernization, Democracy, and Islam* (Westport, CT: Praeger, 2005).

4. See the excellent critique of Orientalists and neo-Orientalists in Yahya Sadowski, "The New Orientalism and the Democracy Debate," *The Middle East Report* (MERIP), July–August 1993.

5. Mohammed Arkoun, *L'Islam. Approche critique* (Islam: A Critical Approach) (Paris: J Grancher, 1992), pp. vi–vii (all translations in this chapter are the author's unless otherwise indicated).

6. It should be pointed out that Rida deviated from the teachings of his master, Mohammed Abduh, by moving closer to Wahhabism. Thus his appellation as a reformer should be qualified to mean that he was a traditionalist reformer, i.e., one who praises the virtues of the early, golden years of Islamic society, which today's Islamists wish to recreate.

7. Malek Bennabi, *Vocation de l'islam* (Islam's Vocation), 2d ed. (Ouled Fayet, Tipaza, Algeria: Société d'Edition et de Communication, 1970). Bennabi believed that Muslims could not modernize without espousing Western values, i.e., they could achieve modernity while preserving their "Islamic authenticity." Although Bennabi was a reformist, his thinking with respect to women was somewhat archaic. See Nora Amira, "Le point de vue de Bennabi sur les femmes" (Bennabi's Views on Women), *NAQD-revue de critique sociale* (Algiers), Special Issue; "Intellectuels et Pouvoirs au Maghreb" (Intellectuals and Power in the Maghreb), *Itinéraires pluriels*, no. 11 (Spring 1998): 69–83. Bennabi had great influence over many university students, especially those enrolled in the physical sciences. A section of the Islamic Salvation Front known as al-Jazara claimed to be inspired by his teachings. See Yahia H. Zoubir, "'Algerian Islamists' Conception of Democracy," *Arab Studies Quarterly*, vol. 18, no. 3 (Summer 1996): 65–85. However, it should be pointed out that Bennabi was favorable to a democratic order. See Yahia H. Zoubir, "Islam and Democracy in Malek Bennabi's Thought," *American Journal of Islamic Social Sciences*, vol. 15, no. 1 (Spring 1998): 107–12.

8. The expression "Algerian Nahda" is from the late Algerian historian Mahfoud Kaddache, *L'Algérie des Algériens de la préhistoire à 1954* (Algeria of the Algerians from Prehistoric Times to 1954) (Paris: Editions Méditerranée, 2003), p. 720.

9. The best book on the subject remains Ali Merad, *Le Réformisme musulman en Algérie de 1920 à 1940, essai d'histoire religieuse et sociale* (Muslim Reformism in Algeria from 1920 to 1940) (The Hague: Mouton, 1967). For a good succinct treatment of the *ulema*, see Michael Willis, *The Islamist Challenge in Algeria: A Political History* (New York: New York University Press, 1996), pp. 8–21.

10. El Hadi Chalabi, "Un juriste en quéte de modernité: Benali Fekar" (A Jurist in Search of Modernity: Benali Fekar), *NAQD-revue de critique sociale* (Algiers), Special Issue; "Intellectuels et Pouvoirs au Maghreb," *Itinéraires pluriels,* no. 11 (Spring 1998): 41–55.

11. Sadek Sellam, "Le Cheikh El Oqbi au cercle du progrès: un précurseur d'une 'laïcité' islamique" (Sheikh El Qobi in the Circle of Progress: A Precursor of an Islamic Secularism), *NAQD-revue de critique sociale* (Algiers), Special Issue, "Intellectuels et pouvoirs au Maghreb," *Itinéraires pluriels,* no. 11 (Spring 1998): 84–90.

12. See Mohamed Charfi, *Islam et liberté, le malentendu historique* (Islam and Liberty: The Historic Misunderstanding) (Paris: Albin Michel, 1998), pp. 20, 41; Kenneth J. Perkins, *A History of Modern Tunisia* (Cambridge: Cambridge University Press, 2004), p. 88. Note that Charfi's book is now available in English: *Islam and Liberty: The Historical Misunderstanding*, trans. Patrick Camiller (London and New York: Zed Books, 2005).

13. Cited in Mohamed Tozy, *Monarchie et islam politique au Maroc* (Monarchy and Political Islam in Morocco) (Paris: Presses de Sciences Po, 1999), p. 140.

14. Henri Sanson. *Laïcité islamique en Algérie* (Islamic Secularism in Algeria) (Paris: Editions du CNRS, 1983), p. 8. *Laïcité* in this context is also understood as the absence of a religious hierarchy and where, despite Islam's preponderance, power is exercised in a secular manner (p. 52).

15. Franck Frégosi, "La régulation institutionnelle de l'Islam en Tunisie: entre audace moderniste et tutelle étatique" (Islam's Institutional Regulation in Tunisia), *Policy Paper* (Institut français des relations internationales [IFRI]), no. 11 (March 2005): 7.

16. Ibid., p. 24.

17. This section draws mostly from Malika Zeghal, "Religion et politique au Maroc aujourd'hui" (Religion and Politics in Morocco Today), *Policy Paper* (IFRI), no. 11 (March 2005): 32–50.

18. On the relationship between religion and politics in Morocco, see ibid.

19. For more details, see Yahia H. Zoubir, "Libye: Islamisme radical et lutte antiterroriste," *Revue Maghreb-Machrek*, no. 184 (Summer 2005): 55–66.

20. Arkoun is the author of innumerable books and articles, among which one should cite: *Essais sur la pensée islamique* (Essay on Islamic Thought), 3d ed. (Paris: Maisonneuve-Larose, 1984); *Pour une critique de la raison islamique* (A Critique of Islamic Reason) (Paris: Maisonneuve-Larose, 1984); *La pensée arabe* (Arabic Thought), 5th ed. (Paris: P.U.F., 1997); *L'Islam, morale et politique* (Moral and Political Islam) (Paris: Desclée de Brouwer, 1986).

21. Malek Chebel, *Manifeste pour un islam des lumières* (Manifesto for an Islam of Enlightenment) (Paris: Hachette, 2004); *L'islam et la raison, le combat des idées* (Islam and Reason: The Battle of Ideas) (Paris: Perrin, 2005); *Le sujet en islam* (The Subject in Islam) (Paris: Seuil, 2002); *L'imaginaire arabo-muslman* (Paris: P.U.F., 2002).

22. Ghaleb Bencheikh, *La laïcité au regard du Coran* (Secularism from Qur'an's Perspective) (Paris: Presses de la Renaissance, 2005); *Alors, c'est quoi l'islam?* (Now, What Is Islam?) (Paris: Presses de la Renaissance, 2001); with Philippe Haddad, *L'islam et le judaïsme en dialogue: salam shalom* (Islam and Judaism in Dialogue) (Paris: Ed. de l'Atelier, 2002).

23. Soheib Bencheikh, *Marianne et le Prophète, l'islam dans l'espace laïque* (Marianne and the Prophet: Islam in a Secular Space) (Paris: Grasset, 1998).

24. Mohamed Talbi, *Plaidoyer pour un islam moden e* (In Defense of a Modern Islam) (Paris: L'Aube Edition, 2004; originally published in 1998, Cérès Edition). Note that Abdelmadjid Charfi wrote the preface to the book, pp. 5–8; *Mohamed Talbi. Penseur libre en islam, un intellectuel musulman dans la Tunisie de Ben Ali.. Entretiens avec Jarczyk Gwendoline* (Mohamed Talbi, A Free Thinker in Islam) (Paris: Albin Michel, 2002); *Islam et dialogue* (Islam and Dialogue) (Tunis: Maison tunisienne d'édition, 1972).

25. In *Penseur libre en islam,* Talbi says that he is Turkish from his mother's side, and Berber from Algerian origin from his father's side (p. 181).

26. Abdelmadjid Charfi, *L'Islam entre le message et l'histoire* (Islam Between the Message and History), trans. André Ferré (from Arabic) (Paris: Albin Michel, 2004). All of his contributions are purposely written in Arabic.

27. M. Charfi, *Islam et liberté.*

28. Youssef Seddik, *Coran, autre lecture, autre traduction* (The Qur'an: Another Reading, Another Translation) (Paris: L'Aube Edition, 2006); *Nous n'avons jamais lu le Coran* (We Have Never Read the Qur'an) (Paris: L'Aube, 2004).

29. He was part of the Islamic Tendency Movement, also known as an-Nahda (Awakening); Rashid Ghanouchi became the party's president in 1984. He left the party because of doctrinal and operational differences. Emad Edin Shaheen, *Political Ascent: Contemporary Islamic Movements in North Africa* (Boulder, CO: Westview Press, 1997), pp. 79–80.

30. Abdelwahab Meddeb, *La maladie de l'islam* (Paris: Seuil, 2002); the book has been translated into English as *The Malady of Islam* (New York: Basic Books, 2003).

31. Abdou Filali-Ansary, *Réformer l'islam? Une introduction aux débats contemporains* (Reforming Islam: An Introduction to Contemporary Debates) (Paris: Editions la Découverte, 2003, 2005); *L'islam est-il hostile à la laïcité?* (Islam: Is It Hostile to Secularism?) (Casablanca: Le Fennec, 1997; Paris: Sindbad, 2001).

32. Mohamed Abed Al-Jabri, *Introduction à la critique de la raison arabe* (Paris: La Découverte, 1994); *Arab-Islamic Philosophy—A Contemporary Critique* (Austin: University of Texas Press, 1999).

33. Rachid Benzine, *Les nouveaux penseurs de l'Islam* (Islam's New Thinkers) (Paris: Albin Michel, 2004).

34. Cheikh Khaled Bentounes, *L'homme intérieur à la lumière du Coran* (The Inner Man in the Light of the Qur'an) (Paris: Pocket, 2006); *Vivre l'islam. Le soufisme aujourd'hui* (Living Islam: Suphism Today) (Paris: Albin Michel, 2006); and *Pour un islam de paix* (For an Islam of Peace) (Paris: Albin Michel, 2002).

35. Soroush argued: "Islam is a series of interpretations of Islam. Christianity is a series of interpretations of Christianity. And since these interpretations are historical, the element of historicity is here. This is the reason why you need to have good knowledge of the history of Islam. Going directly to the Qur'an and the hadiths will not provide you with much. You need to study the history and, from there, come back to the Qur'an and the *hadith,* in order to set the interpretation in its historical context." Cited in Benzine, *Les nouveaux penseurs,* p. 59.

36. Rachid Benzine, Interview, *Tel Quel* (Morocco), no. 128 (2004), available at www. telquelonline.com/128/sujet3.shtml.

37. Mohamed Talbi, "Pour une Charte du musulman moderne" (A Charter for a Modern Muslim), Interview, *Kalima Tunisie* (www.kalimatunisie.com), no. 17 (September 2003), available at www.plmonline.info/id313.html.

38. Ibid.

39. Benzine, *Les nouveaux penseurs,* p. 12.

40. Bencheikh, *La laïcité au regard du Coran,* p. 61.

41. Seddik, *Coran, autre lecture, autre traduction,* p. 8.

42. Jabri discusses these issues in his *Ad-din wa ad dawla wa tatbiq ash-shari'a* (Religion, State, and the Implementation of Religious Laws) (Beirut: Centre d'Etudes pour l'Unite Arabe, 1996).

43. Seddik, *Coran, autre lecture, autre traduction,* pp. 11–12.

44. In France, the new thinkers publish in the series "L'islam des lumières" (Enlightened Islam), published by Albin Michel in Paris.

45. Chebel, *Manifeste pour un islam des lumières,* p. 11.

46. Arkoun, *L'Islam. Approche critique,* p. xxiii.

47. Mohammed Arkoun, *Pour une critique de la raison Islamique* (Paris: Maisonneuve et Larose, 1984), cited in Benzine, *Les nouveaux penseurs,* p. 96.

48. Mohammed Arkoun, *Penser l'islam aujourd'hui* (Algiers: Laphomic/ENAL, 1993).

49. See Benzine, *Les nouveaux penseurs,* pp. 100–109.

50. Seddik, *Coran, autre lecture, autre traduction,* pp. 12–13.

51. Ibid., p. 14.

52. Talbi, *Plaidoyer pour un Islam moderne,* pp. 65–66.

53. Ibid., p. 69.

54. See also Malek Chebel, *Rencontre avec Marie de Solenne. Islam et libre arbitre—la tentation de l'insolence* (Paris: Editions Dervy, 2003), p. 174.

55. Abdou Filali Ansary, "Can Modern Rationality Shape a New Religiosity? M.A. Jabri and the Project of Reduction of Islamic Apories," available at www.aljabfiabed.net/index.htm.

56. A. Charfi, *L'islam entre le message et l'histoire,* p. 45.

57. Ibid., p. 68.

58. Ibid., p. 186.

59. M. Charfi, *Islam et liberté,* p. 147.

60. Alberto Fernandez, "Liberating Islam from Bondage: The Radical Democratic Discourse of Al-Sadiq al-Nayhum," paper presented at the seventh Conference of the Center for the Study of Islam and Democracy, Washington, DC, May 2006, p. 6, available at www.csidonline.org/images/stories/pdfiles/alberto_fernandes[1].pdf.

61. A. Charfi, *L'Islam, entre le message et l'histoire,* p. 100.

62. See Filali-Ansary. *Réformer l'islam?* p. 253.

63. Salah Eddin Al Jourshi, Muhammad al-Quomai, and Abdel Aziz al-Tamimi, *Al-Muqadadimat al-nadhariyya al-taqq dumiyyin* (The Theoritical Basis of the Progressive Islamists) (Tunis: Dar al Buraq li al Nashr, 1989).

64. See Rachid Benzine, Interview, *L'Economiste,* available at www.yabiladi.com/article.php?cat=culture&id=445.

65. In 1967, Nayhum published in the daily Libyan newspaper, *al-Haqiqa,* a series titled *Al-ramz fil qur'an* (Symbolism in the Qur'an), which infuriated the conservative religious establishment. See Suha Taji-Farouki, "Sadiq Nayhum: Introduction to the Life and Works of a Contemporary Libyan Intellectual," *The Maghreb Review,* vol. 25, nos. 3–4 (2000): 254. The article provides the best narrative of Nayhum's life and career.

66. Suha Taji Farouki, "Modern intellectuals, Islam and the Qur'an: the example of Sadiq Nahyum," in *Modern Muslim Intellectuals and the Qur'an* (Oxford: Oxford University Press in association with The Institute of Ismaili Studies, 2004), pp. 309–12.

67. Al-Sadiq Al-Nayhum, *Mihnat thaqafat muzawara: sawt al-nas am sawt al-fuqaha* (The Affliction of a Forged Culture: The Voice of the People or the Voice of the Clerics) (Beirut: Riad El Rayyes Books, 1991), p. 36, cited in Alberto Fernandez, "Liberating Islam from Bondage: The Radical Democratic Discourse of Al-Sadiq al-Nayhum," paper presented at the seventh Conference of the Center for the Study of Islam and Democracy Washington, DC, May 2006, p. 6, available at www.csidonline.org/images/stories/pdfiles/alberto_fernandes[1].pdf.

68. Cited in Fernandez, "Liberating Islam from Bondage," p. 6.

69. Ibid., p. 9.

70. Mohamed Houni, "The Arabic [sic] Dilemma in Face of the New American Strategy," March 10, 2005, available at www.metransparent.com/texts/mohamed_el_houni_arabic_dilemma_book.htm. The book was published in French as Mohamed Abd El Motaleb Al Houni, *L'impasse arabe—Les Arabes face à la nouvelle stratégie américaine,* with a Preface by the Paris-based Tunisian reformist thinker Lafif Lakhdar. Paris: L'Harmattan, 2004.

71. Ibid.

72. A. Charfi, *L'islam entre le message et l'histoire*, pp. 9–10.

73. Bencheikh, *La laïcité au regard du Coran*, pp. 19–20.

74. Henri Tincq, "Soheib Bencheikh, mufti de Marseille: 'Ou l'islam marche avec son siècle, ou il reste à la marge de la société moderne,' Entretien avec Soheib Bencheikh, mufti de Marseille," Interview with the Mufti of Marseille, Either Islam Moves with Its Century or Remains at the Margins of the Modern World), *Le Monde*, November 11, 2001.

75. Meddeb, *La maladie de l'islam*, p. 68.

76. Ibid., p. 74. Ghaleb Bencheikh, too, is very critical of Wahhabism. He declared: "Saudi Arabia exports [to Nigeria] its austere and archaic vision of religion. [Nigerians] are mimicking what is happening in Saudi Arabia, where speedy public executions are carried out, where young people are lashed, where women's freedom is very restricted." Ghaleb Bencheikh, Interview, "Pour une théologie de la minorité," *Géopolitique africaine*, December 2002, available at www.africangeopolitics.org/show.aspx?ArticleId=3350.

77. Yasmina Dahim, "Entretien avec le Cheikh Khaled Bentounes: Nous ne sommes pas ce que vous croyez-I," Interview with Sheikh Bentounes: We Are Not as You Think We Are, *Revue Outre Terre*, 2, no. 3 (2003): 96.

78. Charfi, *Islam et liberté*, p. 34; Meddeb, *La maladie de l'islam*, p. 18.

79. Charfi, *Islam et liberté*, p. 35.

80. Talbi, *Plaidoyer pour un islam moderne*, pp. 42–43.

81. Chebel, *Manifeste pour un islam des lumières*, p. 13.

82. Ibid., p. 9.

83. Bencheikh, *La laïcité au regard du Coran*, p. 121.

84. Abdou Filali-Ansary devotes a whole chapter to Abdul Raziq in his *Réformer l'islam?* pp. 95–114.

85. Raziq's groundbreaking work, published in Cairo in 1925, *Al-islam wa usul al-hukm*, was translated by Abdou Filali-Ansary under the title *L'islam et les fondements du pouvoir* (Paris: La Découverte, 1994).

86. Jabri, *Ad-din wa ad dawla wa tatbiq ash-shari'a*, p. 113.

87. Filaly-Ansary, "Can Modern Rationality Shape a New Religiosity?"

88. Charfi, *Islam et liberté*, p. 193.

89. Ibid., pp. 195–96.

90. Filali-Ansary, *Réformer l'islam?* pp. 233–34.

91. Bencheikh, *La laïcité au regard du Coran*, p. 33.

92. Ibid., p. 39.

93. *Sura* 88, 21, 22.

94. Bencheikh, *La laïcité au regard du Coran*, pp. 50–51.

95. Ibid., p. 57.

96. Ibid.

97. Ibid., p. 70.

98. Ibid., p. 62.

99. Bentounes, "Nous ne sommes pas ce que vous croyez-I," p. 96.

100. M. Charfi, *Islam et liberté*, p. 22.

101. Talbi, *Plaidoyer pour un islam moderne*, p. 110.

102. "Entretien avec l'islamologue tunisien Abdelmajid Charfi: Le pari sur le progrès et la raison," May 15, 2005, available at nawaat.org/portail/article.php3?id_article= 572.

103. Cited in Abdou Filaly Ansary, "Can Modern Rationality Shape a New Religiosity?"

104. Talbi, *Plaidoyer pour un islam moderne*, p. 102.

105. Meddeb, *La maladie de l'islam*, p. 90.

106. Charfi, *Islam et liberté*, p. 173.

107. Ibid., p. 154.

108. Ibid.

109. Ibid., p. 211.

110. Ibid., p. 120.

111. Mohamed Talbi, *Penseur libre en Islam* (Paris: Albin Michel, 2002), available at www.acat.asso.fr/courrier/Cour_dec_2002/talib_cour230.htm.

112. Henri Tincq, "Soheib Bencheikh, mufti de Marseille: 'Ou l'islam marche avec son siècle, ou il reste à la marge de la société moderne,' Entretien avec Soheib Bencheikh, mufti de Marseille," *Le Monde,* November 11, 2001.

113. M. Charfi, *Islam et liberé,* p. 151.

114. Fernandez, "Liberating Islam from Bondage," p. 13.

115. Talbi, *Penseur libre en islam,* p. 269.

116. Ibid., 265. The Qur'an, 2: 256.

117. Sûrah 2. Al-Baqarah, 256 from *The Noble Qur'an in the English Language* (Riyadh, Saudi Arabia: Darussalam Publishers and Distributors, 1985).

118. *Sura* 18. Al-Kahf (The Cave), 29.

119. M. Charfi, *Islam et liberté,* p. 78.

120. Talbi, *Plaidoyer pour un islam moderne,* p. 21.

121. Cited in Fernandez, "Liberating Islam from Bondage," p. 13.

122. Talbi, *Penseur libre en islam,* p. 169.

123. Mohamed Talbi, *"La charia ou l'islam, il faut choisir,"* propos recueillis par Dominique Mataillet, *Jeune Afrique/L'Intelligent,* December 25, 2005, available at www.minorites.org/article.php?IDA=14200.

124. Chebel, *Manifeste pour un islam des lumières,* p. 133.

125. Houni, "The Arabic [*sic*] Dilemma in Face of the New American Strategy."

126. Chebel, *Manifeste pour un islam des lumières,* p. 26.

127. Houni, "The Arabic [*sic*] Dilemma in Face of the New American Strategy."

128. Talbi, *Plaidoyer pour un islam moderne,* p. 137.

129. Bencheikh, *La Laïcité au Regard du Coran,* pp. 137–226.

130. Ghaleb Bencheikh, Interview, "Pour une théologie de la minorité" (For a Theology of Minority), *Géopolitique africaine,* December 2002, available at www.african-geopolitics.org/show.aspx?ArticleId=3350. See also N. Bouzeghrane, "Interview de Ghaleb Bencheikh (Théologien)," *El Watan* (Algiers), 21 September 2004; CERF, "Face aux obscurantismes (l'islamiste et les autres): le Devoir de Liberté," Interview de Ghaleb Bencheikh, available at www.c-e-r-f.org/fao-033.htm; "L'islam et le statut de la femme," *L'Humanité* (Paris), 7 February 7, 2006, available at www.humanite.fr.

131. "Entretien avec l'islamologue tunisien Abdelmajid Charfi: Le pari sur le progrès et la raison," May 15, 2005, available at nawaat.org/portail/article.php3?id_article=572.

132. "Nous ne sommes pas ce que vous croyez-I," p. 106.

133. "Petit exercice d'exégèse moderne, pour libérer les musulmanes, Avec Olfa Youssef, linguiste spécialiste en islamologie appliquée," *Tel Quel,* available at www.telquel-online.com/158/couverture_158_1.shtml.

134. Bencheikh, *La laïcité au regard du Coran,* p. 63.

135. Chebel, *Manifeste pour un Islam des lumières,* p. 192.

136. Yahia H. Zoubir, "Resilient Authoritarianism, Uncertain Democratization, and Jihadism in Algeria," in William J. Crotty, ed., *Democratic Development and Political Terrorism: The Global Perspective* (Boston: Northeastern University Press, 2005), pp. 280–300.

137. Party conference in Algiers in June 1991, author watched in its entirety.

138. Ibid. I have edited the passages cited because of the poor English in the original.

139. Cited in Kate Zebiri, "Islamic Revival in Algeria: An Overview," *The Muslim World,* vol. 83, nos. 3–4 (July–October 1993): 217.

140. Cited in Mustapha Al-Ahnaf, Bernard Botiveau, and Franck Frégosi, *L'Algérie vue par ses islamistes* (Algeria as Seen by Its Islamists) (Paris: Karthala, 1991), p. 116.

141. Cited in *FBIS—Near East and South Asia* 95–214, November 6, 1995.

142. Program of Election.

143. Fayçal Oukaci, "Algérie: Code de la famille—Le chef d'un parti islamiste contre son abrogation," *Le Monde,* November 14, 2003.

144. See "Appel aux citoyens et citoyennes pour la création du Parti du Renouveau Algérien (P.R.A.)," in Soufiane Djilali, *Que veut le P.R.A.? Histoire d'une démocratie refuse* (What Does the P.R.A. Want? The History of a Democracy Denied) (Algiers: Co-Edition Microedit-PRA, 1993), p. 301.

145. Ibid.

146. On this point, see Yahia H. Zoubir, "Islamist Political Parties in Algeria," *Middle East Affairs Journal,* vol. 3, nos. 1–2 (Winter/Spring 1997): 116–17.

147. "M.L. Mouatassime: L'attitude de l'etat à notre égard viole la constitution," *Le Journal,* November 30–December 6, 2002, available at membres.lycos.fr/albadil/journal_media.htm.

148. Ibid.

149. Abdelmohsin El Hassouni, "Al-badil al-hadari entre en scène," *Aujourd'hui le Maroc,* June 10, 2005, available at www.aujourdhui.ma/nation-details36602.html.

150. Moâtassim, cited in *Gazette du Maroc,* July 1, 2002.

151. See Pierre Vermeren, *Maghreb: La démocratie impossible?* (Maghreb: Is Democracy Impossible?) (Paris: Fayard, 2004), p. 297.

152. See *Le Journal,* no. 234, vol. 10, December 16, 2005, available at www.lejournal-hebdo.com/article.php3?id_article=6335.

153. Fayçal Oukaci, "Rabah Kebir fait l'autocritique du FIS dissous" (Rabah Kabir Makes a Self-Criticism of FIS), *L'Expression* (Algiers), September 30, 2006: 2.

154. The author has searched in vain for a single book by Chebel; none of his numerous works is available in Algeria. Talbi complains that most of his work is unavailable in Tunisia.

4

Islamic Modernist and Reformist Discourse in South Asia

Riffat Hassan

Since the mid-nineteenth century, South Asian Muslim scholars and thinkers have contributed greatly to the development and dissemination of Islamic reformist and modernist discourse. Ideas and methodologies developed by such thinkers as Sir Sayyid Ahmad Khan, Muhammad Iqbal, and Fazlur Rahman have helped reformist thought to flourish throughout the Islamic world, and their legacy still inspires Muslim reformist thinkers from Turkey to Malaysia.

South Asian reformist thinkers' contributions are acknowledged by Muslim and Western scholars of Islam, and they all agree that the emergence of Muslim modernist reformers in the Indo-Pakistani subcontinent was a momentous event with far-reaching consequences. These scholars, however, hold different opinions about the nature and relative importance of the factors that caused this important development.

Some Western scholars have seen this phenomenon as representing a reaction to British presence and rule in India and influences emanating from this presence. But different scholars have accorded varying degrees of importance to different aspects of British influence. Bruce B. Lawrence has attributed it "mainly to commercial expansionism emanating from north-western Europe,"[1] while H.A.R. Gibb has stressed the impact of British education on India's Muslim elite.[2]

Some contemporary Muslim scholars have also considered influences resulting from British presence as significant in the generation and evolution of Islamic modernist and reformist discourses in the Indo-Pakistani subcontinent. Other Muslim scholars, by contrast, have attributed this phenomenon mostly to developments within Islam itself and particularly Islam in India. For example, Fazlur Rahman acknowledged the impact Western political and economic expansionism and its educational system on Muslims. He noted that, under the influence of European education, many educated Muslims came to perceive "the Muslim society as an inert mass suffering from a reaction to the Western impact at all levels."[3] Yet he perceived the modernist movement essentially as the continuation of the pre-modern

Islamic reform movements, and not "primarily the result of the West's impact."[4]

Clearly, the historical and sociopolitical context of post-Mughul India, including the impact of British education, made some form of reaction to British colonialism inevitable. Islamic modernist discourse was one of these responses. As in other Muslim societies, in India, too, responses to the multifaceted British influence and challenge have spanned the spectrum from (a) total rejection of these influences and the advocacy of a strict observance of Islam, later followed by the development of Islam-based models of government and resistance to the British conquest; to (b) total embrace of European-style modernity; and (c) synthesis, represented by Islamic modernism.[5]*

No doubt, many diverse factors were responsible for both the multiplicity of Muslim responses to the British challenge and to the emergence of reformist discourse in India. Yet it is undeniable that intrinsic aspects of Islamic tradition and of what Iqbal has called "the culture of Islam" were critical to the emergence and advancement of an indigenous and proactive movement of social and intellectual reform among India's Muslims.

Notwithstanding their differences regarding the principal impetus behind the emergence of the Islamic modernist phenomenon, most scholars agree that "Islamic modernists advocate flexible, continuous reinterpretation of Islam,"[6] in order to "reform" those aspects of Muslim tradition and law that have become outdated, fossilized, or harmful by scrutinizing those aspects in light of Islam's normative sources—the Qur'an and the authentic *sunna*. This perspective sharply departs from the view that currently prevails in the West. This view sees Muslims as incapable of internal "reform" and holds that any change "for the better" in the Muslim world has to be imposed from outside.

Since the time of its pioneering figures, Islamic reformist and modernist discourse in South Asia has evolved in an uneven fashion. In particular, in the last three decades, there has been a resurgence of non-reformist and even extremist trends in South Asia. Conditions that have led to this development in South Asia are similar to those in other Muslim countries, including the authoritarianism of most post-independence governments; the disappointing results of modernization policies, which have not mitigated socioeconomic disparities; the manipulation of religion by political leaders; regional and international developments; and the continuation of conflicts such as those over Kashmir and Palestine.

The Soviet-Afghan and intra-Afghan wars have been particularly important in

---

*Editor's Note: Among the religious leaders who advocated a strict observance of Islam and resistance to the British conquest was Shah Abdul Aziz (d. 1823). He declared India to be *dar al-harb* (a house of war, i.e., a land ruled by infidels). In response, Sayyid Ahmad Shahid (1786–1831) and Sayyid Ismail Shahid (1779–1831) launched a war of liberation and established an Islamic state that included part of present-day Pakistan's North-West Frontier, where *shari'a* was enforced as the law of the land. In the twentieth century, Abul Ala Mawdudi (1903–1979) developed the idea of the Islamic state and the Islamization of modernity.

strengthening extremist and militant tendencies in Pakistan. It is unlikely that these extremist tendencies, which are also found in the West and in other regions with non-Muslim populations, will be replaced with a culture of peace and moderation unless and until their underlying economic, political, sociocultural, and historical causes are adequately dealt with.

Yet despite the resurgence and strengthening of non-reformist trends, a number of Muslim scholars in South Asia have continued further to develop and advance reformist and modernist readings of Islam. The work of some of the most important of these contemporary scholars will be the focus of this chapter. The analysis of their works will be preceded by a discussion of the ideas of the three pioneers of Islamic modernist, reformist thought in India and Pakistan, namely, Sayyid Ahmad Khan, Muhammad Iqbal, and Fazlur Rahman. These authors are still relevant to reformist discourse in the entire Islamic world and they continue to inspire contemporary thinkers.

The thinkers discussed here have two salient characteristics. First, they all have struggled with issues of power and powerlessness, identity and assimilation, and modernity and traditionalism. Second, they have been determined to stimulate new thinking on contemporary issues and to demonstrate that Islam is a dynamic religion that calls for continuing intellectual review of both "normative" and "historical" Islam, in order to construct modern, enlightened, just, forward-looking, and life-affirming Muslim societies.

The Pioneers of Islamic Reformism and Modernism

Sir Sayyid Ahmad Khan and Muhammad Iqbal were products of post-Mughul India, ruled by Britain. Under British rule, Indian Muslims' social, economic, and political positions had been severely eroded. This reality had a profound impact on both thinkers' intellectual development.

Sir Sayyid, whose family had lost its privileged position following the demise of the Mughul Empire, had been greatly impressed by the Europeans' scientific, technological, economic, and educational achievements and their military and political successes. He wanted to show that Islam is compatible with scientific inquiry and hence capable of progress attained by Europe. He also correctly concluded that, without mastering modern sciences, Muslims would suffer further degradation.

The Sepoy Uprising, or the War of Independence as Indians call it, was a crucial event in the history of Indian Muslims and it deeply influenced the evolution of Sir Sayyid's thinking. Most important, it convinced him "that the best of Western civilization could and should be assimilated by the Muslims because the 'pure' Islam taught by the Qur'an and lived by the Prophet was not simply unopposed to Western civilization but was, in fact, its ultimate source and inspiration."[7]*

---

*Editor's note: This view is similar to Afghani's opinion that Muslims had passed their scientific spirit to the Europeans.

In contrast to Sir Sayyid, Muhammad Iqbal belonged to a generation that was exposed to modern education. Having studied in British-ruled India, England, and Germany, Iqbal took a more critical approach to Western ideas and institutions than did Sir Sayyid. Iqbal did not reject positive aspects of Western civilization, but he did not support their blind emulation by Muslims. Instead he wanted to create a new intellectual framework for a more authentic Islamic modernity and searched for ways to regenerate Muslims and their civilization on the basis of their own religious and cultural heritage. It is this aspect of Iqbal's thinking that makes his discourse so relevant to those contemporary Muslim thinkers who are trying to balance the requirements of modernization with those of cultural authenticity.

Sir Sayyid Ahmad Khan and Muslim Modernism:
Philosophy and Methodology

Sayyid Ahmad Khan was born in 1817. On his paternal side, his family were descendants of the Prophet. They had immigrated to India from Herat in the seventeenth century. His maternal ancestors were originally from Hamadan in Iran. His early education was purely traditional. Later in Delhi he studied medicine and Islamic disciplines, including Greco-Islamic philosophy, and he published many original works and translated others. However, it was his experiences during the period 1858–70, especially his greater exposure to the structures of British political culture, that completed his "change to modernity."[8]

An important aspect of Sir Sayyid's philosophy was his distinction between Islam as a divine religion, and Islam as lived by Muslims in different contexts throughout history and influenced by pre-existing cultures.* This underlying perspective led Sir Sayyid to argue, first, that reform requires the use of a scientific and historical methodology for reading and interpreting Islamic history and textual and other sources; and, second, that "the challenges of Western institutions could only be faced by remodelling Muslim interpretations of religion and history on the basis of modern science."[9]

Thus Sir Sayyid developed "a scientific methodology of historiography in his historical and religious works."[10] His *Essays on the Life of Muhammad* (1870), written to refute the errors that Sir Sayyid saw in Sir William Muir's polemical *Life of Mahomet* (1858), is regarded as "the starting point of modern Indian historiography of Islam."[11]

Reason had a pivotal role in Sir Sayyid's philosophy and methodology. His rationalist mindset was partly due to his interest in Mu'tazili thought. However, unlike the Mu'tazila, Sir Sayyid regarded reason not as a faculty of mind but as

---

*Editor's Note: As demonstrated in various chapters of this volume and especially the one dealing with Iran, the distinction between historical Islam and spiritual Islam is a common thread running through the reformist discourse in different parts of the Islamic world. In this regard, then, Sir Sayyid was a pioneer.

a human function that gets "perfected by use."[12] As he put it, "the error of one person is corrected by the reason of another and the error of an age by the future age."[13] Furthermore, he equated reason with understanding and considered it an acquired quality that enables human beings to distinguish between good and bad, right and wrong, proper and improper. According to Sir Sayyid, who used terms like understanding, reason, and intellect interchangeably, "the only criterion for a person having 'reason,' 'intellect,' or 'understanding,' is behavioural rather than substantive."[14]

In keeping with his rationalist mindset, Sir Sayyid stressed the importance of *ijtihad* and a rational interpretation of the sources of Islamic religious thought. He considered this necessary because he believed that unless Islam was presented in a rational way it would not be understood or accepted by modern Muslims. He also stressed the importance of relying on the Qur'an and sifting the false *hadith* from the reliable ones. He tried to remove "the corrosive elements" and accretions that he believed were seriously detrimental to Islam in his day.[15]

Sir Sayyid believed in the compatibility of religion and science, and he considered natural law and divine law to be the same, because he believed that there could not be disagreement between the word and the work of God. If there was an apparent contradiction between a scientific fact and a religious rule, then the latter had to be reinterpreted according to scientific evidence. Applying his naturalistic rationalism in his exegesis of the Qur'an, Sir Sayyid arrived at fifty-two points of divergence from traditionally accepted Sunni Islam.[16] On the basis of his research, Sir Sayyid came to the conclusion that, "if we keep in view the principles deducible from the Qur'an itself, we shall find that there is no contradiction between the modern sciences, on the one hand, and the Qur'an and Islam, on the other."[17]

Sir Sayyid considered it absurd to believe that God's prophets appeared only in Arabia and Palestine and that other peoples were denied knowledge of the divine. A genuine believer in religious pluralism, he upheld that it was possible for the followers of any prophet from anywhere to achieve their religious goals. In the context of two of the world's largest religions—Christianity and Islam—Sir Sayyid stressed the need to demythologize both religions so that they could be understood rationally and seen as being closely related to each other. He sought through writings and through action to convince both Christians and Muslims that their faiths required them to be friends and allies. Sir Sayyid may be considered a pioneer of what our age calls "interfaith dialogue." Like the more liberal contemporary reformist thinkers, he worked for greater understanding and goodwill among Muslim sects and between Muslims and non-Muslims.

Sir Sayyid had relatively progressive views on women's rights and deplored the fact that the Muslim *umma* had not had the political will to implement women's God-given rights. He opposed veiling but did not actively challenge it. Sir Sayyid recognized that the education of girls was a precondition for the development of Muslim society as a whole, but he was also aware of the sociocultural context in which he lived. He noted that "no satisfactory education can be provided for Muslim girls as long as most of the boys do not receive proper education. . . . enlightened fathers, brothers, and husbands will naturally be most anxious to educate their female relations."[18]

Given his admiration for British political institutions, it is reasonable to conclude that Sir Sayyid viewed democracy favorably, although his understanding of democracy, like that of Britain of the nineteenth century, was elitist.

Some South Asian scholars have questioned Sir Sayyid's intellectual prowess as an Islamic thinker, noting contradictions in his philosophy. For example, Fazlur Rahman believed that Sir Sayyid "was not a keen religious thinker, nor perhaps primarily and deeply religious," but "was led by the inner logic of the Muslim intellectual history to justify his cultural progressive attitude theologically."[19] Rahman considers the result of Sir Sayyid's theological work as "chiefly negative: he produced an Islam that was not against modern scientific progress," and states that, toward the end of his life, Sir Sayyid "was himself disappointed in the first crops that grew at 'Aligarh' (the Muslim university that he founded in 1857). These were gentlemen who wore Western dress, spoke English, prided themselves on a smattering of modern ideas but were either a-religious or anti-religious."[20]

Nevertheless, Sir Sayyid's efforts to liberalize Islamic law have been regarded as a "dynamic and constructive" achievement that made "a tremendous impression" on modern Islam, particularly Indian Islam.[21] Iqbal attributed his "real greatness" to the fact that "he was the first modern Muslim to catch a glimpse of the positive character of the age which was coming, and who felt the need for a fresh orientation of Islam and worked for it. We may differ from his religious views, but there can be no denying that his sensitive soul was the first to react to the modern age."[22]

Sir Sayyid's Disciples

In addition to his own contributions, Sir Sayyid inspired others to adopt a reformist approach to the reading and interpretation of Islam. Three of his associates—Mulawi Chiarq Ali, Mahdi Ali Khan (known as Muhsin al-Mulk), and Sayyid Mumtaz Ali—are especially worth noting.

Mulawi Chriaq Ali: Advancing Sir Sayyid's Reformist Agenda

Mulawi Chiraq Ali (1844–1895) took an even more critical approach than did Sir Sayyid to the interpretation of the principal sources of Islamic law—with the exception of the Qur'an. He was particularly reluctant to accept *hadith* as a reliable source, mainly because *hadith* generally convey the sense of the Prophet's sayings, but not his exact words; and because of the unreliability of the *isnad* (the chain of transmitters) of a *hadith*. Consequently, he dismissed all *hadith* whose content appear unsuited to current conditions. He also refused to accept the consensus (*ijma*) of the Muslim *ulema* because *ijma* is never complete and is rejected by some theologians and jurists at various epochs.[23]

Like many contemporary Muslim reformist thinkers, Mulawi Chiraq Ali distinguished between spiritual Islam and historical Islam, or between Islam as a religion and Islam as a social system. In his view, Islam as a religion and spiritual system reflected progress and has "the vital principle of rapid development, of rationalism and adaptability."[24] He further argued that "the Prophet did not compile a code of law; nor did he enjoin the Muslims to do so. He left it to them in general to frame any code of civil or canon law and to found systems which would harmonize with the times and suit the political and social changes."[25]

Mulawi Chiraq Ali maintained that most of Islamic law, especially as related to personal status and such practices as slavery, "should be viewed in the historical context of pagan Arab practices of that time" (the time of prophecy). He added that the Qur'an actually tried to moderate and eventually eliminate negative aspects of such practices, notably those related to women.[26] In short, like his mentor, Mulawi Chiraq Ali advocated a rationalist, dynamic, and humanist understanding of Islam, and at times adopted an even more progressive position than did his mentor.

Mahdi Ali Khan (Muhsin al-Mulk): A More Cautious Reformism

Mahdi Ali Khan (1837–1907) basically accepted Sir Sayyid's philosophy and methodology and moved from imitation to interpretation—from *taqlid* to *ijtihad*. He does not reject *hadith* outright, but advocated great caution in its use as a source of law. Nor did he reject *ijma* (consensus of the *ulema*), but again he stressed that both *hadith* and *ijma* should be reviewed in light of modern sciences and ethics.

He departed from Sir Sayyid's advocacy of natural theology, arguing that the laws of nature were constantly being reinterpreted by scientists. In his view, the Qur'an's references to extranatural agencies such as angels and miracles in allegorical terms, indicated that it was possible to regard them as exceptions to natural laws. He held that it was God's laws as revealed to the Prophet that were immutable rather than the laws of nature and society. His position is seen by some as a corrective to Sir Sayyid's natural theology.[27]

Sayyid Mumtaz Ali: Defender of Women's Rights

Sayyid Mumtaz Ali (1860–1937) was the author of *Huquq-e-niswan* (The Rights of Women) and the co-founder (with his wife) of a journal titled *Tahzib al niswan* (The Manners and Etiquette of Women). Along with the Egyptian Qasim Amin (1863–1905), he may be considered one of the earliest defenders of women's equality with men in any Muslim country or society.[28]

In his book, Sayyid Mumtaz Ali stated all the traditional arguments used to "prove" women's inferiority to men, and then refuted all of them by using a modern exegetical approach based on reason. He was a strong advocate of women's education and rejected such practices as *purda* (segregation and veiling), polygamy, and forced marriages, which he considered to be unjust and injurious to women.[29]

Muhammad Iqbal: Reconstruction of Islamic Thought

The poet-philosopher, lawyer, political activist, and social reformer Muhammad Iqbal was born in November 1877 at Sialkot, in the Punjab. In childhood, he was deeply influenced by his teacher Maulana Mir Hasan, a renowned scholar of Arabic and Persian, and later by Sir Thomas W. Arnold, whom he met at the Government College in Lahore. Iqbal obtained a master's degree in Arabic in 1890 and proceeded to Cambridge University in England where he studied philosophy under J.E. McTaggart. He graduated from Cambridge in 1907 and was called to the Bar in 1908. The same year he was awarded the Ph.D. for his thesis on *The Development of Metaphysics in Persia* by the University of Munich, Germany.

Iqbal returned to Lahore in 1908 and took up legal practice. Later, he became involved in politics. However, his involvement in politics remained secondary to his other interests. Between 1915 and 1938, twelve volumes of his poetry—seven in Persian and five in Urdu—and his famous lectures on *The Reconstruction of Religious Thought in Islam* were published, making Iqbal the most important poet-philosopher of his time, not only in India but in the world.

Iqbal's Religious Philosophy: The Self and the Purpose of Life

Iqbal's philosophy of *khudi*, or self, built on his conviction that the fundamental fact of human life is the absolute, irrefutable consciousness of one's own being. For Iqbal, humanity's advent on earth is a great and glorious event, not one that signifies human sinfulness and degradation. To him the purpose of the cosmos is to serve as the basis and ground for the emergence and perfection of the self. He rejected the idea that humanity's evolution has come to an end. Iqbal believed ardently that human beings are the makers of their own destiny and that the key to destiny lies in one's character.[30] In his view, art, religion, and ethics must be judged from the standpoint of the self. That which strengthens the self is good and that which weakens it is bad.

E.M. Forster wrote of Iqbal that he believed in the self as a "fighting unit."[31] Although humanity is the pivot around which Iqbal's philosophy revolves, as pointed out by A.M. Schimmel, Iqbal's "revaluation of Man is not that of *Man qua Man*, but of Man in relation to God."[32] Iqbal saw his concept of the ideal person realized in the Prophet of Islam whose life exemplifies all the principles dearest to his heart. The most important teaching of Iqbal's religious philosophy is that a true seeker of God seeks not the annihilation but rather a more precise definition of one's own personality. Iqbal's ideal person does not retreat from the world but regards it as the training ground for spiritual development. Despite his attacks on what he called "degenerate Sufism," Iqbal belonged, as A.J. Arberry has stated, "to the history of Sufism, to which he made both scientific and practical contributions."[33] Iqbal did not deny his indebtedness to "higher Sufism," which did so much to check hypocrisy and artifice in religion. In a letter to Professor Nicholson, he stated that his philosophy of *khudi* "is a direct development out of the experience and speculation of old Muslim Sufis and thinkers."[34] Eager as he was to purge Islam of all alien obscurantist elements, in formulating his own philosophy "not only did he turn back to Rumi and the medieval mystics to discover antecedents within Islam for the system for which he sought acceptance, but he casts his thoughts in the mould of Sufi allegory that has been sanctified by centuries of Persian poetry."[35]

Iqbal's Epistemology

Following the Qur'an, Iqbal maintained that there are two sources of knowledge, the inner consciousness of human beings (*anfus*) and the outer world of nature (*afaq*). He mentioned the study of history, described by the Qur'an as "the days of God," as a source of knowledge. Equating scientific knowledge with *'aql* (reason) and mystic knowledge with *ishq* (love), Iqbal believed that without love, reason becomes demonic.

In Iqbal's view, nature does not confront God in the same way as it confronts humanity, since it is a phase of God's consciousness. God is immanent since God comprehends the whole universe, but also transcendent since God is not identical with the created world. All life is individual. There is a gradually rising scale of egohood running from the almost-inert to God who is the Ultimate Ego. God is not immobile, nor is the universe a fixed product. God is constantly creative and dynamic, and the process of creation still goes on. The Qur'anic saying "Toward God is your limit" (Sura 53: *al-Najm:* 42) gave Iqbal an infinite worldview and he applied it to every aspect of the life of humankind and the universe.

Iqbal and the "Reconstruction" of Religious Thought in Islam

Though much has been written by Muslims for Muslims in the modern period, according to H.A.R. Gibb "one looks in vain for any systematic analysis of new currents of thought in the Muslim world," since almost all the books written in English or French fall in the category of apologetics seeking either to defend Islam or to show its conformity to contemporary thinking.[36] In Gibb's judgment, the "outstanding exception is the Indian scholar and poet, Sir Muhammad Iqbal, who in his six lectures on *The Reconstruction of Religious Thought in Islam* faces outright the question of reformulating the basic ideas of Muslim theology"[37] and demands "a fresh examination of the fundamentals of Islamic belief."[38]

Gibb describes Iqbal's lectures as "the first (and so far the only) thoroughgoing attempt to state the theology of Islam in modern immanentist terms."[39] He also perceived that the theology Iqbal was aiming to reconstruct was not the orthodox theology of Islam but the Sufi theology.[40]

In the view of W.C. Smith, theologically Iqbal "wrought the most important and the most necessary revolution of modern times"[41] by making God not merely transcendent but also immanent. He states: "The revolution of immanence lies in this, that it puts God back into the world. Iqbal's God is in the world, now, with us, facing our problems from within, creating a new and better world with us and through us. Religion is life. And life, this mundane material life, is religious. The present world, of matter, time and space is good. . . . God himself, and all the values, rewards, ideals, and objectives of religion become transferred to the empirical world. Correspondingly, the will of God is not something imposed from without to be accepted resignedly, but surges within (and) is to be absorbed and acted upon."[42]

For Iqbal, the reform of Islamic law is an integral part of the "reconstruction" of religious thought in Islam. According to Islam, the basis of all life is spiritual and eternal, and so in Iqbal's view a society based on this perspective was required to reconcile the categories of permanence and change.[43] While permanent principles are needed to give society "a foothold in the world of perpetual change," they must not be understood "to exclude all possibilities of change which according to the Qur'an is one of the greatest 'signs' of God."[44]

What is eternal and what is changeable is exemplified for Iqbal in the life of the Prophet of Islam, who "seems to stand between the ancient and the modern world. Insofar as the source of his revelation is concerned he belongs to the ancient world; insofar as the spirit of his revelation is concerned he belongs to the modern world. In him life discovers other sources of knowledge suitable to its new direction. The birth of Islam . . . is the birth of the inductive intellect."[45]

In Iqbal's judgment, one of the major reasons for the decline of Muslims in the past many centuries was their inability or unwillingness to subject the legal system of Islam to intellectual scrutiny, particularly with reference to *ijtihad*, which is one of the acknowledged sources of Islamic law. Iqbal refers to *ijtihad*—which "literally means to exert"—as "the principle of movement in the structure of Islam"[46] Seeking "the re-valuation and recodification of the Islamic Fiqh,"[47] he stressed the critical need for *ijtihad* by contemporary Muslims. Iqbal pointed out that the Muslim *ulema* wanted to exclude innovations in classical Islamic law in order to have a uniform social life, forgetting that in an over-organized society, individuals—on whom the fate of the community ultimately rests—are altogether crushed.[48]

Challenging the notion that the gates of *ijtihad* were closed, he asked: "Did the founders of our schools ever claim finality for their reasoning and interpretations?" and answered this question with an emphatic "Never!"[49] His oft-quoted concluding statement reads:

> The claim of the present generation of Muslim liberals to reinterpret the foundational legal principles in the light of their own experience and altered conditions of modern life is, in my opinion, perfectly justified. The teaching of the Qur'an that life is a process of progressive creation necessitates that each generation, guided but unhampered by the work of its predecessors, should be permitted to solve its own problems.[50]

While both Sayyid Ahmad Khan and Iqbal were strong advocates of *ijtihad*, their perceptions of *ijma* were very different. The former regarded it as "the exclusive privilege" of the *ulema* and rejected it categorically.[51] However, Iqbal regarded *ijma* as "perhaps the most important legal notion in Islam,"[52] through which the dormant spirit of life in the Islamic system can be galvanized. In his opinion, in modern times, *ijma* is only possible when the power of *ijtihad* is transferred from individual representatives of schools to a Muslim legislative assembly where diverse persons with insight can give their input.[53]

Iqbal's Views on Democracy

Iqbal was critical of some aspects of democracy, particularly Western democracy, which he saw to be a cover for many corrupt practices. The assumption that Iqbal did not believe in democracy rests largely on a verse he wrote in which he said, "democracy is that form of government in which persons are counted, not weighed."[54] However, he did not reject democracy but was keen to reform it so that it would establish a just social order approximating the concept of the "Kingdom of God on Earth."[55]

Iqbal criticized Nietzsche's belief in "an Aristocracy of Supermen." He argued: "Out of the plebeian material Islam has formed a man of the noblest type of life and power. Is not, then the Democracy of early Islam an experimental refutation of the ideas of Nietzsche?"[56] In an essay on "Islam as a Moral and Political Ideal," Iqbal said clearly, "Democracy . . . is the most important aspect of Islam regarded as a political ideal," and added that "there is no aristocracy in Islam."[57]

Iqbal's Views on Women

In Iqbal's view a woman's most important role was that of a mother, and he likened Motherhood to Prophethood.[58] He considered it crucial for the moral health and development of a Muslim society that its women remain "pure" and expend their energy on being "good" wives and mothers. He was highly critical of the Western woman, whom he pictured as childless[59] and unwomanly due to her education.[60]

Sir Sayyid had opposed *purda* (segregation and veiling), even though he considered it politically inadvisable to become a passionate advocate for the rights of Muslim women. Iqbal supported *purda*, even though he was critical of the Indian Muslim custom of child marriage and polygamy[61] and strongly urged Muslim women to fight for the enforcement of the rights given to them by Islam—for example, the right of inheritance. While he did not want to address "imaginary problems,"[62] he was probably the first to notice the difficulties created for women who sought a divorce under the Hanafi law being practiced in India, and he encouraged Muslims to reflect on this issue.[63] Urging Indian judges to move with the times, he proposed "a lucid methodology" for resolving such "real" problems.[64]

As early as 1904, Iqbal wrote that "The most sensitive issue in the reformation of social life is the rights of women,"[65] but he was well aware of the gap between Islamic theory and Muslim practice. His own views regarding the role of women in society remained culturally conservative. This is disappointing, considering the fact that he was "the most daring intellectual modernist the Muslim world has produced."[66] However, Iqbal's philosophy of the self, grounded as it is in the egalitarian and justice-centered vision of the Qur'an, remains a source of inspiration and empowerment not only to Muslim men but also to Muslim women.

Fazlur Rahman: Pakistan's Influential Reformist Thinker

Fazlur Rahman was one of the most important and influential Muslim reformist thinkers of the second half of the twentieth century. He was born in 1919 in the Hazara district of present-day Pakistan. He studied traditional Islamic sciences under his father, Maulana Shihab al-Din, a scholar of Islamic law, and pursued secular studies at Punjab University and at Oxford. He taught at the University of Durham and at McGill University, served as adviser to President Ayub Khan (1961–68), and directed the Islamic Research Institute. In 1968, a controversy was triggered by the publication in the Institute's research journal *Fikr-o-nazar* (Thought and View) of an Urdu translation of a part of Fazlur Rahman's book *Islam*. Under pressure from a countrywide protest launched by conservative *ulema*, Rahman was forced to leave the country. From 1969 to 1988 he taught at the University of Chicago, where he became the Harold H. Swift Distinguished Service Professor. He died in 1988.

Fazlur Rahman's Philosophy and Methodology

In Rahman's view, "the basic questions of method and hermeneutics were not squarely addressed by Muslims,"[67] although the medieval systems of Islamic law "worked fairly successfully." This was largely due to the realism of earlier Muslims, who took materials from the customs and institutions of conquered lands and modified them where necessary in the light of Qur'anic teaching, with which they were integrated. But attempts to deduce laws in abstraction from the Qur'an—as in the area of penal law, *hudud*—proved to be unsatisfactory. This was because analogical reasoning (*qiyas*), the instrument for deriving law, "was not perfected to the requisite degree."[68] Due to a failure to understand the underlying unity of the Qur'an, and the use of an "atomistic" approach that focused on isolated verses, "laws were often derived from verses that were not at all legal in intent."[69]

Rahman's approach to the Qur'an is holistic and historicist. He argues that the Qur'anic perspective, which stresses the ideas of "a unique God" to whom all humans are accountable and the eradication of socioeconomic justice, is different from the existing realities of the Prophet's time.[70] The Qur'an was a response to these realities, and for the most part gave moral and social directives for dealing with specific problems that arose in concrete historical situations.[71] To substantiate his view, Rahman pointed out that in many cases the Qur'anic verse not only gives an answer to a specific problem, but also provides the reason for that particular answer.

Emphasizing the importance of "context" in understanding the real intent of the Qur'an and even *hadith*, Rahman observed that the Prophet's biographers, the collectors of the *hadith*, and those who wrote commentaries on the Qur'an would not have preserved "the general social-historical background of the Qur'an and the Prophet's activity and, in particular, the background (*shu'un al-nuzul*) of the particular passages, if they had not strongly believed that this background was necessary for understanding the Qur'an."[72]

Based on this contextualist perspective, Rahman proposed a process of interpretation that consists of "a double movement" from the present times to Qur'anic times, then back to the present situation. The first of the two movements consists of two steps:

1. Understanding the meaning of the Qur'an as a whole as well as in terms of the specific tenets that constitute specific responses to specific situations.[73]
2. Generalizing those specific answers and enunciating them as statements of general moral-social objectives that can be "distilled" from specific texts in light of the sociohistorical background.[74]

The second movement takes one from the general principles of the Qur'an to the specific concrete sociohistorical context in which the former have to be applied.[75] Rahman believed that if the two movements are achieved successfully, "the Qur'an's imperatives will become alive and effective once again."[76]

Rahman characterized the intellectual element in both movements as *ijtihad*, which he defined as "the effort to understand the meaning of a relevant text or precedent in the past containing a rule, and to alter that rule by extending, restricting or otherwise modifying it in such a manner that a new situation can be subsumed under it by a new solution."[77] In many respects, Rahman's theory is not fundamentally different from the modernist, reformist ideas of Muslim thinkers of the past, notably Sir Sayyid Ahmad Khan and Muhammad Iqbal, who urged Muslims to "go back to the Qur'an," and "go forward with *ijtihad*." However, equipped with new analytical tools, Rahman was able to develop these ideas into a theory articulated in contemporary terms.

Fazlur Rahman's Views on Revelation

Rahman presented his perspectives on revelation in his book *Islam,* first published in London in 1966. When the Urdu translation was published in 1968, it created great turmoil in Pakistan. Recounting these events, Rahman said in an essay (1976):

> As I feared, the most crucial issue for controversy was about the nature of the Qur'an as Revealed Book. I defended the idea of the verbal revelation of the Qur'an, which is the universal Islamic belief. However, it seemed to me that the standard orthodox accounts of revelation give a mechanical and externalistic picture of the relationship between Muhammad and the Qur'an—Gabriel coming and delivering God's messages to him almost like a postman delivering letters.

The Qur'an itself says that the Angel "comes down to the heart of Muhammad. I stated that the Qur'an is entirely the Word of God insofar as it is infallible and absolutely free from falsehood, but, insofar as it comes to the Prophet's heart and then at his tongue, it was entirely his word."[78]

Rahman wanted to affirm both the external and internal aspects of revelation, as had been done by earlier thinkers including al-Ghazali, Shah Wali Ullah, and Iqbal, although "none of them had stated the position in such a clear-cut and blunt manner."[79] However, the Urdu translation of his view of revelation made it appear as if he was stating that the Qur'an was the joint work of God and Muhammad. Rahman tried to clarify his position, but the campaign launched against him by the conservative religious groups, particularly the Jama'at-e-Islami, became so intense that it intimidated the government. Rahman had to resign his position and leave the country. It appears that the conservatives took this opportunity to punish Rahman for his other reformist views on family law and on interest, which he defined as being different from usury (*riba*) and therefore not un-Islamic.

Fazlur Rahman's Views on Democracy

Rahman referred to the case of the first Caliph, Abu Bakr, who was chosen by the elders from both the Meccan immigrants and the Medinese Ansar and endorsed by the entire community,[80] and acknowledged that he had received his mandate from the people who asked him to implement the Qur'an and the *sunna*.[81] In Rahman's opinion, this "clearly establishes that the Islamic State derives its sanction from the Islamic community and that, therefore, it is completely democratic," but democracy can take various forms and be direct indirect, depending on the prevalent social conditions.[82]

Rahman accepted the notion that, given Islam's underlying egalitarian ethos, governments must be based on popular will through some form of representation and does not think that it is un-Islamic to adopt modern democratic institutions.[83] However, drawing attention to the fact that the vast masses of Muslims are illiterate, he pointed out that it is not "easy to implement democracy under such circumstances."[84] Further, in view of the desire and need for rapid economic development, a common problem "in the under-developed countries, including all the Muslim countries,"[85] a strong government capable of a high degree of centralized planning and control of economic development is needed.[86] Therefore, Rahman saw "no harm" in having "strong men" at the helm of affairs in underdeveloped countries, "provided that, at the same time, the spirit of democracy is genuinely and gradually cultivated among the people."[87]

Fazlur Rahman's Views on Women's Rights

In Rahman's view, the Qur'an recognized the full personhood of a woman and improved her status greatly in numerous ways. He pointed out that "the most important legal enactments and general reform pronouncements of the Qur'an have been on the subjects of women and slavery."[88] To substantiate this point, Rahman referred to several issues that are the subject of much Qur'anic concern and many prescriptions. These include: female infanticide, treatment of daughters, equality of men and women, conjugal relations, a wife's right to sexual satisfaction, family planning, gender segregation, divorce, polygamy, inheritance, and women as witnesses.

Rahman's views regarding women were more progressive than those of most Muslim exegetes. For example, in the context of women's testimony he observes: "to say that no matter how much women may develop intellectually, their evidence must on principle carry less value than that of a man is an affront to the Qur'an's purposes of social evolution."[89]

Rahman was also the architect of Pakistan's Muslim Family Laws Ordinance (1961). This law laid down a procedure for and restrictions upon the contracting of polygamous marriages and a procedure for divorce. Although from today's perspective these reforms appear modest, the Ordinance to this day is denounced by the conservatives. However, despite his progressive views on many issues related to women and his emphasis on social evolution as a basis for changing certain laws that discriminate against women, Rahman's exegesis on women's rights often indicated a patriarchal mindset.

Muhammad Khalid Masud: Keeper of the Reformist Tradition

Muhammad Khalid Masud was born on April 15, 1939, at Ambala, East Punjab, and migrated with his family to Pakistan in 1947. Because of various family-related matters, including financial problems, he began his formal education only in 1950. Nevertheless, he succeeded in joining Punjab University in Lahore and later studied at McGill University, where he obtained an M.A. (1969) and a Ph.D. in Islamic Studies (1973).

Masud was affiliated with the Islamic Research Institute from 1963 to 1999, and he taught in France (1977), Nigeria (1980–84), and Malaysia (2003). From 1999 to 2003, he was academic director at the International Institute for the Study of Islam in the Modern World in Leiden. In June 2004 he was appointed chairman of the Council of Islamic Ideology (CII) which advises the Pakistani government on matters relating to Islam.

Masud has had an enduring interest in methodology and the impact of social change on Islamic law. In his master's dissertation he examined the *fatwa* dealing with legal problems for which there is no legal precedent and that could not be resolved within the framework of classical Islamic law. This led him to the works of the Malikite jurist Abu Ishaq al-Shatibi (d. 1388), who adopted the concept of *maslaha* as an independent principle: a method of inductive reasoning that takes into consideration the entirety of Qur'anic verses and *hadith*. According to Shatibi, something is lawful if it is supported by textual evidence and social practice. In this framework of thinking, change is allowed in customs (*'adat*) but not in what is obligatory (*'ibadat*).

Khalid Masud's Philosophy and Methodology

In many respects, notably in its emphasis on context, Masud's methodology is similar to that of Fazlur Rahman. Masud also stresses the importance of linguistic analysis, requiring a thorough understanding of the Arabic of the time of revelation, and a holistic rather than piecemeal approach to the study of the Qur'an. He views the Qur'an and the *hadith* as basic Islamic texts. He does not consider the Qur'an a book of laws but acknowledges its normative character.

In Masud's view, *hadith* need to be recompiled in chronological order. To him, the main methodological problem involved in basing legal reasoning on *hadith* is that there is a large number of inauthentic *hadith*. Moreover, the way a *hadith* is reported in various collections, with fragmentation of "an event or the text of a *hadith* into several reports," its spread "into different chapters," and their repetition "obscures the unity as well as the historicity of the texts of a hadith"[90] and reduces its value as a basis for legal reasoning. He adds that for the *hadith* to be a credible basis for scientific reasoning it is necessary to collect all relevant *hadith* on a particular issue and place them in their historical context.

Khalid Masud's View on Democracy

Masud's view on democracy can be found in his article "Defining Democracy in Islamic Polity."[91] After examining various views on the compatibility of Islam and democracy, he says that the real problem in this context is that, while most scholars speak about the participation of the people in the process of governance and some even ascribe sovereignty to the people, there is mistrust of common people. They are seen as incapable of governing themselves, although they may elect representatives from among the elite, wealthy, or learned, who then govern. Masud sees this mistrust not only in Muslim thinkers but also in Western supporters of democracy.[92] But this is especially true in regard to Muslims, at least according to some scholars He notes, for example, that according to Martin Kramer, "Muslims cannot be democrats unless they give up Islam." He concludes that the real issue in defining democracy is the place and value assigned to the common person as an individual—something not yet fully developed in the present political systems.[93]

Khalid Masud's Views on Pluralism in Islam

In Masud's words, "Pluralism is a part of the project of modernity that favors the freedom of the individual. Pluralism does not stress multiplicity per se as much as it is concerned with questioning the traditional monopoly of certain persons, groups, or institutions on prescribing ethical values authoritatively."[94] Masud maintains that Islam favors pluralism on two grounds: first, because it appeals to human reason, and the Qur'an attaches "pivotal importance to individual choice and responsibility"; and, second, the social acceptance of Islamic values as understood by different communities. This basis also "regulates the permissible scope of dissent from what are widely accepted social norms." Finally, he points out that early in its history Islam developed several approaches to moral issues and was never monolithic.[95]

Khalid Masud and Review of the Hudud Ordinances (1979)

Masud emphasizes the importance of reforming *fiqh*, especially in regard to women and the penal code, as evidenced by his writings on ethics, human rights, *shari'a*, and society. Since his appointment as chairman of Council of Islamic Ideology (CII), he has faced his toughest challenge as a modernist, reformist scholar, and a social-change advocate. Under his leadership, the CII has taken a strong stand against some laws contained in the Hudud Ordinances promulgated by President Zia ul Haq in 1979, holding that they are contrary to the Qur'an and *sunna* and have been used to victimize women.

Masud wrote the Summary of the CII's Interim Report on the Hudud Ordinances presented to the Pakistani government on June 27, 2006. It concludes by stating:

> The Hudud Ordinance does not conform fully to the Qur'an and Hadith. Partial amendments to this Ordinance cannot bring it to accord with the letter and spirit of the Qur'an and Sunna. A thorough revision of the Hudud Ordinance is necessary in order to make it more responsive to the philosophy of crime and punishment in the Qur'an and Sunna as well as more effective in a modern judicial system.

In light of the government's alliance with a religiously conservative grouping, the Muttahida Majlis-e-'Amal (MMA),* which is opposed to any review of the Hudud Ordinance, Masud was not hopeful that his or the CII's efforts would soon succeed in securing any significant changes. However, he continues to struggle.

Riffat Hassan: Theology of Women in the Islamic Tradition

An important development in the context of Islamic reformist discourse has been the emergence of Muslim female scholars who have tried to promote women's rights by providing a correct and dynamic interpretation of Islamic texts and laws. In Pakistan, this author has been part of this pioneering effort and an activist for Muslim women's rights.

---

*Editor's Note: The change in the makeup of Pakistan's parliament and government following the February 2008 elections ended this alliance. Nevertheless, conservative elements are still influential in politics and society.

Despite the existence of prominent women in early Islam, the Islamic tradition has largely remained rigidly patriarchal. Islamic sources underlying this tradition— the Qur'an, the *sunna, hadith,* and *fiqh*—have been interpreted almost exclusively by Muslim men, who have defined the ontological, theological, sociological, and eschatological status of Muslim women. Spurred by this male-dominated tradition on women and the promulgation of anti-women laws in 1983–84 by the government of General Muhammad Zia-ul-Haq under the cover of Islamization, this author became interested in studying the women-related Qur'anic texts from a non-patriarchal perspective.

The conclusion was that, if read without patriarchal bias, the Qur'an does not discriminate against women and is particularly concerned about safeguarding their rights. The analysis began with an examination of the theological ground in which all anti-women arguments are rooted and led to the identification of three theological assumptions on which men's alleged superiority to women rests, not only in the Islamic, but also in the Jewish and Christian traditions, namely:

1. God's primary creation is man, since woman is believed to have been created from man's rib, hence is derivative and secondary ontologically;
2. Woman was the primary agent of man's "Fall," or expulsion from the Garden of Eden, hence all "daughters of Eve" are to be regarded with hatred, suspicion, and contempt;
3. Woman was created not only from man but also for man, which makes her existence merely instrumental and not of fundamental importance.

Of these three questions, the first one pertaining to the issue of woman's creation is the most important one. If man and woman have been created equal by God, who is the ultimate arbiter of value, then they cannot become unequal, essentially, at a subsequent time. On the other hand, if man and woman have been created unequal by God, then they cannot become equal, essentially, at a subsequent time.

The idea that woman was created from man's rib comes from Genesis 2:18–24. It is totally absent from the thirty Qur'anic passages in which reference is made to the creation of humanity inclusive of women and men. However, the story of Eve's creation from Adam's rib became part of the *hadith* literature, including *Sahih al-Bukhari* and *Sahih Muslim,* the two most influential *hadith* collections in Sunni Islam. Theoretically, any *hadith* that conflicts with the Qur'an must be rejected—but this has not happened in the case of *hadith* collections that include the "rib" story, clearly contradicting Qur'anic teaching about creation.

Riffat Hassan's Methodology for Interpreting Islamic Texts

In developing "feminist theology" in the context of the Islamic tradition, the author did not find any ready-made hermeneutical model and developed her own methodology consisting of the following principles:

1. *Linguistic accuracy,* namely knowing the meaning of words, especially key terms, as understood at the time of the Prophet in Hijaz.
2. *Historical context,* namely knowing the larger social and historical background used by the Qur'an, as advocated by Fazlur Rahman and others.
3. *Philosophical consistency.* This is connected to the Muslim belief that the Qur'an is internally consistent. This means that "in investigating a specific topic the interpreter must take into account all instances where that topic is addressed in the text. Similarly, in attempts to understand a particular word, all instances where the word is used in the Qur'an must be considered."[96]
4. *Ethical criterion.* This means that "the Qur'an must be interpreted in the light of God's intentions found in the Qur'an itself."[97] God's categorical self-statement in the Qur'an: "I do absolutely no wrong [literally: I am not a *zallam*—an emphatic form of *zalim*] to My servants!" (Sura 50: *Qaf:* 28)[98]

This means that God can never be guilty of *zulm* (tyranny, oppression, injustice, wrongdoing). Since the Qur'an is God's word, it must reflect God's justice and "any specific passage in the text that seemingly condones 'injustice' has to be reinterpreted in a way that is consistent with this basic notion of divine 'justice.'"[99]

Javed Ahmad Ghamidi: A Contemporary Reformist Thinker in Pakistan

Javed Ahmed Ghamidi was born on April 18, 1951, in Jeevan Shah village, near Sahiwal, a Punjab city. From a young age he studied traditional Islamic disciplines. In 1972, he achieved B.A. Honors in English literature from Government College University, Lahore. From 1973 to 1995 he was a pupil of Amin Ahsan Islahi (1904–1997), a noted Islamic scholar and exegete of the Qur'an who himself had been a student of Hamiduddin Farahi (1863–1930).

Islahi was one of the founding members of the Jama'at-e-Islami, a religious party organized in 1941 by Sayyid Abul Ala Mawdudi (1903–1979), considered by many to be a founding father of the global Islamic revivalist movement. Islahi parted from him after seventeen years, following a difference of opinion on the nature of the party's constitution. Ghamidi also worked closely with Maududi for about nine years before expressing his first differences of opinion, which led to his subsequent expulsion from the party in 1977. For Maududi, the establishment of an Islamic world order was the basic obligation of Islam; for Ghamidi, it is servitude to God.

Ghamidi is the founder-president of the Al-Mawrid Institute of Islamic Sciences. The Institute aims to continue the intellectual process initiated by Muslim scholars of the past because the element of human error can never be eliminated. In 1993, he fulfilled one of his greatest aspirations and founded a modern *madrasa* the Mus'ab School System. The system is made up of a chain of schools spread throughout the country. The schools' objective is to produce students highly qualified in modern disciplines but also knowledgeable about what is best in their religion and culture.

Ghamidi is the chief editor of two monthly journals and has numerous publications. Since 1970 he has been delivering weekly lectures on the Qur'anic text in different venues. He gives lectures on aspects of Islam and is a popular speaker in programs arranged by television channels and local institutions.

Appointed a member of the Council of Islamic Ideology (CII), headed by Dr. Muhammad Khalid Masud, Ghamidi resigned on September 21, 2006, when the government formed a separate Ulema Committee to review the bill regarding women's rights. He said that this was a breach of the CII's jurisdiction. Furthermore, in his view, the amendments in the bill proposed by the Ulema Committee were against Islamic injunctions. Ghamidi's resignation was not accepted by President Musharraf, and he continues to be an active member of the CII.

Javed Ahmad Ghamidi's Approach to Interpreting Islamic Texts

Ghamidi developed his approach to interpreting Islamic texts (which he limits to the Qur'an and *sunna*) under the tutelage of his teacher Islahi, who based his exegesis on his teacher Farahi's thesis that the Qur'an has structural and thematic unity. Ghamidi distinguishes between the content of the Qur'an and its interpretation. While the former is immutable, the latter is always subject to critique and analysis.

In his view, the Qur'an, compiled and arranged by the Prophet under divine guidance, possesses *nazm* (coherence) at both the structural and the thematic level.[100] Similarly, each *sura* of the Qur'an is a complete unit in itself with its own structural, thematic, and linguistic features. In Ghamidi's hermeneutics, understanding this *nazm* has a direct bearing on interpretation, and primary importance is placed on *tafsir al-qur'an bi'l qur'an* (exegesis of the Qur'an through the Qur'an). These include *naza'ir* (clues) from parallel usage in the Qur'an, language, context, and theme.[101]

Javed Ahmad Ghamidi's Views on Governance and Democracy

Referring to Sura 42: *al-Shura*: 38, Ghamidi states that the style and pattern of the verse demands that an Islamic government should be established and maintained only through the consultation of the believers and should conduct its affairs in all cases on the basis of a consensus or majority opinion of the believers. He states that human beings need social order and political organization.[102] To achieve this purpose, they should develop a social contract that creates a fair and righteous government. To succeed in this goal, humans need divine guidance. For Muslims this guidance is provided by the Qur'an and the *sunna*.

Javed Ahmad Ghamidi's Views on Women

In Ghamidi's view, while men and women are absolutely equal in their capacity as human beings, they have different responsibilities and obligations.[103] Since men and women are different, he thinks that a good society is based not on the principle of equality but on the principle of justice. Equality means that all persons should be dealt with equally, irrespective of their needs or abilities, strengths or weaknesses, while justice means that a person should be dealt with on the basis of his or her capabilities and qualities.

Ghamidi believes, that according to the Qur'an, man should be the head of the family for two reasons: first, because he is given the responsibility of earning the livelihood for the family; and second, because he is given the mental, physical, and emotional qualities that are more suitable for this responsibility. It is only in this sphere of the husband-wife relationship that God has given the man a degree of authority over the woman. Aside from this sphere, both are considered equal.

In Ghamidi's judgment, head covering for women is a preferred part of Muslim social custom and tradition, but it is not a directive of the *shari'a*.[104] A review of his views on women-related issues, such as women's testimony, indicates that patriarchal assumptions about women's role in society that color the analysis of the majority of Muslim exegetes may also be found in his work. However, despite his traditional background and training, Ghamidi is more "modernist" and "reformist" than most Muslim scholars, challenging some generally prevalent interpretations in what is the most sensitive of all subjects for most Muslims.

Asghar Ali Engineer: India's Reformist Scholar-Activist

Asghar Ali was born at Salumbar, Rajasthan (near Udaipur) on March 10, 1939. He belongs to an orthodox priestly family of Bohras who are Shi'a Isma'ili Muslims. His father, Sheikh Qurban Husain, was a scholar of Islam. Asghar Ali learned Arabic from his father, who also taught him *tafsir* (exegesis of the Qur'an), *ta'wil* (hidden meaning of the Qur'an), *fiqh*, and *hadith*. He also attended the municipal school where he acquired modern secular knowledge. He graduated with distinction in civil engineering from Indore, and served for twenty years as an engineer in the Bombay Municipal Corporation, thereafter taking voluntary retirement to devote himself to the Bohra reform movement. Due to his profession he came to be known as Asghar Ali Engineer.

Asghar Ali Engineer: Leader of the Dawoodi Bohra Reform Movement

From an early age, Engineer upheld the view that a truly religious person could not support an unjust order or remain silent in the face of gross injustice. He pointed out that "the faithful should bear in mind that absolute faith could lead to blind surrender to an authority which leads to highly exploitative practices."[105] He believes that a religious person has to continue "to wage jihad against all forms of exploitation and injustices. Even a religious establishment can become highly oppressive and one must fight against such oppressive religious establishment."[106]

From 1972, Engineer began to play a leading role in the Dawoodi reform movement, which protested against what it perceived to be the exploitative practices of the Bohra leader Sayyidna Burhanuddin. Engineer was one of the reformers who set up the Central Board of the Dawoodi Bohra Community to conduct the reform campaign. The reformers defined themselves as believing Bohras and stated that their sole concern was for the Sayyidna and his family to strictly abide by the principles of the Bohra faith and end their authoritarian and tyrannical control over the community. Engineer devotes a great deal of his time to the reform movement, which he has internationalized through his writings and speeches.

Yoginder Sikand has observed "In the course of the struggle against the Sayyidna, Engineer developed his own understanding of Islam as a means and a resource for social revolution. One can discern in his thought and writings a multiplicity of influences: Mu'tazilite and Isma'ili rationalism, Marxism, Western liberalism, Gandhism, and Christian liberation theology, and the impact of the Iranian 'Ali Shariati as well as Indian Muslim modernists such as Sayyid Ahmad Khan and Muhammad Iqbal."[107]

Engineer's involvement in the Bohra reformist movement led him to make contact with other progressive groups in India and internationally. He has done a great deal of work on communalism and communal violence in India since the first major riot in India in Jabalpur in 1961, and he has written extensively about Hindu-Muslim relations. In 1997 he was awarded the first National Communal Harmony Award by the Government of India.

Asghar Ali Engineer's Philosophy and Methodology

Engineer's view of the relationship between reason and faith is stated in an article titled "What I Believe," in which he states: "A careful study of the Qur'an makes it very clear that revelation is in no way contradictory to reason. Both, in fact, are complementary to each other and one is incomplete without the other. While reason helps us understand the physical aspects of this universe (whole development of natural sciences depends on human intellect), revelation helps us find the ultimate answers to our origin and destination. While reason is an important source of enrichment of our material life, revelation is necessary for our spiritual growth."[108]

In Engineer's judgment, the Qur'an emphasizes four important teachings: (1) *'adl* or justice, (2) *ihsan* or benevolence, (3) *rahma* or compassion, and (4) *hikma* or wisdom. He believes that "a person must be just, benevolent, compassionate and wise in order to be a good human being. Mere performance of certain rituals cannot qualify one for being a spiritual person."[109]

Engineer's methodology is based on the twin principles of rationality and justice, reflecting his affinity with Mu'tazili thought. He also believes in distinguishing between the essence of religion (*din*) and its interpretations.

On the question of secularism, Engineer states that both non-Muslims and ortho-dox Muslims feel that Islam is not compatible with secularism because in a secular state there is no place for divine laws. Orthodox Muslims also think that secularism is atheistic and atheism has no place in Islam, which puts great emphasis on faith in God. They feel uneasy with the very word "secularism," which pertains only to matters of this world, whereas Islam attaches great importance to life hereafter. Also, since there is a well-developed *shari'a law* that most Muslims consider to be divine in origin, the very notion of secular law is unacceptable to them.

In Engineer's opinion, the sacral and the secular should not be treated as being mutually antagonistic but as being complementary to each other. He stresses the need to maintain a balance between reason and faith, which are both of fundamental importance to human existence. In his opinion, if reason does not become arrogant and faith does not become blind, then secularism can coexist with Islam and other religions. Engineer thinks that secularism should be taken in a political rather than in a philosophical sense, and he states: "Secularism in a political sense creates a social and political space for all religious communities."[110]

Engineer believes in the democratic spirit of Islam as exemplified by the Qur'anic emphasis on the principle of *shur'a*, or governance by mutual consultation. He points out that Islam accepts freedom of conscience as a fundamental human right. He substantiates Islam's acceptance of religious pluralism by referring to the Qur'anic teaching that all prophets are to be revered and to the example of Prophet Muhammad, who provided equal social and religious space to all religions present in Medina through the Covenant of Medina. Engineer states that Islam expressly upholds respect for human dignity and human rights, which are regarded as core characteristics of secular democracy. Furthermore, he thinks that a democratic form of government that strives to establish a just society reflects the spirit of Islam, which is profoundly concerned about safeguarding the human rights of all peoples, especially those who are socially or politically marginalized or disadvantaged.[111]

Engineer is an advocate of women's rights and argues that, from a Qur'anic perspective, women and men are equal and women should not be regarded either as inferior or as subordinate to men. Keeping in mind the egalitarian spirit of the Qur'an and the principle of justice, Engineer advocates the revision of discrimina-tory laws pertaining to women.[112]

Yoginder Singh Sikand: A Moderate Muslim Voice in India

Yoginder Singh Sikand was born in October 1967 in Bangalore, India. He received his M.Phil. in sociology from Jawaharlal Nehru University, New Delhi, and his Ph.D. in history from Royal Holloway, University of London. His doctoral thesis on Tablighi Jama'at has been published by Orient Longman. He completed his postdoctoral work on "Islamic Perspectives on Inter-Faith Relations in Contem-porary India" at the International Institute for the Study of Islam in the Modern World, in Leiden, The Netherlands.

In February 2007, Sikand converted to Islam and is now teaching at Jam'ia Millia in Delhi. A prolific writer, he has published many books[113] and contributed numerous articles on Islam and Muslims in contemporary India to publications ranging from learned journals to popular periodicals and daily newspapers. The primary focus of Sikand's academic work has been in the disciplines of economics, sociology, and history. But as shown above, he has also studied many aspects of contemporary Islam, particularly in the context of India, and has written about it. He is a progressive intellectual who aspires to give a balanced account of issues pertaining to Muslims. Sikand is committed to promoting a dialogue among religiously diverse groups. While Sikand's work is at a different level from that of the modernist, reformist thinkers discussed in this chapter, his writings have generated a discourse that encourages open-mindedness, moderation, and tolerance among Muslims and between Muslims and people of other faiths.

Conclusion

To do full justice to the work of South Asian modernist, reformist thinkers would require more space than is available in this chapter. Nevertheless, the foregoing account presents compelling evidence of the enduring significance of their ideas.

Reference has been made here to the retrogressive trends and activities of recent decades which have sought to undermine if not reverse the progress made by modernist reformist thinkers, not only in the context of South Asia, but also of the Muslim world in general. No doubt, today's modernist and reformist Muslim thinkers face great difficulties and even danger as they continue to disseminate their message. In some way this message echoes the rallying-cry of Muslim modernist reformers of the nineteenth and twentieth centuries, namely, "Go back to the Qur'an and go forward with *ijtihad*."

The progressive spirit of the historic Aligarh movement founded by Sayyid Ahmad Khan for the intellectual, moral and social regeneration of Indian Muslims, and which Iqbal enshrined in the hearts of millions through his passionate poems, remains a source of inspiration and empowerment for those who want to create communities and societies that embody the highest ideals and best practices of Islam.

Charles Dickens opened his great novel *A Tale of Two Cities* with the following unforgettable words:

> It was the best of times, it was the worst of times,
> it was the age of wisdom, it was the age of foolishness,
> it was the epoch of belief, it was the epoch of incredulity,
> it was the season of Light, it was the season of Darkness,
> it was the spring of hope, it was the winter of despair,
> we had everything before us, we had nothing before us.

The times we are living in today are reminiscent of these lines from Dickens. A fierce battle is raging between reformist thinkers and their opponents, a battle to capture the hearts, minds, and souls of Muslims, especially young Muslims. The outcome of this battle depends on how well contemporary Muslims understand, internalize, and actualize the message of reformist thinkers such as the ones referred to in this chapter.

Internal and external forces casting a shadow over the Muslim world are impelling a significant number of people in the direction of extremism and life-negating attitudes and actions. Despite these challenges, it is this author's conviction that the voices of reformist thinkers, with their forward-looking, life-affirming vision, will prevail over the negative forces. This conviction is not based on naive optimism but upon the author's lived experience both as a thinker and as an activist.

Notes

1. Bruce B. Lawrence, "Islam in South Asia," in *The Oxford Encyclopaedia of the Modern Islamic World,* ed. John L. Esposito (New York: Oxford University Press, 1995), vol. 2, p. 282.

2. H.A.R. Gibb, *Modern Trends in Islam* (Chicago: University of Chicago Press, 1947), p. 63.

3. Fazlur Rahman, "Revival and Reform in Islam," in *Cambridge History of Islam,* ed. John P. Holt et al. (Cambridge: Cambridge University Press, 1970), vol. 11, p. 641.

4. Ibid.

5. Hafeez Malik, *Sir Sayyid Ahmad Khan and Muslim Modernization in India and Pakistan* (New York: Columbia University Press, 1980), p. 8.

6. David Commins, "Modernism," in *The Encyclopaedia of the Modern Islamic World,* vol. 3, p. 118.

7. Christian Troll, "Sayyid Ahmad Khan," in *The Encyclopaedia of Religion,* ed. Mircea Eliade (New York: Macmillan Publishing Company, 1987), vol. 1, p. 15.

8. Hafeez Malik, *Sir Sayyid Ahmad Khan and Muslim Modernization in India and Pakistan,* p. 82.

9. Muhammad Aslam Syed, "Islamic Modernism," in *Islam in South Asia* (Historical Studies [Muslim India] Series) 11, ed. Waheed-uz-Zaman and M. Salim Akhtar (Islamabad: National Institute of Historical and Cultural Research, 1993), p. 343.

10. Ibid.

11. Aziz Ahmad, *Islamic Modernism in India and Pakistan: 1857–1964* (London: Oxford University Press, 1967), p. 39.

12. Manzoor Ahmad, "Islamic Response to Contemporary Western Thought," in *Islam in South Asia* (Proceedings of an International Seminar on Islamic History, Art, and Culture in South Asia, Islamabad, Pakistan, 1986), ed. Rashid Ahmad Jullundhri and Muhammad Afzal Qarshi (Lahore: Institute of Islamic Culture, 1995), p. 11.

13. Sir Sayyid Khan quoted in ibid.

14. Ibid.

15. S.T. Lokhandwalla, ed., *India and Contemporary Islam* (Simla: India Institute of Advanced Study, 1971), p. 55.

16. Aziz Ahmad, *Studies in Islamic Culture in the Indian Environment* (Oxford: Clarendon Press, 1964), p. 57.

17. Sayyid Ahmad Khan cited in Abdul Khaliq, *Sir Sayyid Ahmad Khan: On Nature, Man and God—A Critique* (Lahore: Bazm-e-Iqbal, 1993), p. 12.

18. Sayyid Ahmad Khan cited in J.M.S. Baljon, *The Reforms and Religious Ideas of Sir Sayyid Ahmad Khan* (Leiden: E.J. Brill, 1949), p. 44.

19. Fazlur Rahman, "Muslim Modernism in the Indo-Pakistan," *The Bulletin of the School of Oriental and African Studies,* vol. 21, no. 2 (1958): 83.

20. Ibid., pp. 83–84.

21. Aziz Ahmad, *Islamic Modernism in India and Pakistan, 1857–1964* (London: Oxford University Press, 1967), pp. 53–54.

22. S.A. Vahid, "Reply to Questions Raised by Pandit Jawahar Lal Nehru." In *Thoughts and Reflections of Iqbal,* ed. S.A. Vahid (Lahore: Shaikh Muhammad Ashraf, 1964), p. 277.

23. See Aziz Ahmad, *Islamic Modernism In India And Pakistan, 1857–1964,* pp. 59–60.

24. Ibid, p. 60.

25. Ibid.

26. Ibid, p. 61.

27. Ibid, pp. 67–71.

28. See Qasim Amin, *The Liberation of Women,* trans. Samantha Sidhorn Peterson (Cairo: American University in Cairo Press, 2000).

29. Ibid, pp. 72–76.

30. See Aziz Ahmad, *Islamic Modernism in India and Pakistan,* p. 38.

31. E.M. Forster, *Two Cheers for Democracy* (London: Harcourt, 1962), p. 296.

32. A.M. Schimmel, *Gabriel's Wing* (Leiden: E.J. Brill, 1963), p. 382.

33. A.J. Arberry, *An Introduction to the History of Sufism* (London: Longmans, Green & Company, 1942), p. 47.

34. Vahid, ed., *Thoughts and Reflections of Iqbal,* p. 161.

35. A.J. Arberry, *Sufism* (London: Dover, 1950), p. 133.

36. Gibb, *Modern Trends in Islam,* p. ix.

37. Ibid., pp. ix–x.

38. Ibid., p. 77.

39. Ibid., p. 60.

40. Ibid., p. 82.

41. W.C. Smith, *Modern Islam in India: A Social Analysis* (London: Victor Gollancz, 1946), p. 105.

42. Ibid., pp. 105–6.

43. Muhammad Iqbal, *The Reconstruction of Religious Thought in Islam* (Lahore: Shaikh Muhammad Ashraf, 1962), p. 147.

44. Ibid., pp. 147–48.

45. Ibid., p. 126.

46. Ibid., p. 148.

47. Mazheruddin Siddiqi, *Modern Reformist Thought in the Muslim World* (Delhi: Adam Publishers and Distributors, 1993), p. 77.

48. Iqbal, *Reconstruction of Religious Thought in Islam,* p. 151.

49. Ibid., p. 168.

50. Ibid.

51. Ahmad, *Islamic Modernism in India and Pakistan,* pp. 154–55.

52. Iqbal, *Reconstruction of Religious Thought in Islam,* p. 173.

53. Ibid., p. 174.

54. Muhammad Iqbal, *Zarb-e-kalim* (Lahore: Sheikh Ghulam Ali and Sons, 1936), p. 150.

55. H.H. Bilgrami, *Glimpses of Iqbal's Mind and Thought* (Lahore: Orientalia, 1966), p. 91.

56. Vahid, ed., *Thoughts and Reflections of Iqbal,* pp. 83–84.

57. Ibid., pp. 51–53.

58. Rumuz-e-Bekhudi, *The Mysteries of Selflessness,* trans. A.J. Arberry (London: John Murray, 1953), p. 63.

59. Iqbal, *Zarb-e-kalim,* p. 90.

60. Ibid., p. 95.

61. Iqbal cited in Muhammad Khalid Masud, *Iqbal's Reconstruction of Ijtihad* (Lahore: Iqbal Academy, 1995), p. 155.

62. Ibid., p. 165.

63. Ibid., p. 164.

64. Ibid., pp. 165–66.

65. Ibid., p. 155.

66. Fazlur Rahman cited in *The Muslim Almanac,* ed. Azim Nanji (New York: Gale Research, 1996), p. 67.

67. Fazlur Rahman, *Islam and Modernity: Transformation of an Intellectual Tradition* (Chicago: University of Chicago Press, 1982), p. 2.

68. Ibid.

69. Ibid., pp. 2–3.

70. Ibid., p. 5.

71. Ibid.

72. Ibid., p. 143.

73. Ibid., p. 6.

74. Ibid.

75. Ibid., p. 7.

76. Ibid.

77. Ibid., pp. 7–8.

78. Fazlur Rahman, "Some Islamic Issues in the Ayyub Khan Era," in *Essays of Islamic Civilization,* ed. Donald P. Little (Leiden: E.J. Brill, 1976), p. 299.

79. Ibid.

80. Fazlur Rahman, "Implementation of the Islamic Concept of State in the Pakistani Milieu," *Islamic Studies* (Karachi: Central Institute of Islamic Research), vol. 6, no. 3 (1967): 207.

81. Ibid.

82. Ibid.

83. Rahman, "Revival and Reform in Islam," p. 654.

84. Ibid.

85. Ibid.

86. Ibid.

87. Ibid.

88. Fazlur Rahman, *Islam,* 2d ed. (Chicago: University of Chicago Press, 1979), p. 38.

89. Rahman, *Islam and Modernity,* p. 19.

90. Muhammad Khalid Masud, "Hadith and Violence," *Oriente Moderno,* vol. XXI (LXXXII) n.s., no. 1 (2002): 6–18. Special issue on Hadith and traditions in modern Islam. Manuscript provided courtesy of the author.

91. Muhammad Khalid Masud, "Defining Democracy in Islamic Polity," (paper presented at the International Conference, "The Future of Islam, Democracy, and Authoritarianism in the Era of Globalization," International Centre for Islam and Pluralism, Jakarta, December 5–6, 2004. Manuscript provided courtesy of the author. Also available at http://www.maruf. org/frames/Articles/article-3.htm.

92. Ibid., p. 18.

93. Ibid., p. 20.

94. Muhammad Khalid Masud, "The Scope of Pluralism in Islamic Moral Traditions," in *The Many and the One, Religious and Secular Perspectives on Ethical Pluralism in the Modern World,* ed. Richard Madsen and Tracy B. Strong (Princeton: Princeton University Press, 2003), p. 181.

95. Ibid.

96. Jonas Svensson, *Women's Human Rights and Islam: A Study of Three Attempts*

at Accommodation (Lund Studies in History of Religions 12) (Lund: Lunds Universitet/ Almqvist & Wiksell, 2000).

97. Ibid.

98. Toshihiko Izutsu, *The Structure of the Ethical Terms in the Koran: A Study in Semantics* (Tokyo: Keio Institute of Cultural and Linguistic, 1959), pp. 113–44.

99. Svensson, *Women's Human Rights and Islam,* p. 90.

100. Asif Iftikhar, "Jihad and the Establishment of Islamic Global Order: A Comparative Study of the Interpretative Approaches and Weltanchauungs of Abu'l A'la Mawdudi and Javed Ahmad Ghamidi," thesis, Institute of Islamic Studies, McGill University, 2004, p. 54. Provided in manuscript form courtesy of the author.

101. Ibid., p. 57.

102. This section is based on Javed Ahmed Ghamidi, "The Political Law of Islam" (paper). Provided in manuscript form courtesy of the author.

103. Javed Ahmad Ghamidi, personal communication to author, October 2, 2006.

104. Javed Ahmad Ghamidi, "Norms of Gender Interaction," trans. Saleem Shehzad, available at http://www.renaissance.com.pk/novislaw2y2.html.

105. Asghar Ali Engineer, "What I Believe," November 18, 2006, available at http:// ecumene.org/IIS/csss16.htm.

106. Asghar Ali Engineer, "Engaged Islam," November 15, 2006, available at http://www. religiousconsultation.org/engaged_islam.htm.

107. Yoginder Sikand, "Asghar Ali Engineer's Quest for an Islamic Theology of Peace and Religious Pluralism," November 15, 2006, available at http://www.svabhinava.org/ MeccaBenares/YoginderSikand/AsgharAliEngineerIslamicTheology-frame.php.

108. Asghar Ali Engineer, "What I Believe."

109. Ibid.

110. Asghar Ali Engineer, "Islam and Secularism," October 1–15, 2000, available at http:// andromeda.rutgers.edu/~rtavakol/engineer/secular.htm.

111. Asghar Ali Engineer, "Islam and Pluralism," October 18, 2006, available at http:// andromeda.rutgers.edu/~rtavakol/engineer/plural.htm.

112. Asghar Ali Engineer, "Reconstruction of Islam Thought," October 18, 2006, available at http://andromeda.rutgers.edu/~rtavakol/engineer/recon.htm.

113. Yoginder Sikand, *Sacred Spaces: Exploring Traditions of Shared Faith in India* (New York: Penguin, 2003) and *Muslims in India Since 1947: Perspectives on Interfaith Relations* (New York: Routledge/Curzon, 2004).

5

Liberal and Progressive Voices in Indonesian Islam

Martin van Bruinessen

The Beginnings of Islamic Reform in Indonesia

The Islamization of the Indonesian archipelago was a long process and took centuries. Indonesian scholars and students of Islamic legal and other disciplines played important roles in the process.[1] Indonesians who made the annual pilgrimage to Mecca (*hajj*) were one channel of communication between Indonesian Muslims and those of the Arab world.[2] During the nineteenth century, it became common practice for young men aspiring to become religious scholars, *ulema*, to study at religious schools in the holy cities of Mecca and Medina and, later at Al-Azhar in Cairo. By the late nineteenth century, the number of Indonesian Islamic scholars and students residing in those cities was substantial.

Upon their return to Indonesia, each generation of these scholars attempted to "correct" belief and practice at home, and to bring local practices more in line with religious currents in Islam's heartlands.* Returning scholars rejected intercession, the visiting of saints' graves, and other local practices they deemed un-Islamic, they rejected *taqlid* (imitation), and called for *ijtihad* (independent interpretation) based on the Qur'an and *sunna*.[3]

Reformist Movements and Organizations: A Brief History

Indonesia's first major Muslim reformist organization, the Muhammadiyya, was founded by Haji Ahmad Dahlan in 1912, in Yogyakarta. Dahlan had studied in Mecca and was familiar with the ideas of the Egyptian reformers Muhammad Abduh and Rashid Rida. Initially, the organization's main objectives were education

---

*Editor's Note: The reformism referenced here is reform in the traditional sense of eliminating exogenous and often syncretistic influences on Islam.

and social reform; only later reform of belief and ritual became a central issue for the organization. In pursuance of these goals, Muhammadiyya organized public sermons to educate the public on religious matters (*tabliq*), and distributed alms (*zakat*) among the poor and needy instead of for the maintenance of mosques and the *ulema*, as was common until then. Over time, Muhammadiyya established schools and orphanages, in order to counter the efforts of the Christian missions, whose activities were facilitated by the Dutch colonial government.

Another reformist organization, Persatuan Islam ("Islamic Union," known as Persis), was established in 1923. It was almost exclusively focused on religious reform and approximated a homegrown Salafi movement. Persis rejected *taqlid* and the *madhhab* system in favor of exclusive reliance on the Qur'an and *sunna*. It fought syncretistic and local Islamic practices, especially those involving belief in spirits, worship of saints, and other devotional relations with the dead. It also opposed lavish life-cycle rituals, Sufi spiritual exercises, and litanies and prayers, which it considered *bid'a*.[4] The activities of Persis, joined by reformists in other parts of the country who shared its beliefs, also led the Muhammadiyya to focus more on religious issues.

The Traditionalist Reaction

The increasing assertiveness of Indonesian reformists, coupled with international developments such as the Saudi conquest of Mecca in 1924, were viewed by many *ulema* as threatening to traditional religious practices. To counter these threats and defend their own style of scholarship and ritual practices, the leading *ulema* of East Java in 1926 established a traditionalist association, Nahdatul Ulama (NU) (Awakening of the Scholars). Despite its conservative objectives, the NU propelled many *ulema* toward participation in the modern public sphere.

Politicization of Islamic Reformism

The Japanese occupation (1942–45) interrupted Dutch rule in Indonesia, politicized Muslim religious leaders, and prepared them for a role in the independence struggle. The Japanese merged all Muslim associations into a single umbrella organization, Masyumi (an acronym for "Consultative Council of Indonesian Muslims"). After the war, and Indonesia's independence, Masyumi transformed itself into a political party. Following this change, the NU broke away from Masyumi and became a party in its own right, defending traditionalist interests. After this break, Masyumi became dominated by the reformists and pursued a liberal economic and political agenda. However, both parties favored a more central role for Islam in the new state and tried to add a phrase to the Constitution that would oblige Muslim citizens to follow the *shari'a* (a phrase that would become known as the Jakarta Charter). These efforts were shelved in 1945 because of the opposition of Christian nationalist leaders and were finally defeated in the Constitutional Assembly in 1959.[5] Both

Islamic parties had considerable constituencies, and in the free elections of 1955 they each obtained approximately 20 percent of the popular vote. However, most Indonesia Muslims preferred non-religious political parties and showed no interest in the establishment of an Islamic state.

Muhammadiyya provided the bulk of Masyumi activists, but the religious ideas of its most prominent leader, Muhammad Natsir, had been shaped in Persis. He was one of the few reformist politicians fluent in Arabic and had a solid knowledge of Islamic scripture. An eloquent speaker, he was equally at ease discussing religious questions and issues of international politics or economic policy. As a puritan, modern-minded Muslim, Natsir abhorred the nativism and religious syncretism, magic and mysticism that became an important component of the Sukarno and Suharto regimes' political culture. Under his leadership, Masyumi followed a liberal-democratic and pro-Western course, and became the major force of democratic opposition to Sukarno's increasingly authoritarian, patrimonial style of politics. A number of Masyumi leaders, but not Natsir, took part in an abortive, CIA-supported rebellion against Sukarno in 1958, as a result of which the party was dissolved and many of its leaders jailed.

Sukarno was finally brought down in 1965, in the wake of a coup attempt by left-leaning officers, followed by a rapid counter-coup by General Suharto and a wave of mass killings of Communists and student demonstrators against Sukarno. In 1966 Suharto assumed presidential powers and established a pro-Western, development-oriented authoritarian regime that became known as the New Order. Under Suharto's New Order there was no place for Muhammad Natsir and other Masyumi leaders, and attempts to resurrect the Masyumi party met with a strict ban by the regime. Natsir and his closest collaborators decided to devote themselves to *da'wa*, or efforts to further Islamize the country's Muslims, since they could not Islamize the state.

From Party Politics to Da'wa

In 1967, Natsir and his colleagues established the Indonesian Council for Islamic Predication (Dewan dakwah Islamiyah Indonesia—DDII). The DDII established close relations with the Islamic World League and became a conduit for contemporary Middle Eastern Islamist thought. The council trained large numbers of preachers and, despite official discouragement, managed to have a great impact on religious discourse in urban lower- and lower-middle-class circles as well as among university students. It developed into the most consistent moral critic of the Suharto regime and its policies, speaking in the name of democracy as much as Islam. Whereas the Masyumi party had been liberal and pro-Western in outlook, the council gradually shifted toward a more anti-Western and anti-liberal position, and it adopted much of the worldview of the Muslim Brotherhood.

Not all Masyumi leaders joined Natsir in this course. Some second-echelon Masyumi politicians established an alternative government-controlled reformist

Muslim party, while others joined the government party, Golkar. The most explicit departure from the policies set out by Natsir and his colleagues was that of the movement for "Renewal of Religious Thought" (*pembaruan pemikiran agama*), a small group of young men of Masyumi background, who challenged the older generation over the latter's failure to carry out true reform. The charismatic leader of this movement was Nurcholish Madjid.

Nurcholish Madjid and the Movement for "Renewal of Religious Thought"

Nurcholish Madjid's career as a public intellectual coincided with Indonesia's New Order. He delivered his first provocative and widely discussed speech in 1970, and remained a prolific writer and speaker until his death in August 2005. He was a prominent member of the student "generation of 1966." Student demonstrations had helped weaken the Sukarno regime and prepared the way for Suharto's final takeover in that year. Afterwards, many members of this student movement became part of the New Order's civilian elite.

Nurcholish was born in Jombang, East Java, in 1939 to a religious family affiliated with Masyumi. He received his secondary education in the "modern *pesantren*" of Gontor. This school offered a curriculum that combined the traditional religious education offered in *madrasa* with the teaching of modern general subjects, and it enjoyed a high reputation for the quality of its teaching of Arabic and English.[6] He then attended the State Institute of Islamic Studies (IAIN) in Jakarta. There he joined the most important Muslim student association of the time, Himpunan Mahasiswa Islam (HMI), and rapidly became an influential student leader. In the crucial year 1966, he was elected chairman of this association and held this position for two consecutive three-year terms. His education, his gifts as a speaker, and his career as a student leader appeared to make him the ideal successor to the respected Muhammad Natsir as leader of Indonesia's reformist Islam. By the late 1960s he had acquired the nickname of "the young Natsir," and many people expected him to take responsibility for the survival of Masyumi and its ideals.

First Provocative Ideas

Given these expectations, the programmatic speech that Nurcholish delivered in early 1970, at a joint meeting of all reformist Muslim student unions, came as a shock. Speaking on "the need for renewal of Islamic thought and problems of the integration of the *umma*,"[7] Nurcholish firmly distanced himself from Masyumi and the sort of Muslim politics it represented, as well as from the established reformist Muslim associations (Muhammadiyya, Persis, Al-Irshad), because he thought they had lost their dynamism and had become conservative. He perceived that there was a growing interest in and devotion to Islam among the population at large. But he also noticed that Muslim parties and their ideas held little attraction for the Muslim public: their ideas were stagnant and even fossilized, and the parties projected an image of unpleasant infighting and even corruption.[8] The attitude of the Muslim public, Nurcholish claimed, could be summarized as "Islam yes, partai Islam no!"

The older generation of Masyumi leaders saw this statement as a betrayal of their struggle and as proof of Nurcholish's collusion with the regime's efforts to depoliticize Islam. Yet Nurcholish did not oppose Muslim parties as a matter of principle, but considered them irrelevant to most Muslims' religious concerns. The speech also generated other misunderstandings. Nurcholish called for "secularization" and distinguished it from secularism, which he rejected, yet, he was accused of being a secularist wanting to reduce Islam to a matter of private piety. In reality, his intention was more iconoclastic: he explained "secularization" as the "de-sacralization" of all concepts and institutions, including Islamic political parties.

The Yogyakarta Group and Intellectual Influences on the Renewal Movement

Some ideas espoused by Nurcholish were discussed among a select group of HMI members who shared his intellectual curiosity and open-mindedness. They came to be known as the Renewal (*pembaruan*) movement. A significant contribution was made by a group studying in Yogyakarta in the late 1960s. Yogyakarta is Indonesia's city of culture and education and the site of some of the country's best universities (general, Muslim, and Christian) and rich libraries, with a tradition of lively student discussion circles and easy communication across ethnic and religious boundaries. The leading lights of the Yogyakarta Renewal group were Djohan Effendi and Dawam Rahardjo. Much of the discussions in this circle is reflected in the posthumously published diaries of a younger member of the group, Ahmad Wahib.[9] These were very serious young men, strongly drawn to religion and willing to question the certainties of their upbringing. Intellectual curiosity drew them to a weekly study club of the Lahore Ahmadiyya movement and to discussions with their Christian peers.

A major intellectual influence on this group was a discussion circle led by A. Mukti Ali, a professor of comparative religion at the IAIN. Mukti Ali had studied in Pakistan in the early 1950s, partly because of his admiration for the modernist thinker Sayyid Ahmad Khan, and later at McGill University. The "limited group" discussions he organized included non-Muslim clerics, thinkers, and artists and were the freest intellectual forum in Indonesia in the late 1960s. As Dawam Rahardjo later wrote, Mukti Ali may have inspired the call for liberal and reformist Islamic thought in Indonesia. He criticized Muhammadiyya for its religious conservatism and considered it lagging behind reformist religious thought in Egypt and the Indian subcontinent.[10]

Djohan Effendi established especially close relations with the Ahmadiyya, but all the members of the Yogyakarta group were strongly attracted to the South

Asian rationalistic school of Islamic reform, beginning with Sayyid Ahmad Khan (d. 1898), with which they became acquainted through their Ahmadiyya contacts.* Strongly influenced by the Mu'tazila, Sayyid Ahmad Khan and his followers harmonized their interpretations of the Qur'an with modern science, sought rational explanations of miracles, and presented the divine commands as reasonable and intelligible in the context of their revelation.

A more recent South Asian thinker who became a major influence among the Yogyakarta group was Muhammad Iqbal (d. 1938), whose application of *ijtihad* to modern problems of Muslim society they found stimulating. Iqbal had defended Turkey's abolition of the caliphate as an exercise of *ijtihad* by which sovereignty was transferred from a single person to the national assembly. The Renewal group adopted a similar style of reasoning, recognizing in modern institutions the spirit of those of early Islam. Thus the multireligious Indonesian nation state, with its official ideology of Pancasila, was declared an appropriate application of the spirit of Medina under the Prophet. (This was a recurring element in the arguments against the idea of an Islamic state.)

In the 1980s, another South Asian thinker, Fazlur Rahman (1919–1988), became the main intellectual mentor of the Renewal movement. In his case too, it was his rational and contextual interpretation of the Qur'an that constituted his strongest appeal to Indonesians.

The Renewal Movement and the New Order

In the beginning, the ideas of the Renewal movement did not find much support even within HMI.[11] The participants long remained isolated and subject to fierce criticism by their seniors and peers. However, helped by the regime's recognition and strong endorsement, they achieved positions of influence and eventually changed the public Islamic discourse. There was an obvious congruence between the Renewal group's discourse and the New Order's development policies, which demanded the depoliticization of religion and inter-religious harmony. Mukti Ali, the mentor of the Yogyakarta group, was appointed Minister of Religious Affairs from 1972 to 1978, and he brought Djohan Effendi to his department as his chief advisor for inter-religious dialogue. Dawam Rahardjo joined the Institute for Economic and Social Research, Education, and Information (LP3ES), the first major development-oriented NGO in Jakarta, and eventually became its director.

Due to the group's efforts, Renewal ideas attracted followers at university campuses. The IAIN of Jakarta, where Nurcholish had studied and later taught, became a stronghold of the movement. The rector of this institute was Harun Nasution, another McGill graduate and nonconformist, a self-professed follower of the Mu'tazila. Like Mukti Ali, Nasution may not have shared all of the

---

*Editor's Note: Orthodox Muslims consider the Ahmadiyya a heretical sect.

Renewal ideas but he promoted independent and critical thinking and debate among students. In this environment, rational and liberal Muslim thought could flourish; ideas of the Renewal movement interacted with those of the Mu'tazila and with philosophy.[12]

Among the members of the Renewal group, Nurcholish maintained the highest national and international profile. His public prominence won him a scholarship to the University of Chicago, where he studied theology and philosophy under the supervision of Fazlur Rahman. This experience deeply influenced his intellectual development. When he returned to Indonesia in 1984, he was a more mature thinker, well prepared for the task of disseminating a modern and moderate Islamic discourse among political and business elites and the emerging Muslim middle class.

This middle class, many of whose members had belonged to HMI, had benefited from the New Order, and were self-consciously social climbers. They were looking for a modern religious discourse compatible with their new social and economic status, and Nurcholish and his associates provided them with such a discourse.

Institutionalization of the Renewal Movement: Paramadina

The establishment of the "religious study club" Paramadina in 1986 provided the movement with an institutional base. Dawam Rahardjo was the principal inspiration behind Paramadina, as he stressed the need for associations that could replace the Masyumi political party format. However, it was Nurcholish who coined the name and became its leader and spokesman.[13] Paramadina offered a new type of religious sermons or, more correctly, seminar lectures, catering to the spiritual needs and intellectual ambitions of its target group. Over time, the number of lectures and the range of religious subjects discussed were increased. Paramadina participated in the establishment of an elite boarding school, Madaniyya, and established the Universitas Paramadina Mulya, which employs many liberal reformists.

Core Elements in Nurcholish's Thought

Nurcholish was essentially an effective communicator of moral teachings rather than a systematic and rigorous thinker.[14] His writings consist mostly of his speeches and do not include a single book. The most coherent of his writings are those written for Paramadina's monthly study meetings.[15] His writings and speeches address a wide range of subjects and often are responses to specific historical situations. Nevertheless, certain themes appear in most of them, thus giving his work a thematic consistency.

This consistency can be partly attributed to his ongoing debate with the Dewan Dakwah and other textualists. For Nurcholish, Islam is first and foremost a system of moral teachings and not strict prescriptions. He therefore strongly rejected the idea of the Islamic state and the formalization of the shari'a into legal prescriptions. Modernity, the nation state, democracy, human rights, liberal values, and religious pluralism all reflect Islamic values. He saw those values first embodied in the "Constitution of Medina," the document that regulated relations between the Muslims and the Jewish tribes of the city in Prophet Muhammad's time.[16] In Nurcholish's view, Medina was an early nation state and the ideal civil society, and modern Indonesia, with its official ideology of harmonious interethnic and inter-religious relations, replicated this model in important respects.[17]

Nurcholish rejected the Arabizing thrust of puritan Islamic reform and affirmed the essentially Islamic nature of Indonesian culture and the national ideology of Pancasila. It was Islam and cultures shaped by Islamic influences that had united Indonesia's diverse ethnic and religious groups into a single nation. He maintained that Christians and Jews, but also Hindus and Buddhists, were to be treated as *ahl al-kitab* (people of the Book), the recipients of valid divine revelations, and as citizens with equal rights. He supported this thesis with the argument that the terms *Islam* and *Muslim* occur in the Qur'an not only in the narrow sense, to refer to the followers of Muhammad, but also in certain contexts to refer to the followers of all prophets, thus subsuming Jews and Christians and even the followers of other unnamed religions.[18] On Islam's compatibility with modernity, he often quoted approvingly Ernest Gellner's observation that "Islam is, of the three great Western monotheisms, the one closest to modernity," and Robert Bellah's analysis of early Islam as a secularizing impulse in world history.[19]

The encounter with Fazlur Rahman had a great impact on Nurcholish's thought and that of his associates. He acquainted them with previously unexplored aspects of Muslim intellectual tradition, notably philosophy, and with his contextual understanding of the Qur'an. Upon his return to Indonesia, Nurcholish published a collection of translations of Muslim philosophical thinkers, from Kindi and Farabi to Afghani and Abduh, with an introduction on the intellectual heritage of Islam.[20] He frequently referred to these thinkers and to selected quotations from the Qur'an in support of his arguments. He maintained that Qur'anic verses must be understood in the historical and social contexts of their revelation. However, his understanding of "context" was much broader than the traditional concept of "circumstances of revelation" (*asbab al-nuzul*) and included the sociology of seventh-century Mecca and Medina. Nurcholish found the study of *sira* (early biographies of the Prophet) to be more helpful in this respect than *hadith*. He gratefully adopted insights from Western historians like Marshall Hodgson and Ira Lapidus.

The idea of the fundamental importance of social context for the understanding of sacred texts has remained a central hermeneutic principle in the Renewal movement. From this principle, many of the movement's followers have concluded that Islam's universal teachings needed reformulation for the Indonesian cultural context: they defend the legitimacy of vernacular expressions of Indonesian Islam and consider them a source of pride.

The positive appreciation of other religious traditions has also remained a conspicuous element in thinking and teaching at Paramadina, and some of its members are attracted to the idea of underlying unity of all religions, represented by authors of the Perennialist or Traditionalist schools such as Seyyed Hossein Nasr and Fritjof Schuon.

During the final years of the Suharto regime, characterized by rising Muslim–Christian tensions and violent riots, Paramadina and its affiliates openly supported religious pluralism and interreligious understanding. Paramadina published a controversial book on the *"fiqh* of interreligious relations," which offered theological arguments in support of cooperative and friendly relations and against exclusivist views of conservative Muslims.[21]

Traditionalist Islam, the *Pesantren*, and the Search for a Socially Relevant *Fiqh*

These debates occurred in urban middle-class circles belonging to the reformist strand of mainstream Indonesian Islam. Until the mid-1980s, when a new generation of leaders took control of Nahdatul Ulama (NU) and created the conditions for the flourishing of social activism and intellectual debate, the vast majority of Muslims remained unaffected by the reformist discourse.

Abdurrahman Wahid, the NU's general chairman from 1984 to 1999, played a key role as a cultural and political broker between his large conservative constituency on the one hand and the worlds of international human rights activism, liberal Islamic reform, and religious minorities, on the other.

Abdurrahman Wahid: Maverick Modern Traditionalist

From the late 1970s, Abdurrahman Wahid regularly participated in the Renewal discussions and supported some of the same views that had made Nurcholish controversial.[22] Wahid had studied at a *pesantren* and at a modern school, and at Al-Azhar and the University of Baghdad. He found Al-Azhar an intellectually stifling environment but used this time to become acquainted with contemporary Arab culture. He was a voracious reader and acquired a better knowledge of European and American cultures than did many Indonesians who studied in the West. Wahid's family background—his father and grandfathers had been among NU's most respected *ulema*—meant that he commanded respect and did not have to prove his Islamic loyalty and credentials. He successfully explained controversial views in a language accessible to his constituency, maintained close links with his grass-roots supporters, and helped transform the NU from an intellectual backwater to the site of lively thinking and debate. After moving to Jakarta he interacted with artistic, political, business, governmental, religious, and journalistic groups of diverse ethnic and religious backgrounds, as well as with the Renewal group, and gained their respect.

Wahid rejects the idea that Islam prescribes a specific type of state, strongly supports Indonesia's secular state ideology of Pancasila, and advocates equal rights and state protection for religious minorities, including those not recognized by the state. He defends the notion of "cultural Islam," associated with the Renewal movement and New Order policies, against varieties of political Islam represented by legal Islamic parties and radical underground movements. In his usage the term "cultural Islam" acquires overtones of local culture, traditional religious practices, bottom-up social activism, individual moral values and, implicitly, religious tolerance and protection of non-Muslims and heterodox Muslim sects.

Wahid's views have often been more liberal than those of Nurcholish and his friends. Unlike them, he has also defended the legal rights of Communists and heterodox sects, as well as the economic rights of the poor. He did this within the framework of universal human rights that he explained by reference to principles from Islamic legal theory, *usul al-fiqh*. For this reason, religious minorities have looked to him rather than to the Renewal group as their protector. Women activists who challenged gender inequality in Islam also found him supportive, whereas Nurcholish shied away from this sensitive issue. Wahid has understood the central concerns of community development, empowerment, and grassroots democracy, and he has been able to translate them into the language of *fiqh* and *usul al-fiqh* and defend them as genuinely Islamic concerns, thus stimulating intellectual debate and creative thought among the younger generation of NU thinkers and activists.

Nahdatul Ulama, NGO Activists, and the "Fiqh of Social Questions"

The NU represented the world of the *pesantren* and the *ulema*, or *kyai*, the traditional Islamic boarding schools and their charismatic teachers, who exerted a strong influence in rural Java and on some of the other islands. In this world Shafi'i *fiqh* is the dominant intellectual tradition, great *ulema* of the past are venerated, life is punctuated by religious ceremonies, and belief in the intercession of saints is strong.

Abdurrahman Wahid and several others who took over NU's leadership in 1984 had for a decade been involved in efforts to involve the *pesantren* in community development. Their encounter with international NGOs and the grand narratives of development from below, human rights, gender equality, civil society, and democratization was a major factor in the reorientation of the NU. The shift from party politics to social welfare activities exposed many of the NU's younger and more active members to NGO activities and discourse, taught them useful skills, and broadened their mental horizons. An entire generation of *pesantren* students grew up with an awareness that there should be a relationship between religious discourse and social and economic activities.[23]

In the late 1980s, the NGOs realized that, on the one hand, to be accepted as legitimate the discourse of development had to be "translated" into the language of *fiqh* and, on the other hand, the discourse of *fiqh* had to be expanded to accommodate modern ideas and become relevant to contemporary social problems. Consequently, an NGO specialized in *pesantren*-based activities—P3M—initiated the first efforts to develop a new, relevant *fiqh* discourse.[24] It organized a series of seminars—announced as *halqa* (study circles); involved relatively open-minded *kyai* (religious leader) with specialists in various fields in discussions; and challenged them to find Islamic answers to issues ranging from organ transplants and euthanasia to the state's expropriations of private lands, popular representation, and women's rights. The organizers tried to develop "progressive" perspectives and get them endorsed by the participating *kyai*.

The chief organizer and thinker behind these *halqa* was the nonconformist NU intellectual Masdar F. Masudi. Masdar's strength was that he had a thorough *pesantren* education and naturally thought like a *kyai*, in the categories of *fiqh*, but due to his intelligence and his wide-ranging contacts with NGO activists of different backgrounds, he also had a much broader perspective on society. He wrote thought-provoking discussion papers. In these papers he took classical *fiqh* as his point of departure but, with an original analysis, he supported peasants' rights in cases where the state had expropriated land without compensation, and he stressed the duty of elected deputies to speak out in support of the oppressed.[25]

The P3M *halqas* were facilitated by NU's progressive new leadership and by a few influential senior *kyai*. They influenced the content and form of the *fatwas* issued by the leading NU *ulema*. NU's national congresses and conferences had always been occasions for the leading *ulema* to deliberate on topical questions and issue collective *fatwas*. In the late 1980s, NU established a special body to prepare and coordinate these deliberations, or *bahth al-masa'il* (discussion of questions), with the intention of ensuring the discussion of important contemporary problems. Its members prepared discussion materials on major practical and ethical questions, ranging from buying and selling shares in the stock exchange to *in vitro* fertilization. They invited lay experts to explain various subjects before the *ulema* discussed their permissibility or proscription under different conditions.[26]

This type of question could not be reduced to those already discussed in the classical *fiqh* texts, which relied heavily on the rulings (*qawl*) of the leading scholars of the *madhhab*, and the practice of reducing a new question to an older one on which a ruling existed (*ilhaq*). Reformists had replaced this practice with a return to the Qur'an and *hadith* and the exercise of reasoned interpretation, *ijtihad*.

As a result of these efforts, the NU's *ulema* agreed on a compromise between *ijtihad* and tradition, by distinguishing the literal words (*qawl*) of the great *ulema* of the *madhhab* and their method (*manhaj*) of reaching their verdicts. In cases where there was neither a relevant *qawl* nor a possibility of *ilhaq*, they decided that the *ulema* could legitimately exercise "collective *ijtihad*," following the *manhaj* of the founding fathers. Theoretically, this allowed the use of reason and much greater flexibility, while remaining loyal to the *madhhab*. In practice, however, such collective *ijtihad* was not often exercised and, after promising beginnings in the 1990s, the NU's *bahth al-masa'il* reverted to more conventional topics and more conservative *fatwas* in the 2000s.

Gender Issues, Liberation Theology, and Human Rights in Traditionalist Circles

The limited opening of the gates of *ijtihad* that NU's *ulema* allowed themselves did not satisfy the demand for a more relevant and progressive religious discourse that had developed among young NU members active in discussion circles and NGOs.

Women's Rights

One area where the need for a drastic change in the existing *fiqh* discourse and its complete reconstruction was strongly felt concerned women's rights. There was also a growing belief that women's rights should be discussed from an Islamic perspective. This interest was spurred by contacts with secular women's NGOs, foreign sponsors, the emergence of Islamic feminist discourse, and acquaintance with the works of Muslim feminists such Riffat Hassan and Asghar Ali Engineer. Consequently, P3M devoted one of its *halqa* to a critical discussion of women's rights and obligations as reflected in the literature studied in the *pesantren*. Meanwhile, Muslim women's groups emerged that engaged in activities aimed at raising awareness of gender issues.

By the mid-1990s, P3M started a large project on women's reproductive health that included the development of a woman-friendly *fiqh* discourse and its dissemination. The dynamic Muslim feminist activist Lies Marcoes-Natsir was the inspiration for this project. The project resulted in the development of a vast network of women activists in the *pesantren* world and a new, gender-sensitive discourse grafted on, but critical of, traditional *fiqh*, called *fiqh al-nisa* (women's fiqh).[27]

The *fiqh al-nisa* project led to the emergence of new Muslim women's NGOs involved in gender awareness activities for *pesantren*, educating female preachers, establishing women's crisis centers and shelters, and the critical discussion of the dominant *pesantren* discourse on gender.[28] Masdar Masudi, was an early and major contributor to this rights-based discourse. But Kyai Husein Muhammad, a highly respected *kyai* from the Cirebon region with solid traditionalist credentials, became its leading thinker.

Developing a Rights-Based Islamic Discourse

The Muslim feminist movement was part of a broader trend to develop a progressive, rights-based Islamic discourse. This trend was especially strong among student activists with an NU background who studied or had studied at one of the IAINs, a principal channel of social mobility for rural Muslim youth. Many of them had also been active in *pesantren*-based community development projects or in actions in support of displaced villagers. Many were familiar with English and Arabic and were interested in postmodernism and contemporary Arab philosophers. In the mid-1980s, they had become aware of Catholic liberation theology as developed in Latin America and in the Philippines. Encouraged by Abdurrahman Wahid, some tried to develop a Muslim theology of liberation, a religious discourse that unambiguously sided with the oppressed and powerless. The result was that the young generation of NU thinkers and activists of the 1990s demanded a more radical rethinking of traditionalist Islamic discourse. They argued that, in order to eliminate the injustices and inequalities of traditionalist discourse, it was not sufficient to replace the *qawl* of the great *ulema* of the Shafi'i *madhhab* by their *manhaj*. Istead they favored the construction of a new *fiqh*. They went beyond the earlier reformists involved in the Renewal and drew inspiration from such Western thinkers as Michel Foucault and the deconstructionists as well as from contemporary Arab philosophers and thinkers. The latter included the Sudanese scholar Mahmud Muhammad Taha, introduced to them through Abdullahi An-Na'im's book on Taha.[29] Taha's revisionist reading of the Qur'an allowed for a new understanding of the faith that permitted gender equality and equality for religious minorities. Others who aroused their admiration were Hassan Hanafi, one of the originators of the Islamic left, Mohammed Abed al-Jabri, a critic of Arabic thought, and Nasr Hamed Abu Zayd, a pioneer in the hermeneutics of the Qur'an.

Institutional Networks

In the course of the 1990s, several informal discussion groups transformed themselves into NGOs. The Yogyakarta-based NGO, LKiS, later joined by its Surabaya-based counterpart LSAD, emerged as the major brokers of alternative religious ideas, most of them critical of the political and religious establishment.[30] LKiS published numerous books and organized training courses for *pesantren* youth on Islam and human rights. These NGOs were not formally affiliated with NU, and external funding gave them a degree of independence from the parent organization. Moreover, Abdurrahman Wahid strongly endorsed their search for a rights-based Islamic discourse.

These activists were aware that, in order to get a hearing and make an impact on thought and attitudes in NU circles, they had to formulate their critique and revisions in the language of traditionalist Islam. Many *kyai* had always been suspicious of foreign ideas, and they were subjected to a stream of publications from the Middle East warning of a Western ideological offensive (*al-ghazw al-fikri*) to subvert Islam. Foreign-sponsored community development programs in the *pesantren* environment had already faced some suspicion but were accepted because of the obvious benefits that they brought. However, when LKiS proposed to give training courses on human rights and direct democracy in 1997, as the Suharto regime was weakening, it ran into strong opposition from the *kyai*. Because of the tense political conditions at the time, the *kyais'* objections reflected political caution in addition to religious concerns.

To overcome their reticence, the activists replaced overt discussion of democracy and human rights with discussion of the classical Islamic concept of the "five basic needs" (*al-daruriyyat al-khamsa*). This had earlier been proposed by Abdurrahman Wahid as the proper Islamic basis for a human rights discourse and had been discussed in a series of P3M *halqas*.[31]

The "Five Basic Needs" as a Basis for an Islamic Human Rights Discourse

The concept of the "five basic needs" was well known to the *kyai* because Imam Abu Hamid al-Ghazali had discussed it at length in *al-Mustasfa*, his work on the principles of *fiqh*.

The objective of *shari'a* in al-Ghazali's discussion and that of later authors is *maslaha*, defined as that which brings benefit or prevents harm (to the *umma*). There are different categories of *maslaha*, ranging from the necessary (*daruri*) to the commendable (*tahsini*). In the former category, al-Ghazali lists five basic needs: the protection of religion (*hifz al-din*), self (*hifz al-nafs*), family (*hifz al-nasl*), property (*hifz al-mal*), and intellect (*hifz al-'aql*).

The concept of *maslaha* was further developed and given a more central place in Islamic legal thought by the fourteenth-century jurist Abu Ishaq al-Shatibi. The latter's treatment of the subject was judged to be more conducive to a modern rights-based discourse. The discussions in *halqa* organized by P3M and the human rights and democracy training courses set up by LKiS were based on Shatibi's conception of the objectives of the *shari'a* (*maqasid al-shari'a*).[32] The participants in the LKiS training sessions read Mohammed Abed al-Jabri's comparison of al-Ghazali's and al Shatibi's treatment of the basic needs (*daruriyyat*) and Jabri's arguments on why he considers Shatibi's definition to be superior. They then discussed how concepts of democracy and human rights could be derived from the five basic needs.[33]

The P3M and LKiS activists interpreted the five basic needs very differently from al-Ghazali and from the early generation of the NU leaders who had a utilitarian if not opportunistic approach to the concept of *maslaha*. For al-Ghazali, the imperative of *hifz al-din* justified the death penalty for apostasy, while the activists interpreted it as freedom of religion in the widest possible sense, including the freedom to choose any religion (i.e., freedom from the charge of apostasy) and the freedom to spread any religion.[34] They gave human rights–related interpretations to the other "basic needs" as well. *Hifz al-nafs* was said to entail not only the right to life but also freedom from torture, the right to medical services, and respect and human dignity. *Hifz al-nasl* implied the freedom to choose one's spouse and the right of both spouses to sexual enjoyment. *Hifz al-mal* meant the right to defend property against expropriations by the state or other institution and the right to employment and fair pay. *Hifz al-'aql* encompassed the right to education, freedom of opinion, expression, and association, as well as protection of (local) cultural practices.[35]

Eclecticism, Social Activism, and Discourse

The religious discourse developed by the young NU activists is eclectic and reflects selective borrowing from *usul al-fiqh*, modern Arabic philosophers, Western cultural studies, social sciences, and Oriental studies. It also reflects the influence of international NGOs and later the anti-globalization movement. Yet the result is uniquely

Indonesian and reflects the background of the activists and the context in which they operated. Most of them had a *pesantren* education and were among the first of their families to have had extensive exposure to other social circles and intellectual influences. They were not primarily thinkers but activists who developed their ideas in the course of their social and political action. They were guided by an inner moral conviction, which only later they attempted to justify on the basis of scriptural arguments.

The concept of *maqasid al-shari'a*, the objectives (rather than the letter) of the divine law, and of *maslaha*, interpreted as the common good, had a self-evident appeal to activists who were convinced that Islam is a religion of social justice. It provided a useful connection between social activism directed toward the common good and the mental world of the *pesantren*. The training courses on democracy and *al-daruriyyat al-khamsa* were a great success, and the concept of *maqasid al-shari'a* gained considerable popularity.[36] These NU activists have actively supported the rights of villagers whose land was confiscated for development projects, as well as the rights of threatened religious minorities, and they have fought for education for the poor. Their discourse stresses religious and political pluralism and tolerance, including toward the left.

A prominent representative of this combination of discourse and social activism is Kyai Husein Muhammad, the leading progressive thinker on Islam and gender relations. Together with his wife, he gives marriage counseling, runs a shelter for battered women, and fights human trafficking. He has tried to find scriptural support for his progressive ideas on gender issues in *tafsir* and *usul al-fiqh* literature, and he has also drawn on the work of progressive Arab thinkers. The arguments developed by Kyai Husein have been published by various NGOs and have found immediate application in training courses.[37]

Post-Suharto Developments

The last years of the Suharto regime in Indonesia witnessed both a growing visibility and influence of radical Islamic groups in public debate and a sharp rise in inter-religious tensions. These developments, in turn, generated different reactions on the part of other Indonesians aimed at combating the threat posed by radical Islam to the country's inter-religious peace.

Interreligious Tensions and the Defense of Religious Pluralism

One reaction to these developments was an increase in the appeal of Sufism among the urban middle classes, partly because it represented a more irenic and "inclusive" version of the faith. However, this was not the only Muslim response to radical Islam. Many felt that these events gave the theme of religious pluralism practical relevance and urgency and led to numerous manifestations of inter-religious solidarity. For example, since the burning of a number of churches at Christmas 2000, the NU youth organization Anshor has been guarding churches at times of great tension. Communal conflicts in the Moluccas attracted not only jihadists but also Muslim women's NGOs that organized relief for both Muslim and Christian victims.

NU activists became involved in the defense of other forms of pluralism. One NGO, Desantara, developed a special interest in local adaptations of Islam and acted as an advocate of "syncretistic" communities. Another NGO, Syarikat, engaged in a dialogue with the relatives of victims of the 1965–66 mass killings of Communists which had involved NU leadership and members. The basis of reconciliation was sought in the Javanese syncretistic culture that united political opponents.[38]

The Liberal Islam Network

The most direct response to radical Islam has come from the Liberal Islam Network (*Jaringan Islam Liberal*—JIL), which has gained a high media profile.[39] The JIL has campaigned for the acceptance of religious pluralism and against narrow, literalist interpretations of the faith. In terms of background and intellectual orientation, the Liberal Islam Network is even more heterogeneous than the Renewal movement, of which it is, in some sense, the successor. There is a small core group that frequently presents its own views in newspaper columns, radio commentaries, and essays posted on its Web site and electronic mailing list. Several members of the core group have an NU background and a thorough education in the classical Islamic disciplines, as well as a considerable knowledge of less conventional literature. In an important sense, the group combines the intellectual strengths of the Renewal and NU-based movements.

The most prominent member and most interesting thinker of the group, Ulil Abshar-Abdalla, is *pesantren*-educated and was active in an NU-affiliated NGO. He improved his Arabic in Jakarta at the Institute of Arabic and Islamic Studies (the institute had been established by Saudi Arabia to spread Salafi teaching). He also sharpened his analytical skills at the (Catholic) High School of Philosophy.

The clearest programmatic statement of the group is to be found in a newspaper column that Ulil wrote in 2002. In content and even in title it echoes Nurcholish's provocative speech of the 1970s: "Making Islamic Thought Fresh Again."[40] This well-written piece caused much controversy and led some self-appointed arbiters of orthodoxy to sentence Ulil to death for insulting Islam. "I consider Islam a living organism," Ulil began his declaration, "and not a dead monument erected in the seventh century . . ."

> There is a strong tendency these days to treat Islam as a monument, petrified and immutable, and it is time to challenge that attitude. We need interpretations that are non-literal, substantive, contextual, and consonant with the heartbeat of a human civilization that is ever-changing.
>
> The substance of Islam should be separated from the culture of the Arabian Peninsula, and it is that universal substance that has to be interpreted in accordance with the local cultural context. Whipping, stoning and the cutting of hands, the *jilbab* and beard are Arab cultural peculiarities, and there is no reason why other Muslims should follow them. There is not really a detailed divine law, as most

Muslims believe, but only the general principles known as *maqasid al-shari'a*, the objectives of Islamic law, and these basic values have to be given concrete content in accordance with the social and historical context. We have to learn to understand and accept that there cannot be a single interpretation of Islam that is the only or the most correct and final one. We must open ourselves to what is true and good, even if it comes from outside Islam. Islamic values can also be found in Christianity and other major religions, and even in minor local religious traditions. Islam should be seen as a *process*, never completed and closed; new interpretations may emerge, and the major criterion to judge interpretations by is *maslaha*, i.e., what is beneficial to mankind.[41]

Such views are shared by many well-educated Muslims in Indonesia, although few would state them with the same bluntness. However, unlike the original Renewal movement, which emerged in a favorable political context and enjoyed a degree of official protection, the Liberal Islam group has from its inception opposed resurgent puritan and radical Islamist movements that have significant political muscle.

Conclusions

Indonesian Islamic reformists of the early twentieth century focused on purging Islam of "syncretistic" practices, and liberating Muslims from exclusive reliance on the views of scholars of the past (*taqlid*), and replacing this by independent interpretation (*ijtihad*) of the original sources, Qur'an and *hadith*. Traditionalists organized themselves in defense of the established ritual practices and scholarly styles that were under attack. In the process, they modernized the tradition.

As organized movements, reformism and traditionalism have constituted the twin main streams of Indonesian Islam, and after the country's independence they became competing political movements. Within both, second-generation reform movements emerged that took issue with the emphasis on the political struggle and instead stressed the importance of moral values.

The Renewal (*pembaruan*) movement associated with Nurcholish, Madjid, and the emerging Muslim middle class of New Order Indonesia broke ranks with established reformism. Due to favorable political circumstances it became extremely influential. It represented a sophisticated, liberal, and "contextual" reading of Islam, embraced modernity and the Indonesian nation state, and became a staunch defender of religious pluralism, human rights, and democracy.

Other segments of the old reformist movement, in opposition under President Suharto, came increasingly under the influence of conservative Middle Eastern currents and were instrumental in a sweeping turn to conservatism after Suharto's fall in 1998. Meanwhile, within the traditionalist stream, activists and critical thinkers made efforts to develop a rights-based discourse rooted in *fiqh*, Islamic legal thought. Identifying with the weak and oppressed whom they wished to empower, they challenged established authority but had to clothe their arguments in appropriate terms in order to gain a hearing. However, in recent years, there has also been a turn to conservative interpretations of Islam in traditionalist circles and a rejection of everything that smacks of "liberalism" and Western influences.

The current confrontation between the Muslim world and the West, whether perceived or real, has strengthened the conservative backlash. But this new conservatism has in turn released a new wave of reformist thought that builds on the achievements of the Renewal movement and the traditionalist NGO activists and thinkers. This conservative trend is reflected in demands, made in June 2008 by large numbers of Muslim protesters, that the government ban the Ahamadiyya sect. These protests led to a ministerial decree that members of the group could get up to five years in jail for "tarnishing religion," although it stopped short of banning the group.

Notes

1. Christiaan Snouck Hurgronje, *Mekka in the Latter Part of the 19th Century* (Leiden: Brill, 1931); also Michael F. Laffan, *Islamic Nationhood and Colonial Indonesia: The Umma Below the Winds* (London: RoutledgeCurzon, 2003).

2. Ibid.

3. Merle C. Ricklefs, "Six Centuries of Islamization in Java," in *Conversion to Islam,* N. Levtzion, ed. (New York: Holmes and Meier, 1979), pp. 100–28; and Deliar Noer, *The Modernist Muslim Movement in Indonesia, 1900–1940* (Kuala Lumpur: Oxford University Press, 1973). In Indonesia the term "Modernist" is used to indicate all Muslim reformist trends, and not only the followers of Sayyid Ahmad Khan or Muhammad 'Abduh.

4. Howard M. Federspiel, *Islam and Ideology in the Emerging Indonesian State: The Persatuan Islam (PERSIS), 1923 to 1957* (Leiden: Brill, 2001).

5. B.J. Boland, *The Struggle of Islam in Modern Indonesia* (The Hague: Martinus Nijhoff, 1971).

6. Lance Castles, "Notes on the Islamic School at Gontor," *Indonesia,* no. 1 (1966): 30–45.

7. "Keharusan pembaruan pemikiran Islam dan masalah integrasi umat" (The Need for Renewal of Islamic Thought and Problems of Integration of the Umma). The text of this speech is reproduced in Nurcholish Madjid, *Islam, kemodernan dan keindonesiaan* (Islam, Modernity and Indonesian-ness) (Bandung: Mizan, 1987), pp. 204–14.

8. Nurcholish probably referred to the events surrounding the party that was established to replace Masyumi, the Partai Muslimin Indonesia. See Ken E. Ward, *The Foundation of the Partai Muslimin Indonesia* (Ithaca, NY: Cornell Modern Indonesia Project, 1970).

9. Djohan Effendi and Ismed Natsir, eds., *Pergolakan pemikiran Islam: catatan harian Ahmad Wahib* (The Effervescence of Islamic Thought: The Diary of Ahmad Wahib) (Jakarta: LP3ES, 1981). Ahmad Wahib died young in a traffic accident in 1973. On Wahib, see also Anthony H. Johns, "An Islamic System or Islamic Values? Nucleus of a Debate in Contemporary Indonesia," in *Islam and the Political Economy of Meaning,* W.R. Roff, ed. (London and Sydney: Croom Helm, 1987), pp. 254–80.

10. M. Dawam Rahardjo, "Pembaharuan pemikiran Islam: sebuah catatan pribadi" (The Renewal of Islamic Thought: A Private Note), Freedom Institute, May 20, 2003, available at http://www.freedom-institute.org/id/index.php?page=artikel&id=121. For a more extensive analysis of Mukti Ali's thought and his impact, see Ali Munhanif, "Islam and the Struggle for Religious Pluralism in Indonesia: A Political Reading of the Religious Thought of Mukti Ali," *Studia Islamika,* vol. 3, no. 1 (1996): 79–126.

11. Djohan Effendi and Ahmad Wahib in fact resigned from HMI in September 1969 because they felt the local leaders of the association did not tolerate their questioning of established truths and wished to impose doctrinal conformity. See Johns, "An Islamic System or Islamic Values?" pp. 266–70.

12. Saiful Muzani, "Mu'tazilah Theology and the Modernization of the Indonesian Muslim Community: Intellectual Portrait of Harun Nasution," *Studia Islamika*, vol. 1, no. 1 (1994), pp. 91–131.

13. The name is made of the Sanskrit word *parama,* meaning "supreme," and *dina,* meaning "religion." It also alludes to Medina, the city of the Prophet, which for Nurcholish remained the ideal Muslim society.

14. More extensive discussion of the thought of Nurcholish and associates in Ann Kull, *Piety and Politics: Nurcholish Madjid and His Interpretation of Islam in Modern Indonesia* (Lund: Department of Anthropology and History of Religions, 2005); and Gregory James Barton, "The Emergence of Neo-Modernism: A Progressive, Liberal Movement of Islamic Thought in Indonesia. A textual study examining the writings of Nurcholish Madjid, Djohan Effendi, Ahmad Wahib and Abdurrahman Wahid, 1968–1980," Ph.D., Monash University, Clayton, 1995.

15. The most substantial and systematic collection of these papers is Nurcholish Madjid, *Islam doktrin dan peradaban. Sebuah telaah kritis tentang masalah keimanan, kemanusiaan, dan kemoderenan* (Islam: Doctrine and Civilization. A Critical Study on Problems of Faith, Humanism, and Modernity) (Jakarta: Yayasan Wakaf Paramadina, 1992).

16. On this document, see William Montgomery Watt, *Muhammad at Medina* (Oxford: Clarendon Press, 1956), pp. 221–28.

17. Nurcholish frequently referred to the Constitution of Medina, especially after he became involved in the pro-democracy movement of the mid-1990s. The idea of the Indonesian nation state as Medina writ large is developed in several texts of that period, most extensively in his *Indonesia kita* (Our Indonesia) (Jakarta: Gramedia, 2004). His lasting fascination with Medina is also reflected in the names of the Paramadina foundation and the Madaniyya school.

18. Anthony H. Johns and Abdullah Saeed, "Nurcholish Madjid and the Interpretation of the Qur'an: Religious Pluralism and Tolerance," in *Modern Muslim intellectuals and the Qur'an,* S. Taji-Farouki, ed. (London: Oxford University Press, 2004), pp. 67–96.

19. Madjid, *Islam doktrin dan peradaban,* p. 594. Nurcholish also lists the criteria on the basis of which Gellner speaks of Islam's modernity: "universalism, scripturalism, spiritual egalitarianism, the extension of full participation in the sacred community not to one, or some, but to *all,* and the rational systematization of social life" (Ernest Gellner, *Muslim Society* [Cambridge University Press, 1981], p. 7). Bellah's argument (Robert N. Bellah, "Islamic Tradition and the Problems of Modernization," in Bellah, *Beyond Belief. Essays on Religion in a Post-Traditional World* [New York: Harper & Row, 1970], pp. 146–67) had inspired Nurcholish's plea for secularization in his famous 1970 speech and has a prominent place in *Indonesia kita.*

20. Nurcholish Madjid, *Khazanah intelektual Islam* (The Intellectual Resources of Islam) (Jakarta: Bulan Bintang, 1985).

21. Zainun Kamal et al., *Fiqih lintas agama: membangun masyarakat inklusif-pluralis* (The *Fiqh* of Inter-Religious Relations: Building an Inclusive, Pluralistic Society) (Jakarta: Yayasan Wakaf Paramadina, 2004).

22. Some observers, notably Greg Barton, have for this reason lumped him together with the Renewal movement as representing Indonesian Islamic "Neo-Modernism." See Barton, "The Emergence of Neo-Modernism." The distinctiveness of Abdurrahman Wahid, his background and his thought is brought out more clearly in a judicious article by Mujiburrahman, "Islam and Politics in Indonesia: The Political Thought of Abdurrahman Wahid," *Islam and Christian-Muslim Relations,* no. 10 (1999): 339–52.

23. The story of the various NGO activities in the NU environment is told in Martin van Bruinessen and Farid Wajidi, "Syu'un Ijtima'iyah and the Kiai Rakyat: Traditionalist Islam, Civil Society and Social Concerns," in *Indonesian Transitions*, ed. H. Schulte Nordholt (Yogyakarta: Pustaka Pelajar, 2006), pp. 205–48.

24. P3M stands for Perhimpunan Pengembangan Pesantren dan Masyarakat—Association for the Development of *Pesantren* and Society.

25. Masdar F. Mas'udi, *Fiqh permusyawaratan/ perwakilan rakyat* (The *Fiqh* of Consultation and People's Representation) (Jakarta: P3M-RMI-Pesantren Cipasung, 1992); idem, *Agama dan hak rakyat* (Religion and the Rights of the People) (Jakarta: P3M, 1993).

26. Martin van Bruinessen, "Traditions for the Future: The Reconstruction of Traditionalist Discourse Within NU," in *Nahdlatul Ulama, Traditional Islam and Modernity in Indonesia*, ed. G. Barton and G. Fealy (Clayton, VIC: Monash Asia Institute, 1996), pp. 163–89.

27. Lies M. Marcoes-Natsir and Syafiq Hasyim, *P3M dan program fiqh an-nisa untuk penguatan hak-hak reproduksi perempuan* (P3M and the Program of Women's *Fiqh* for the Empowerment of Women's Reproductive Rights) (Jakarta: P3M, 1997). This is both a training manual and a description of the program.

28. See chapter 7 of Djohan Effendi, "Progressive Traditionalists: The Emergence of a New Discourse in Indonesia's Nahdlatul Ulama during the Abdurrahman Wahid Era," Ph.D. diss, Department of Religious Studies, Deakin University, Melbourne, 2000. Also, Andrée Feillard, "Indonesia's Emerging Muslim Feminism: Women Leaders on Equality, Inheritance and Other Gender Issues," *Studia Islamika*, vol. 4, no. 1 (1997): 83–111.

29. Abdullahi Ahmed An-Na'im, *Toward an Islamic Reformation: Civil Liberties, Human Rights, and International Law* (Syracuse, NY: Syracuse University Press, 1990). Shortly after, Taha's own works in Arabic and the English translation, *The Second Message of Islam* (Syracuse University Press, 1987) were being passed from hand to hand. The latter was published in Indonesian under an equally significant title: *Syari'ah demokratik* (Surabaya: LSAD, 1996).

30. LKiS stands for Lembaga Kajian Islam dan Sosial (Institute of Islamic and Social Studies); LSAD for Lembaga Studi Agama dan Demokrasi (Institute for the Study of Religion and Democracy).

31. Abdurrahman Wahid may have been the first in Indonesia to connect the concept of *al-daruriyyat al-khamsa* with a modern concept of human rights, as he did in several discussions in Jakarta in the late 1980s and a number of published articles, briefly discussed in Mujiburrahman, "Islam and Politics," p. 344. The P3M *halqa* on this subject, and the interpretations that emerged there, are discussed in Effendi, "Progressive Traditionalists," pp. 162–72.

32. Shatibi's treatment of *maslaha* and the five *daruriyya* is discussed in Muhammad Khalid Masud, *Shatibi's Philosophy of Islamic Law* (Islamabad: Islamic Research Institute, 1995), pp. 151–62.

33. This paragraph is based on discussions with Jadul Maula and Luthfi, the LKiS activists who devised and organized the training course. The training is also briefly discussed in Mochamad Sodik, *Gejolak santri kota: aktivis muda NU merambah jalan lain* (The Urban Santri as Torch-Bearer: Young NU Activists Paving a New Way) (Yogyakarta: Tiara Wacana, 2000), pp. 59–62.

34. The last-named point is significant: in Indonesia, proselytization is prohibited except among the marginal populations that do not adhere to one of the five officially recognized religions. See Mujiburrahman, "Feeling Threatened: Muslim-Christian Relations in Indonesia's New Order," Ph.D. diss., University of Utrecht, 2006, pp. 72–91, available at http://igitur-archive.library.uu.nl/dissertations/2006-0915-201013/index.htm.

35. Effendi, "Progressive Traditionalists," pp. 168–72.

36. The dangers of reliance on this utilitarian argument were brought home to the activists a few years later, when one of the Bali bombers, Amrozi, justified his act of terrorism with a reasoning that also appeared based on the protection of the five *daruriyyat*: protection of religion from foreign domination, etc. It made them aware that they needed additional arguments to support their own interpretation of *maslaha* against other versions.

37. KH. Husein Muhammad, *Islam agama ramah perempuan: pembelaan kiai pesantren* (Islam, a Woman-Friendly Religion: Defense by a Pesantren Kyai) (Yogyakarta: LKiS & Fahmina Institute, 2004). A book of training materials developed by Kyai Husein and his collaborators was recently translated into English: Husein Muhammad, Faqihuddin Abdul Qodir, Lies Marcoes-Natsir and Marzuki Wahid, *Dawrah Fiqh Concerning Women: Manual for a Course on Islam and Gender* (Cirebon: Fahmina Institute, 2006).

38. Farid Wajidi, "Syarikat dan eksperimentasi rekonsiliasi kulturalnya (sebuah pengamatan awal)" (Syarikat and Its Experiment of a Cultural Reconcilation [A First Observation]), *Tashwirul Afkar,* vol. 15 (2003): 55–79.

39. The name was taken from the title of Charles Kurtzman's collection of readings, *Liberal Islam: A Source Book* (New York: Oxford University Press, 1998). JIL has a syndicated radio program, a weekly page in a major newspaper, a very lively email discussion list, and an active Web site that also has English pages, available at http://islamlib.com/.

40. "Menyegarkan kembali pemikiran Islam," originally published in the daily *Kompas,* November 18, 2002; reprinted in Ulil Abshar-Abdallah, *Menjadi muslim liberal* (Becoming a Liberal Muslim) (Jakarta: Nalar, 2005), pp. 3–10.

41. This is a short translation of the first part of the text; much of the second part consists of a fierce critique of the Islamists' project of implementing the *shari'a* as a ready-made solution for all problems and of their Manichaean worldview opposing "Islam" and "the West."

6

Reformist Muslim
Thinkers in Malaysia

Engaging with Power to Uplift the *Umma?*

Farish A. Noor

*The option elected by any religious community will be determined—not by the
timeless truths of scripture but by the struggle for the influence among rival
bearers of the Word.*
　　　　　　　　　　　　　　　　　—Robert Hefner, *Civil Islam* (2000)[1]

In the years since the United States launched a "war on terror," geopolitical considerations have compelled Western and Muslim governments to seek allies and
partners for dialogue, and they have called for "reformist" and "moderate" and
"progressive" Muslim voices to be heard. Yet they have not attempted to define
what those descriptions might actually mean. Does a quiescent Islam that does not
challenge the existing power structures or Western policies qualify as reformist?
Or does the term "reformist Islam" refer to a methodology of interpreting Islamic
sources that is based more on reason and offers a more liberal interpretation of
Islam, especially on human and gender rights? Malaysia, Indonesia, and Turkey
have been singled out as "model" Muslim states where "moderate Islam" prevails.
Why might this be, and on what criteria is this judgment based?

　　The aim of this chapter is to try to answer some of these questions by examining the challenges and prospects of reformist Islam in Malaysia, a country where
contests over the form, meaning, and content of Islam have been raging since long
before the country gained independence. The chapter will assess the viability of
the project of reformist Islam and will question some of its fundamental premises.
It will also inquire into the political, cultural, historical, economic, and theological
factors that shape the form and content of this discourse and guide its workings.

　　The chapter will first focus on historical factors that have given rise to the
phenomenon of reformist Islam and have shaped its discourse. It will ask how and
why reformist Islamic thought appeared in Malaysia. What were its antecedents,

who were its early primary proponents, and what were their motives? What was the connection between the rise of reformist Islam and the struggle for power and influence in Malaysia? This analysis is necessary for understanding the complex mechanics involved in the evolution of, and disputation over, reformist Islam.

This analysis will be done by examining the lives and work of a number of prominent Malaysian Muslim intellectuals; locating their standing and subject-positions vis-à-vis both the state and Malaysian society; and comparing their stands on issues of social equality, state power, democracy, pluralism, and gender equality, as well as their methodologies and modes of representation. Finally, the chapter will assess the long-term prospects of reformist Islam in Malaysia and will consider whether the entire project of reformist Islam will be dashed on the hard rocks of realpolitik.

In the context of this chapter, reformist Islam will be defined as rationalist in its methodology and liberal in its aspirations: specifically, an Islam that is more concerned with the faith's ultimate goals, which are justice, compassion, and human dignity.

Reformist Islam in Historical Context

In Malaysia, different manifestations of Islam, including reformist Islam, have been directly connected with issues related to the rise of national consciousness, the anticolonial struggle, nation building, and the effort to shape the character of the Malaysian state and society. In other words, different manifestations of Islam have been intimately connected with the question of power and who wields it.

The close interaction between Islam and politics in Malaysia dates from the late-nineteenth century, when Muslims throughout the world were trying to organize and mobilize against internal and external threats. The Muslims of colonial Malaya had to contend with both the pressure imposed by living under secular Western colonial rule and the threat of other Asian powers, such as the Kingdom of Siam, which had territorial ambitions on the weakened Malay-Muslim kingdoms in the peninsula.

In Malaysia, the discourse and normative expression of Islam were used to mobilize the masses against the combined threat of Western colonialism, foreign economic exploitation, and competition with non-indigenous and non-Muslim communities. However, different groups had different interpretations of Islam, as well as different visions for a postcolonial Malaysian state and society. These groups included both secular nationalists and various groups inspired by Islam.

Early Reformist Thinkers

Reformist Muslim thinkers were a component in the connection that developed between Islam and politics in Malaysia. From the very beginning, they were deeply concerned with realities of power and its differentials, and they were engaged in the ongoing debate about the country's political and cultural future. Their goal and ambition were to develop a school of Islamic praxis and norms that could elevate the Malay Muslims' political and economic status and offer guidance about dealing with realities of life under colonial rule, while also opposing it.

In pursuance of this vision, early on a group of Muslim reformist thinkers, including Sheikh Muhammad Tahir Jalaluddin and Syed Sheikh al-Hadi, played a key role in encouraging reform and mobilizing the masses against what they regarded as the entrenched interests of the conservative feudal elite. These Malay and Peranakan (mixed ancestry)[2] reformist thinkers looked for inspiration to Japan and the Ottoman state and the works of such Muslim reformers as Jamal al-Din al-Afghani and Muhammad Abduh.

Sheikh Muhammad Tahir Jalaluddin, perhaps the most important early Malay reformer, had studied in Mecca with Malay *ulema* based there—notably, Sheikh Umar al-Sumbawi, Sheikh Uthman al-Sarawaki, and Shaikh Ahmad Khatib of Minangkabau—and at Al-Azhar University in Cairo with Muhammad Rashid Rida, a disciple of Abduh's. Through his educational efforts, the reformist ideas and analytical methods of Abduh and Rashid Rida were introduced to the Malay Muslims.

Like their counterparts in the western part of the Islamic world, the Malay and Peranakan Muslim reformers of the archipelago saw education as vital for improving people's conditions and reducing foreign domination, and so they set up modern reformist Islamic seminaries (*madrasas*) and established a vernacular Islamic press. They also sought more fundamental social, economic, and political reform. The reformist thinkers then widely known as the *kaum muda* (younger generation) were mostly Malay. The Peranakan Muslims had grown up in the British colonial settlements of Penang, Malacca, and Singapore. They were the inheritors of a different intellectual tradition dating back to the time of the writer and educator Munshi Abdullah (also known as Abdullah bin Abdul Kadir), whose works were written in the mid-nineteenth century. Being urban-based, both the Malay and Peranakan Muslims were shaped by the values and lifestyle of a modern, cosmopolitan mercantile community where economic and political success was the key to survival.

The Traditionalist/Reformist Encounter

Reformist Muslim scholars were strongly opposed by the "old," or traditionalist, Muslims, known as *kaum tua*. They advocated a more conservative interpretation of Islam, which emphasized the importance of tradition, deference to authority (both political and religious), and a literalist reading of the Qur'an and *hadith*. The intense political, discursive, and at times physical struggle between the traditionalist *kaum tua* and the reformist *kaum muda* introduced terms such as *pembaruan* (renewal), *nahda* (rebirth, renaissance), and *modernisme* (modernity) into the discursive economy of normative Islam.

The entry of these novel terms and ideas into Islamic hermeneutics radically changed the Malay Muslims' understanding and perception of Islam. Renewal (*pembaruan*) meant a shift from the old to the new, the rethinking and reconceptualization of all things (normatively) Islamic, and a rejection of antiquated and outdated elements, such as saint worship and veneration of tombs, that were deemed no longer relevant or necessary.

The introduction of these new ideas opened the way for the drawing of new chains of equivalences. Reformists equated "true" Islam with modernization, material and economic progress, and the spirit of rationalism and critical enquiry. Related to this was a secondary chain of equivalences that equated "old" Islam with traditionalism, obscurantism, the occult, economic stagnation, and underdevelopment in its most comprehensive sense.

The *kaum muda* reformists lived and worked in the British Crown Colonies of Singapore, Malacca, and Penang, which were governed under British secular law and not traditional Islamic and *adat* (customary) laws, as was the case in the Malay sultanates. This situation made them realize their own precarious position as British colonial subjects in need of British protection and help. In the Malay-ruled states of the Peninsula, they would have suffered persecution at the hands of traditional *ulema* and royal houses. There their writings were often banned. This situation explains both the liminal status of these reformists and their ambiguous relationship to colonial rule and the institution of the state.

Islam's reform in British Malaya was thus facilitated via an adaptation to the realities of power, or more specifically, colonial rule. Ironically, it was the fact of living under foreign rule that protected the Malay reformist and modernist Muslims. They, in turn, were acutely aware of both the practical necessity of power and patronage and the need to gain power themselves. These early reformers opened the way for the rise of reformist Islam in Malaysia. Their discourse remains part of Malaysia's intellectual terrain to this day.

Fighting Islam with Islam: Malaysia's State-Sponsored Islamization

> The State has become the primary determinant of the dominant discourse on Islam in Malaysia to which all alternative groups must or have necessarily responded.
>
> —Shanti Nair, *Islam in Malaysian Foreign Policy* (1997)[3]

Malaysia gained independence on August 31, 1957, without having to fight for it. The first generation of postcolonial leaders in Malaysia, led by Tunku Abdul Rahman (the country's first prime minister) and the United Malays National Organization (UMNO), were mostly products of British colonial education. Malaysia inherited a system of secular democracy based on the Westminster model. Malaysian leaders like Tunku did not favor a politicized Islam and resisted calls to establish an Islamic state, as demanded by the opposition Pan-Malaysian Islamic Party (PAS), founded in 1951.[4] Tunku used the argument of Malaysia's ethnic and religious diversity to oppose such demands: "Our country has many races and unless we are prepared to drown every non-Malay in the sea, we can never think of an Islamic administration."[5]

Yet successive Malaysian governments could not ignore the country's religious, economic, and political realities. Among those realities was the fact that Malaysia's first Islamist party, the Hizbul Muslimin, had been banned and its leaders arrested by British authorities in 1948. It was succeeded by the PAS in 1951. Committed to the establishment of an Islamic state, PAS proved to be UMNO's staunchest opponent. The existence of PAS meant that other political parties, UMNO included, could not leave the discursive field on Islam to PAS. Rather, they have had to develop their own Islamic discourse, thus giving rise to a state-sponsored Islamic project.

Imperatives of Development and Islam

For Malaysia's first-generation postcolonial leaders, the priority was rapid economic development. The Malaysian government was concerned that the country's import-substitution economy would be left vulnerable to the vicissitudes of the global market and the disruptive and unpredictable consequences of the Cold War. It therefore decided to embark on an ambitious policy of expanding public education programs, intensifying infrastructure development, and redirecting the economy from reliance on heavy industries to export-led growth. The short-term goal was to break out of the economic and intellectual dependency that blighted so many postcolonial states.

Malaysia's development was thus left entirely in the hands of secular-educated technocrats and bureaucrats. Islam and its normative expression and practice were left to the ordinary *ulema* and religious leaders, whose power and charismatic authority lay in their enormous cultural capital.

The development process was uneven however, and the distribution of its benefits was skewed in favor of urban populations. The wide urban-rural gap coincided with class, race, and religious cleavages. The urbanized elite tended to come from the Western- and secular-educated middle and professional classes, with an over-representation of Chinese, Indian, and other "migrant" races.

Meanwhile, the urbanized, university-educated Muslim intelligentsia felt both alienated from the state and cut off from other Muslims because of their own relative distance from them. This situation offered opportunities for Islamist opposition parties, social movements, and pressure groups to fill the gap. In the process, like their counterparts in other Muslim countries, they formed close partnerships and organic links to the "lumpen" *umma*, who felt abandoned by statist elites, the urban bourgeoisie, and Muslim intellectuals alike.

Consequently, the Islamists of PAS and groups like ABIM (Angkatan Belia Islam Malaysia, the Malaysian Islamic Youth Movement) and the neo-Sufi Darul Arqam movement gained support among rural Malays in the underdeveloped, mostly agrarian-based northern states. This situation eventually compelled UMNO to embark on its wooing of underprivileged Muslims, since it was unwilling to allow PAS, ABIM, and Darul Arqam to win the contest to define the meaning and content of Islam. Thus, in response to the proliferation of Islamic groups in the 1970s and their demands for the establishment of an Islamic state, UMNO attempted to play its role as "protector" of not only the Malay race but of Islam as well.

Statist, Modernist, Developmentalist Islam

The response of the Malaysian government to the challenge of extremist and even some traditionalist groups was to offer its own version of reformist Islam. Malaysia's experiment with "statist-developmentalist-modernist" Islam began in 1981, when the country experienced its fourth peaceful transition of power and the beginning of the premiership of Dr. Mahathir Muhammad. Mahathir's credentials and popularity lay in his claim of being a modernist leader who wanted to propel the country into the modern age through rapid development, modern education, and reform of the normative understanding and practice of Islam itself. He rose to power with the backing of millions of ordinary middle-class professional Malay-Muslims who also supported his calls for affirmative action and pro-Malay economic policies.

The 1980s witnessed the implementation of an UMNO-led state Islamization policy. Mahathir had his own way of addressing the challenge posed by the Islamist opposition. He did not favor the confrontational approach of Tunisia's Habib Bourguiba, the Sudanese leader Ja'far Muhammad Numayri's spectacular displays of piety, or the vague conciliatory maneuvers of Suharto. As Shanti Nair (1997) puts it, Mahathir's vision meant that:

> Domestically, Islamization focused on the distinction between a "moderate" Islam deemed more appropriate in the context of Malaysian society against more radical expressions which were unacceptable to the government. The conflict between "moderate" and "extreme," in effect, encompassed intra-Malay rivalry.[6]

UMNO's brand of state-sponsored modernist Islam was based on a chain of equivalences that equated Islam with all that was positive, such as modernity, economic development, material progress, rationality, and economic liberalism (though, interestingly, not with democracy, freedom of speech, and free media). The UMNO understanding of Islam was framed against a negative chain of equivalences that equated PAS's brand of Islam with obscurantism, extremism, fanaticism, intolerance, backwardness, and militancy.

The bone of contention between UMNO and PAS at the time was not whether Islam was "liberal" or "tolerant" in the Western sense, but rather whether as a system of belief and values it could be used to promote a dynamic outlook on economic and political issues. To this end, the machinery of the state was directed toward an Islamization program that was meant to eliminate discrepancies between different sites and sources of Islamic authority while outdoing the claims and promises of PAS and other Islamist movements.[7]

By initiating its own Islamization program, the government of Dr. Mahathir effectively stole the initiative from the Islamists of PAS, ABIM, and Arqam. In time, the labors of the Mahathir administration began to pay off: Malaysia's International Islamic University (IIU) project received considerable financial assistance from Arab governments, the bulk of which was for Islamic *dakwah* (Arabic *da'wa*), or proselytizing, activities.[8] Mahathir himself gained recognition for his efforts as a Muslim leader. In 1983 he was given the "Great Leader" award by General Muhammad Zia ul-Haq, president of Pakistan.

To foreclose any possibility of further doctrinal conflict in the area of religion and religious practice, the UMNO-led government empowered the religious arm of the bureaucracy and in 1991 set up the International Institute of Islamic Thought and Civilization (ISTAC)[9] under the leadership of the influential Islamist thinker, Syed Muhammad Naquib al-Attas. The creation of ISTAC and the appointment of Naquib al-Attas as its head was another attempt by the Malaysian state to co-opt the voice of Muslim intellectuals in its bid to gain hegemonic leverage over the Islamist opposition, while also suturing the discourse of Islam once and for all.

The Institute was promoted as an attempt by the Malaysian state to showcase its brand of modernist, moderate, and progressive Islam Yet the institute and the man chosen to lead it were firmly embedded within the power structures of the state and were thus part of the state's expansive machinery. In the workings of ISTAC one can see the difficulties that may be faced by Muslim intellectuals who have to operate within the confines of state patronage and power.

Power and Patronage: Syed Muhammad Naquib al-Attas and the Pitfalls of State Power

Syed Muhammad Naquib al-Attas is one of the most influential Muslim intellectuals in Malaysia today. His influence extends well beyond the confines of academia, and he has played an important role in cultivation of the Islamic elite in the country. He comes from a famous aristocratic family in the southern state of Johore and is of mixed Malay-Arab (*Hadrami*) stock. He studied at Eton, Sandhurst Military Academy, and the School of Oriental and African Studies (SOAS), University of London. He is known as the proponent of the "Islamization of knowledge" project, now a major international effort.

By co-opting al-Attas into its expansive network of Islamic institutions and research centers, the government succeeded in gaining the upper hand in its competition with Islamist opposition. Al-Attas's early works tried to establish that Malaysian society in general and the Malay society in particular were definitively and permanently shaped by the arrival and consolidation of Islam. Islam's arrival in the Malay world marked a radical rupture from the past and a total break from the pre-Islamic era. Moreover, al-Attas the reformist-modernist equates Islam with modernity per se and posits that Islam's arrival also meant the arrival of modernity to the Malay world. In his *Preliminary Statement on a General Theory of the Islamization of the Malay-Indonesian Archipelago* (1963), he wrote: "The coming of Islam, seen from the perspective of modern times, was the most momentous event in the history of the (Malay) Archipelago."[10] This thesis was a comfortable notion for conservative Malay Muslims, who saw themselves as a separate constituency distinct and apart from other racial and religious groups. Al-Attas insisted on Islam's superiority while belittling as superficial the achievements of the Malays' pre-Islamic ancestors.[11]

After eliminating any other worthy ideological competitors, al-Attas then proceeded to backdate and post-rationalize Islam's arrival to the region with a view of presenting Islam in modernist terms. In his *Commentary on the Hujjat al-Siddiq of Nur al-Din al-Raniri* (1986), he insisted on the modern aspect of Islamic philosophy, which for him remains a viable alternative to Western logic and epistemology.[12] Al-Attas explained Islam's ascendancy in modern, rational, and positivist terms. For al-Attas, Islam's victory in the Malay Archipelago had less to do with conquest or the realities of shifting trade patterns in Asia in the sixteenth to eighteenth centuries than with Islam's ideational superiority as a value and belief system.

But his own reading of Islam and his undue emphasis on the rites and rituals of Islamic mysticism, in particular, betrayed his leanings toward the state and the question of power. This penchant for the trappings of ritualized and performative power has been noted by his critics, such as Mona Abaza, in her study of the work and ideas of al-Attas and his place within Malaysian politics and academia.[13] Al-Attas's engagement with state power in many ways reflected the concerns of the earlier generation of Malay and Peranakan Muslim reformists who understood the need to possess power and to control the state. His own accommodation with power came in the form of his acceptance of the post of head of ISTAC.

In 1978, al-Attas's most influential book, *Islam and Secularism*, was published by the Malaysian Islamist movement ABIM.[14] In it, he proposes a bifurcated and dichotomized worldview opposing Islam and Western secularism to one another. He defined the latter in purely negative terms as bereft of morality, ethics, and the sense of the sacred, beauty, spirituality, and God. He severely criticized Western philosophical systems for being de-sacralized, and regarded modern-day journalism as one of the vices of Western life and values. He blamed the West for developing the cult of public opinion that equalizes all worldviews in a relativist way and neglects the superior role and status of the wise and the learned to lead the society. He therefore insisted that Islamic norms of respect for authority, deference to the learned, and obedience to the just state should be lauded and promoted by Muslim leaders and ordinary Muslims alike. In doing so, however, he contradicted other Islamic injunctions that emphasize equality among Muslims and the importance of people's acceptance of the ruler enshrined in the concepts of *baya* (swearing of allegiance) and *shura* (rule by consultation), and he overlooked the frequent Qur'anic references to *al-nass* (the people). These important lapses in the end make al-Attas's reformism of a limited and lopsided nature and placed in the service of the legitimization of state power and its developmentalist project.

The Failure of State-Sponsored Islamic Reformism

By creating ISTAC, the Malaysian government had hoped to control and counteract the influence of resurgent forces of Islam. But by trying to fight the tide of oppositional Islam with its own brand of statist-developmentalist-modernist Islam, the government effectively inflated the Islamic discourse and raised levels of expectations among its own constituency. It was this inflation of Islamic discourse and normative practices, along with the normalization of religion in public life, that ultimately made it impossible for the government to control the form and content of Islamic discourse and the area of its circulation.

The nation-builders of Malaysia regarded normative Islam as a factor that could be inculcated into the development process to produce the desired results. But they overlooked the fact that Islam—like all religions—is a *variable* factor that is beyond anybody's control. In time, the modernist-developmentalist model of statist Islam collapsed under the weight of its own contradictions and the impossibility of policing the discursive frontiers of Islamism.

The modernist message failed to get through to the *umma* because of inadequate and faulty tools of dissemination; its proponents' lack of eloquence, their alienation from the believers, and the lack of credibility of its primary articulator—the state. Institutions like ISTAC and the Institute of Islamic Understanding (IKIM) were seen as institutions that had been set up under the patronage of the Mahathir administration as part of the government's Islamization campaign. They were thus seen as disconnected from the people and their needs.

Thus while the research and academic staff of the institute busied themselves with questions about the need for a radical paradigm shift that would bring about an essentially Islamic epistemology, ordinary Malay Muslims went about their lives as they had always done. These institutions therefore came to be seen as representing "refeudalization" and the institutionalization of an "Islam of power."[15]

Meanwhile, the opposition and the traditional *ulema* dismissed state-sponsored Islamization as cosmetic, a view that appealed to more orthodox Muslims. Such an "Islam of power" was obviously not able or meant to speak truth to power or even to question its operational and working premises. Against such a backdrop, what hope was there of ever creating an Islam that spoke for the powerless? What was needed was a "third voice" that could speak the language of the man in the street, the farmer in the field, and the corporate manager in the high-rise apartment block. Between the ideologues and Islamist intellectuals of the state on the one hand and the strident voices of the Islamist opposition on the other, Malaysian society was still in need of an independent Muslim voice that could maintain a degree of objective distance from both polarities. In other words, Malaysia needed a truly reformist voice of Islam.

Liminality and Critique: Chandra Muzaffar and the Struggle for Reform in Islam

> *The challenge that awaits the progressives is to harness this Islamic discourse and to recreate the conditions in which an open, tolerant and pluralistic society can emerge. . . . These are contemporary problems that need modern solutions, and the answer lies in part in the creation of a modern and progressive school of thought that is firmly rooted in the politics of the here-and-now, and which operates through the democratic process. What the Muslim world needs more than ever is a living, vibrant culture of dignity consonant with one of the most vital concepts of the Qur'an: the status of the human being as khalifatullah, the vicegerent of God.*
>
> —Interview with Chandra Muzaffar, "What the Muslim world needs more than ever is a culture of dignity"[16]

If Syed Muhammad Naquib al-Attas represents statist Islamic reformism, Chandra Muzaffar epitomizes the intellectual who remains independent from the state. A former academic based at the Scientific University of Malaysia (USM) and the University of Malaya (UM), Muzaffar is the founder and leader of well-known Malaysian NGOs like Aliran and the International Movement for a Just World (JUST). He has campaigned for human rights and been imprisoned for it.

Muzaffar is of Indian origin and a convert to Islam.[17] He pursued his academic and activist career simultaneously during his student days at the University of Malaya in the 1960s. In many respects, Chandra remains a liminal figure in Malaysia's constellation of intellectuals and activists. His ethnic and religious background enables him to straddle Malaysia's racial and religious schisms. Chandra experiences the realities of Malaysian life from the point of view of both insider and outsider. His identity as a Muslim makes him welcome and trusted by the Muslim community, while his Indian background makes him the member of one of the marginalized racial minority groupings. This dual perspective lends his work a uniquely objective critical distance.

He demonstrated his political scientist's bent in his powerful study of the nature and form of Malay political culture. The study highlighted the extent to which contemporary Malaysian politics was still dominated by residual influences of Malay traditionalist feudalism. Published in 1979, the work, titled *Protector? An Analysis of the Concept and Practice of Loyalty in Leader-led Relationships within Malay Society*,[18] was the first sustained critique of modern modes of Malay feudalism that attempted to explain, analyze, and deconstruct the workings of power and governance among the ruling Malay elite and their leaders, and particularly the ruling UMNO party. It was lauded as a landmark work that exposed the structural inequalities of Malaysia's Malay-dominated and Malay-colored politics, but it was rejected by the ruling elite of UMNO.

In *Protector?* Chandra questioned the extent to which Islam's arrival in the thirteenth century had reformed the political mindset of the Malay ruling elite. He maintained that Islam had superficially converted the Malays of the archipelago, while itself being converted and instrumentalized by the Malay feudal elite, who saw it as an effective means to legitimize their power.

In another work, *The Universalism of Islam* (1979),[19] Muzaffar again criticized the elite instrumentalization of Islam and emphasized Islam's fundamental universalism and its non-recognition of differences of age, gender, class, caste, and social status because they were irreconcilable with the fundamental Islamic notion of *tawhid* (the unity of God and creation).

The underlying theme of Chandra's philosophy is how to translate Islam's values and goals into a living reality that is relevant in the here-and-now and to extend its universalism to its utmost inclusive domain, thus bridging the gap between Muslims and non-Muslims. In his own words: "The struggle for justice in politics is the struggle to translate that principle into policy."[20] But how is the struggle for justice and its application to be carried out if the state itself is a double-edged tool that one has to be wary of? A committed anti-racist who has campaigned against sectarian race-based politics, Chandra's position in the Malaysian political scene has been equidistant between the state and the Islamist opposition. Skeptical of the workings of power, he has called on Muslim governments and leaders (including the government of Malaysia) to understand and apply Islam's principles in a non-superficial manner. In his essay "Islam: Justice and Politics" (1993) Chandra states:

> Our first and foremost challenge if we want to create a responsible Ummah committed to the Qur'anic ideal of justice into reality is the total eradication of illiteracy among Muslims. Perhaps the Organisation of the Islamic Conference (OIC) with its vast material resources could make this its goal. . . . If Muslim countries can spend so much money on producing world cup football teams, surely they can do something to ensure that every Muslim can read the Qur'an.[21]

Cognizant of political realities and the need to secure power prior to effecting any form of social change, Chandra does not dismiss the state per se or deny the necessity of power:

> If there was a government committed to reformist Islam, it should take the lead. It should be a government that feels strongly about the legitimacy of Qur'anic justice and which has a good track record of protecting the dignity and welfare of its people. We emphasise the role of government in this because we know that without political power it will not be possible to put into practice the values and principles of justice contained in the Qur'an.[22]

While recognizing the necessity of power, Chandra is aware of its abuse by both secular and superficially religious elites. Bemoaning the deliberate instrumentalization of Islam for sectarian ends, he criticizes Muslim political and theological elites' excessive focus on the details of religious dogma and their failure to address the real issues of the day:

Instead of seeing the Qur'an and the Sunna in a holistic manner [such elites] have adopted a selective, sectarian approach which in itself is an injustice to God's revelation. This is why the Qur'an's fundamental proclamation of justice and compassion is often lost in a cacophony of trivialities.[23]

Pointing to the failure of nominally "Islamic" regimes such as that of postrevolutionary Iran, Sudan, and Saudi Arabia, Chandra criticizes the Muslim states' and elites' tendency to focus too much on matters of religious praxis and dogma such as the veiling of women, public demonstrations of piety, and other forms of spectacular religiosity such as the construction of grand mosques, while failing to build hospitals and libraries or to provide them with adequate resources.[24] Warning of the "idolisation of mainstream Islamic tradition" that leads to the growing conservatism of Islamic movements, Chandra cautions against relinquishing too much power and authority to religious theocratic elites, for they, too, are susceptible to the temptations of power and its abuses.[25] He bluntly states that "there is perhaps not a single country in the whole world where Islamization or Islamic resurgence has brought Muslims closer to the ideal of a just and compassionate society."[26]

This skepticism about power and the state compels him to warn the public against what he terms the "car-sticker approach to religion"[27] that overstates the importance of form over substance and to restate again and again the primacy of the individual and his role in his own religious and political salvation:

It must be emphasised time and again that understanding the Qur'an is a task that the individual alone must undertake on his own and not through someone else. For in Islam there is no intercessor. The relationship with God is direct. . . . We may seek guidance of those who are well-versed in the Qur'an as we try to learn God's word but the responsibility of understanding and applying it to ourselves is our own.[28]

Chandra the political analyst and Muslim intellectual is thus thoroughly skeptical about the capacity of the state—as a tool in the hands of ordinary human beings—to deliver justice and Islamic justice in particular. Yet the Muslim intellectual in Chandra wishes to defend Islam both from the state and from the theocratic elites who may try to instrumentalize it for their own ends.

Finally, he finds refuge in the abstract concept of the rational, individual human being, who, in his eyes, remains the dignified bearer of the message of religion and God's vicegerent on earth. This sums up both the philosophy and the methodology of Chandra when he interprets both Islamic texts and history for the sake of contemporary political and social struggles in the here-and-now. Adopting a rationalist approach while paying close attention to the specificity of Muslim history, Chandra scrupulously reads through normative Muslim history and Islamic law to identify the essential ideas and values of humanism and universalism that can be taken as resources for a transformative project in the present. From this belief in the universal message of the religion, he takes the foundational ideas of Islam—such as the universal equality of all human beings before God—as the starting point for an emancipatory project that embraces other contemporary struggles such as gender and racial equality. It is therefore hardly surprising that many of his students and followers come from other faith-based NGOs and civil society groups such as the Malaysian Muslim feminist organization, Sisters in Islam (SIS).

Chandra's calculated distancing from power makes him an ambiguous figure in Malaysian politics. The Malaysian state views him as a respected and world-renown intellectual-activist who has raised Malaysia's profile thanks to his own global voice, but is wary of his criticisms of the government. Malaysia's Islamist opposition parties and movements welcome his critiques of the government, but remain worried about his criticism of Islamist governments, regimes, and parties at home and abroad.

Other Reformist Voices

Kassim Ahmad, the Critic of Hadith

Chandra stands alone as the most eloquent voice of Islamic reformism in Malaysia, but there are a number of other individuals and organizations who offer a progressive view of Islam.

Kassim Ahmad is one of these voices. His influence today is not significant—his career peaked in the 1980s. Nevertheless, with his criticism of reliance on the *hadith* and his call for a return to the Qur'an, he played a pioneering role in generating a more rationalist discourse in Malaysian Islam.* Ahmad's philosophy is best elaborated in his book *Hadith: A Re-Evaluation*. Ahmad begins by challenging both the modernist and the traditionist explanations of Muslims' decline and then offers his own view. According to him, Muslims declined because they lost their dynamic ideology based on the Qur'an and relied on the *hadith*, codified two centuries after Prophet's death, as a source on a par with the Qur'an.[29]

To reverse the process of decline and stagnation, Ahmad recommends reliance on the Qur'an. He then offers what he calls a scientific methodology for interpreting the Qur'an based on guidance provided by the Qur'an itself. This methodology is based on the following principles:

1. The distinction between the clear and unequivocal (*muhkam*) and allegorical (*mutashabihat*) verses of the Qur'an (3:7);

---

*Editor's Note: Kassim Ahmad is a controversial figure in Malaysia because of his political and religious ideas. Some question his mastery of Islamic sciences and hence his credentials for making sweeping judgments and recommendations about a major source of Islamic jurisprudence—*hadith*. Others go further and question his commitment to Islam.

2. Recognition of the unity of the Qur'an and the harmonious nature of its verses (4:82);
3. Recognition of the self-explanatory nature of the Qur'an, meaning that Qur'anic verses explain one another (55:1–2; 75:18–19);
4. The importance of good intention: the Qur'an cannot be comprehended by anyone who approaches it with bad intention (41:44; 56:77–79; 17:45–46);
5. The importance of topical context. This means that the meaning of a verse or verses must be understood in the context of the topic under discussion (17:58; 53:3–4; 59:7);
6. The importance of historical context (4:25, 92; 4:3);
7. The principle of easy practicability, because the Qur'an's teachings are meant to facilitate things for humankind and not render them difficult (22:78; 20:2; 5:6,101–2; 4:28); and
8. The importance of distinguishing between principle and methodology and putting principle above methodology (22:67; 2:67–71).[30]

Ahmad also emphasized the fact that the Qur'an acknowledged existing conditions, such as slavery, and recommended changing those conditions. Thus he recommended freeing of slaves. Based on this principle, Ahmad argued that a number of Islamic laws, including those regarding women, should be changed in accordance with new realities.[31] Ahmad's views posed a challenge both to conservative scholars and to the state religious authorities. Consequently, he was attacked by both groups and his book was banned.*

---

*Editor's Note: Another important figure in the Malaysian Islamic reformist movement is Anwar Ibrahim. He started his public career as a member of the ABIM. As part of his strategy of co-opting Muslim radical youth, Prime Minister Muhammad Mahathir gave Anwar a ministerial position in government, and later made him his deputy. In 1998 he fell from favor because of disagreements with Mahathir. Anwar was accused of various moral and financial wrongdoings and was imprisoned. The accusations and subsequent imprisonment of Anwar caused considerable international criticism of Prime Minister Mahathir as well as an internal outcry. He returned to politics in 2007, planning a return to parliament. The opposition coalition led by Anwar's wife scored a considerable electoral victory in the March 2008 general elections. In the summer of 2008 Anwar was again accused of immoral conduct by a twenty-three-year-old male aide. Fearing arrest and imprisonment, Anwar briefly took refuge in the Turkish embassy. He firmly denied the accusations, which he said were fabricated for political reasons in a repeat of the old script, and launched a lawsuit against the accuser. In August 2008 he won his wife's parliamentary seat and assumed leadership of the opposition.

Anwar always has been more of an activist and politician than a thinker and theoretician. Nevertheless, since the mid-1990s he has advocated a reformist and politically more liberal vision of Islam. He has called this vision a third way between the West's absolute secularism and strict traditionalist Islam. His vision balances Islamic values with the requirements of the modern world, and is open to the outside world and committed to dialogue with others.

Islamic Feminism

The Muslim women's organization Sisters in Islam (SIS) is perhaps the best-known Muslim feminist organization in Malaysia. It was established in the early 1980s by a group of Muslim women academics, writers, researchers, and students, including the well-known activist Zainah Anwar and the academic Noraini Othman. In many ways the development of SIS was an indirect result of the opening of discursive space occasioned by the writings of Chandra Muzaffar. Over the past two decades, SIS has championed the cause of Muslim women and men in the country, challenging the increasingly conservative interpretation of Islamic law and praxis promoted by both the more conservative Islamist opposition movements and the state religious bureaucracy.

During the 1980s and 1990s, most of SIS's campaigns were directed toward protecting the interests and legal status of Muslim women whose marriages were regulated by the state-sponsored religious bureaucracy. SIS made its name by fighting for the equality of Muslim women and launching several campaigns to ensure that fundamental rights such as the freedom to marry and divorce were not compromised by latter-day revisions of Islamic family law in Malaysia.

In terms of their approach to religious issues, the members of SIS have taken a page out of the book of Chandra Muzaffar. They have adopted a rationalist outlook that seeks to find the message of the Qur'an in the here-and-now. They advocate a reading of the Qur'an and, more important, Islamic law, in the present-day context. The fundamental subject of SIS's campaigns is the universal human being, grounded on the idea of the universal equality of human beings (*insan*) in Islam.

While accepting the view that gender inequalities are the result of very real differentials of power and economic wealth in society, SIS has challenged Muslims in Malaysia to rethink the workings of power, both on domestic and international levels. Its critique of many of the *shari'a* law reforms in Malaysia (carried out both by the state and the Islamic opposition party) has been based on the idea that any attempt to return to a historical interpretation and praxis of Islam (as in the seventh to eighth centuries) would negate the realities of the present time, when women in the country are highly educated, independent economic agents and actors in their own right.[32]

Emerging Reformist Clergy

Another group with reformist tendencies that should be mentioned is a younger generation of reformist religious leaders who are challenging the conservative clergy. Some of them are inspired by early Muslim reformists such as Muhammad Abduh and are engaged in offering more reformist interpretations of Islamic religious sources and laws. Their reformism is of a more limited nature compared to that of some of the lay intellectuals, but potentially very important in the context of the reformist project.

A prominent representative of this young generation of clergy is Dr. Mohd Asri Zainul Abidin, the mufti of the state of Perlis; in his mid-thirties, he is the youngest person to hold such a position. In his capacity of mufti, he is supposed to advise the Perlis sultan and the state government on all matters related to Islamic law. He has been critical of the conservative clergy who, according to him, "seek to stuff the mouths of the public and tell them 'Don't speak about religion. Religion is our [exclusive] right. . . . stop what you are doing and just listen.'"[33] Asri has said that the young generation cannot accept this attitude on the part of the conservative clergy and that it could push the youth toward secularism. As an example of this attitude, he has criticized the clergy for discussing the issue of punishment for apostasy instead of talking about what leads some Muslims to leave the faith. He adds that the religious leaders of the past "stressed the need to answer the questions posed by the apostates and to clarify any confusion they may have about Islam."[34] But now this practice has been abandoned.

Asri is also critical of those reformist thinkers whom he calls "liberal Muslims" because they question even those aspects of religion established by the Qur'an and the *sunna*. He maintains that the Salafi movement in Malaysia, which seeks through *tajdid* (renewal) to make the Qur'an and the *sunna* the terms of reference for Islamic discourse and to bring them up directly against the challenges of modern times, provides the best way to avoid extremism of conservatism and liberalism.* In his words: "This Salafiyyah movement says we have the right to think, as the intellect has a function in religion, though the exercise of our thought should not go against the Qur'an and the Sunna."[35]

Has "Reformist Islam" Become a Hostage to Malaysian Politics?

> *The problem of religion as an instrument of political ends is as old as history.*
> —Abdulaziz Sachedina, *The Islamic Roots of Democratic Pluralism*[36]

Muslim reformist thinkers played an important role in the political mobilization of the people of Malaysia, the struggle for independence, and the early educational and social reforms in the nineteenth and twentieth centuries. However, these reformers formed a relatively small community that was isolated in many ways. A number of their characteristics also limited their appeal to significant portion of Malaysians.

The reformist intellectuals of the *kaum muda* generation were mostly urban-based professionals of cosmopolitan outlook and often of mixed racial origins—Malay-Indian, Malay-Arab, Eurasian. They lived and worked in the British Crown

---

*Editor's Note: Dr. Asri's Salafism is of the more reformist version promoted by Muhammad Abduh and other early Muslim reformist thinkers rather than the more conservative and literalist type. The use of the term *tajdid* reflects the reformist bent of his type of Salafism.

Colonies of Singapore, Malacca, and Penang. This meant that they were doubly disadvantaged from the start and were seen as outsiders by both the British and the Malaysians.

This early generation of reformist Malay and Peranakan Muslims concerned themselves with the questions of modernity, scientific progress, economic development, and political independence more than did their counterparts in the traditionalist camp. Their concerns were neither accidental nor unexpected. They were themselves colonial subjects who had to live under foreign and secular colonial law and had to negotiate the particular politics that then prevailed in the colonies. But this also meant that their sphere of concerns and interests was in many ways different from that of their more traditionalist counterparts. Their position and status as liminal figures gave them the ability and opportunity to articulate ideas that were deemed unacceptable or novel at the time, but it also placed them in a precarious state of perpetual dependency and vulnerability that affected the form and content of their work and ideas.

Being colonial subjects also meant that they had to seek protection from colonial authorities. Freedom of speech and the freedom to disseminate their teachings were granted to them by the *secular* constitution of the Crown colonies. Thus, from the outset their own relationship with and understanding of secularism was radically different from that of traditional Muslims.

After independence, the government's tight grip on all Islamic movements and forms of public discourse meant that Muslim reformists were monitored, controlled, and policed. They had to develop and spread their ideas in a society where freedom of speech and the free circulation of ideas were constantly threatened. In addition, they had to contend with the ever-present threat of persecution by conservative and, worse, radical Muslims. Moreover, many of the ideas and values of reformist Muslims were tapped and instrumentalized by the state in order to justify developmentalist policies, while largely ignoring the reformists' other concerns such as democracy and freedom of speech and belief.

No wonder, then, that reformist Islamic thinking and Muslim reformers have not been able to develop adequately and increase in numbers. The collaboration of some reformist thinkers with the state has further undermined their position. By contrast, mainstream orthodox and traditional Islamist organizations and parties such as PAS have learned how to develop their own grassroots support networks without state patronage and, therefore, have gained in popular support. The fact is that reformist Islam cannot and will not succeed until and unless it breaks loose from its own dependency complex and becomes independent from the state.

Malaysia today is promoted as a model of modern, reformist Islam at work. Yet, until now the space for reformist Islamic discourse has been controlled and curtailed by the very same centralizing authoritarian state that also promotes *ijtihad* (rational interpretation). The modernist-reformist tradition in Malaysia is kept alive by a younger generation of Muslim academics and activists across the country, many of whom have been educated overseas and who have a mixed Islamic-secular educational background. However in the context of rising religious tension following the events of September 11 and the onset of the "war on terror," the stakes in the struggle for the meaning and content of Islamic discourse have risen, making it increasingly difficult for younger activists to make themselves heard in society. If reformist Islam is to grow and flourish, then Malaysia's own Muslim intellectuals will have to grapple with, and possibly even resist, the state's monopolization of power, authority, and modes of patronage and control.

Notes

1. Robert Hefner, *Civil Islam: Muslims and Democratization in Indonesia* (Princeton: Princeton University Press, 2000), p. 220.
2. The term Peranakan refers to Malays of mixed Indian or Arab ancestry. It is no longer in use.
3. Shanti Nair, *Islam and Malaysian Foreign Policy* (London: Routledge and ISEAS, 1997), p. 41.
4. The nucleus of the Pan-Malaysian Islamic Party actually lay in the Bureau of Religious Affairs of the Conservative-Nationalist Malay party, UMNO. In 1951, PAS was formed under the leadership of Haji Fuad Hassan, who was the head of the UMNO bureau of religious affairs. The radical nationalist and Islamist thinker Dr. Burhanuddin al-Helmy was invited to take over as president of PAS in December 1956.
5. Quoted in K.J. Ratnam, *Communalism and the Political Process in Malaysia* (Kuala Lumpur: University of Malaya Press, 1965), p. 122.
6. Nair, *Islam and Malaysian Foreign Policy,* p. 91.
7. In 1981 the UMNO General Assembly issued a resolution to the effect that the Federal and state Islamic councils should enforce and defend the "purity of Islam." Nair, *Islam and Malaysian Foreign Policy,* p. 36. The state set to identify deviant sects and prevent their activities.
8. In 1982, Kuwait donated more than RM 120 million for projects launched by the Pusat Islam (Islamic Centre). Later in 1986 eight loans totaling RM 390 million were secured from the Saudi Fund to help with other missionary and welfare projects for Muslims.
9. The International Institute for Islamic Thought and Civilisation (ISTAC) was officially opened in 1991. In the preface to the second edition (1993) of his book *Islam and Secularism,* al-Attas outlines the mandate and agenda of his institute: "Among its most important aims and objectives are to conceptualise, clarify, elaborate scientific and epistemological problems encountered by Muslims in this modern age; to provide an Islamic response to the intellectual and cultural challenges of the modern world and various schools of thought, religion and ideology; to formulate an Islamic philosophy of education; including the definitions, aims and objectives of Islamic education, to formulate an Islamic philosophy of science" (p. xiii).
10. See Syed Muhammad Naquib al-Attas, *Preliminary Statement on a General Theory of the Islamization of the Malay-Indonesian Archipelago* (Kuala Lumpur: Dewan Bahasa dan Pustaka, 1963), p. 4.
11. Ibid., p. 2.
12. See Syed Naquib al-Attas, *A Commentary on the Hujjat al-Sadiq of Nur al-Din al-Raniri* (Kuala Lumpur: Ministry of Culture, 1986). Mona Abaza notes that in his reading of Raniri al-Attas was attempting to find and promote a Malay-Muslim thinker who could rival not only the philosophers and intellectuals of the West, but also of the Muslim world in the sixteenth and seventeenth centuries. As she puts it: "Al-Attas was the first to highlight the idea that al-Raniri was for the Malay world the equivalent of Ibn Khaldun. Al-Raniri's

Bustan-as Salatin was considered (by al-Attas) as the first piece of scientific modern, historical Malay writing." Mona Abaza, *Debates on Islam and Knowledge in Malaysia and Egypt* (London: Curzon Press, 2002), p. 99.

13. See Abaza, *Debates on Islam and Knowledge,* pp. 88–106.

14. The anti-secular worldview of Naquib al-Attas was taken up by ABIM leaders. Chandra noted that ABIM criticized secularism for limiting "the concept of existence to 'this world' and the 'here and now,' thus resulting in a modern society 'inflicted by such diseases as hedonism, materialism, individualism, utilitarianism, permissiveness, relativistic values and anomie.'" See Chandra Muzaffar, *Islamic Resurgence in Malaysia* (Petaling Jaya: Fajar Bakti), p. 48.

15. Abaza, *Debates on Islam and Knowledge,* p. 105.

16. Farish A. Noor, *New Voices of Islam* (Leiden: ISIM, 2002), p. 49.

17. Chandra's conversion to Islam was a matter of personal choice, undertaken in his twenties. His family remained non-Muslim.

18. Chandra Muzaffar, *Protector? An Analysis of the Concept and Practice of Loyalty in Leader-Led Relationships Within Malay Society* (Penang: Aliran, 1979).

19. Chandra Muzaffar, *The Universalism of Islam* (Penang: Aliran, 1979).

20. Chandra Muzaffar, *Rights, Religion and Reform: Enhancing Human Dignity Through Spiritual and Moral Transformation* (London: RoutledgeCurzon, 2002), p. 191.

21. Muzaffar, *Rights, Religion and Reform,* p. 176.

22. Ibid., pp. 178–79.

23. Ibid., p. 177.

24. Ibid., pp. 204–6.

25. Ibid., pp. 214–15.

26. Ibid., p. 221.

27. Ibid., p. 219.

28. Ibid., p. 176.

29. Kassim Ahmad, *Hadith: A Re-Evaluation,* trans. Syed Akbar Ali, 1997, available at http://www.submission.org/HADITH2.HTM.

30. Ibid.

31. Ibid.

32. For information on the activities and publications of ISI, see http://www.sistersin-islam.org.my.

33. Fauwaz Abdul Aziz, "Nation's Youngest Mufti Speaks Out on Apostasy," *Malaysiakini,* November 22, 2006, available at http://www.malaysiakini.com/news/60114.

34. Ibid.

35. Fauwaz Abdul Aziz, "Religious Leaders Can Be Challenged," *Malaysiakini,* November 27, 2006, available at http://wwwmalaysiakini.com/news/60114.

36. Abdulaziz Sachedina, *The Islamic Roots of Democratic Pluralism* (Oxford: Oxford University Press, 2001), p. 4.

7

Islamic Reformist Discourses and Intellectuals in Turkey

Permanent Religion with Dynamic Law

Recep Şentürk

As early as the late eighteenth century, Ottoman Turkey became the first Muslim state to reform its administrative, educational, military, and, eventually, political systems. It was also first to introduce religious reform, including measures such as granting equal rights to religious minorities and development of a religious theoretical framework to legitimize its overall reform project. Despite this history, in terms of theory Islamic reformist discourse in Turkey has remained underdeveloped.

Unlike Iran, the Arab world, or South Asia, no major thinkers espousing a reformist discourse on Islam have emerged in modern Turkey. In fact, because of the particular characteristics of the Turkish Republic and the process of its evolution since its founding in 1923, post-Ottoman Islamic discourse in Turkey has been more concerned with Islam's preservation and revival as a social and political force than with its reform. Therefore, in order to understand the nature of the contemporary reformist Islamic discourse in Turkey and its sociocultural context, it is important first to review the sociopolitical and cultural evolution of republican Turkey.

The Fall of the Empire and the Rise of the Republic

The dismantling of the Ottoman Empire after World War I, the abolition of the Caliphate in 1923, and their replacement with a secular Turkish republic were momentous events in the history of the Islamic world. The demise of the Ottoman Empire was not only the disappearance of a particular system of government but also the end of an indigenous process of reform in an Islamic country. The main objectives of this process were: (1) to generate reform from within Islam in order to bring it closer to modern concepts of governance and people's rights; (2) to create a synthesis between Turkish-Islamic ideas and values and Western thought and science; and (3) to develop a theoretical basis for reform that met the approval of the religious establishment and the people.

Most important, the ultimate purpose of Ottoman reforms was to make Turkey into a strong and progressive country and not drastically alter its Islamic identity and culture. In other words, Ottoman reforms were in the category of "inner reform." This type of reform emanates from within the religious establishment, is gradual, and results from a long and continuous process of debate and consensus-building. It also tends to be longer-lasting and enjoy public support.

By contrast, the objective of the republican state in Turkey has not been merely to reform Islam or to develop a theoretical framework based on a synthesis of Western and Turko-Islamic principles and values. Rather, its goals have been complete reshaping of Turkey and Turkish culture according to a European model and the establishment of a secularist, rather than merely secular, political system. In respect to political and religio-cultural issues, the republican reform project has been both revolutionary and ideological. Its ideological dimension derives from the fact that the ideas of the republic's founder, Mustafa Kemal Atatürk, known as Kemalism, have been offered as a blueprint for reform and as a modern and scientific alternative to a religion-based (i.e., Islam-based) worldview.

The philosophical underpinnings of this ideology are sociological and legal positivism. Sociological positivism assumes that religion is a transitory phenomenon that will disappear with the progress of science and modernization. Legal positivism, meanwhile, maintains that enactment by the state bestows legitimacy upon laws without further need for justification. In other words, according to republican ideology, modernization and Europeanization are sufficient justification for state action, and state action carries its own legitimacy. Furthermore, at least the early republican system was based on charismatic leadership and a cult of Atatürk. This has meant that Atatürk's example provided justification for state actions.

Consequently, among the principal aspects of the republican project for Turkey's Europeanization have been the elimination of an independent *ulema* class; closure of religious schools (*madrasa*); abolition of the Sufi brotherhood (*tariqat*) and the Islamic endowments (*waqf*); the replacement of Islamic laws with secular laws; and the elimination of public displays of Muslim religiosity, such as the veil, the clerical turban, the fez, and the call to prayer (*adhan*) in Arabic. The republican state also brought religion under state control, adopted secularism as the official state ideology, and prohibited the mentioning of Islam as the official state religion. Furthermore, as part of the project of Turkey's Europeanization and the dilution of its Islamic culture, the republican state adopted the Latin script and purged Persian and Arabic words from Turkish. Republican reforms were imposed by the state in a top-down fashion, without much concern for either public debate or public approval. This was particularly true during the period 1923–39. Even today, despite considerable progress in the development of Turkish democracy, basic tenets of Kemalism are viewed as sacrosanct and not subject to debate or revision.

Because of these characteristics, the republican-era reforms are of the type that can best be described as "outer reform." This type of reform comes from the state rather than society, including the religious establishment, and is in sharp contrast to Ottoman reforms. The ideological aspect of the republican state, coupled with a paternalistic approach to governance, has thus limited the boundaries of discourse in Turkey. A casualty has been reformist discourse on Islam.

Other factors contributing to the relatively underdeveloped state of reformist discourse in Turkey include the following:

1. The republican state has implemented far-reaching reforms that exceed what is suggested today by many reformist thinkers in other Muslim countries. For example, a principal preoccupation of reformers in the Muslim world is to change Islamic penal and family laws. This has already happened in Turkey. Thus a major concern of Turkish reformist thinkers is not so much to reform the *shari'a* but rather to resist secularist orthodoxy; and
2. The republican state has viewed Islamic reformists as a more serious rival than the traditionalists or even the radicals because the latter can be more easily dismissed.

Opposition, Resistance, and the Development of Turkish Democracy

The ideas and reforms of the republican state and the manner in which they were implemented were not favorably received by several segments of Turkish society, including ethnic minorities such as the Kurds, leftists, Islamists, liberals, and even pan-Turkists, all of whom for different reasons were unhappy with the reforms. Islamists were especially concerned because they believed that the new regime had abandoned Islamic ideals and principles and had isolated Turkey from the rest of the Muslim world.

The newly established state successfully silenced all of its opponents by temporarily allying itself with some of them against the others. In this effort, it was helped by the lack of unity and coherence within the ranks of the opposition. It also used military force, notably against Islamic and Kurdish resistance. No effort was made to engage these diverse groups in a national dialogue. In the long run, this approach led to the ossification of Kemalist ideology and, by the 1950s, to a revival of leftist and Islamic discourses.[1]

For most of Atatürk's rule, Turkey was governed by a single party, the Republican People's Party (RPP). Despite occasional talk of going to the people (*halka inmek*), the RPP was committed to democracy only if it served to legitimize its own power. However, because of economic, social, and cultural dislocations caused by the rapid, drastic reforms of the new state, the RPP was in constant fear of losing power. Consequently, any democratic experiments were short-lived.

The situation began to change after the end of World War II, Turkey's alliance with the West, and its membership in NATO. As a full-fledged Western ally, Turkey was subjected to pressures to democratize, especially by the United States. These pressures finally led to the holding of multiparty elections in 1950, during which the RPP suffered a crushing defeat and lost to the newly established Democrat Party (DP).

The democratization process, although halting and often interrupted by military coups d'état, prepared the ground for Islam's return to the public sphere, as politicians competed for the votes of the silent masses, which had remained loyal to Islam. Even the RPP, under the leadership of İsmet İnönü, Atatürk's successor, had to make concessions to people's religious sensibilities. Thus,

> Although İnönü was known as a devout laicist/secularist, he allowed the government to restore religious instruction in schools. Religious concessions were considered of prime importance to isolate the Democrat Party as well as the Nation Party, formed in 1948 by conservative DP dissidents, who wanted even greater religious freedom. İnönü seemed to be abandoning three of the principal pillars of Kemalist ideology: Statism, revolutionism, and laicism, and even embracing Islam.[2]

Yet these concessions were too late and too little to eradicate the memory of past grievances. Meanwhile, the Democrat Party developed the slogan of making Turkey into "a little America." In addition to economic prosperity, this slogan meant establishing freedom of religion and expression.

After coming to power, the DP reinstated the practice of calls to prayers in Arabic. This act was viewed by the public as a victory of the "national will" (*milli irade*), and it garnered more votes for the DP in the 1954 elections. In the following years, Islam's revival in Turkish society acquired a political dimension and led to the formation of Islamist parties, notably the party under the leadership of Necmettin Erbakan, which operated under different names over the years because of the periodic suspension of the parliamentary process by the military and the dissolution of political parties.[3]

Later, Turgut Özal, an economic liberal and a pragmatic politician who served both as Turkey's prime minister and as president and the leader of the Motherland Party (Anavatan Partisi), made freedom of religion and conscience a pillar of his political discourse. Özal, who became Turkey's prime minister following the first democratic elections held in 1982 after the military coup of 1980, was a prominent representative of a new breed of Turkish politicians who combine modern education with Islamic faith.

During the republican era, religiosity and secularism had acquired a class dimension: by and large, the poorer and less-educated classes were more religious. According to Şerif Mardin:

> Because value socialization in the lower-class families remained an Islamic process, a barrier was set to the transition from this background into the Westernized educational establishment. Cultural boundary between a lower-class Islamic culture and an upper-class Western culture caused alienation on both sides.[4]

However, by the 1980s this distinction was no longer valid. A new generation of highly educated engineers, scientists, and other professionals, businessmen, and entrepreneurs had emerged. These elites openly acknowledge their Islamic loyalties while remaining committed to the goal of a modern, secular, and pro-Western Turkey.

Özal's statement in his inaugural speech as president in 1990, in which he emphasized the importance of freedom of expression, freedom of religion and conscience, and freedom of enterprise aptly reflects this new elite's philosophy. He noted that the consolidation of these three freedoms was essential if Turkey were to become part of the civilized world. Özal, who came from a religious family and was a member of the Naqshibandi Sufi order, had a pragmatic and non-ideological approach to social and political issues. Through his policies and his own behavior, he showed that one can be both Muslim and progressive. Özal's policies were also influenced by the view that emerged in the 1980s, that in order to prevent the spread of radical Islam, mainstream Islam and its progressive interpretations should be allowed a greater presence in the public sphere.[5] By his pragmatic policy, especially his linking of Turkey's future to Europe while allowing a greater space for Islam in Turkish society, Özal exerted a positive influence on the way Islam was viewed by both intellectuals and the masses. It was Özal's policies that allowed Islamist politicians to compete more effectively in democratic elections at the municipal and national levels and even to become prime ministers, as happened with Erbakan in 1997 and Recep Tayyip Erdoğan in 2003.

This involvement in politics and competition with secularist politicians created a greater awareness of the need for a reformist Islamic discourse. It also helped the evolution of Islamist politicians in the direction of a reformist Islam, as best illustrated by Erdoğan's personal transformation from a mildly radical Islamist to a reformist politician.

Islamic Reformist Thinkers in the Republican Era

Despite the interruption of the process of Islamic reform following the republican cultural and political revolution, Islamic reformist thinking, although overshadowed by other discourse including that of Islamic revivalists, never completely disappeared from Turkey's intellectual scene. Indeed, it is possible to identify three generations of reformist Muslim intellectuals in Turkey.

Transitional Figures

Reformist thinkers who grew up during the late Ottoman era but produced their work during the republican period constitute the first generation of post-Ottoman reformist thinkers. Prominent representatives of this generation included: İzmirli İsmail Hakkı, Said Halim Pasha, Elmalılı Muhammed Hamdi Yazır, Seyyid Bey, Ömer Nasuhi Bilmen, Said Nursî, and Mehmet Akif Ersoy. Ziya Gökalp can also be considered part of this group because he tried to combine sociology and *usul al-fiqh* as a new science called *ijtimai usul al-fiqh* (social scientific methodology of *fiqh*).[6] These thinkers' goal was to revive and reform Islam in the sense of *tajdid* and *islah*, and their methodology was essentially based on *usul al-fiqh.*[7]

Second Generation

Reformist scholars who grew up during the republican period included Hayrettin Karaman (Islamic law), Bekir Topaloğlu (Islamic theology), Tayyar Altıkulaç (*qira'a*), Ali Osman Koçkuzu (*hadith*), Said Hatipoğlu (*hadith*), and Yaşar Kandemir (*hadith*). Three non-Turkish scholars contributed to the academic education of this generation and influenced it with their reformist ideas: Muhammad Hamidullah from India, Muhammed b. Tavit Tanci from Morocco, and Muhammed Tayyib Okiç from Bosnia. Methodologically, they are similar to the transitional generation. These first two generations of republican-era Islamic reformist scholars are now viewed as conservative compared to some scholars from the new generation of reformist thinkers.

Third Generation

The third category includes the most prominent contemporary reformist thinkers, whose ideas and works are the primary focus of this chapter. This group is divided into those thinkers who methodologically still subscribe to *usul al-fiqh* and those who use modern Western methods of scriptural interpretation.

Most Islamic intellectuals and academics within this category still hold on to *usul al-fiqh* and refuse to use Western methods when trying to solve new problems presented by the modern age.[8] The reformist discourse of this group reflects the continuity in Turkish reformist thought since the time of Ottoman reforms known as *Tanzimat* (1839). However, another group of scholars tries to reinterpret fundamental Islamic sources using modern tools derived from Western culture such as historicism, structuralism, deconstructionism, phenomenology, process philosophy, and hermeneutics. These methods are usually used eclectically and are commonly referred to as historicism (*tarihselcilik*). However, because of the increasing critique of historicism and its application to Islamic scriptures, some members of this group would no longer like to be called historicists or even reformists.

In this context, it is also important to note the contribution of the Presidency of Religious Affairs (PRA). The PRA tries to play a mediating role between the strictly secular state and reformist intellectuals and religious segment of the population. Ali Bardakoğlu, the current president of the PRA, has embarked on reformist policies. He has appointed female deputy muftis and increased the number of women preachers and teachers of the Qur'an. The Directorate has also launched a project to produce a new collection of *hadith* by selecting from the old *hadith* books the ones that do not contradict modern notions such as gender equality.[9]

The Center for Islamic Studies, based in Istanbul and funded by the Foundation of the PRA, also contributes to reformist discourse on Islam. It is the publisher of the Turkish Encyclopedia of Islam.[10] It also houses such young Islamic scholars as Tahsin Görgün (philosophy), Adnan Aslan (philosophy), Şükrü Özen (Islamic law), Sait Özervarlı (theology), and Mustafa Sinanoğlu (theology). These scholars combine modern and classical education and write both in Turkish and in European languages.

Reforming Islam from Within: Revival or Inner Secularization?

The two major categories of Islamic reformist thinkers in Turkey have different understandings concerning how reform should be carried out and what methods should be used, namely the principles of Islamic jurisprudence (*usul al-fiqh*) or historicism.

The term *reform*, which was adopted into the Turkish language from French at the turn of the last century, is closely associated in the Turkish mind with the Christian (Protestant) reformation. Most scholars and the population would not want to reform Islam in Turkey on such a model. They do accept the need for change and adaptation to new conditions but they call for reform that is more suitable to Islamic historical experience. Accordingly, the meaning of the English term "reform" as used in this chapter corresponds to the Turkish word *yenilenme*, meaning renewal.

The following thinkers are the most prominent figures associated with the above-mentioned two groups. The purpose here is to provide representative examples and not to enumerate all the members of each group.

Reform via Usul al-Fiqh

Hayrettin Karaman

Hayrettin Karaman was born in 1934 to a middle class family in a small Anatolian town. After graduating from elementary school, he studied Arabic and traditional Islamic disciplines. Once religious education was allowed by the Democrat Party and Imam-Hatip schools were established, Karaman studied at an Imam-Hatip High School in Konya and in 1959 became one of its first graduates. After that, he studied at the newly opened High Islamic Institute (Yüksek İslam Enstitüsü) in Istanbul and in 1963 became one of its first graduates. Upon graduation, he taught at an Istanbul Imam-Hatip high school for two years. Later, he was assigned as a teacher to the High Islamic Institute in Istanbul, where he continued to teach until 2001. In 2001, the High Islamic Institutes in Turkey were transformed into schools of theology and integrated into the secular university system.[11] Karaman was one of the editors of the *Nesil* (Generation) journal, published between 1976 and 1980, which tried to disseminate revivalist ideas. Along with Bekir Topaloğlu and Tayyar Altıkulaç he was also one of the founders of the Center for Islamic Studies.

Karaman is among those reformist thinkers who believe that reform must follow the methodology offered by *usul al-fiqh*. His underlying thesis is that reform should be achieved through interpretation—*ijtihad*.[12] It is through *ijtihad* that qualified Muslim scholars can find answers to problems that Muslims face in the modern world. Karaman is best known for declaring that the gate of *ijtihad* is not closed, and for emphasizing the need for new *ijtihad*. In 1975 he published a book on the subject, titled *Ijtihad in Islamic Law*. The expression of such views caused an uproar among traditionalist Muslims and led to attacks on Karaman by figures such as Ahmed Davudoğlu, a traditionalist scholar, Necip Fazil Kisakurek, a poet and intellectual, and Mehmet Şevket Eyg, a journalist and publisher.

In Karaman's view reform should be understood as *tajdid* and *islah* (renewal and removal of harmful accumulated traditions often exogenous to Islam) as elaborated in traditional and more recent Islamic thinking. This perspective reflects the intellectual influence of different types of reformists, ranging from Ibn Taymmiyya and Imam Rabbani to Muhammad Abduh and Jamal al Din Afghani. What these figures have in common is their emphasis on reform and renewal, though their understanding of what constitutes reform differs greatly and they have been adopted by widely different contemporary Islamic tendencies. Karaman has argued against zealously following a particular school of Islamic law and in favor of adopting positive elements from different schools. This view was severely criticized by Hanafi scholars.

Karaman pays great attention to the question of human rights in Islam, with particular emphasis on women's rights and freedom of religion, conscience, and expression. According to Karaman, "There is no other system or religion that can compete with Islam where freedom of religion and conscience is concerned."[13] This view leads Karaman to oppose the death penalty for apostasy. Basing his view on traditional Hanafi doctrine, he argues that the death penalty for those who left the Islamic community was done not because of change of religion, but because of the charge of sedition or active combat against Muslims. His focus on these issues is partly due to a desire to answer those who criticize Islam's position on these matters. Another motivation is to challenge the present notion and practice of laicism in Turkey, which are used to restrict freedom of religion and to exclude religion from public sphere. Karaman stands for freedom of conscience and religion as an alternative to authoritarian laicism.

His focus on women's rights derives from similar motives. Islam is attacked for not giving equal rights to women, but meanwhile the rights of observant Muslim women are a strenuously debated legal, political, and social issue in Turkey. Karaman states clearly that in Islam men and women are equal as human beings and that women can achieve spiritual perfection (*insan kamil*). However, he adds that each should play the part within the family unit and society that is best suited to their particular abilities. He recognizes the right of women to work if they so choose but stresses that no one should force them to do so. He acknowledges that the Qur'an permits polygamy, albeit with very strict legal and moral conditions.

However, he recognizes the right of the state to outlaw the practice if it is deemed harmful to women's rights.

Karaman supports women's right to religious freedom and opposes the official ban on *hijab*, specifically head covering, on the grounds that it violates Muslim women's rights to religious freedom as well as to education, work, and free expression.* Nevertheless, Karaman has issued a *fatwa* allowing young Muslim women who have to choose between continuing their education and their religious duty to continue their education even without *hijab*. Karaman based his *fatwa* on the principle of public benefit, *maslahah*, because educated Muslim women would contribute more to Muslim society. However, viewed from a modern perspective, Karaman may seem to have a relatively narrow definition of women's equality with men. Within the family unit he considers the husband to be the head of the family, although he mentions that in many areas the husband should act in consultation with his wife.

Karaman maintains that religious minorities have the right to inviolability of life, religion, property, honor, family, and freedom of speech. He also maintains that atheist parents living in a Muslim state have the right not to allow their children to embrace Islam. On other issues, he leaves it to the state to determine the rights and duties of minorities. Another area of Karaman's focus is the problem of reconciling Islamic injunctions on issues such as interest and insurance within a global capitalist system. Classical Islamic law has no solution to offer to such questions. Karaman's answer is that Muslims need new *ijtihad* to solve these dilemmas. In the absence of such *ijtihad*, he has said, Muslims will become "perplexed and may even leave Islam."[14]

Karaman is very critical of Turkey's secularist system because it oppresses pious Muslims, in particular women. Indeed, he rejects the Turkish version of secularism. He argues that Muslims in Turkey must find ways to practice their religion even under an authoritarian secularist system. He has written a two-volume work on the subject, titled *Practicing Islam in a Laique System*.[15] Karaman maintains that Muslims who live under an authoritarian secularist regime need different type of *fatwa* than those who live under systems that recognize freedom of religion. In other words, Muslims living in a secular society need a new *fiqh*.

Fethullah Gülen

Another important figure who should be mentioned is Fettullah Gülen. He and his movement have been extremely influential with the educated youth and middle-class Muslims in Turkey, partly as a result of establishing a vast educational system as well as electronic and print media operations in Turkey and in Muslim Central Asia.

---

*Editor's Note: In February 2008 the Turkish parliament voted to change the part of the Constitution that prohibits women wearing a headscarf from attending university. Turkey's Constitutional Court then upheld the ban, precipitating a political crisis in the country.

Much has been written on Gülen and his movement, and only the basic underpinnings of his philosophy can be discussed here. Gülen's movement is rooted in the ideas of Said Nursî (1878–1960) and his followers, commonly known as Nurculuk, and represents its moderate branch.[16] Gülen's ideas on issues such as modernization, democracy, and the West have undergone considerable change over the years; the Özal years were particularly important. Gülen emphasizes the importance of scientific education in the schools because of his strong conviction that that there is no conflict between Islam and modern sciences, and he champions democracy. Methodologically, he favors the traditional *usul al-fiqh* in dealing with legal and moral questions of the modern age, as well as interpreting the Qur'an and *hadith* in light of modern scientific discoveries. Despite his relatively progressive views, Gülen, like his inspiration Said Nursî, has been accused of wanting to undermine Turkey's secular system. So far, however, the courts have acquitted him of such charges.

Reform via Historicism

The advocates of using novel methods other than traditional *usul al-fiqh* in Islamic studies consist of a small group of avant-garde reformist theology professors from Ankara University. They first gathered in 1986 around the magazine *İslami Araştırmalar* (Islamic Studies), which is still being published. Their methodology, which in Turkey is commonly known as "historicism" (*tarihselcilik*), is eclectically derived from various Eastern and Western sources. Foreign thinkers who have influenced this group in various degrees include Fazlur Rahman, Ignaz Goldziher, Joseph Schacht, G.H.A. Juynboll, Erich Fromm, Hassan Hanafi, M. Abed Jabri, Alfred North Whitehead, Hasan Khalaf Allah, Nasr Hamed Abu Zayd, and Abdolkarim Soroush,[17] with Fazlur Rahman being the most influential.

Said Hatipoğlu, a senior professor of *hadith* at Ankara University's Divinity School, played a significant role in promoting a critical approach to tradition among his students, especially by introducing them to the works of Goldziher. Hatipoğlu did not view Goldziher as a role model. Rather, he used him to promote a critical understanding of classical sources. Later, Fazlur Rahman's influence exceeded that of Goldziher. His ideas were first introduced to Turkish intellectuals by Alpaslan Açıkgenç, who studied under him at the University of Chicago. Mehmet Aydın, a philosophy professor who did his Ph.D. in England on Whitehead's process philosophy, also played an important role in introducing and promoting Rahman's reformist ideas.

Fazlur Rahman defined his project as modernist and liberalist.[18] However, because of criticism raised against the historicist approach by traditional Muslims, young scholars from Ankara University Divinity School refuse to be called "reformist" and emphasize their being Muslims.[19] For example, Ömer Özsoy, a professor of *tafsir* (exegesis) at Ankara University's Divinity School, declared that "Fazlur Rahman is a Muslim and not a modernist."[20] Mehmet Paçacı, another professor of *tafsir* from the same school, tries to portray Rahman as an opponent of liberalism.[21] Following Rahman's historicism, these young scholars advocate a critical approach to the analysis and interpretation of sources of Islamic theology and law, notably the Qur'an and the *hadith*. Their primary goal is to demonstrate that legal rules in the Qur'an are not applicable to the present age because they were addressed to Arab society of the seventh century. In other words, they maintain that legal principles in the Qur'an are historical and not universal and timeless. This position implies that their applicability is limited to the period of their revelation.

According to this view, what is universal in the Qur'an are fundamental principles such as justice and the establishment of a just and ethical society. During Islam's early days these goals were achieved through certain rules, but today the same goals can be achieved through different means. These scholars are very much concerned with human rights, women's rights, democracy, and the way laicism is practiced in Turkey.

Unlike Karaman, who refuses to accept laicism, they accept it as a practical system, but criticize the authoritarian and coercive manner of its implementation in Turkey. However, their primary concern is to develop a new theoretical framework for the interpretation and application of Islamic sources. They believe that before turning to practical issues they need to justify their new ways of interpreting the Qur'an and the *hadith*.[22]

Historicity of the Qur'an: Ömer Özsoy and Mehmet Paçacı

Ömer Özsoy is a faithful follower of Fazlur Rahman and his historicist methodology. He was born in 1963 in Kayseri, a conservative town in central Anatolia.[23] His doctoral thesis was on "The Concept of Sunnatullah in the Qur'an" (1986). He did postdoctoral work in Germany (1991–93) and served as the general manager of *İslamiyat* journal from 1997 to 2003. Özsoy argues that the Qur'an is a historical text, as indicated by the following features: it is in Arabic, God-centered, anthropomorphist, and meaning-giving rather than explanatory. An objective interpretation of the Qur'an is only possible by translating its verses into physical and historical domains.[24]

Özsoy praises the work of two Egyptian scholars, Amin al-Khuli and Nasr Hamed Abu Zayd, for approaching the Qur'an as a literary text and applying to it the methods of literary interpretation. He sees the work of Abu Zayd as a significant contribution because, in his view, it offers the first comprehensive critique of traditional Qur'anic disciplines, *ulum al-qur'an*.[25] However, Özsoy disagrees with Abu Zayd's argument that social conditions during the Meccan period shaped the Qur'an (*tashakkul*). Instead, he argues that the Qur'an impacted its environment from the very beginning.

For Özsoy, the Qur'an has an original meaning that can be determined through historicist interpretation.[26] He poses the question whether the Qur'an was addressed only to the audience who lived during the time of Prophet Muhammad or to all humanity and to following generations. His answer is that the Qur'an is not above history, and the logical conclusion is that it was addressed only to the Arabs of the Prophet's time. This is against the dominant dogma in the Muslim world, which considers the Qur'an above history. In a polemical exchange with the editors of *Hak Söz* (The True Word) magazine, who accused historicists of denying Islam's universality, Özsoy claimed that the opposite of historicity is not universality; it is being above history.[27]

Mehmet Paçacı, a professor of *tafsir* at Ankara University Divinity School, was at one time a follower of Fazlur Rahman and part of the historicist movement. More recently, he has become skeptical of Rahman's ideas and methods of interpretation of Islamic sources. Now he argues that Islamic hermeneutics is *usul al-fiqh*, which must also be adopted by contemporary scholars of Islam. He argues that *usul al-tafsir* cannot replace *usul al-fiqh* because they serve different functions. Paçacı maintains that the Qur'an is not historical but that *ijtihad*, which is used in the interpretation of the Qur'an and the derivation of rules from it, is historical. He further notes that the use of historicist methodology is not completely new to the interpretation of the Qur'an, and that classical Muslim commentators dealt with the role of history in the formation of the Qur'an and Islamic legal principles. He argues that traditional methods of interpretation, which are embodied in *usul al-fiqh* and *usul al-hadith*, approach the text with the help of both literary and historical methods of interpretation. The latter include emphasis on the study of circumstances attending the revelation (*asbab al-nuzul*) and the process of abrogation (*naskh*) of one verse by another. He also notes that the same historical methods have been used in the interpretation of the *hadith* because the study of *hadith* requires looking at the social setting in which it was initially uttered (*asbab wurud al-hadith*).[28]

In short, Paçacı still subscribes to the historical approach but wants to redefine it by reconciling it with traditional methods of interpretation. He emphasizes that *tafsir* and *fiqh* are two different endeavors and the former should not be used to produce change in the latter. As a scholar of *tafsir* he does not think that he is obliged to derive legal and moral rules from the Qur'an and leaves this task to the specialists of Islamic law. In other words, he is limiting the role of *tafsir*, and thus that of historical interpretation, to the verses that are not related to legal issues. Such a limitation, however, would disrupt the efforts of historicist scholars, who by using this methodology want to change existing Islamic rules on the grounds of changed conditions.

Historicity of the Hadith: *Hayri Kırbaşoğlu*

M. Hayri Kırbaşoğlu is a professor of *hadith* at Ankara University's Divinity School.[29] He was born in 1954 in Manisa, a town in central Anatolia. He graduated in 1978 from the same school where he now teaches. He received his Ph.D. in 1983, and from 1985 to 1987 taught at Imam Muhammad bin Saud University in Saudi

Arabia. He has also served as an editor for the journals *İslami Araştırmalar* and *İslamiyas*. Kırbaşoğlu's main project is to set up an "alternative *hadith* methodology" in order to solve current problems that Muslims face concerning *hadith*. His methodology is eclectic and is derived from various Islamic and Western sources. Kırbaşoğlu argues that, if Muslims are incapable of distinguishing the true *hadith* from the false, it is because they have been applying the wrong methodology to determine the authenticity of *hadith*. Yet, there is no serious project in the Muslim world to overcome this problem.[30] Kırbaşoğlu demonstrates that these problems have been articulated by many prominent scholars, including Abu Shama al-Maqdisi (d. 665/1266), Musa Jarullah Bigiyef (1871–1949); also known as Musa Jarullah Bigi), Fazlur Rahman, Münir Şefik, and Perviz Mansur, as well as Western scholars such as Juynboll.[31]

Their main criticisms relate to the following issues: (a) *isnad*—the chain of transmitters of a *hadith*—may be fabricated even if it looks reliable, yet this has been ignored; (b) there are no criteria for the critique of a *hadith*'s content; and (c) dubious narrations of the first generations of transmitters, such as the *irsal* of al-Hasan al-Basri and Sa'id bin al-Muthayyab, have not been questioned. The main features of Kırbaşoğlu's alternative *hadith* methodology are the following:

- It is not an independent method but part of a general method
- It does not belong to any particular school (*madhhab*)
- It is based on an interdisciplinary approach
- It relies on methodological doubt and critical reasoning
- It is not a "sponge" but a "filter"
- It is rationalist
- It is open to change and dynamic
- It relies on *ijtihad*
- It is a practical method that takes present needs into consideration
- It is a synthesis of the traditional and the modern; and
- It is a normative and not historical and descriptive method.

The most significant contribution of the methodology proposed by Kırbaşoğlu is the critique of content along with the critique of *isnad*. His methodology of authenticating and interpreting *hadith* would enable Muslims to judge the *hadith* on the merits of its content. This would allow sifting of those *hadith* that contradict modern notions of science, human rights, and women's rights. This, in his view, could be a great contribution to the advancement of reform in Islam.*

---

*Editor's Note: In February 2008, the project of removing harmful *hadith*, under the guidance of the Ministry of Religious Affairs, was made public and received significant attention in Turkey and internationally. See "Turkey Is Radically Revising the Hadith," available at http://nielsenhayden.co/makinglight/archives/009994.html.

Historicity of Theology: İlhami Güler

İlhami Güler, born in Tortum, near Erzurum in northeastern Turkey, is a professor of Islamic Theology at the Ankara University's Divinity School,[32] where he completed his studies. Unlike most other Turkish reformists, he is methodologically eclectic and does not subscribe to Fazlur Rahman's historicism alone. Instead, he uses diverse methods that are seen as contradictory, ranging from deconstructionism to historicism, from phenomenology to hermeneutics. On some occasions, he even calls for the revival of *usul al-fiqh*. As a theologian, Güler's focus is on the relationship between human beings and God. His doctoral thesis was titled "The Relationship Between Morality and Faith in the Hereafter According to the Qur'an" (1991).[33] It was published in 1998 under the title of *The Problem of God's Morality: A Critical Approach to the Sunni Concept of God from a Moral Perspective.*[34] In this work he critically examines the Sunni view of God and aims his critique toward the folk understanding of God among the Sunnis, but his criticisms could also largely apply to the Shiites.

According to Güler, the source of the problem is the image of God: those who read the verses in the Qur'an from a "partial-scripturalist" perspective see it as the universal word of an Omnipotent God whose power penetrates everything. Yet the image of God derived from the Qur'an is at odds with that constructed by Muslim theologians of later generations.[35] This particular image of God as omnipotent and omnipresent generates destructive beliefs, such as predestination, which are used by religious and political powers to oppress people.

Like the "idealist" historian Sabri Ülgener, who has worked on the causes of the late Ottoman decline, Güler believes that this image of God and superstitious beliefs derived from it have been the main cause of Muslim societies' and civilization's decline. To resolve this problem, Güler believes the image of God must be reconstructed on the basis of the Qur'an. In the Qur'an God is a moral being whose relationship with humanity is based on morality rather than power. God does not command to be obeyed because he is omnipotent but does so by moral arguments. For the same reasons, nothing that is immoral should be attributed to God as His actions or attributes. Viewed from this perspective, the word "servant/slave" (*'abd*), which occurs frequently in the Qur'an, should be understood as "human being" and not literally as "servant" or "slave."

Güler distinguishes between religion and law, and states that religion must remain stable and permanent while law must be dynamic and changeable.

> The last experience with the divine law, *shari'a*, is framed by scholars of Islam as the Eternal Word, *kelam-i kadim*. This approach has turned it into something as sacred and absolute as God. Here lies the authority of the scripture and of early generations, Salaf. Yet, this scripture, which emerged within life, can only be understood within life. The correct understanding of law depends on grasping the reasons behind legislation, and then legislating like God. The only person who understood this was the Caliph Umar.

Those who write thirty volumes of commentary on the Qur'an or derive hundreds of meanings from a single letter of it have a feeble willpower and weak intelligence, because they cannot see the reality (social and moral reality) in themselves. This reflects the decadence of Islamic thought. It is a regression from the duty to make *ijtihad* even when there is a rule, as was done by the Caliph Umar. Instead they say "*ijtihad* is not permissible if there is a rule in the scripture (*nass*)."[36]

Güler calls for *ijtihad* even if there is a rule regarding an issue in the scriptures. This is a clear departure from the *fiqh* tradition and at odds with *usul al-fiqh*. He also calls for the deconstruction of Islamic intellectual legacy.[37] Güler criticizes Imam Shafi'i for claiming that all events in the present and in the future have been ruled about in the scriptures and that the *shari'a* offered solutions to all social problems even before their emergence.[38] He considers Imam Shafi'i as the founding father of the Sunni paradigm and therefore as the source of stagnancy and decay in Islamic thought. By contrast, he believes Abu Hanifa and Imam Malik had dynamic methods; Abu Hanifa developed the method of *istihsan* (a type of analogy), and Malik that of *al-masalih al-mursala* (expected public good). According to Güler, Shafi'i confused religion and law, and made law permanent as religion.[39]

Güler believes in the historicity of the Qur'an and says that when God in the Qur'an addresses the believers, he means the believers at the time of revelation of the Qur'an, and not, for example, the present-day Turks.[40] For Güler, claiming that *shari'a* is universal and unchangeable violates this rule. Many Qur'anic regulations, including those about the status of women, are historical but not universal nor eternal principles. Güler tries to support his position by citing Fazlur Rahman and Roger Garaudy, the French Muslim philosopher.[41]

Historicity of the Law: Practical Questions

The reformist thinkers discussed so far try to develop a methodology with which to justify their ideas and views. There is another group, one that is not interested in theoretical and methodological questions. Instead, they focus on practical questions such as the permissibility of unveiling, interest, and slaughtering animals by means other than the traditionally prescribed method.

Yaşar Nuri Öztürk (Sufism), the former dean of the School of Theology at Istanbul University, and Zekeriya Beyaz (sociology), the former dean of the School of Theology at Marmara University, are the most prominent representatives of this group. Their lack of interest in theory and methodology may be connected with the fact that both Öztürk and Beyaz have political ambitions. Öztürk calls for a "Qur'anic Islam," meaning Islam without the *shari'a*. He contends that law is a product of history. Contemporary Muslims should read the Qur'an directly and interpret it by themselves, disregarding previous commentaries. Öztürk ignores or uses arbitrarily the corpus of *hadith* and dismisses most of it as unreliable.

Although these scholars are not interested in constructing a sophisticated method for their reform projects, their main argument revolves around relegating to history all traditional religious norms that contradict modern norms. These norms are categorized as reflections of Arab customs and not as part of Islamic religion. For instance, regarding the controversial issue of *hijab*, Beyaz argues that the Qur'anic command is a reflection of the Arab customs of that time. With drawings he demonstrates how the slave-girls were not required to cover a significant part of their body even during prayers.

However, both Öztürk and Beyaz's political activities, their power ambitions, their cooperation with government to implement certain restrictive policies, and accusations of corruption against them in the media have undermined their intellectual and Islamic credibility. There is also the question whether their views result from scholarly research or are motivated by their professional ambitions. Although Öztürk and Beyaz play an important role in introducing historicist ideas to the general public, their lack of moral and scholarly credibility may undermine the cause of reformist Islam.

Reform and Sufi Thought

Although outlawed in 1925, Sufi orders have survived in Turkey, albeit unofficially. They have been influential with both secular and Islamist politicians, and have a strong cultural influence. The most important Sufi orders with branches throughout Turkey are the Naqshibandi, Khalwati, Qadiri, and Rufai. The official state ideology portrays Sufis as being against science, technology, democracy, and progress. Yet in practice, some Sufi orders, in particular the Khalidiyya branch of the Naqshibandis, have emphasized the role of science, technology, and economic prosperity. Both Özal brothers (Korkut and Turgut), Necmettin Erbakan, and many other political figures were in the circle of Abdulaziz Bekkine, a Sufi from the Khalidiyya tradition. Mehmet Zahid Kotku and Esat Coşan succeeded Bekkine in maintaining the same discourse with an explicit emphasis on the importance of scientific, technological, and economic progress. This branch of the Naqshibandiyya can be seen as the order most involved in worldly affairs.

The late sheikh of the Khalwatiyya order, Muzaffer Ozak, and his living successor, Tuğrul İnançer, have had a very open-minded approach to contemporary human needs.[42] The Rufai Sufi order, whose great master at the turn of the twentieth century was Kenan Rufai, also has an open-minded interpretation of Sufi thought. Today, women, including Samiha Ayverdi, Safiye Erol, Nezihe Araz, and Sofi Huri, play important roles in this order, suggesting that it puts some emphasis on gender equality. Broadly speaking, Turkish Sufis approach issues such as science, democracy, and human rights from moral rather than legal or political perspectives.

From the Sufi perspective, morality, like all other issues, revolves around love of God. Humans are obliged to love and respect the rights of creation as a whole—humans, animals, plants—because God created them.[43] *Keşkul,* a quarterly magazine dedicated to Sufi tradition and life, published a special issue on questions related to women. The articles emphasized the equality of men and women in the Sufi path and argued that women can attain the highest levels of spiritual perfection. They also emphasized respect for women's rights and dignity on moral grounds and love of their creator.

Conclusions

The current Islamic discourse in Turkey reflects the legacy of its Ottoman past and its republican experience. The Ottoman past has shaped this discourse in two ways. First, many religious Turkish intellectuals, like their secular counterparts, have attributed Ottoman decline to cultural factors, in particular the contamination of religion by superstitious beliefs and the wrong perception of God. Thus, as was demonstrated in this study, a characteristic of contemporary reformist discourse in Turkey has been its efforts to develop a different vision of God, religion, and law in Islam. Second, the history of Ottoman reforms continues to provide a worthy example for those reformist thinkers who want to effect reform through traditional Islamic methodology.

The sociocultural and ideological revolution carried out by the republican state, by radically transforming Turkey's Islamic institutions and religious class, along with the vast secularization policy of its legal and political systems, have deeply affected the content of reformist discourse and the character of its agents in Turkey. Thus, in Turkey, unlike in some other Muslim countries, the question preoccupying reformist Muslims is not how to legitimize secularism in the eyes of religious establishment, but rather, as İlhami Güler puts it, to secularize Turkey from Kemalist ideology.[44] Meanwhile, the elimination of a clerical class (*ulema*) has meant that today reformist discourse is carried out mainly by academics.

The republican state has ideologically been opposed to Islamic reformist discourse as a means of justifying secularism and modernization. Indeed, ultrasecularists like Emre Kongar have argued that Islamic reformist discourse is undermining the Kemalist regime and must be stopped.[45] However, because of Islam's strength and resilience in Turkey, the authoritarian dimensions of the official ideology, coupled with broader problems of the Islamic world, have led to awareness in Turkey of the need for reform in Islam. Yet Islamic reformism remains a contested concept in contemporary Turkey. For some it is a pejorative term, and for others it is positive. It is debated not only among conservatives who oppose it but also among reformists who call for it.

There is also debate about the methodology of effecting reform. Some advocate reform via *usul al-fiqh* while others favor the use of modern methodologies. These disagreements among Muslim scholars, in addition to the secular character of the Turkish Republic, have meant that Islamic reformist discourse in Turkey is under-theorized and most reform projects are merely action-oriented. However, as Turkey's democratization advances, the need for popular justification for state policies will increase. Here, reformist discourse can become an important mediator between the secularist state and the considerable number of devout Muslim Turks.

Notes

1. The habit of silencing society through various coercive measures still persists.

2. Feroz Ahmad, *Turkey: The Quest for Identity* (Oxford: Oneword, 2003), p. 103.

3. Erbakan's party operated under the names of the National Order Party (Milli Nizam Partisi), the National Salvation Party (Milli Selamet Partisi), the Prosperity Party (Refah Partisi), and the Virtue Party (Fazilet Partisi). In 2000 Fazilet was banned. Its more progressive elements formed the Justice and Development Party (Adalet ve Kalkınma Partisi) in 2001 under the leadership of Recep Tayyip Erdoğan, and the followers of Erbakan formed the Happiness Party (Saadet Partisi).

4. Şerif Mardin, *Religion, Society and Modernization in Turkey* (Syracuse, NY: Syracuse University Press, 2006), p. 123.

5. "Strategies to Fight Fundamentalism Viewed," *Turkish Probe,* November 4, 1994.

6. For Gökalp's ideas on *ictimai usul-i fıkıh,* see Recep Şentürk, *Modernleşme ve Toplumbilim* (Modernization and Sociology), 2d ed. (Istanbul: İz Yayıncılık, 2006), pp. 284–319.

7. For a critique of their ideas by the Ottoman Sheikhulislam, see Mustafa Sabri Efendi (1373/1954), *Dini Müceddidler: Türkiye İçin Necat ve İtila Yollarında Bir Rehber* (Religious Reformers: A Guide for Turkey in the Paths of Salvation and Progress) (Istanbul: Evkaf Matbaası, 1340).

8. Bedir, Murteza, "*Fıkh* to Law: Secularization Through the Curriculum," *Islamic Law and Society,* vol. 11, no. 3 (2004): 378–401.

9. See Mustafa Akyol, "[Sexism Deleted] in Turkey," *Washington Post,* July 16, 2006, B2, available at http://www.washingtonpost.com/wp-dyn/content/article/2006/07/14/AR2006071401381_pf.html. This is a report about the new *hadith* project of the Directorate of Religious Affairs. It aims to eliminate *hadith* derogatory toward women, such as "Women are imperfect in intellect and religion" or "The best of women are those who are like sheep." Whether this media account reflects the intentions behind the ongoing project is still unclear.

10. The full title in Turkish is *Türkiye Diyanet Vakfı İslam Ansiklopedisi* (The Encyclopedia of Islam by the Turkish Religious Foundation) (Istanbul). The encyclopedia is expected to be forty volumes when completed. To date thirty-one volumes have been published.

11. These schools offer a B.A. to their graduates.

12. For Hayrettin Karaman, see http://www.hayrettinkaraman.net. Karaman is a prolific author who has written fourteen books. His published books include: (joint work by a committee) *Kur'an-ı Kerim ve Açıklamalı Meali* (Translation of the Qur'an to Turkish); (with B.Topaloğlu) *Arapça-Türkçe Yeni Kamus* (Arabic-Turkish Dictionary); (with a committee) *İlmihal* (Islamic Catechism); (with a committee) *Kur'an Yolu* (The Qur'anic Path) (five volumes of commentary on the Qur'an); *Mukayeseli İslam Hukuku* (Comparative Islamic Law) (3 volumes); *İslam Hukuk Tarihi* (History of Islamic Law); *İslam Hukukunda İctihad* (*Ijtihad* in Islamic Law): *İslam'ın Işığında Günün Meseleleri* (Contemporary Problems in the Light of Islam) (3 volumes); *Günlük Hayatımızda Helaller ve Haramlar* (Lawful and Unlawful in Our Daily Life); *İslam'da İşçi-İşveren Münasebetleri* (Labor Relations in Islam); *Anahatlarıyla İslam Hukuku* (Main Ideas of Islamic Law) (3 volumes); *İslam'da Kadın ve Aile* (Woman and Family in Islam); *İslamlaşma ve Önündeki Engeller* (Obstacles Before Islamization); *İmam-Hatip şuuru* (Ideology of Imam-Hatip Community); *İnsan Hakları* (Human Rights); *Gerçek İslam'da Birlik* (Unity in True Islam); *Laik Düzende Dini Yaşamak* (Practicing Religion Under a Secular Regime) (3 volumes); *Türkiye ve İslam* (Turkey and Islam); *Her şeye Ragmen* (Despite Everything) (interviews); *Hayatımızdaki İslam* (Islam in Our Life) (2 volumes.); *Dert Söyletir* (Troubles Make You Speak) (poems). Besides publishing his own works, Karaman has translated several books from Arabic and French.

13. Hayrettin Karaman, *İnsan Hakları: Din, Vicdan ve Düşünce Hürriyeti* (Human Rights: Freedom of Religion, Conscience and Thought), Istanbul: Ensar Neşriyat, 2004, p. 13.

14. Hayrettin Karaman, *Her şeye Ragmen* (Despite Everything) (İstanbul: İz Yayıncılık, 2001), p. 28.

15. Hayrettin Karaman, *Laik Düzende Dini Yaşamak* (Practicing Religion in a Secular Society), 3d ed. (İstanbul: İz Yayıncılık, 1998).

16. Şerif Mardin, *Religion and Social Change in Modern Turkey: The Case of Bediüzzaman Said Nursî* (Albany: State University of New York Press, 1989).

17. İlhami Güler, *Özgürlükçü Teoloji Yazıları* (Writings on Liberal Theology) (Ankara: Ankara Okulu, 2004), p. 38.

18. Fazlur Rahman wrote: "What is true is that Muslim modernism represents Islamic liberalism; it has accepted certain key liberal social values from the modern West and has interpreted the Qur'an to confirm those values and not just to 'legitimize' them as a social scientist is so fond of putting the matter." Fazlur Rahman, "Islam and Political Action: Politics in the Service of Religion," in *Cities of Gods,* ed. N. Biggar and J.S. Scott (Westport, CT: Greenwood Press, 1986), p. 160.

19. Omer Özsoy, *Kur'an ve Tarihselcilik Yazıları* (Writings on the Qur'an and Historicity) (Ankara: Kitabiyyat, 2004), p. 91.

20. Ibid., p. 81.

21. Mehmet Paçacı, "*Kur'an ve Tarihsecilik Tartışması,*" *Kur'an'ı Anlama'da Tarihsellik Sempozyumu* (Symposium on the Role of Historicity in Understanding the Qur'an) (Bursa: Kurav-Bayrak, 2000), p. 28.

22. The debate on historicist methods of interpretation is still going on in Turkey among scholars and intellectuals. For examples of the range and nature of debate see among others: Hayrettin Karaman et al., eds., *Kur'an-ı Kerim, Tarihselcilik ve Hermenötik* (The Holy Qur'an, Historicism and Hermeneutics) (Istanbul: Işık Yayınları, 2003); Necdet Subaşı, *Ara Dönem Din Politikaları* (Religious Politics in Transitional Periods) (Istanbul: Küre Yayınları, 2005); Şevket Kotan, *Kur'an ve Tarihselcilik* (The Qur'an and Historicism) (Istanbul: Beyan Yayınları, 2001); Yasin Aktay, *Türk Dinin Sosyolojik İmkanı* (The Sociological Possibility of a Turkish Religion) (Istanbul: İletişim 1999).

23. Ömer Özsoy, *Sünnetullah: Bir Kur'an İfadesinin Kavramlaşması* (God's Laws: Conceptualization of a Qur'anic Expression) (Ankara: Fecr Yayınevi, 1994); Rudi Paret, *Kur'an üzerine Makaleler* (Essays on the Qur'an), trans. Ömer Özsoy (Ankara: Bilgi Vakfı, 1995); *Kur'an ve Tarihsellik Yazıları* (Writings on the Qur'an and Historicity) (Ankara: Kitabiyat, 2004).

24. Omer Özsoy, *Kur'an ve Tarihselcilik Yazıları,* p. 19.

25. Ibid., pp. 21–37.

26. Ibid., p. 53.

27. For a similar approach, see Mustafa Öztürk, *Kur'an Dili ve Retorigi: Kur'an Metninin Dokusu üzerine Tartışmala*r (The Language of the Qur'an and Its Rhetoric: Discussions and Debates on the Fabric of the Qur'anic Text) (Ankara: Kitabiyat, 2002); *Kur'an'ın Mu'tezili Yorumu: Ebu Müslim el-İsfahani Örnegi* (The Mu'tazilite Interpretation of the Qur'an: The Example of Abu Muslim al-Isphahani) (Ankara: Ankara Okulu, 2004).

28. On the changing views of Mehmet Paçacı, see "*Kur'an ve Tarihsellik Tartışması*" *Kur'anı Anlamada Tarihsellik Sorunu Sempozyumu,* pp. 17–56; "Din Bilimleri ve çağdaş Sorunları üzerine" (On Religious Disciplines and Their Contemporary Problems), paper presented at Modern Dönemde Dini İlimlerin Temel Meseleleri Sempozyumu (Symposium on the Fundamental Problems of Religious Disciplines in the Modern Era), ISAM, Istanbul 14–17 April 2005.

29. His works include: *Ebu Muhammed Abdullah b. Müslim İbn Kuteybe* (d. 276/889), *Hadis Müdafası* (In Defense of the Hadith), trans. Mehmet Hayri Kırbaşoğlu (Istanbul: Kayıhan Yayınevi, 1979); Muhammed Avvame, *İmamların Fıkhi İhtilaflarında Hadislerin*

Rolü (The Role of Hadith in the Jurisprudential Disagreements of Jurists of Legal Schools), trans. Mehmet Hayri Kırbaşoğlu (Istanbul: Kayıhan Yayınevi, 1980); İslam Düşüncesinde Sünnet: Yeni Bir Yaklaşım (Sunna in Islamic Thought: A New Perspective) (Ankara: Fecr Yayınevi, 1993); İslam Düşüncesinde Sünnet: Eleştirel Bir Yaklaşım (Sunna in Islamic Thought: A Critical Perspective) (Ankara: Ankara Okulu Yayınları, 1996).

30. Hayri M. Kırbaşoğlu, *Alternatif Hadis Metodolojisi* (An Alternative Methodology of Hadith Studies) (Ankara: Kitabiyat, 2002), p. 14.

31. Ibid., pp. 17–20.

32. His works include: *Allah'ın Ahlakiligi Sorunu: Ehl-i Sünnetin Allah Tasavvuruna Ahlaki Açıdan Eleştirel Bir Yaklaşım* (The Problem of God's Morality: A Critical Approach to the Sunni Concept of God from a Moral Perspective) (Ankara: Ankara Okulu, 1998); *Sabit Din, Dinamik Şeriat* (Permanent Religion, Dynamic Shari'a) (Ankara: Ankara Okulu Yayınları, 1999); *Politik Teoloji Yazıları* (Writings on Political Theology) (Ankara: Kitabiyat, 2002); *İman Ahlak İlişkisi* (The Relationship Between Faith and Morality) (Ankara: Ankara Okulu Yayınları, 2003); *Özgürlükçü Teoloji Yazıları* (Writings on Liberal Theology) (Ankara: Ankara Okulu Yayınları, 2004).

33. In Turkish: *Kur'an'a Göre Allah ve Ahiret İnancının Ahlakla İlişkisi* (The Relationship Between Faith in God and the Hereafter According to the Qur'an) (A.Ü. Sosyal Bilimler Enstitüsü, 1991).

34. Ilhami Güler, *Allah'ın Ahlakiligi Sorunu: Ehl-i Sünnet'in Allah Tasavvuruna Ahlaki Açıdan Eleştirel Bir Yaklaşım.*

35. Güler, *Sabit Din, Dinamik şeriat,* p. 97.

36. Ibid., p. 8.

37. Ibid.

38. Ibid., p. 31.

39. Ibid.

40. Ibid., p. 91.

41. Ibid., pp. 152–62.

42. A significant number of Muzaffer Ozak's works have been translated into English by his American disciples. Tosun Bayrak is among his leading successors in North America.

43. Inancer O. Tuğrul, "Vakte Karsi Sozler" (Words Against Time), in *Keşkul,* ed. Ayse Sassa and Berat Demirci (2006).

44. İlhami Guler, "Türkiye'nin Kemalizmden Laikleşme Zorunlulugu" (The Necessity of Turkey's Secularization from Kemalism), *Özgürlükçü Teoloji,* pp. 117–20.

45. Kohgar's views are available at http://www.kongar.org/aydinlanma/2006/506_Dinde_Reform.php.

8

Reformist and Moderate Voices in European Islam

Farhad Khosrokhavar

Today, there are between 12 and 18 million Muslims in Europe from diverse immigrant backgrounds. They are living in countries with predominantly secular cultures, values, and environments. The immigrant Muslim minorities are trying to adapt to these realities while retaining some measure of separate religious and cultural identity. As European Muslims, especially the second and third generations who came of age during the 1990s, they try to achieve these twin goals. In the process they face new religious, cultural, and legal questions and challenges requiring answers and solutions that do not exist in traditional Islamic sources. Since the 1990s, new discourses have emerged in response to these questions and challenges. They cover a wide spectrum from conservative to moderate and reformist. Despite philosophical differences, these discourses are all products of European Muslims' varied experiences in their adopted countries and reflect their ethnic, sectarian, and socioeconomic diversity.

Muslim Immigration to Europe

The overwhelming majority of Muslim immigrants arrived in Europe in the 1960s to help in its postwar economic reconstruction. They were mostly poorly educated, unskilled workers with rural backgrounds. The pattern of Muslim immigration reflected past colonial links or special relations between different European and Muslim countries. These relations explain why most immigrants to France are from French North and sub-Saharan Africa, to Britain from the Indian subcontinent, and to Germany from Turkey.

Both the immigrants and the receiving countries viewed this pattern of immigration a temporary phenomenon and not a permanent feature of European societies. The immigrants wanted to make enough money to return home, and their European employers expected them to leave once their task was done. This state of temporariness is best captured in German appellation of immigrants as "guest workers" (*Gastarbeiter*).[1]

However, events did not develop the way both sides had imagined. Restrictive laws on migration in Europe in the 1970s, coupled with high unemployment and bleak economic prospects in the immigrants' home countries, convinced Muslims to stay in Europe. The number of Europe's Muslims increased in the 1970s, because of the policy of family reunification and in the 1980s and 1990s, because of the arrival of a new wave of immigrants as a result of wars and revolution.

Until the 1970s, the overwhelming majority of Europe's Muslim immigrants were single men who were intent on returning home. They did not establish organizations or conspicuous places of worship, such as proper mosques, and they largely remained invisible to the public. Consequently, until the mid-1970s Europeans felt no need to think about Muslims and their problems. Nor did Muslims feel compelled to focus on questions such as how to live in secular European countries as Muslims; how to integrate into European societies without becoming totally assimilated; how to organize socially and politically and protect their rights; how to educate their children, and many other questions.

Economic Downturn and Social Revolution: Challenges to Europe's Muslims

The recession that gripped European economies in the 1970s, coupled with changes in the patterns of industrial production, had a devastating impact on Europe's Muslim immigrant workers, most of whom lost their jobs. Left to fend for themselves by management as well as trade unions and syndicates, they were forced to organize. The late professor Remy Leveau dates the emergence of a strong Muslim identity among France's immigrant workers to this development.[2] It was also during this time that a Muslim underclass began to form in key European countries, notably France, which has become a permanent feature of European social landscape and has deeply influenced the content and evolution of Islamic discourse among Europe's Muslims. This phenomenon at least partly explains the appeal of certain extremist ideas to Europe's Muslim youth, a large number of whom have not experienced life in a Muslim country.[3] Meanwhile, cultural changes in Europe, particularly related to gender relations, have widened the gap between Islamic and European moral codes.

These developments have resulted in widespread feelings of economic and social disenfranchisement and cultural alienation among Muslim youth and have encouraged many of them to look to Islam as the core of their individual and collective identity.[4] These developments have also endowed Islam with greater significance as a vehicle for expressing non-religious grievances and seeking redress.

The greater consciousness of individual and collective Islamic identity has also been enhanced by events happening in the Muslim world, especially those seen by Muslims as victimizing them. Events perceived as anti-Islam and anti-Muslim, such as the publication of Salman Rushdie's *Satanic Verses* or, more recently, the publication of cartoons depicting the prophet of Islam as a terrorist, have further consolidated European Muslims' Islamic identity.[5] Meanwhile, the growing numbers of Europe's Muslims, their greater visibility, their apparent lack of willingness to assimilate, and the violent actions of some extremist Muslims, coupled with Europe's own cultural and identity crisis, have generated resentment and anti-Muslim feelings among a significant portion of European populations. Despite these negative trends, there is also an understanding on both sides that some form of *modus vivendi* must be reached between European societies and their Muslim minorities. The role of those Muslim organizations, intellectuals, and religious leaders who espouse a moderate and/or reformist perspective on Islam have been central to efforts to reach such an understanding.

Major Questions Facing Europe's Muslims

Europe's Muslims face a number of significant challenges and questions as a religious minority living in secular societies. These challenges relate to the private and public spheres of their lives with considerable overlaps between the two. Examples include dietary rules, religious education (particularly in Germany), recognition of the *umma* as a community, and the issue of veiling. In many European countries, notably France, Britain, Germany, and the Netherlands, the veil is a question of public policy and not merely of private life. Gender relations within the family, especially the issue of polygamy, also straddle public and private domains. Other traditional practices such as honor killing, although unrelated to Islam, also raise problems of public policy because of human rights concerns.

Despite these observations, major issues facing Muslims can be broadly divided into two categories, private and public. Issues related to the private sphere include daily prayers, especially in workplaces, most of which lack space allocated to this purpose; the problem of exclusive cemeteries for Muslims; animal sacrifice during the Eid al-Adha at the end of the *hajj*; and the problem of ritual ablutions prior to prayer.

Issues related to the public sphere include whether Muslims should integrate into European societies and, if so, on what terms; whether integration should be total (assimilation); whether Europe is part of *dar al-Islam*; what loyalty Muslims owe to European governments and under what conditions; how far Muslims should go in order to be accepted by majority societies; whether Muslims should become involved in politics as Muslims or as anonymous citizens; and whether there should be political parties in Europe bearing the name of Islam.

Moderate and Reformist Muslim Responses:
Defining Moderation and Reform

Muslims and native Europeans have different understandings of the terms moderation and reform. There are even differences of opinion among Muslims themselves on this subject. What Muslims may consider a normal pattern of behavior may be viewed by the Europeans as fundamentalist or even extremist. For some Europeans, anything short of total assimilation is considered a form of fundamentalism. The issue of veiling is a good example. Many European Muslims resent native Europeans' view of the veil as a sign of underdevelopment, women's servitude, resistance to becoming full-fledged citizens, or "fundamentalism." Many young Muslim women consider veiling a way of asserting their Muslim identity, do not accept these characterizations, and may even see themselves as "moderate" and "modern." The same holds true for daily prayers and many other religious attitudes, like not drinking alcohol.

Partly depending on their definitions of these terms, moderate Muslims behave according to the following four distinct patterns:

1. Practicing Islam in an individualistic way, which includes abstaining from behavior viewed as divisive by the Europeans, and in effect, assimilationist;
2. Retaining religious identity without insisting on the supremacy of Islamic law over secular laws or challenging the legitimacy of European political structures;
3. Retaining Islamic identity and observing Islamic rules without making political claims in the name of Islam; and
4. Living within closed religious boundaries, renouncing integration in the name of safeguarding Islam's purity, but rejecting violence. For many secular Europeans, this is a "hyper-fundamentalist" attitude, sometimes ending up with radicalization. For many Muslims this attitude prevents radicalization because it gives a sense of belonging to the *umma* alongside the secular world therefore eliminating reasons for fighting it.

In terms of their attitude toward violence, the last two groups are moderate. But in terms of their interpretation of Islam they are similar to Salafis and have a conservative and literalist perspective. This pattern is represented by those Muslims belonging to the Tabliqi organization (Tabliq wal Da'wa), whose European center is in Dewsbury, England, and sympathizers of the Muslim Brotherhood (Ikhvan al Muslmin), such as the Union of Islamic Organizations in France (UOIF) and Germany's Islamische Gemeinschaft Milli Görüs. Yet European publics do not consider these groups to be moderate; they view them as a Trojan horse that might cause a clash between secular European and Islamic values.

The last two groups have created their own organizations, which in most cases coexist with traditional mosques and religious and cultural centers. These associations are mostly voluntary and are organized at city, regional, national, and transnational levels. They produce new types of intellectuals who question the supremacy of traditional imams and structures. In France and Switzerland, Tariq Ramadan, one of the most prominent Muslim intellectuals in Europe, is known to have been close to the UOIF, although he claims to have preserved his autonomy. Tariq Oubrou and Hassan Iquioussen[6] are other examples of these new intellectuals. By contrast, the Paris mosque, which is the most "moderate" among France's religious organizations, lacks any notable intellectuals or new thinkers. In Great Britain the late Sheikh Muhammad Abulkhair Zaki Badawi (1922–2006), rector of the Islamic College, was both a religious leader and to some extent a reformist thinker. In Germany, the head of the Central Council of Muslims (Zentralrat der Muslime in Deutschland) is a convert, Ayyub Axel Köhler. The council is dominated by the Islamic Community in Germany (Islamische Gemeinschaft in Deutschland), an organization made up of Arab Muslims and close to the Muslim Brotherhood. Köhler, however, rejects violence and publicly asks Muslims to act in a way compatible with Europe's democratic rules, particularly regarding matters related to contested attitudes of European leaders toward Muslims in the Middle East and elsewhere.

These new associations have resulted from efforts by younger generations of Muslims who are dissatisfied with traditional religious institutions based on ethnic affiliations. The latter are still important, but they are increasingly challenged by the new organizations. This development has also resulted in the emergence of what could be characterized as "free-floating" individuals, often charismatic figures, who attract new groups of Muslims from the emerging middle class and the excluded lower class. They combine old and new religious functions with modern ways, within a diversified religious "market." To these must be added a new type of religious preachers similar to Christian televangelists, and mystical, Sufi, and other cult leaders. This diversification of Islamic discourse and its proponents reflects a more individualistic approach to religion among Muslim youth. European converts to Islam from the educated middle or lower classes provide another source of new Islamic leadership.

Traditional, Moderate, and Reformist Muslim Associations

Muslim organizations in Europe reflect the ethnic and ideological diversity of Muslim communities. The character of their relations to the state reflects the traditions of each European country. In France, the UOIF, the Paris mosque, and the National Federation of Muslims in France (FNMF) are the most influential organizations under the umbrella organization the French Council of Islamic Faith (CFCM). The Tabliq organization, which is particularly powerful in the poor suburbs in France, is also represented within the CFCM. But the new fundamentalist religious associations called "Salafis" are not represented. The principal Muslim organizations in England are the Muslim Council of Britain (MCB) and the Conservative Muslim Forum, which is directly linked to the Conservative party. A newly formed organization is the Sufi Muslim Council, but it lacks grassroots support and is not very influential. Most organizations in Germany and other European countries are still ethnically based.

Positions of Muslim Organizations on Key Issues in European–Muslim Relations

Most mainstream Muslim organizations hold moderate and even reformist positions on key issues related to both the private and public spheres. For example, institutions such as the MCB in Britain, CFCM in France, the Executive of the Muslims of Belgium (EMB), and similar associations in Germany and other European countries believe that Muslims should be law-abiding citizens of their adopted countries and participate fully in social and political life. They oppose any form of violence and condemn terrorism. The MCB condemns terrorist attacks in Britain and elsewhere in the West; but it also notes the impact of some British domestic and foreign policies in promoting terrorism in the country.[7] On issues related to the private sphere their positions are also moderate, although to varying degrees.

Other organizations, such as UOIF in France, have a more mixed approach, being moderate on most public issues and more conservative on private matters. The UOIF is critical of the French government's policy on veiling, but it has negotiated with Jewish organizations in France to oppose anti-Semitism. Mainstream Muslim organizations in other European countries, too, have moderate positions, especially regarding questions of law and order and other public policy matters.

Transnational Organizations

The most important transnational organizations is the European Fatwa Council, headed by Sheikh Yusuf al-Qaradawi. Its explicit aim is to adapt Islamic jurisprudence (*fiqh*) to the needs of Muslim minorities in Europe in what is called "jurisprudence for the minority." On most social and religious issues, the council is fairly conservative, although its rulings regarding issues facing European Muslims are, out of necessity, becoming less strict. In terms of rejecting violence and calling on Muslims to respect the laws of European countries and respect the rights of non-Muslims, the Council is definitely moderate. For example, at the conclusion of its annual meeting on July 2004, the Council recommended that "Muslims in the West should observe all duties and provide a good example for others in words, actions and behaviours" and should "respect the lives and properties of non-Muslims."[8]

More recently, the council gave its support to an "historic code of conduct" agreed upon by 400 Muslim organizations, and based on an initiative by the Federation of Islamic Organizations in Europe. According to Farid El Machaoud, spokesperson for the League for Muslims in Belgium (LMB), the code urges Muslims to take an active part in European societies, and to realize that European societies are secular and allow Muslims to practice their religion, but that there are some things that are not allowed, like wearing the veil.[9]

The New Muslim Intellectuals

Most first-generation Muslim immigrants were poorly educated. Until recently their religious leaders were mid-level clerics with limited education in Islamic law, theology, and even less so philosophy. Nearly all of them came from the immigrants' countries of origin. Europe's Muslim communities thus lacked the intellectual base from which to develop new religious and philosophical discourses and frameworks capable of providing guidelines for life in secular societies.

This situation has begun to change with the spread of education among second- and third-generation Muslims, coupled with the ability of European Muslims to tap into the resources of the Islamic world through expanded communication networks. In the last decade, distinctive European voices have been heard on important issues facing Muslims in Europe. These new voices include religious leaders and intellectuals who help legitimize Muslims' claim to living a "modern Islam" within Europe. They lead new institutions and prepare European public opinion to accept Islam as an "internal" religion rather than merely a foreign implant.

Global Islamic Intellectuals: Tariq Ramadan

The most representative figure of a global Muslim intellectual is Tariq Ramadan. He transmits new messages to European Muslims in ways that transcend culturally particularistic tendencies. The grandson of the founder of the Muslim Brothers, Hassan Al Banna, Ramadan, is a Swiss citizen, born in Geneva in 1962, and married to a French woman. He is fluent in French, English, and Arabic, well-versed in European philosophy and Islamic studies, and highly articulate. He attracts many second- and third-generation Muslims from among the excluded and the new middle classes in French-speaking Europe and, through the translation of his works, in other European countries, notably the United Kingdom. In his ability to touch the public and enhance the sense of identity of alienated and rootless Muslims, he resembles Christian televangelists. He gives a new dignity to Muslims, who are perceived by Europeans as second-class citizens. His partially defiant attitude encourages Muslims' identification with an Islamic subculture that is not respected by secular or non-Muslim majorities. Through him, Islam becomes a subject of pride, with reasoning and rationalizations that symbolically bestow equality and dignity on Muslims.

Ramadan defends Muslims' rights, emphasizes their duties, and calls for restoration of their rights, self-respect, and pride. These views have gained him a large audience among Muslim youth, while his criticism of autocratic Arab regimes and Israeli and Western policies regarding the Palestinian issue have made him a controversial figure. For example, it has been alleged that he has refused unreservedly to condemn the September 11, 2001, attacks, thus depriving him of a U.S. visa and a professorial position at the University of Notre Dame. His support for a "public Muslim identity" is viewed as illegitimate by some French intellectuals, but he is welcome in Britain, where his charisma is viewed as preventing Muslim youth from succumbing to extremist temptations.

Many people see Ramadan's ideas as contradictory, and they view him as lacking a coherent view on Islam and its relation to European Muslims' problems. Yet these contradictions are more apparent than real and reflect the difficult position of European Muslims as they struggle to reconcile being Muslim and part of the Islamic *umma* with being European citizens.

This task has become more difficult to achieve since the late 1980s. Events such as the Salman Rushdie affair in Britain, multiple confrontations over the Islamic veil in France and other European countries, terrorist acts committed by Muslims in the United States and Europe, the 2004 killing of the Dutch film director Theo van Gogh, and the controversy over the Danish cartoons of the prophet Muhammad have reinforced the Europeans' view of Islam as a "fundamentalist religion" incompatible with democracy and have intensified anti-Muslim feelings. This response has enhanced Muslims' belief that their faith suffers too much by making too many concessions to majority societies.

Ramadan considers himself a "fundamentalist" (*salafi*) in the good sense of the word: adhering to the "fundamentals" of Islam while trying to be a European citizen. He emphasizes that the two are compatible. To achieve this goal, Ramadan believes that a distinction must be made between *shari'a* and *fiqh*. He argues that Muslims should discover *shari'a*'s original meaning, which is "the way to the source" and not a body of laws made by jurists (*fuqaha*). In Ramadan's view, *shari'a* is a global perception of how to relate to God. Although normative, this reading of the *shari'a* would enable Muslims "to extract a global meaning" from their particular norms and thus find commonalities with European principles.[10] He urges Muslims to discover the good points in European traditions and constitutions, such as freedom and justice, and to make them part of their *shari'a*. He says that this is allowed by the original permission, *ibaha al-asliya*.[11] Like many other reformist thinkers, Ramadan distinguishes between those aspects of Islam that are unchangeable (*sabit*), and those that are changeable (*mutaqayer*); and between what is essential (*asl*) and what is secondary (*far*).[12] In essential and unchanging matters, which mostly relate to *ibadat* (worship), there is no room for compromise. But on secondary matters dealing with societal relations (*muamelat*), there is wide scope for compromise and adaptation.

In a short book titled *Dar as-Shahada: The West, the Sphere of Bearing Witness* (published in French), Ramadan discusses various theories on where Europe stands as between *dar al-islam* and *dar al-harb*, and concludes that Europe should be considered the abode for bearing witness (*shahada*), where Muslims should observe their religion and present its message while respecting the law of the land.[13] This interpretation of Islam allows both for the preservation of Islamic identity, a goal that Ramadan advocates, and the creation of a European Muslim, which he also supports. The problem he and most Muslims face is how to delineate the respective realms of religion and secular law in Europe—what to do when the scarf is legally forbidden in government schools in France and some other European states, or outlawed for female teachers as in Switzerland? Should Muslims follow the law or their religion?*

Most Muslims do not feel comfortable with a clear-cut answer to this type of question. A minority might choose one or the other of the radical answers, observing either secular law or Islamic commandment. But most choose not to challenge the secular law but contest its legitimacy by legal and religious arguments. This attitude leads to a "dual system of reference," which does end the claim of being a Muslim while avoiding a confrontational attitude toward secular European systems. In this ambiguity resides a new type of identity, and Ramadan best articulates it in theoretical terms.

From the Europeans' perspective, especially that of the exceedingly secular French, here emerges the major problem of coping with Islam, which Ramadan and other new Muslim thinkers try hard to address. The contradictions find no easy solution when it comes to gender issues or to problems related to the public sphere where Islamic norms and secular laws become incompatible. The French consider any open displays of religiosity as threatening secular republican values, hence their difficulty in accommodating certain Muslim demands, such as the freedom for women to wear a headscarf. Ramadan does not challenge the validity of the French system but reserves Muslims' right to live their lives according to their faith, in particular in matters of worship (*ibadat*). He resists what he sees as European demands that Muslims "relativize and to put into context—social, geographical/cultural—their sense of their faith's divinity and universality." He refuses to accept that his faith is "a relative creed or aspiration."[14]

Ramadan says the main issue is "how my sense of universality will be able to deal with diversity; how my link to God, the revelation, will force me to understand and to respect the diversity of humanity and its civilizations. . . . Muslims do not want to relativize their universal values, but from their universal values they can, and must, deal with diversity."[15] Ramadan argues that "if there is to be a true and equal dialogue between Europeans and Muslims, Europe's universal values should enter into a dialogue with Islam's universal values. . . . In short, Europeans must accept that Muslims have universal values. It does not mean that Muslims cannot understand concepts of diversity and relativity. But, in order to manage a sense of diversity within society, one has to promote a dialogue from within Islamic and European senses of universality." Only in this way is it possible that "a sense of transcendent universality can coexist with a sense of human relativity."[16]

It is precisely this concept of the equality of universalities that is unacceptable to the West; hence the perceptions of Ramadan as a two-faced and dangerous dema-

---

*Editor's Note: The attitude of European countries toward veiling has hardened in the last few years as some Muslims have turned to wearing even stricter forms of the veil, covering their face completely except for the eyes.

gogue, perhaps worse even than an outright extremist.[17] As proof, they quote some of his statements, such as the following in an interview with "Radio Beur" in Paris: "There is a reformist rationalist stream, and there is a Salafi stream that is trying to remain faithful to the foundations (of Islam). I belong to the (latter) stream. That is, there are a number of principles that I consider to be basic, and that as a Muslim I cannot deny."[18] Or his statement at a UNESCO conference: "I am not a Salafi. A Salafi is someone who clings to the written word (*harfi*) and I am not like that."[19] Again, the confusion is caused by definitions of Salafi. Currently Salafism is mostly of the strict Wahhabi version, but in the nineteenth century Muslim modernists such as Muhammad Abduh considered themselves as Salafi.

Many reformist intellectuals believe that notions such as *shura* (consultative council) and *ijma* (consensus among the *ulema*) should serve as a means of re-interpreting and if necessary marginalizing some verses in the Qur'an. Ramadan disagrees and sees this as apostasy (*ridda*). Again the problem derives from what is meant by revision. Ramadan has said that "The Muslims' new situation in Europe will allow them to get back to the sources of their religion and reread its principal sources. In the new European context, some sources must be reread and reinter-preted, and this is what is meant by *tajdid* (renewal). It does not mean changing the text, but rather reading it with a new perspective."[20] This clearly allows for offering new interpretations. In his book *The Faith, the Way, and Resistance*, Ramadan calls for a rereading of Islamic sources in order to eliminate discriminatory practices against women that he says are justified by traditions falsely described as Islamic or by cultural pretexts.[21]

Some observers accuse Ramadan of putting religious identity over citizenship. As proof they cite his saying that: "These two affiliations (the Islamic and the national) are not of an identical nature or degree. Being a Muslim means that you have an entire outlook on life . . . while being French means that you have a role as a citizen."[22] However, the confusion again derives from a misunderstanding of religious, social, and political domains. In response to those who ask Muslims whether they are Muslims first or French, Belgian, or British, Ramadan answers that the question is wrongly posed. He says "if we are talking about questions of life or death, we will say that we are Muslims, but if they ask us about a social issue we say that we are French, Belgian or Swiss as does any humanist or Christian."[23] In short, Muslims are being judged by a standard of citizenship that is not applied to the followers of other religions. Thus Ramadan argues for Muslims' active par-ticipation in Europe's social, political, and economic life, but he says this does not mean merely voting but rather actively working for equality and justice.

Some have argued that Ramadan is at best ambivalent about terrorism in the name of Islam. They point out that while rejecting the September 11 terrorist attacks on the United States, he has cast doubts about the role of al-Qaeda and Bin Laden in them arguing that the beneficiaries of the September 11 attacks were not the Muslims but the U.S. government.[24] This is a serious misjudgment on his part and certainly questions his sincerity in condemning violence in other contexts. Nevertheless, his position more generally has been that "political violence such as killing tourists, priests, women and children by blind bombs should be condemned."[25] But he also condemns the violence that Muslims are subjected to by their governments and others. This latter commentary makes him vulnerable to accusations that he somehow condones violence.

Despite some ambiguities and contradictions in Ramadan's works and speeches, he enjoys great credibility with a large number of Europe's Muslim youth who are at a crossroads between secularization and return to Islam. He provides them with a new identity that is modern and at the same time faithful to Islam's prescriptions in a manner that is not specifically culture-bound. His aim is to build a "hyphen-ated identity" among European Muslims, enabling them to be "modern" without renouncing their religious roots. Many of his works are devoted to this task.[26] The problem is how to construct this dual identity and distribute the weight between its "Muslim" and "European" dimensions. He waivers in this respect, sometimes overstressing the Islamic dimension to the detriment of the national and the secu-lar. This is a false dichotomy, however, since for him the domain of religious and civil are separate. Like many believers of other faiths, Ramadan is not willing to subordinate his Islamic values to the laws of the land, without, however challeng-ing those laws.

Ramadan is seen by many secular Europeans as a "wicked" intellectual who pushes European Muslims toward fundamentalism. Yet, his role is far from negligible in the dual process of "modernizing" Islam as well as "Islamizing" modernity for a European Muslim youth in quest of its Islamic roots. Europe's and Muslims' main problem is not that Ramadan leaves so many questions un-answered, but that there are not many more people like him who could open new vistas for debate to the new generations of Muslims who feel insecure both as citizens and as Muslims.

Building Bridges Between Muslims and British Society: Zaki Badawi

After his death in January 2006, the London *Independent* characterized the Egyp-tian-born Zaki Badawi as a "global Muslim." Indeed, he was a pioneer in dialogue between Muslims and followers of other faiths with a global vision. Beyond this, however, his influence was largely confined to middle-class British Muslims who sought integration into society. Badawi could best be characterized as a practical reformist. He subscribed to the contextual rather than the literalist school, holding that all matters except those relating to the fundamentals of the faith (*ibadat*) are subject to change in accordance with the requirement of time and space.[27]

After the rise in anti-Muslim sentiments in Britain, he ruled that, in order to remain safe, Muslim women could take off their *hijab*. This ruling showed his pragmatism, although more liberal Muslims did not consider this enough.[28] This pragmatism allowed him to be the first to develop the concept of "British Muslim," that is a Muslim without another cultural heritage but integrated into British society.

He also did much to reconcile Islamic and British values. His goal was to build the institutional and theoretical framework for an Islam that would fit with British values: a moderate, tolerant religion, not hostile toward Western values. To this end, in 1984 he founded the Council of Imams and Mosques in Britain, in 1986 he established the Muslim College in West London as a postgraduate seminary, and later he founded the Shari'a Council in order to reconcile British and Islamic laws. To justify his own moderate stance, he often referred to the farewell sermon of the Prophet at the foot of the Mount of Mercy.

He defended women's rights, condemned female circumcision as un-Islamic, and promoted interfaith dialogue. He called on Muslims to spare Rushdie's life, condemned the terrorist attacks of September 11, and urged Muslims to obey military orders as British soldiers. His political stance as a moderate Muslim in close cooperation with British institutions and government can be compared to that of Dalil Boubakeur, the head of the Paris Mosque.

Badawi devoted his life to promoting a modern Islam in tune with British realities, and the development of a British Muslim whose loyalty is to Britain and not to another country of origin or the Muslim *umma*. His efforts and those of like-minded Muslims in other countries have had mixed results, largely because his ideas appeal to the middle class and already integrated Muslims.

Most Muslims who are economically excluded and culturally despised (due to Islamophobia and racism) do not find any response to their questions in this type of attitude. The idea of "British Muslims," "French Muslims," or any other hyphenated Muslims loses its credibility for most Muslims when they feel they are rejected by European societies. Therefore, the success of people like Badawi is at best limited. The terrorist events in Britain in 2005, as in France in 1995 (many other attacks were thwarted afterward), stress the existence of serious stumbling blocks to the integration of Muslims in Europe. People like Tariq Ramadan or Tariq Oubrou see more acutely the social and cultural problems of Muslims in Europe, whose integration cannot be a mere problem of their identification with European values but also raises the problem of Europe's ability to accept as citizens those Muslims who do not want to entirely renounce their religious and cultural identity.

Zaki Badawi in England and Dalil Boubakeur or Soheib Bencheikh (the so-called mufti of the Marseille mosque) in France attempt to make Islam palatable to non-Muslim Europeans. For them, a good Muslim is all but invisible, somebody who identifies with European values and culture and gives up his peculiar identity. In this respect, assimilation rather than integration is in view. This is so explicit in the case of Bencheikh, who subscribes to a republican Islam, and it is implicit in the case of Badawi, who speaks of British Muslim—that is those Muslims who espouse British values and do not care anymore about the specificity of their religion and faith. Some mainly middle-class and modern Muslims who support an individualist version of Islam find their ways through this new identity. But many Muslims who would like to preserve their communal identity to some degree and who care about the fate of their fellow Muslims in other parts of the world find it increasingly difficult to abide by this type of ideal. They see it as "taming Muslims" rather than as recognizing them in their hyphenated identity, as Muslim and British or Muslim and French in equal fashion.

The New Middle-Class Intellectual: Ziauddin Sardar and "Mere Islam"

Ziauddin Sardar was born in 1951 in Dipalpur, northern Pakistan, and migrated to Britain as a small boy. He studied physics and information science at the City University in London. He has worked as a journalist, a television reporter, and as a visiting professor of science and technology policy at Middlesex University between 1994 and 1998.[29] Sardar takes an anticolonial stance and believes that the present backwardness of non-European countries in science is mainly due to their colonial past. He believes that lack of financial resources rather than cultural peculiarities are behind this scientific backwardness. However, he also is critical of Muslims because of what he sees as their parochialism and traditionalism.

> Muslim people have been on the verge of physical, cultural and intellectual extinction simply because they have allowed parochialism and petty traditionalism to rule their minds. We must break free from the ghetto mentality.[30]

As a prolific author, Sardar endeavors to reconcile scientific modernity with an Islam that relativizes some parts of the Holy Scripture (the Qur'an) by giving an historical interpretation of them. He is a contextualist who believes that each generation must reinterpret the holy texts in light of their own worldview. The exegesis must change periodically. Sardar has introduced the notion of "mere Islam" in his weblog, following in the footsteps of a popular Christian theologian C.S. Lewis, who talked of "mere Christianity." For Sardar, mere Islam means

> Islam just as it is—straight from the mouth of a Muslim—unadulterated by the bigotry of Islamophobes, the snide remarks of pundits and the distortion of Orientalists. By that, I certainly don't claim to be speaking for all Muslims, but rather I'm only presenting my own subjective views—views which hopefully fit within the limits expounded by the large majority of Sunni Muslims for the past 1,400 years.[31]

Sardar wants to free himself from the straitjacket of an ossified tradition represented by the *ulema* and their parochialism. If each Muslim tries to use his own reason and feeling toward Islam and expounds it in his own way, traditions lose much of their weight. By this process of individualizing Islam, modernization occurs, and each Muslim's subjectivity becomes the yardstick for the understanding of Islam according to his needs and aspirations.

This view of Islam is in tune with the modern Muslim middle classes. They have internalized the mottoes of individualism and seek salvation through their own personal view of the religion. According to this individualized Islam, notions like the *umma* or *jihad* as a duty of Muslims toward their community lose their traditional sense. This interpretation of Islam does not speak to most Muslims, however, who feel uprooted, disenfranchised, marginalized, and stigmatized as second-class citizens. For them Islam cannot be merely a private matter, related to the subjectivity of the believer alone and without any roots in a tradition that warrants an identity and brings solace to the individual in a situation of non-recognition and rejection. Even many middle-class Muslims feel that tradition and a communal conception of Islam are relevant to their lives as minorities in non-Muslim countries.

Sardar is also incapable of understanding the sense of Muslim resentment toward Europeans, policies vis-à-vis other Muslim countries, because he strongly identifies with the views of Westerners.[32] The result is that his ability to mediate between disenfranchised Muslims and British or European societies is limited.

Other British Muslim Reformists

Two other British Muslim reformist thinkers should be noted here: Sheikh Abdul Hakim Murad, born Timothy J. Winter, and Mona Siddiqui. Both of them, especially Tim Winter, have high visibility in the media and are frequently interviewed on various television programs. Yet for reasons noted earlier, their appeal to most Muslims, and hence their ability to shape Muslims' views and modes of behavior, is limited. They both preach a flexible, contextualist, and peaceful Islam, although there are some differences on certain issues between them. Sheikh Abdul Hakim Murad is a convert to Islam and teaches Islamic studies at Cambridge University. He has studied at Al-Azhar and lived in Jeddah, Saudi Arabia. He is an adept of Sufi traditions and holds classes and groups (*halaqa*).[33] He has spoken strongly against violent acts committed by extremist Muslims, but at the same time he holds relatively conservative views on certain issues such as women's position in Islam. Mona Siddiqui teaches at the University of Glasgow and has published on Islam, political authority, and pluralism. She maintains that Islam favors pluralism.

Free-Floating Muslim Intellectuals

Another category of intellectuals invite European Muslims to moderation and reform. These Muslim reformist thinkers were forced to leave their home countries because of repression and spread new ideas on Islam in Europe and in the West in general. Some stay permanently in one country, while others move among different countries, or between European countries and their birthplace. Their views carry some weight within their home countries, other reformist circles in Muslim countries, and the West.

A good representative of the first group is Nasr Hamid Abu Zayd, who was forced to migrate from Egypt to Holland for fear of assassination after being declared apostate. The Yemeni intellectual Elham Manea defends the right of women to take off the veil. She traces the origins of the veil to the Islamic Revolution in Iran, political Islam, or Wahhabi Islam.[34] Her position is not historically valid, however, and thus is unlikely to carry much weight with believers. Others, like the Tunisian-born Lafif Lakhdar, promote an "Islam within the bounds of reason," in other words a rationalist Islam. He rejects Islamic radicalism as a crime against humanity and promotes the "Meccan Islam" of the time of the Prophet when the most progressive and egalitarian concepts in Islam were developed. He rejects the "Medina Islam" of the time when the Prophet acted both as political and religious leader. He believes the memory of this period has served as inspiration for fundamentalism and extremism.[35]

Self-Proclaimed Preachers: The Case of Hassan Iquioussen

Another type of Muslim intellectual in Europe, particularly in France, is the charismatic preacher. He mostly lacks credentials in Islamic jurisprudence (*fiqh*) or in theology (*kalam*) but has the support of young Muslims. These preachers lack the scholarly turn of mind of traditional imams. Their strength derives from their language skills: many are fluent and even eloquent in European idioms, and are thus capable of communicating with their audiences. A prominent representative of this category is Hassan Iquioussen in France. He is characterized as a "predicator." He is neither an imam, nor a scholar versed in traditional Islamic knowledge (*alim*); his legitimacy derives from his recognition by part of the Muslim population (mostly the Muslim youth), thus bestowing on him a measure of success. Iquioussen was born in France in 1964 of Moroccan parents.[36] He has become well known among the Muslim youth of poor suburbs and popular districts, especially in Lille, and is close to the Union of Islamic Organizations.

In his preaching, he combines ethical approaches to Islam with protest against the injustices committed against Muslims with defense of Palestinian rights. He insists on the self-determination of the individual Muslim, who should not allow his destiny to be shaped by either the non-Islamic Western societies or the traditional imams. The following words from a sermon he delivered in La Courneuve, a poor suburb of Paris, reflect well his thought and style: "Don't be parrots, don't follow anyone, and do not indulge in mimicry. You don't need any spiritual father." Meanwhile, he insists on the dignity of being both a Muslim and a French citizen and refuses to disconnect the two dimensions by relegating to the private realm the Islamic side of the personality:

> Be proud to be Muslims, for God's sake! Be proud of your cultural particularities. To distinguish between Frenchness and the Islamic side of one's personality is devoid of any meaning. As a Frenchman I can only live simultaneously according to my citizenship and my religion.[37]

Iquioussen fights against the "inferiority complex" of Muslims in Western societies and against "integration by (eating) pork," which he characterizes as a kind of "prostitution." Integration through rejection of Islam and adoption of European (French) patterns of behavior can still result in rejection by French society, as illustrated in the extreme right's slogan: "You don't have a place in France!" He advances new ideas regarding how Muslims should adapt to the European context, including a liberal attitude toward women's rights, and he rejects the paternalistic attitude of traditional imams toward youth. He intersperses his preaching with humorous remarks and uses the slang of the poor French suburbs.

People like Iquioussen are much more likely to be found in France. This is because of the special features of French secularism (*laïcité*); the impact of the long fight between the Catholic Church and the state on the French political and cultural system which has made rejecting religion in the name of freethinking a faith on its own,[38] and the French tradition of open controversy and debate. Yet because the public style in places like Britain, Germany, and Holland does not allow putting religion at the center of public debate, preachers like Iquioussen do not exist there, even though new Muslim middle classes and political elites are stronger in these countries than in France.

Imam of Muslims as a Religious Minority: The Case of Tariq Oubrou

Imams are the main type of Muslim religious leaders in Europe. Most of them still come from the immigrants' countries of origin. They have a more or less solid knowledge of Islam, read at least the Qur'an in Arabic, and are able to give advice about what kind of attitude to adopt in non-Muslim societies where it is not always easy to live according to Islamic rules. They are either based in specific towns or cities (like Tariq Oubrou, the imam of the mosque in Bordeaux) or they belong to larger structures like the European Council of Fatwas.

Among imams, the case of Oubrou is exemplary because he encourages many Muslims who otherwise might be attracted to extremist ideas, toward moderation. He was born in Agadir, Morocco, in 1959, and is leader of a traditional Muslim community in Bordeaux.[39] He tries to reconcile some tenets of European culture with Islamic values, notably the individual's right and duty to judge for himself about many aspects of his life without referring excessively to communal values. His major contribution has been to emphasize the role of reason and the right of the individual in deciding about matters related to daily life and to restrict religious rules to matters of worship, *ibadat*. He writes books and articles in the style of European intellectuals, defends his views in French (not Arabic), and engages in critical dialogue with female scholars on equal ground.

Oubrou tries to vindicate secular European laws in regard to what he calls the "*shari'a* of the minority," which is different from the *shari'a* in Muslim majority countries. He argues that because Muslims are a minority in Europe and are likely to remain so, the rules for them cannot be as they were in their countries of origin.

Muslims have three choices: they can adopt Europe's secular laws and become totally disconnected from Islam; they can choose to live according to Islamic laws in isolation from broader society; or they can try to find an intermediary discourse that would allow them to remain Muslims while observing the laws of the majority societies. Preferring the third option, Oubrou endeavors to create a legal and moral structure for those whom he calls "minimal Muslims." In answers to questions such as what to do when the job requirements inhibit praying five times a day, he offers practical solutions such as one daily prayer. Such a ruling is considered a harmful innovation (*bid'a*) by many traditionalists, but Oubrou justifies it through his interpretation of the *shari'a*, and by recourse to the fact that Islamic rulings (*hukm*) are adaptable to concrete situations through *fatwas* (religious rulings).

He also gives mystical justifications for the renewal of the faith by seeking the *haqiqat* (truth), thus questioning Islamic orthodoxy. In this vein, he argues that daily prayer is not a mere ritual act. It is the internalization of faith, a communication with God, both of which presuppose a spiritual attitude. In this way, "spiritual faith" as opposed to "ritualistic faith" solves the difficulties of performing formal rituals. Oubrou proposes a version of religion adapted to secular and individualistic European societies that precludes public displays of religious belief. Oubrou's ideas could attract Europe's young Muslims and provide a bridge between Muslim communities and European societies.

Transnational Ulema: The al-Qaradawi Paradigm

To this category belong those religious leaders who are recognized in Muslim countries as scholars and pious men whose religious recommendations (*fatwa*) are followed by many Muslims. Some of them seek and attract disciples by establishing institutions or taking part in existing ones. Yusuf al-Qaradawi, the head of the European Council for Fatwa and Research as well as the International Association of Muslim Scholars, is probably the most prominent representative of this category. He gives religious advice to Muslims in Europe, setting new rules for the *umma* living in the situation of a "minority."[40] These *fatwas* inevitably become less stringent in relation to daily life because the European context makes many stringent Islamic rules either inapplicable or difficult to apply to the letter. Thus Qaradawi encourages a timid liberalization of Islamic laws on inheritance, marriage, and divorce.[41] He has ruled that Muslims wanting to buy a house are allowed to get a mortgage, although interest is prohibited in Islam. While clearly very conservative, Qaradawi's rulings send a new message to many traditionalist Muslims in Europe and open new possibilities for gradual change.

Conclusions

Europe's Muslims face serious dilemmas and challenges. Their most serious dilemma is how to integrate fully into European societies without totally losing their

Islamic identity and, worse their faith. Some find any form of adaptation impossible, and thus withdraw into their isolated communities, with all that implies in terms of their economic and political future in Europe. Others choose total assimilation and lose their Islamic identity.

Moderate and reformist religious leaders and intellectuals are trying to offer Muslims a third way. This holds the best promise for peaceful integration of Muslims into European societies and preventing the radicalization of underprivileged Muslim youth. Among these leaders, those who can relate to the needs and aspirations of the disenfranchised and alienated Muslims, offer them a credible way of integrating into European societies, and show them how to mediate the demands of faith and life in modern societies have a better chance of being credible mediators between Muslim communities and European societies.

Excessively individualistic readings by largely secularized intellectuals are less able to perform this task and their appeal is likely to remain limited to already integrated Muslims. Similarly, those Muslim religious leaders, like the late Zaki Badawi, Dalil Boubakeur, or Soheib Bencheikh, who in fact preach assimilation rather than integration, will have limited appeal for those Muslims who wish partially to preserve their communal identity, and who care about the fate of other Muslims. This approach seems more suited to "tame Muslims" rather than to those with a hyphenated identity both as Muslims and Europeans.

In order to succeed in spreading their moderate message, these intellectuals and religious leaders will need the native Europeans' cooperation. If the Europeans cannot accept anything short of complete assimilation of Muslims, the task of these intellectuals will become more difficult. Worse, if the Europeans condemn and victimize all Muslims for the sins of a radical minority, or accuse those intellectuals who dare criticize aspects of European policies, or object to the religious bigotry of some political or other groups and personalities, then in all likelihood they will doom the prospects of a reformist Islam taking root in Europe. Yet reformist Islam holds the best hope of providing a bridge between Europe's absolute secularism and Muslims' attachment to their religious beliefs.

Notes

1. For a detailed analysis of the pattern of migration of Muslims to various European countries, see Shireen T. Hunter, ed., *Islam, Europe's Second Religion: The New Social, Cultural, and Political Landscape* (Westport, CT: Praeger, 2002).

2. See Remy Leveau and Shireen Hunter, "Islam in France," in ibid., pp. 29–51.

3. The exact percentage of the second- and third-generation Muslims is not known, but their numbers are increasing.

4. Farhad Khosrokhavar, *L'islam des jeunes* (Paris: Flammarion, 1997).

5. Some scholars date the emergence of political activism of British Muslims to the Rushdie affair.

6. They will be discussed in more detail below.

7. The Muslim Council of Britain (MCB) takes a firm position that all parents, both Muslim and non-Muslim, have an important responsibility for being vigilant and ensuring

that their children are not misled by criminal and extremist elements in society. However, the MCB notes that the government needs to also recognize the impact of some of its own policies, domestic and foreign, in contributing to the spread of extremist ideas: "It is as though in response to the threat of Global Warming and the threat of rising water levels, the government were to ask all of us merely to place sandbags outside our homes to prevent flooding. Surely, the more sensible way forward would be to tackle the causes of Global Warming. Similarly, in continuing to ignore the damage that some of our foreign policies, particularly in the Middle East, have done to our national security, the government is not facing up to a major contributory factor behind the rise of extremism." Dr. Muhammad Abdul Bari, Secretary-General of the Muslim Council of Britain, press release, The Muslim Council of Britain, September 20, 2006.

8. Ali Al-Halawani, "European Fatwa Council Urges Muslims to Respect Laws," Islam-Online.net, July 11, 2004, available at http://www.islamonline.net/English/News/2004-07/11/article06.shtml.

9. See "Muslims to sign 'Historic Code of Conduct'" *Islam in Europe*, available at: http://islamineurope.blogspot.com/2008/01/muslims-to-sign-historic-code-of.html.

10. Tariq Ramadan, "Europeanization of Islam or Islamization of Europe?" in *Islam, Europe's Second Religion*, ed. Hunter, pp. 211–12.

11. Ibid., p. 210.

12. Ibid., p. 213.

13. Tariq Ramadan, *Dar as-shahada. L'occident, espace de temoignage* (Lyon: Tawhid, 2002), pp. 65–74.

14. Tariq Ramadan, "Europeanization of Islam or Islamization of Europe?" p. 208.

15. Ibid.

16. Ibid., pp. 208–9.

17. Caroline Fourset, *Frère Tariq* (Paris: Grasset, 2004).

18. A. Dankowitz, "Tariq Ramadan, Reformist or Islamist?" MEMRI, February 17, 2006.

19. See ibid.; see Women Living Under Muslim Laws, "Actualités et points de vue. Mondial: Ramadan et Bencheikh s'expliquent," May 15, 2006, available at www.wluml.org/french/newsfulltxt.shtml?cmd[157]=x-157-537329 for excerpts of that dialogue.

20. Ramadan, "Europeanization of Islam or Islamization of Europe?" p. 211.

21. Tariq Ramadan, *La foi, la voie et la résistance* (Lyon: Tawhid, 2002), p. 42.

22. See Tariq Ramadan, *Les Musulmans dans la laicite: responsabilites et droits des Musulmans dans les societes occidentales* (Muslims in Secular Society: Responsibilities and Rights of Muslims in Western Countries) (Lyon: Tawhid, 1998), p. 15.

23. Tariq Ramadan, *Musulmans d'Occident: Construire et contribuer* (Muslims of the West: Constructing and Contributing) (Lyon: Tawhid, 2002), pp. 32–33.

24. See Tariq Ramadan, "Condamner et résister ensemble," *Le Monde,* October 3, 2001.

25. Tariq Ramadan, *Jihad, violence, guerre et paix en Islam* (Jihad, Violence, War and Peace in Islam) (Lyon: Tawhid, 2002), p. 75.

26. See Ramadan, *Les Musulmans dans la laicite* and *Musulmans d'Occident.*

27. Zaki Badawi, "Civilisation & Dialogue in the 21st Century," Islam21.com, September 3, 2007, available at http://islam21.net/main/index.php?option=com_content&task=view&id=437&Itemid=39.

28. Ahmed Fathy, "Take off Hijab to Avoid Harm: UK Muslim Scholar," IslamOnline. net, July 28, 2005, available at http://www.islamonline.net/English/News/2005-07/28/article05.shtml.

29. Ziauddin Sardar's Web site is http://www.ziauddinsardar.com.

30. Ziauddin Sardar, "Reformist Ideas and Muslim Intellectuals," in *Today's Problems,*

Tomorrow's Solutions: The Future Structure of Muslim Societies, ed. Abdullah Omar Naseef (London and New York: Mansell, 1988), quoted from "Ziauddin Sardar," Wikipedia.org, available at http://en.wikipedia.org/wiki/Ziauddin_Sardar.

31. See "Ziauddin Sardar, C.S. Lewis and 'Mere Islam,'" MereIslam.info, September 18, 2004, available at http://www.mereislam.info/2004/09/ziauddin-sardar-c-s-lewis-and-mere.html.

32. See Sardar's series of articles—Ziauddin Sardar, "I do not know what drives Muslim terrorists. . . ," *The Evening Standard,* September 13, 2001; "My Fatwa on the Fanatics," *The Observer,* September 23, 2001; "Where Is the Hand of My God in This Horror?" *New Statesman,* September 17, 2001.

33. For examples of Murad's views, see "Feature Interview: Tim Winter (aka Abdul Hakim Murad)," Sunday Nights with John Cleary on ABC Local Radio, 18 April 2004, available at http://www.abc.net.au/sundaynights/stories/s1237986.htm; and Abdal-Hakim Murad, "The Poverty of Fanaticism" *Islam for Today* (n.d.), available at http://www.islamfortoday.com/murad02.htm.

34. See his writings in www.middleeasttransparent.com.

35. See his English interview, "Lafif Lakhdar: Religion Within the Limits of Reason," Special Dispatch Series, No. 1157, May 5, 2006, available at http://memri.org/bin/latestnews.cgi?ID=SD115706.

36. See Telquel Online, 21 March 2006, www.telquel-online.com. Hassan Iquioussen does not have French citizenship, despite of the fact that he was born in France. His status as "Moroccan" is sometimes used by the authorities to pressure him toward moderation in his preaching.

37. Ibid.

38. Jean Baubérot, *Laïcité 1905–2005. Entre Passion et Raison* (Paris: Seuil, 2004).

39. Alexandre Caeiro, "An Imam in France: Tariq Oubrou," *ISIS Review* 15 (Spring 2005). See Tareq Oubrou, "Introduction théorique à la charî'a de minorité," Oumma.com, May 26, 2000, available at http://oumma.com/Introduction-theorique-a-la-chari. Catherine Coroller, "Portraits: Lieu d'attaches (2,7): Tareq Oubrou, imam de la mosquée de Bordeaux, dans sa bibliothéque. Le goût du sacré," *Libération,* August 20, 2002, available at http://www.mafhoum.com/press3/108S27.htm.

40. See Alexandre Caeiro, *La normativité islamique á l'épreuve de l'Occident: le cas du Conseil Européen de la fatwa et de la recherche* (Paris: EHESS, 2002); Rémy Leveau and Khadija Mohsen-Finan, eds., *Musulmans de France et d'Europe* (Paris: CNRS Editions, 2005).

41. See the French translation of the Arabic *fatwas* of European Council for Fatwa and Research, *Recueil de fatwas* (Lyon: Tawhid, 2002).

9

Voices of Reformist Islam in the United States

Tamara Sonn

Muslims have a long and distinctive history in the United States, dating back to the slave trade of the seventeenth to nineteenth centuries. It is estimated that some 30 percent of the ten million Africans brought to America as slaves were Muslims, one notable example being Omar Bin Said from Senegal. Bin Said was highly literate and, upon his death in 1864, left numerous religious documents written in Arabic.[1] Because of slaveholders' policies, especially separation of family members, prevention of literacy, and rewarding of conversion to Christianity, little evidence of Muslim slaves' religious traditions has survived intact. Nevertheless, scholars have suggested the indirect impact of certain aspects of African Muslim culture, especially in music, where some have detected the traces of the *muezzin*'s call to prayer.[2]

After Emancipation, many African-Americans undertook concerted efforts to reclaim their Islamic heritage. Some of the earliest efforts resulted in heterodox approaches to doctrine and practice, but today most African-American Muslims are indistinguishable in ideology and practice from other Muslim Americans.[3] Most of the American Muslim community, which numbers from five to seven million, is now made up of immigrants from South Asia, the Middle East, and Africa who have arrived over the last century.[4] Most are Sunni but there is also a significant Shi'a minority; Sufism—a highly spiritual and mystical version of Islam—is also well represented.

Like adherents of other faiths and Muslims worldwide, American Muslims are engaged in the discourses of modernity and postmodernity, including debates on how to integrate religious and political life, as well as on pluralism, democracy, human rights, and gender issues. Like other Americans, some Muslims hold conservative, traditionalist views; they focus on the importance of exclusive religious identity and privileging religious authority. Others favor more liberal positions that emphasize the importance of pluralism, democracy, and human rights, including gender justice.

The American Muslim community includes thinkers who have produced significant works on issues that have engaged intellectuals throughout the Muslim world for over a century and a half. Some of their ideas have had significant influence on the evolution of Islamic discourse, ranging from the need for more dynamic interpretation of Islamic sources to how to mediate between Islam and modernity. In no small measure, this influence has resulted from the fact that these senior scholars have trained generations of Muslim students from various Muslim countries in American universities. Some of them are still productive, but a younger generation of American Muslim scholars is also emerging. Unlike the earlier generation of scholars who addressed the global Muslim community, the younger scholars tend to be more concerned with specific challenges facing American Muslims, but their views are nevertheless significant for ongoing discourses throughout the Muslim world.

The focus of this study is the contributions made by those scholars who belong to the more liberal part of the spectrum of Islamic thought in America, along with their role in the development and propagation of reformist Islamic discourse. However, the views of moderate, if not exactly liberal, Muslims will also be addressed.

Terminology and Methodology

The term "liberal" in this context does not refer to policy positions such as those implied in contemporary partisan usage in the United States.[5] Instead, it is used it in the classical sense, characterizing the prevailing values of American democracy such as the freedoms guaranteed in the United States Bill of Rights. In the context of Islamic discourse, these views are often called "reformist." This does not mean revision of basic Islamic beliefs, but rather rethinking traditional understandings of those beliefs and their implications for social and political organization in the modern world. It is essentially a discourse of Islamic law, focusing on basic principles that inform specific legal codes.[6]

The methodology of American Muslim reformist thinkers in interpreting the Qur'an and the *sunna* is similar to that of other reformist thinkers discussed in this volume. This methodology involves distinguishing between the foundations of Islamic faith, the Qur'an and the *sunna*, which are considered infallible, and human interpretations of them and their social and political implications. These interpretations are subject to revision according to the specifics of various times and places.[7] They also distinguish between the *shari'a*, the path traced by God for humanity, which is unchangeable, and *fiqh*, the codification of the *shari'a* as a result of human endeavor, which can be changed according to new needs through interpretation, *ijtihad*. In addition to the traditional methodology of *ijtihad* as articulated in *usul al-fiqh*, reformist thinkers employ methodologies partly or wholly derived from other disciplines, including history, sociology, phenomenology, and anthropology.

Pioneers of Muslim Reformist Thought in the United States

Reformist Islamic discourse has developed gradually over the past half-century. Its earliest leaders were immigrants from Muslim majority countries, and their thought reflected their backgrounds. They tended to address the global Muslim community rather than Muslims in the United States or the West. This was so partly because, until the last two decades, the number of Muslims in the West was not very significant and, with few exceptions, Muslims were largely invisible in Western countries, including the United States.

Ismail al-Faruqi and the Islamization of Knowledge

Ismail al-Faruqi (1921–1986), a Palestinian activist, scholar of Islam and Western philosophy, professor at Syracuse University (1964–68) and Temple University (1969–86), was one of the early major figures of Islam in America. Early in his career he focused on "Arabism" (*uruba*) as the central core of Islam.[8] He maintained that only those Muslims who master Arabic, thus becoming honorary Arabs, are true Muslims and can understand Islam's message.[9] For most Muslims, who are non-Arab and lack a mastery of Arabic, al-Faruqi's Arabism is difficult to understand, let alone to accept.

By the late 1960s, al-Faruqi had distanced himself from Arabism and Islam became his defining identity. At the same time, he developed the view that Islam was the vehicle of perfected universal religious values. This perspective informed the intellectual program "Islamization of knowledge" with which he is most closely associated.

Al-Faruqi advocated the Islamization of knowledge as a way to integrate Islamic values and modern learning, particularly in the social sciences.[10] He believed that Muslims had become alienated from learning, partly because of the perception of modern learning as foreign. Therefore, in order to rehabilitate Islamic society and empower Muslims, the body of modern knowledge had to be "Islamized." This meant that modern knowledge had to be processed through essentially Islamic categories and methods of analysis, as had been done in Islam's classical age. In this way, Islamic values or ethics would guide the use of knowledge. Al-Faruqi also believed that Muslims had a mission to bring this ethical message to the West in order to "save the West."[11] This is why al-Faruqi participated in establishing the International Institute of Islamic Thought (IIIT) in northern Virginia in 1981. The Institute's goal is

> the revival and reform of Islamic thought and its methodology in order to enable the *Umma* [global Muslim community] to deal effectively with present challenges, and contribute to the progress of human civilization in ways that will give it a meaning and a direction derived from divine guidance. The realization of such a position will help the *Umma* regain its intellectual and cultural identity and reaffirm its presence as a dynamic civilization.

Methodologically, therefore, al-Faruqi was different from reformist thinkers. The latter want to reinterpret Islam in light of modern sciences and use other disciplines in their work because they believe that traditional Islamic tools are no longer sufficient. However, to the extent that al-Faruqi tried to find a way to reconcile Islam and modernity, he was a reformist.

Seyyed Hossein Nasr and the Perennialist School

Another major proponent of an Islamic approach to knowledge is the Iranian-born philosopher of science Seyyed Hossein Nasr (b. 1933). Nasr's perspective is informed by his Shi'a upbringing, his Sufi orientation, and his study of perennialist philosophy, particularly that associated with the traditionalist school of Rene Guenon and Frithjof Schuon. This school teaches that the material world is only a pale reflection of a higher, non-material or spiritual reality.[12] According to this school of thought, all people are capable of transcending the material world, and all religions aspire to do so. This transcendence is the route to liberation from falsehood and suffering and thus to true happiness, the goal of human life. Unfortunately, the modern world, particularly in the West, obscures this higher reality and distracts people from its pursuit.

Like al-Faruqi, Nasr focuses on knowledge, although his approach is neither political nor exclusivist. It is both spiritual and universalist. It involves a quest for knowledge that begins in the physical world but its goal is metaphysical, an inquiry into the nature of things, and the goal of life. This concern is clearly reflected in Nasr's works on science.[13] His physical-metaphysical epistemological holism is expressed in a model of science informed by values that are at once Islamic and, in his view, global. For example, his scientific scrutiny of the environment, in the context of the Islamic notion of human beings as stewards of the earth, resulted in one of the earliest public warnings about ecological degradation. In lectures given at the University of Chicago in 1966, Nasr noted the impending environmental crisis and observed that this looming physical disaster reflected current spiritual or religious failures.[14] Thus Nasr's work is comprehensive, reaching beyond what is considered in Western categories to be strictly scientific.

Nasr is also an ardent advocate of respect for religious diversity, and believes that American Muslims have a special responsibility. He says that American Muslims must promote not only mutual respect among Muslims, Jews, and Christians, but respect for religious diversity in general. This entails countering the "thousand-year history" of Christian attacks on Islam and especially the vindictive post–9/11 attacks. This must be done "with reason and logic, with compassion rather than anger." But it must be done not simply in the interest of setting the record straight but also because of the enormously negative impact such attacks have when broadcast, as they are, throughout the Muslim world. This, Nasr believes, is all part of "authentic Islamic intellectual activity in this country" that Muslims must develop.[15]

Also, like al-Faruqi, Nasr keeps a keen eye fixed on the Muslim world. He says that, for the first time in history, "a number of very important Islamic thinkers live outside the borders of Islam and have an influence on the Islamic world itself." By responding with enlightened Islamic models to Western ideologies such as Marxism, liberal capitalism, existentialism, feminism, socialism, and nationalism, American Muslims may assume influential positions within the broader Islamic world. He compares them with the Muslims of medieval Spain and says, "The modern-day Islamic community in the United States could possibly become another Andalusian intellectual community for the rest of the Islamic world."[16]

Al-Faruqi and Nasr are among the most well-known figures in American Islam, but neither is particularly strongly associated with reformist Islam. Al-Faruqi's Islamization of knowledge program was meant to be global. It was, moreover, multi-generational and the necessary precursor to the exercise of *ijtihad* (the hermeneutics of reform). But under present circumstances, *ijtihad* was not a central concern for him. Nasr unquestionably encourages Muslims, American and worldwide, to assist in curing modern humanity of its spiritual malaise. And like al-Faruqi, his impact both in the United States and abroad has been widespread. But stressing the strengths and depth of spirituality in classical Islam, his approach is not essentially reformist nor is its focus primarily on America. Nasr, in fact, cautions against excessive enthusiasm for *ijtihad*. For him "authenticity" is a prior concern, and its test is whether or not Muslims in the Middle East accept the viewpoints expressed. He notes that there is already criticism of American Muslims in the Muslim world, "and [it] is going to become much more accentuated if far-fetched interpretations of Islamic matters by Muslims living in the West begin to inundate the Islamic world."[17] In addition, Nasr is a harsh critic of modernity. In his native Iran he is viewed as a traditionalist and has been criticized for this by some reformist thinkers.

Fazlur Rahman Malik and the Theory of Double Motion

Of all the earlier thinkers, Fazlur Rahman Malik (1919–1988), popularly known as Fazlur Rahman, is closest to the contemporary reformist thinkers and has inspired many of them. Some of these thinkers studied under him either at UCLA or at the University of Chicago, where he taught until his death, and have translated his works into their native languages. Rahman's views are discussed in more detail elsewhere in this volume. However, given the fact that his more productive and influential years were spent in the United States, his underlying philosophy will be briefly mentioned here.*

Like al-Faruqi and Nasr, Fazlur Rahman believed in the need to work out an "Islamic worldview."[18] But working out that worldview was, for Rahman, a dynamic process that required constant reference to revelation and ongoing intellectual effort to identify core values exemplified there and ways to implement those values in changing circumstances.

---

*Editor's Note: See the chapter on reformist thinkers in South Asia.

Rahman did not predict a time when core Islamic values would be conclusively understood and realized, and consequently he believed that Islamic laws must be constantly reinterpreted and adapted to new circumstances. He noted that what was appropriate at the time of revelation in Arabia may no longer be appropriate in the twenty-first century. He saw the Qur'an and *sunna* as eternally perfect sources to be returned to again and again for inspiration and guidance as human beings struggle to implement the will of God. To undertake that struggle is, in Rahman's view, to obey the command to participate in *ijtihad*.

Rahman maintained that Islam itself was a process of constant reform, and he argued that the human condition is one of "creative" or "dynamic tension" between the values revealed in the Qur'an and exemplified by the Prophet and the constantly changing circumstances of life. Those values were repeatedly described and exemplified in the Qur'an and may be subsumed under the general notion of justice. But they were implemented in the specific circumstances in which revelation took place. The challenge of Islam is to find ways in other times and places to realize those values. Meeting that challenge requires ongoing efforts to assess current conditions in light of revealed models and to make adjustments in modes of implementation when they appear to be warranted. He called this process of assessment and adjustment in light of Qur'anic values a "double motion." For him, it was the essence of faith to accept the limitations of human understanding and maintain receptivity to divine guidance. But he believed that the Muslim community as a whole had failed to establish institutions reflecting their limitations and the consequent need for periodic reassessment.

Fazlur Rahman shared the concern with Islamic education found in the work of both al-Faruqi and Nasr. But unlike al-Faruqi, he did not believe today's Muslim community perceived Islamic values clearly or sufficiently to be able to "Islamize" secular knowledge. Like Nasr, he believed the process of mining revelation was deeply spiritual. But unlike Nasr, Fazlur Rahman believed that well-educated Muslims, working in community, not only were capable of devising new ways to implement Islamic values in modern circumstances, but, considering the challenges facing Western Muslims, they had the responsibility to do so.

Fathi Osman and the Dynamics of Change

Like Fazlur Rahman, Fathi Osman (b. 1928) is convinced of the need to rethink the classical sources of Islam in order to implement their teachings in the contemporary world. Still prolific in retirement, Osman has published over thirty books including, most recently, *Islamic Law and the Contemporary Society: Shari'a Dynamics of Change*, a massive commentary on the Qur'an; *Concepts of the Qur'an: A Topical Reading;* and *Children of Adam: An Islamic Perspective on Pluralism.* His overall approach, again like Fazlur Rahman's, is based on recognizing that the Qur'an delivered a universal and eternal message, contextualized in a specific society in seventh-century Arabia. The challenge for all generations of Muslims, then, is to distinguish between the eternal values of the Qur'an and the specific examples of how to implement those values. Once the values are clearly understood, Muslims must then determine appropriate ways to implement those values in changed circumstances. As he puts it, Muslims must "draw the line between what is transitional and what is permanent in Islamic sources."[19] Osman gives the example of slavery, noting that Muslims now universally reject slavery even though it was permissible in the Qur'an. That is because Muslims recognize that slavery, transitional at the time of revelation, violates the permanent values of human dignity and equality in the Qur'an.

In *Children of Adam,* Osman outlines his views on the Qur'anic demands for three issues that continue to occupy Muslim reformers: democracy, pluralism, and women's rights. He bases his argument on interpretations of classical elements of Islam, beginning with the Qur'anic command that governance—even that conducted by Prophet Muhammad—be participatory. "Shura means a serious and effective participation in decision making, and the example of the Prophet proves that it cannot be merely a formal or ceremonial exercise."[20] While the means of implementing *shura* may have been relatively informal in the past, in today's world, Osman insists, *shura* should be implemented through democracy. In response to traditionalists, who argue that nothing may be introduced to Islamic governance that was not directly indicated by the sources, Osman cites classical legal principles whereby Muslims are required to adopt the most effective means to achieve the obligatory goals established by Islamic law: "their life, families and children, minds, freedom of faith, and their private or public possessions."[21] Provided a system achieves these goals, which are agreed upon by all the major schools of Islamic legal thought, that system may be called just and therefore Islamic. Osman further argues that the Qur'an's insistence on equality for all human beings means that women should enjoy equal rights, including in political matters. Thus they must be allowed to vote and hold office. He also favors political equality for religious minorities and says, "A Muslim majority should have no misgivings about a non-Muslim voting, since votes are taken regarding matters related to common sense, not to a particular faith."[22]

Contemporary Developers of Reformist Islam in America

As a minority, American Muslims face some key challenges in coping with modernity more immediately than do their fellow Muslims in Muslim-majority countries. These include the interrelated issues of pluralism and democracy. Classical Islamic law, with no jurisdiction outside Muslim lands, provides little guidance for Muslims facing these challenges. As minorities enjoying democratic rights, therefore, Western Muslims are confronted daily with what the South African scholar Farid Esack has called the challenge of "living with integrity with non-Muslims," in a way that Muslims living as majorities, often in non-democratic societies, are not.[23] A number of Muslim scholars have taken up this challenge and have endeavored to provide guidance to Muslims on how to live as Muslims in pluralistic societies.

Abdulaziz Sachedina: Islamic Roots of Democracy and Pluralism

One of today's major voices of pluralism in Islam is Abdulaziz Sachedina of the University of Virginia. Traditionalists may argue that the Qur'an's early acceptance of pluralism was abrogated with Prophet Muhammad's mission. In this view, after receiving the Prophet's message, members of other faith communities failed to join the Muslim community and therefore they should be considered outside or, at best, subordinate to the community of believers. But Sachedina holds that the Qur'an's pluralism is timeless. He bases his conclusion on the Qur'an's respect for religious freedom. "[T]he concern for human autonomy, especially freedom of worship (or not to worship), is as fundamental to the Koranic vision of human religiosity as it is to that of other civilizations."[24] In fact, "without recognition of freedom of religion," he says, "it is impossible to conceive of religious commitment as a freely negotiated human-divine relationship that fosters individual accountability."[25] Thus, for him, when the Qur'an declares, "Who so desires another religion than *Islam,* it shall not be accepted of him; in the next world he shall be among the losers" (3:85), it is referring not to Islam as a distinctive faith community but to "submission [to the will of God]"—that is, monotheism in general. As in Nasr's and Fazlur Rahman's analyses, it is no less true now than during the Prophet's lifetime that the Qur'an accepts the legitimacy of multiple monotheistic religions. He reasons that this is because the divine guidance is of two orders, universal and particular. Universal moral guidance is the basis upon which humans "qua humans" agree on certain values that may be enforced; they are "objective and universally binding." But "on the basis of particular guidance through scripture, it is crucial to allow human beings to exercise their volition in matters of personal faith."[26] Religious choice, then, is part of the relationship between God and the individual; human beings may not interfere.

There is no doubt that intolerance has been a factor in Islamic history, Sachedina says, "even to the exclusion of the other from the divine-human relationship. Such an exclusivist theology can envision a global human community only under Islamic hegemony."[27] But under current circumstances, such a position is untenable. However, Sachedina does not simply subscribe to the "secular liberal theory" whereby religious belief is irrelevant to governance. Instead, he believes that "Abrahamic traditions in general and Islam in particular have much to contribute to a discourse about the desirability of including universal religious argument calling for human cooperation in establishing a just public order."[28] He recognizes that traditional Islamic law has no provision for "egalitarian citizenship—the core of civil rights and responsibilities in a modern nation-state." But that does not mean that the Qur'an offers no guidance for modern civil society. Muslims must develop "a fresh reading of this heritage . . . retrieving the core values of Islamic system to offer this fresh paradigm."[29]

Sachedina is also a keen proponent of democracy as an Islamic value. In his book *The Islamic Roots of Democratic Pluralism,* and even more emphatically since September 11, 2001, Sachedina has argued that Islam's essential pluralism demands democracy. He says that Muslims "need to learn how to guide [themselves] and [their] community back to the sources, to the living heart of Islamic belief, and take seriously the emphasis that [they] find there on building nurturing, constructive relationships of justice and charity at all levels of human existence." By doing so, he says, Muslims will come to understand more clearly that the kinds of relationships their faith enjoins them to build "cannot exist without respect for the equal dignity of all human persons and a broad appreciation for the God-given liberty of human conscience."[30]

Sachedina believes that, given that Islam provides comprehensive guidance, it is virtually unthinkable that it would not concern itself with governance. According to Sachedina,

> Shari'a regulates religious practice with a view to maintaining the individual's well being through his or her social well-being. Hence, its comprehensive system deals with the obligations that humans perform as part of their relationship to the Divine Being, and the duties they perform as part of their interpersonal responsibility.[31]

Thus in the modern pluralistic state, Islam need not be marginalized. Instead, its heritage of respect for religious diversity and human initiative offers clear guidance, if not governance, for Muslims to participate fully in democratic governance. Thus, for Sachedina,

> Fostering a positive understanding of democratic ideals within an Islamic framework . . . is not a matter of superficial "Islamizing" verbiage, but rather of a deep and comprehensive effort to show . . . that democratic ideas can and must be thought from within the authentic ethical culture of Islam and its teachings about the awesome accountability of human beings in this world and the next.[32]

Integrally related to Sachedina's views on democracy is his commitment to women's rights, particularly their right to participate in Islamic legislation. In an article subtitled "Crisis of Male Epistemology in Islamic Jurisprudence," Sachedina argues that the personal status of women in Islamic law "demand[s] rethinking and reinterpretation of the normative sources like the Qur'an and the Sunna (Tradition) to deduce new directives under changed social conditions."[33] However, it is not only the changed social conditions that call for rethinking the status of women; Sachedina's argument turns on the observation that women's voices were inappropriately excluded from the formulation of Islamic laws concerning them in the first place. He cites a *hadith* report according to which even Prophet Muhammad had recourse to the voice of a woman—his wife Aisha—when dealing with matters that pertain specifically to women. He is therefore critical of the traditional legal designation of women's voices as inappropriate for public discourse, a designation that renders women "legally silenced." In his analysis, Islam's insistence on human equality "dictates that women need to represent their own concerns in all matters of family and maternity care."[34]

Khaled Abou El Fadl: Advocate of Human Rights in Islam

Khaled Abou El Fadl, who teaches at UCLA Law School, is another proponent of Islam's basically democratic and pluralistic ethos as well as Islam's commitment to the protection of basic human rights. In his *Islam and the Challenge of Democracy,* Abou El Fadl examines the foundational texts of Islam and argues that Islam is not only compatible with democracy but that Islamic values can best be expressed today in constitutional democracies that protect individual rights—that is, in liberal democracies.

In this analysis, Islamic tradition is pluralistic and incorporates a number of concepts comparable to those of modern democracies. One is the need for consultation in government. The Qur'an instructs even Prophet Muhammad to rule in practical matters in consultation with the community. In addition, Abou El Fadl says that early Muslim jurists "agreed on the notion that government exists by contract . . . between the ruler and the ruled."[35] There were differences of opinion regarding the status of this contract, but all agreed that there must be popular approval of the government in some form. This is based on the classical concept of *bay'a,* or pledge of allegiance. Based on the example of Prophet Muhammad, governments must receive popular approval in order to be legitimate. Jurists disagreed about how to get this pledge and from whom, and what to do if it was not forthcoming. But all agreed on the principle of government by consent.

Abou El Fadl offers a further argument in support of democratic forms of government, namely that the Qur'an has charged human beings collectively to implement its principles. Abou El Fadl acknowledges that some Muslims reject the idea of democracy on the basis of the belief that God is the sole legislator. But he argues that this is "a fatal fiction . . . indefensible from the point of view of Islamic theology, because it assumes that some human beings have perfect access to the divine will."[36] He insists that no human being or group of human beings can claim to have direct access to the divine will other than through the guidance of revelation. The Qur'an is a divinely revealed source of guidance for all aspects of life and contains specific legislation for some areas of human life, including worship and diet. But beyond these basic regulations, the Qur'an challenges human beings to use their reason to find ways to implement its principles. Abou El Fadl believes that Muslim jurists over the ages have correctly identified justice and mercy as foremost among the Qur'an's principles. In his view, then, Muslims have a collective responsibility to establish governmental structures that promote justice and mercy. Putting it another way, to the extent that a social order (government) is successful in establishing justice and mercy, it reflects divine sovereignty. The opposite also holds true; no government that fails to establish a social order characterized by justice and mercy can claim to have truly implemented the divine mandate. Thus the determining characteristic of a government reflecting divine guidance or sovereignty is not its legislative structure; rather, "[P]rinciples of mercy and justice are the primary divine charge, and God's sovereignty lies in the fact that God is the authority that delegated to human beings the charge to achieve justice on earth by fulfilling the virtues that approximate divinity."[37]

For Abou El Fadl, in today's world a just and merciful government is one that protects the basic human rights identified by Islamic classical jurists. But traditional interpretations of the appropriate way to protect these rights are not always tenable in today's world. Protecting those essential rights must be "re-analyzed in light of the current diversity of human existence." In particular, he calls for the rights of free speech, association, and suffrage. In other words, he concludes, "[D]emocracy . . . offers the greatest potential for promoting justice and protecting human dignity, without making God responsible for human injustice or the degradation of human beings by one another."[38] By recognizing the human responsibility for articulating, executing, and adjudicating that government, divine sovereignty remains intact.

According to Abou El Fadl, the issue of human rights is closely related to arguments in favor of pluralism and democracy. He believes that Islam has a rich tradition of human rights. Classical legal sources contain detailed discussions of this topic, the *maqasid* (goals or purposes of Islamic law). In Islamic legal discourse, rights are divided into two kinds: the rights accorded to God (*huquq allah* or *ibadat*), and the rights of human beings or individuals (*haqq al-'abd* or *huquq al-ibad*). The rights of God have to do with ways of worshiping: prayer, fasting, pilgrimage, and so on. The rights of human beings were definitively described by the fourteenth-century legist Imam Abu Ishaq al-Shatibi: religion, life, family, reason, and wealth.[39] Establishing and protecting these rights is considered one of the primary purposes of Islamic law. The question then becomes: How are these rights to be established and protected? Traditionally, preservation of religion is described as making sure people are allowed to carry out their religious duties. *Jihad* is often described as the means for defending religion. Some scholars describe preservation of life (*nafs*) as the most basic human right, taking precedence over even the rights of God. According to that line of reasoning, if a life is at stake, the requirement for prayer or fasting may be suspended.[40] Other scholars point out that preservation of religion has priority over protection of life, since people must potentially take lives and risk their own lives in a war justified on the basis of protecting the right to carry out religious duties. In any case, human life is considered inviolable (*isma*) or sometimes *hurman* (sacred), except in the case of a just war or duly adjudicated capital punishment. It is preserved by making sure people have enough to eat and the ability to assure good health, and it is protected by effective penalties for those who take life without legal justification. Preservation of family (*nasl*) includes the right to legal marriage and inheritance, for example, and is protected by providing penalties for those who undermine those rights. Preservation of intellect includes the right to education and the prohibition of substances that interfere with the intellect (such as intoxicants). And preservation of property (*mal*) is traditionally interpreted as maintaining conditions for creating and increasing wealth, including the right to private ownership of property, and it is protected by implementing penalties for theft or misappropriation of wealth or property. Abou El Fadl indicates that scholars need to discuss ways to implement these essential Islamic values in contemporary circumstances.

For example, on the issue of women's rights, Abou El Fadl is known for his forthright position. In his 2001 monograph *Speaking in God's Name,* he argues from unassailable position that women and men share full legal and ethical equality in Islam.[41] Other scholars who argue in favor of pluralism and democracy also support gender equality, but Abou El Fadl takes the argument a step further. For example, he assumes a position that is very rare among contemporary legal scholars and challenges the traditional view that only men may lead congregational prayers. In response to a question about the subject, Abou El Fadl issued a *fatwa* in which he describes two traditional positions held by scholars concerning the qualifications of the prayer leader. According to the more liberal of the two, a prayer leader (*imam*) may be anyone who knows how to pray. The more conservative position is that the imam should be the person in the community who knows the Qur'an best and is the most learned in both religion and community affairs. Abou El Fadl opts for the latter position. He then notes that the Prophet "on more than one occasion allowed a woman to lead her household in prayer—although the household included men—when the woman was clearly the most learned in the faith."[42] Furthermore, he claims that scholars agree on the permissibility of women teaching both women and men about religion. In view of the Prophetic precedent and the permissibility of women teaching men about religion, he argues that the subsequent exclusion of women from leading congregational prayer would have to be based on unequivocal evidence. But, he says, there is nothing in the Qur'an that precludes women's leadership of prayer, and the Sunna holds no firm position on the matter. The exclusion of women is based only on custom and "male-consensus." He then cites the standard legal position that the common good should take precedence over custom and concludes that "a female ought not be precluded from leading *jumu'a* [Friday congregational prayer] simply on the grounds of being female."[43]

Abdullahi Ahmed An-Na'im: Controversial Methodology

Abdullahi Ahmed An-Na'im teaches law at Emory University and directs its program on Religion and Human Rights. He is perhaps the most controversial Muslim reformist thinker in America. An-Na'im argues that Islam supports the modern conception of human rights as articulated in the Universal Declaration of Human Rights of 1948: "universal claims of rights that are due to all human beings by virtue of their humanity, without distinction on such grounds as race, sex (gender), religion, language, or national origin."[44] But he does so through a methodology judged to be problematic by many Muslims. An-Na'im argues that there is a disconnect between the values expressed in the Qur'anic verses revealed in Mecca and those from the later Medinan period. He sees the former as more authentically Islamic in that they respect human equality in general, while the latter seem to privilege males over females and Muslims over non-Muslims. Therefore, he favors the Meccan model of Islam as a basis for a modern articulation of human rights and recommends that standard principles of abrogation (*naskh*), whereby later verses supersede earlier verses, be ignored.

An-Na'im's unique language of "evolutionary" Islam is inspired by his Sudanese mentor Mahmud Muhammad Taha, who was executed on charges of heresy. Few other scholars embrace this language, although most reformist thinkers support An-Na'im's contention that the Qur'an is a rich source of inspiration for modern views of universal human rights and that, as Fazlur Rahman taught, its message must be understood in context.

Louay M. Safi: Developing Islam-Based Human Rights

Louay M. Safi is the executive director of the Islamic Society of North America's Leadership Development Center. He is critical of An-Na'im's approach and instead argues for the development of Islam-based human rights. He justifies his position on the grounds that proper understanding of Islam "is bound to evolve a human rights tradition," one in which "the civil and political liberties of all citizens—regardless of gender, ethnic, or religious distinctions—are protected." This, he says, is preferable to simply importing human rights from the Universal Declaration; basing the discussion on the Qur'an will produce the same set of rights but they will have the advantage of being recognized as authentic to Muslims. He says that such an understanding rests on distinguishing classical formulation of Islamic laws "from the socio-political structure of early Muslim society."[45]

Safi presents a detailed discussion of human rights based on the Qur'an that follows essentially the methodology outlined by Fazlur Rahman. It begins by distinguishing between Qur'anic teachings and human interpretation of these teachings in specific contexts. In Safi's analysis, the Qur'an establishes human dignity as a core value. It places human beings at the pinnacle of creation, endowed with the ability and the need to distinguish right from wrong. Safi uses the language of "moral autonomy" to describe this phenomenon and believes it is consistent with Western, Kantian ethics. But he believes that the Qur'an goes beyond the Western vision of individual moral autonomy and establishes moral autonomy for communities, as well. Thus diverse religious communities are granted both the right and responsibility to act with moral autonomy, each according to its divinely revealed laws. However, he says, Muslim jurists developed legal codes that failed to protect this autonomy in some cases; they restricted religious freedom and discriminated against non-Muslims. Beginning in the eighth century of Islam, with the turmoil created by the Crusades, the Mongol invasions, and the Reconquista, "mistrust and suspicion" of the religious Other set in. This, in turn, led to the development of discriminatory laws and practices rationalized on the basis of an agreement between Caliph Omar and Syrian Christians, an agreement that, according to Safi, is of dubious authenticity. Nevertheless, Islamic legal codes still reflected recognition of "the intrinsic dignity of non-Muslims . . . even when they failed to provide a complete and comprehensive list of rights for its protection."[46]

Safi also argues, again like Fazlur Rahman, that *ijtihad* must be exercised in order to reestablish religious freedom in modern circumstances. Following classical procedure, jurists must examine the ultimate purposes (*maqasid*) of Islamic legislation. In a further parallel to Fazlur Rahman's methodology of reform, Safi argues that legislation concerning these values must be informed by a holistic reading of the Qur'an and not be based on individual verses. Moreover, interpretations based on *hadith* reports must not contravene Qur'anic evidence. Applying this methodology, Safi concludes that the Qur'an is "unequivocal in supporting religious freedom." The juristic rules that restricted religious freedom and the rights of non-Muslims were based not on the Qur'an but on specific *hadith* and were developed under specific conditions that no longer obtain. Legal reform through *maqasid*-based *ijtihad* must therefore be undertaken and, when it is, will result in full protection of human rights on both individual and communal levels.

Safi follows the same line of reasoning for guaranteeing women's rights through reformed Islamic legislation, although he says that the traditional legal codes are "more perplexing" on this issue than on that of other human rights. On the one hand, he says they recognize women as "autonomous persons with full legal capacity: they enjoy full control over their property; their consent is required for marriage and they have the right to initiate the process of divorce; they can initiate legal proceedings and can grant or receive the power of attorney; they can even assume public office and serve in the capacity of judges." Yet there is also a "historical prejudice against women in general" and that is reflected in the undermining of their rights through "a host of legal devices."[47] In some cases, legal codes permit a father to force a daughter into a marriage, in some cases a woman requires consent of a guardian to marry the person of her choice, and in some cases a woman's right to terminate a marriage is so severely restricted as to be virtually nonexistent. But he argues that these restrictions are not based on a holistic reading of the Qur'an. The Qur'an does differentiate between men's and women's responsibilities within the family, he says, but "all limitations on women's rights imposed by classical scholars in the public sphere were based on either faulty interpretation of Islamic text or practical limitations associated with the social and political structures of historical society."[48] In particular, he takes issue with interpretations of the Qur'an's designation of men as protectors (*qawwamun*) of women. He believes that the relevant verse and those that require women's obedience apply only within the family. Again, he says, jurists who extended these restrictions to the public sphere as well relied upon *hadith* material. Safi argues that the impact of the *hadith* and the legislation based on it are at odds with the overall thrust of the Qur'an on the issue of women's status. "We have to conclude therefore that the Islamic sources support the right of women to have full access to public office, and to enjoy complete equality with men in public life."

Amina Wadud: Champion of Women's Rights

Amina Wadud, an African-American scholar of Islam who teaches at Virginia Commonwealth University, is the best known and most outspoken champion of women's rights among American Muslim thinkers. She admits that women's status in the Muslim world is distinctly beneath that of men, but she refuses to accept that this situation is a reflection of Islamic values because, she says, the fundamental Qur'anic ethos is "equity, justice, and human dignity" as derived from a holistic understanding of the Qur'an.

Based on this understanding of the Qur'anic ethos, Wadud undertakes a "gender jihad" in order to reform gender-related practices in the Muslim world and bring them into accord with Qur'anic ideals. To achieve this goal she uses a methodology that she calls a "hermeneutics of *tawhid*," emphasizing the Qur'an's overall unity and how this unity permeates all of its parts.[49]

In her choice of methodology, Wadud is influenced by Fazlur Rahman. She uses his notion of "double motion" in interpreting the Qur'an, going "from the present situation to the Qur'anic times and then back to the present." Like other reformist thinkers, she, too, stresses the importance of the historic and social context of the time of revelation in understanding Islam's essential principles and applying them to society under new conditions. In support of her approach, Wadud cites the specific example used by Rahman, namely the verses pertaining to women's testimony. In verses discussing the permissibility of borrowing and lending, the Qur'an advises that such transactions may be undertaken but should be recorded and witnessed by two men. But "if two men be (not at hand) then a man and two women, of such as you approve as witnesses, so that if the one errs (*tudilla*) the other can remind her" (2:282). Wadud, following Rahman, disagrees with the interpretation of classical jurists whereby the import of the verse is that women's testimony is only half as reliable as that of a man. She notes that the unreliability of women's testimony was specific to the historical context of the verse rather than a universal principle:

> Since the testimony of a woman being considered of less value than that of a man was dependent upon her weaker power of memory concerning financial matters, when women become conversant with such matters—with which there is not only nothing wrong but which is for the betterment of society—their evidence can equal that of men.[50]

Wadud proceeds to apply the same hermeneutic to other major issues in the legal status of women, including men's authority over women, inheritance, the right to initiate divorce, and child custody in case of divorce. In all cases, she derives conclusions from the Qur'an, which she believes views women as "primordially, cosmologically, eschatologically, spiritually, and morally . . . full human being[s] equal to all who accepted Allah as Lord, Muhammad as prophet, and Islam as *din*."[51] Following Fazlur Rahman's "double motion" hermeneutic, she argues that modern implementation of Qur'anic views of women would yield full equality and social empowerment for women.

Acting upon these conclusions, Wadud has become a highly controversial figure within the Muslim world. When she has challenged the traditional segregation of sexes in the mosque, she has received widespread criticism, from both Muslim men and women. Nevertheless, her insistence on human equality in all matters, including gender, based on a holistic reading of the Qur'an, is broadly accepted among reformist thinkers.[52]

Conclusions: Identification of Trends

Contemporary American Muslim reformist thinkers owe a great deal to the pioneering work of intellectual giants of the earlier generations. Through the work of al-Faruqi, Nasr, Osman, and Rahman, they have found their voices. The focus on knowledge and the importance of addressing contemporary concerns in an Islamic context may even be seen as fulfillment of the dashed dreams of America's first Muslims, the African slaves. The early scholars emphasized issues that were of concern to the global Muslim community, although their work had significant implications for American Muslims and other Muslims living in the West. But the generation of Muslim reformers in America represented by Sachedina, Abou El Fadl, Safi, and Wadud are more concerned with specific challenges facing Muslims who live in Western liberal democracies. Perhaps more important, their influence goes beyond the scholarly and intellectual communities and is being felt within the Muslim community at large, as shown by the changing character of the leadership of the Islamic Society of North America (ISNA).

Established in 1963, ISNA is the largest organization of Muslims in North America. Its mission is to provide "a common platform for presenting Islam, supporting Muslim communities, developing educational, social and outreach programs and fostering good relations with other religious communities, and civic and service organizations." Included in its activities is the training of religious leaders (imams). The executive director of ISNA's Leadership Development Center is Louay Safi, a fact that indicates the organization's reformist orientation. Further indication of this orientation is the election of Ingrid Mattson as president of ISNA in 2006. Mattson holds a Ph.D. in Islamic Studies from the University of Chicago. She teaches Islamic Studies at the Macdonald Center for Islamic Studies and Christian-Muslim Relations at Hartford Seminary and directs its Islamic Chaplaincy Program. Clearly, there is strong support for the democratic processes, pluralism, and women's rights, particularly among America's Muslim students.

The influence of Islamic reformist thought is registering strongly among popular religious leaders, such as Hamza Yusuf and Imam Zaid Shakir. They offer a uniquely American perspective on issues of concern particularly to younger generations. Both unequivocally condemn those who commit violent acts in the name of religion, as well as those whose support for unjust policies reflects a lack of spiritual or moral awareness. Born in the United States and thoroughly at home in the secular West, both encourage critical awareness of the strengths and faults in both Western and Islamic countries. Sheikh Yusuf studied Islam in Saudi Arabia, Egypt, and elsewhere in the Arab world. He returned to the United States and founded the Zaytuna Institute in Hayward, California, where Zaid Shakir, who studied Islam in Syria, is scholar-in-residence. The Zaytuna Institute offers courses for both males and females in classical Islamic studies as well as special programs and conferences addressing contemporary issues. Through these programs, Sheikh Yusuf and Imam Zaid encourage Muslims to develop profound spirituality through which they can engage with their world and bring Islamic values of justice and peace to bear. Although Imam Zaid Shakir cherishes the belief that someday the United States will rule according to Islamic law, both Yusuf and Shakir express distinctly pluralist views.[53]

Imam Feisal Abdul Rauf, the leader of the al-Farah mosque in New York City, represents another aspect—Sufi—of the broad spectrum of moderate Islamic views in the United States. Imam Feisal is committed to interfaith understanding and solidarity, and when he founded the American Sufi Muslim Association in 1997 he identified as its objectives helping non-Muslims and Muslims overcome mutual misunderstandings and developing Islamic arguments in support of the principles of separation of powers, justice, women's rights, and freedom of religious practice.[54] Imam Feisal has been particularly active since 9/11, which he considers a dire warning of the need for concerted effort among all people of conscience. He described his work in a 2004 interview: "I am not here to condemn one side or the other, but to tell Muslims what they must do differently and tell Christians and Jews what they must do differently. I want people to understand the things that have fueled this violence against us—not to excuse it, but to work to find ways to stop it."[55]

Elements of reformist thought are also beginning to appear in the work of more centrist and even conservative members of the American Muslim community. In 1993, the United Kingdom branch of the International Institute of Islamic Thought published a work by the president of the Fiqh Council of North America, Taha Jabir al-Alwani, advocating the use of *ijtihad*. In the preface, the editors wrote:

> Ijtihad, for long codified and confined to history, needs to be redeemed and put to effective use. . . . Consigning the salubrious factor to the annals of history is a denial of the rationalistic, egalitarian, and human aspects of a realistic and durable Faith. The act would also be a repudiation of the requisites of changing times and of the clamoring need to rid the Ummah of its present baggage of malaise and miseries and enable it to forge ahead, inspiring other nations and communities.

The preface also noted that "the debate is not an open-and-shut issue," but that "it needs to widen quickly in view of the urgency of a solution for the civilizational future of the Muslim world."[56]

In 2003 the same institution published another work by Sheikh al-Alwani, advocating the exercise of *ijtihad* on the specific question of the status of Muslims living as minorities. That work was introduced by the venerable Sheikh Dr. Zaki

Badawi (1922–2006), principal of the Muslim College of Britain and founder of the Imams and Mosques Council of the United Kingdom.* These works take a decidedly cautious approach; they do not directly claim to be exercising *ijtihad*, only that it should be exercised, and that Muslims living in the West deserve special attention in Islamic law.

Clearly, the reformist approaches discussed above are not yet at the center of debate in the Muslim world, and the views of reformist thinkers are not considered mainstream. But Sheikh al-Alwani's insistence in 2003 on the need for a new *ijtihad*, one that privileges the Qur'an over *hadith* and supports legislation based on the ultimate objectives of the *shari'a*, indicates that American thinkers may be part of the vanguard of future developments in Islamic thought. Indeed, their approaches may well have implications not just for Muslims living as minorities in liberal democracies, but also for Muslims worldwide, where people are still awaiting the development of functioning democracies. Certainly, with the growing interaction between Muslim intellectuals and activists in the West and those in Muslim-majority countries, there will be greater cross-fertilization of ideas. Such cross-fertilization could potentially be highly beneficial to the cause of reform in the Islamic world, thus enabling Muslims to mediate between their religious and cultural values and the imperatives of living in the modern and increasingly globalized world.

Notes

1. Marc Ferris, "America's First Black Muslims," *American Legacy*, vol. 3, no. 4 (Winter 1998): 33–39; N. Painter, *Creating Black Americans: African-American History and Its Meanings, 1619 to the Present* (New York: Oxford University Press, 2005).

2. John Storm Roberts, *Black Music of Two Worlds* (New York: Schirmer Books, 1998); and Gerhard Kubik, *Africa and the Blues* (Jackson: University Press of Mississippi, 1999).

3. Jane I. Smith, *Islam in America* (New York: Columbia University Press, 2000).

4. The exact number of Muslim Americans is impossible to determine since U.S. Census Bureau figures do not reflect religious identification and estimates by other surveys range widely. See Zahid H. Bukhari, "Demography, Identity, Space: Defining American Muslims," in *Muslims in the United States: Demography, Beliefs, Institutions,* ed. Philippa Strum and Danielle Tarantolo (Washington, DC: Woodrow Wilson International Center for Scholars, 2003).

5. Ann Coulter, *Godless: The Church of Liberalism* (New York: Crown Forum, 2006).

6. As modern Islamic scholar Fazlur Rahman Malik put it, Islamic law is "an endless discussion on the duties of a Muslim rather than a neatly formulated code or codes." Fazlur Rahman, *Islam and Modernity: Transformation of an Intellectual Tradition* (Chicago: University of Chicago Press, 1982), p. 32. For a discussion of the various terms used to describe contemporary Islamic trends, see Meena Sharify-Funk, "From Dichotomies to Dialogues: Trends in Contemporary Islamic Hermeneutics," in *Contemporary Islam: Dynamic, not Static,* ed. Abdul Aziz Said, Mohammed Abu-Nimer, and Meena Shaify-Funk (London and New York: Routledge, 2006), pp. 64–66.

---

*Editor's Note: See the chapter on Europe for more information on the views and contributions of Sheikh Badawi.

7. Islamic law distinguishes between matters considered to be between the individual believer and God, and social matters. Laws concerning the former concern such things as how to pray and perform pilgrimage and are not subject to rethinking. The rethinking that informs reformist Islam pertains only to social (including political and economic) matters.

8. Ismail al-Faruqi, *'Urubah and Religion: An Analysis of the Fundamental Ideas of Arabism and of Islam as Its Highest Moment of Consciousness,* vol. 1 of *On Arabism* (Amsterdam: Djambatan, 1961).

9. Ibid., p. 3.

10. See Ismail al-Faruqi, *Islamization of Knowledge* (Herndon, VA: International Institute of Islamic Thought, 1982).

11. See Ismail al-Faruqi, "The Path of Da'wah in the West," *The Muslim World League Journal,* vol. 14, nos. 7–8: 55; cited in Behrooz Ghamari-Tabrizi, "Loving America and Longing for Home: Ismail al-Faruqi and the Emergence of the Muslim Diaspora in North America," *International Migration,* vol. 42, no. 2 (June 2004): 75.

12. Seyyed Hossein Nasr, ed., *The Essential Frithjof Schuon* (Bloomington, IN: World Wisdom, 2005).

13. Seyyed Hossein Nasr's, *An Introduction to Islamic Cosmological Doctrines* (Cambridge, MA: Harvard University Press, 1964), *Science and Civilization in Islam* (New York: Barnes & Noble, 1992), *Islamic Science: An Illustrated Study* (Chicago: Kazi, 1976), *Man and Nature: The Spiritual Crisis in Modern Man* (San Francisco: HarperCollins, 1991), *Religion and the Order of Nature* (New York: Oxford University Press, 1996).

14. Nasr's Rockefeller Lectures were the basis for his *Man and Nature.*

15. Seyyed Hossein Nasr, "American Islamic Intellectual Activity and the Islamic World," in *Muslims in the United States: Identity, Influence, Innovation,* ed. Strum and Taraublo, p. 76.

16. Nasr, "American Islamic Intellectual Activity," p. 82.

17. Ibid., p. 81.

18. Fazlur Rahman, *Islam and Modernity,* p. 86.

19. Shimaila Matri Dawood, "We Are Not Remaking Islam. Interview with Dr. Fathi Osman," *Newsline,* December 2004, available at http://www.newsline.com.pk/NewsDec2004/religion2dec.htm.

20. Fathi Osman, "Shura and Democracy," in *Islam in Transition: Muslim Perspectives,* John J. Donohue and John L. Esposito, ed., 2d ed. (New York: Oxford University Press, 2007), p. 288.

21. Ibid.

22. Ibid., p. 291.

23. Farid Esack, "Between Mandela and Man Dalla: Rethinking Kaffirs and Kafirs," unpublished proceedings of the conference, Islam and Civil Society in South Africa: Prospects for Tolerance and Conflict Resolution, University of South Africa, August 5–7, 1994.

24. Abdulaziz Sachedina, "The Role of Islam in the Public Square: Guidance or Governance?" in *Islamic Democratic Discourse: Theory, Debates, and Philosophical Perspectives,* ed. M.A. Muqtedar Khan (Lanham, MD: Lexington Books, 2006), pp. 180–81.

25. Ibid., p. 181.

26. Ibid.

27. Ibid., p. 176.

28. Ibid., p. 177.

29. Ibid., pp. 185–86.

30. Abdulaziz Sachedina, "Why Democracy, and Why Now?" in *Islam in Transition,* ed. Donohue and Esposito, pp. 308–9.

31. Abdulaziz Sachedina, "The Role of Islam in the Public Square," p. 174.

32. Abdulaziz Sachedina, "Why Democracy, and Why Now?" p. 308.

33. Abdulaziz Sachedina, "Woman, Half-the-Man? Crisis of Male Epistemology in

Islamic Jurisprudence," available at: http://www.globalwebpost.com/farooqm/study_res/
islam/gender/sachedina_half_man.html.

34. Ibid., p. 6.

35. "Islam's Forgotten Heritage: A Conversation with Khaled Abou El Fadl," Ethics
and Public Policy Center, June 24, 2003, available at http://www.eppc.org/programs/islam/
publications/pubID.1588.programID.36/pub_details.asp.

36. Khaled Abou El Fadl, "Islam and the Challenge of Democracy," Boston Review, no.
28, 2 (April/May 2003), available at http://www.bostonreview.net/BR28.2/abou.html.

37. Ibid.

38. Ibid.

39. Based on a hadith according to which the Prophet Muhammad said that the soul,
body, property, and honor of Muslims are inviolable.

40. On the concept of necessity (darura), see Subhi Mahmassani, The Philosophy of
Jurisprudence in Islam, trans. Farhat J. Ziadeh (Leiden: Brill, 1961), pp. 152–59; and Mo-
hammad Hashim Kamali, Principles of Islamic Jurisprudence (Cambridge: Islamic Texts
Society, 1991), pp. 267–81.

41. Khaled Abou El Fadl, Speaking in God's Name: Islamic Law, Authority, and Women
(Oxford: Oneworld, 2001).

42. "Fatwa by Dr. Abou El Fadl: On Women Leading Prayer," Scholar of the House,
2006, available at http://www.scholarofthehouse.org/onwolepr.html.

43. Ibid.

44. Abdullahi A. An-Na'im, "The Synergy and Interdependence of Human Rights,
Religion and Secularism," Forum for Intercultural Philosophy 3 (2001), available at http://
them.polylog.org/3/faa-en.htm.

45. Louay M. Safi, "Human Rights and Islamic Legal Reform," Human Rights Forum,
vol. 18, no. 2 (Spring 2001): 32–59, available at http://www.iiu.edu.my/deed/articles/hu-
man3.pdf.

46. Ibid., Section 2.

47. Ibid., Section 3.

48. Ibid., Section 4.

49. Amina Wadud, Qur'an and Woman: Rereading the Sacred Text from a Woman's
Perspective (New York: Oxford University Press, 1999), p. xiii.

50. Ibid., p. 49.

51. Ibid., p. x.

52. Gisela Webb anthologizes a number of Muslim women reformers in Windows of Faith:
Muslim Women Scholar-Activists in North America (Syracuse, NY: Syracuse University Press,
2000). At one and the same time they argue against non-Muslims who claim that Islam is
misogynist, and traditional Islamic interpretations that appear to violate the egalitarian spirit
of the Qur'an. See also Asma Barlas, Believing Women in Islam: Unreading Patriarchal
Interpretations of the Qur'an (Austin: University of Texas Press, 2002).

53. See Laurie Goodstein, "U.S. Muslim Clerics Seek a Modern Middle Ground," New
York Times, June 18, 2006.

54. See the American Sufi Muslims Association Society's Web site at http://www.as-
masociety.org/about/index.html.

55. Chris Hedges, "A Muslim in the Middle Hopes Against Hope," New York Times,
June 23, 2004.

56. Taha Jabir al-Alwani, Ijtihad (London: International Institute of Islamic Thought,
1993), p. 3.

Conclusions and Prospects

Shireen T. Hunter

This survey of the current Islamic reformist discourse and its proponents in key Muslim countries and in the Muslim communities of Europe and the United States has identified a number of important broad themes. Some of them show that current reformist thinking has many features in common with earlier reform movements, while others highlight its novel aspects and dimensions. These themes also point to both similarities and differences in approaches to critical issues taken by thinkers involved in the current reformist project.

The foregoing chapters have also yielded a number of significant conclusions that concern the following important aspects of the Islamic reformist discourse: origins and evolution; factors behind its emergence, including the current wave; and the causes of its limited success to date. Together, this analysis and its findings and conclusions provide insights into the likely directions in which reformist discourse may evolve, and factors that could help or hinder its future progress and ultimately its success.

Continuity with and Departures from the Past

Current Islamic reformist discourse is a continuation of nineteenth- and early twentieth-century reformist movements that emerged in Muslim societies in response to the twin challenges of modernity and the direct or indirect domination of Muslim lands and peoples by the European powers. Like its predecessors, this latest wave of reformist discourse is nourished by the rationalist heritage of early Islam. The continuity between the current reformist discourse and the earlier movements is particularly evident in the factors behind its emergence, its basic motivations, and its fundamental objectives. Today's Muslim reformist thinkers are motivated by factors similar to those that inspired earlier reformists, namely: Muslim societies' severe economic, political, cultural, and moral problems and, in some cases, the underdeveloped state of their economies and social and political institutions; the low level of their scientific and technological advancement; their growing socioeconomic disparities; and the lack of guarantees for civil and political rights.

At a more fundamental level—and nearly two centuries after Muslims' encounter with modernity and its carriers, the European powers—today's reformist thinkers are still grappling with the same basic conundrum, namely: the causes of the Muslim world's decline, which led to its domination by the European powers; and its current state of stagnation compared not only to Western societies but also to non-European countries such as Japan and China. Just as early reformists asked what had made Muslims "colonizable," today's reformist thinkers are asking what has kept them dependent and vulnerable. Like their predecessors, they are keenly aware of Muslim governments' continued economic and political dependency on the great powers, even after decades of official independence, and Muslim societies' increased vulnerability to external pressures and attacks. Moreover, they know very well that, because of the advent of globalization and the communications revolution, the nature of these pressures has become more complex and opaque and hence more difficult to deal with.

They see Muslims' current predicament as a direct consequence of economic and political underdevelopment; the lack of basic civil and political freedoms, leading to a closed and stagnant intellectual environment inimical to any kind of progress; the lack of serious religious thinking and *ijtihad*, which has left the religious field in the hands of conservatives and radical Muslims; the instrumentalization of religion by both governments and opposition groups for political purposes and repression; and the lack of sufficient popular legitimacy of the ruling elites, and hence their vulnerability to external influences.

Muslim reformists favor open and multidimensional interaction between Muslim societies and the outside world. At the same time they are concerned that, given vast disparities between their respective countries' capacities at every level and in every field of human activity and those of global economic and political actors, such interaction would occur within the confines of an uneven playing field. They fear that the outcome of such interaction could be either total absorption into a dominant global culture and the loss of indigenous cultural identity and/or the reactive strengthening of destructive nativist trends of a religious or secular variety.

Today's reformist thinkers and activists also have many goals and objectives in common with earlier reformers, including the cultural, scientific, political, economic, and social regeneration of Muslim societies; the establishment of rights-based and fair social, economic, and political systems; the encouragement of *ijtihad* and rational thinking, thus making Islam more relevant to Muslims' current needs and aspirations; and the restoration of Muslim societies' independence, thus leading to the creation of a more equal ground for interaction between Muslims and the rest of the world. However, today's reformists are aware that these goals should be achieved within the framework of a far more interpenetrated world and through constructive dialogue and engagement and not by violent and destructive methods.

These patterns of continuity between the current and earlier reformist discourses indicate that the Muslim world is still grappling with challenges posed by the encounter with modernity. Today's Islamic reformist discourse is also a response to these challenges and is an effort to mediate between the need to accommodate modernity and the pull of religion, tradition, and the quest for cultural authenticity.

In many respects, however, especially in their prescriptions for achieving their stated objectives, current reformists differ from earlier reform movements. These differences reflect the impact of the Muslim countries' experiences over the course of a century and a half. The most important of these experiences are related to the failure of various models of social, economic, and political development and modernization that originated in the West and were adopted by Muslim governments. These developmental models were supposed to provide Muslims with decent living conditions, guarantee their basic civil and political rights as citizens and human beings, and to reduce, if not eliminate, their vulnerability to external predatory forces. Yet, as implemented in the Muslim world, none of these models delivered on their promise, and in some cases even caused serious damage. This failure seriously undermined Muslims' faith in various Western utopian mega-narratives, including the entire project of modernity with its underlying belief in a linear trajectory of progress toward a more prosperous, free, and peaceful future.

The treatment of Muslim countries by Western liberal countries and the now defunct Soviet Union has also followed the patterns of traditional great-power behavior toward weaker states and has fallen short of their proclaimed ideals. In the process, such behavior has given credibility to the view that domination is the other and darker side of modernity; consequently it has exacerbated Muslims' sense of disenchantment with Western grand narratives.

Yet as shown in the introduction to this volume and in the chapters detailing the experience of different countries, the process of modernization in Muslim societies, even if flawed and falling short of expectations, has been a major, if not the major, factor in the emergence of today's reformist thinkers and their discourse. This has been so because despite all its shortcomings, the process of modernization has in many important ways—notably in terms of class structure, access to education and information, urbanization, and development of bureaucratic and professional classes—fundamentally transformed Muslim societies. It is noteworthy that, over the last fifty years, both revolutionary and reformist Muslim thinkers have mostly come from lower-middle-class backgrounds and gained access to higher education because of their respective governments' developmental policies.

Islamic Mega-Narratives, Their Discontents, and Islamic Reformists

The emergence of current reformist thinking is also a reaction to Muslims' disappointment with what can best be described as Islamic mega-narratives developed by Muslim revolutionary thinkers in the 1960s and 1970s. These Islam-based mega-narratives were Muslims' first response to their disenchantment with foreign-inspired socioeconomic and political ideologies and the process of modernization inspired by them.

These Islamic counter-narratives explain the past, provide a trajectory of future progress, and offer utopian blueprints for the establishment of an ideal and just Islamic society. Despite their early appeal, however, such Islamic alternatives and their proponents have fared even worse than their secular and foreign-inspired counterparts in terms of resolving Muslims' problems, improving their living conditions, and guaranteeing their basic rights. Iran, Sudan, Afghanistan, and Pakistan, where different versions of the Islamic alternative have been tried, are proof of the inadequacy and failure of Islam-based mega-narratives. In Afghanistan, the implementation of the Taliban's version of the Islamic narrative brought nothing but devastation and war to the country. Even in Malaysia, one of the few Muslim economic and to some degree political success stories, where the government has promoted a development strategy based on a modernist narrative of Islam and a measure of democratic rule, the results in some areas have been less than ideal. These areas include civil and political liberties, gender equality, freedom of conscience, and minority rights.

In places where the proponents of the Islamic alternative have not gained power, some Muslims, notably the Salafis and the Takfiris, have embraced a highly reductionist, literalist, intolerant, and, at times, violent interpretation of Islam. By resorting to violent acts against their own governments and peoples and against foreign nationals and states, some of these Muslims, have helped repressive Muslim governments to justify their authoritarian rule, damaged Islam's global image, and made Muslim countries vulnerable to outside pressures and even military attacks.

The failure of various experiments with Islamic mega-narratives and utopian blueprints to provide effective solutions to Muslims' many problems, coupled with the negative consequences for Muslims of the actions and policies of governments and non-state actors embracing such narratives, has led to growing popular disenchantment with such narratives, to varying degrees in different countries. In Iran, Egypt, the Maghreb, and Southeast Asia, many intellectuals and activists with roots in Islamist ideological and political movements have experienced a process of double disillusionment. They have realized that neither the Western-inspired models of modernization nor the ideologized and idealized narratives of Islam can provide practical answers for Muslims' problems or a viable intellectual framework for their socioeconomic and political development.

These thinkers and activists are keenly aware that, irrespective of its limited success, the discourse of modernity and a century of development have altered the Muslim societies' physical and intellectual landscape, making a return to a traditional Islamic lifestyle and social organization both impossible and undesirable. Yet they also know that one reason for the failure of secular modernizers has been that their discourse is not rooted in indigenous popular cultures and hence is inaccessible to most Muslim populations who are still attached to traditional and religious values.

The conclusion that reformist thinkers draw from these experiences is that, in order to rescue the Islamic world from its present predicament, a homegrown version of modernity with roots in the Muslims' indigenous cultures and hence accessible to most people must be developed. It is thought that such a homegrown concept of modernity will both answer the need to accommodate modernity and prevent a sense of cultural rupture that early modernizing efforts produced, leading to nativist and religious reactions.

The themes of "nativizing modernity" and developing "homegrown modernities" are most openly and extensively discussed by Iranian reformist thinkers, as shown in Chapter 1. Reformists from the Maghreb countries (Chapter 3) talk more in terms of "modernizing Islam" or generating an "Islamic Enlightenment." Others, such as the more reformist elements that have split from the Muslim Brothers in Egypt, do not address these themes openly, but their discourse, as discussed in Chapter 2, points to similar objectives. In sum, despite their different vocabularies of reform and the varying extent of their reformism, the main objective of reformist thinkers and activists is the same: to mediate between Islam and modernity and to find a way of bringing the Muslim countries into the modern age while retaining Islam as a spiritual and cultural referent for society.

Commonalities and Differences Within the Reformist Trend

As gleaned from the chapters in this volume, nearly all reformist thinkers believe that, if Muslim societies are to enter the modern world while maintaining their Islamic culture, character, and values, they will have to observe a number of principles in their interpretation of Islam and its major scriptural and legal sources. These are as follows.

1. To distinguish between the transcendent, universal, and eternal essence of Islam and the historical unfolding of Islamic experience, which has been influenced by many factors exogenous to Islam; as put by the Iranian reformist thinker Hojat al Islam Muhsen Kadivar, to distinguish between *spiritual* and *historical* Islam. Historical Islam is the result of varied interactions between Islam and different preexisting cultures and has been affected by the dynamics of power and politics and the manipulation of religion for dynastic and other group interests. Much of Islamic law is the outcome of these interactions and conflicts, given an aura of sanctity by Muslim religious scholars. More often than not, historical Islam has betrayed the message and prescriptions of spiritual Islam.

2. To distinguish religion (*din*), and the path of life that it has traced (*shari'a*), from *fiqh* (Islamic law as produced by Islamic scholars). The former is eternal and sacred, the latter is changeable and non-sacred.

3. To differentiate between Islam's fundamental sources—the Qur'an and *sunna*—and their interpretations by generations of religious scholars and experts in law (*fuqaha*), and subject the latter to new analysis and scrutiny in order to identify those circumstantial and personal factors that may have influenced these interpretations.

4. To privilege Islam's ultimate goals over its ritualistic and legalistic aspects; to judge Islamic laws in light of Islam's ultimate objectives, and to adjust them on the basis of their contribution to the achievement of these ultimate goals, namely, justice, freedom, and respect for human dignity, irrespective of race, religion, or gender. The Iranian thinker Kadivar calls this "goal-oriented Islam" (*islam e-qayat gera*). Some Indonesian reformist thinkers and activists advocate a similar type of Islam through a more liberal interpretation of a traditional Islamic concept, *maqasid al shari'a*, or the objectives of Islamic law. This kind of Islam would be compatible with modern notions of human rights, participatory politics, and governments chosen by the people and accountable to them. Other reformist thinkers in the Arab world and South Asia use this concept in different ways to promote a goal-oriented Islam.

5. To emphasize rights over duties and create a rights-based Islam; the Iranian thinker Ahmad Qabel calls this a rights-centered (*haq mahvar*) Islam.

6. To distinguish between those Islamic injunctions that are eternal and immutable and those that clearly are bound by time and space, namely, most of the injunctions that deal with worldly affairs, including family relations and gender rights.

7. To emphasize Islam's tolerant and egalitarian dimensions and its stress on the lack of any compulsion in faith, and to adjust the laws that do not meet these fundamental aspirations. This reading will open the way for ensuring the rights of religious minorities, promoting gender equality, guaranteeing freedom of conscience, and doing away with the problem of apostasy and its punishment by death.

8. To adapt through *ijtihad*, Islamic injunctions to Muslim societies' new circumstances and needs, especially with an eye to the promotion of a just society.

9. To break the stranglehold of official clergy on the interpretation of Islamic sources, keeping in mind that in Islam there is no intermediary between God and humankind.

10. To encourage a critical and rational approach to the study of Islamic sources as well as to foreign ideas and philosophies. As put by Muhammad Khatami, the emphasis should be on critical reason (*aql e-naqad*).

11. To interpret Islam as a cultural and spiritual foundation and referent for Muslim societies, not as a detailed and comprehensive political, economic, and social blueprint and manual for managing society's affairs.

12. To keep in mind, in the management of societies' affairs, Islam's message of justice, mercy, and respect for human dignity, and to interpret and apply its laws in light of these principles and in ways best suited to current needs and conditions.

Reformist and moderate thinkers and activists abjure the use of religion as an instrument either to gain power or to prevent others from legally competing for it. Yet they also reject the idea that religion should be excluded from the public sphere, as advocated by secular purists. Rather, like the Tunisian reformist thinker Mohamed Talbi, they consider equating secularism with the total exclusion of religion from the public sphere to be both discriminatory against believers and counterproductive to the goal of advancing a reformist agenda in the Muslim world. This is so because this kind of secularism is often perceived as atheism and as such is rejected by the masses.

There are also significant differences among reformist thinkers. Some of these divergences are related to differences in the national and regional contexts within which they are operating and to which they are responding. Others derive from the varying emphases that individual thinkers put on Islam and modernity in their vision of a reformist Islam. For Mohammed Arkoun, Abdolkarim Soroush, and a number of Maghrebin thinkers along with their followers, the emphasis on the latter is so high that it makes their identification as Islamic reformists problematic. Rather, they seem to fall more in the category of Muslim secularists.[1]

While all reformists oppose the anti-religion type of secularism, some of them, notably those of Maghrebin origin, advocate a strict delineation of the respective domains of religion and politics and the depoliticization of religion. Another area of disagreement concerns economic systems. In Iran and in the Arab East, notably Egypt, many reformists still believe in a mixed economy, a tendency that reflects Islam's own egalitarian dimensions and the lingering influence of leftist ideas on Muslim intellectuals.

The most significant differences relate to the issue of reform of the Islamic penal code and the family and inheritance laws that discriminate against women and in general about the status of women in Muslim societies. Some reformists advocate the elimination of all discriminatory laws and the penal code; others use a variety of religious and other arguments to support the practical suspension of these laws and a more gradual process of revision. In terms of women's rights, some favor complete equality; others emphasize women's role within family while also recognizing their right to take part in their societies' social and political life.

In terms of relations with other cultures and countries, all reformist thinkers support dialogue and unfettered exchanges of ideas across borders. Some, such as Iran's Muhammad Khatami, stress the need for equality in this exchange. Objecting to the view of Islam as a mere subject of inquiry by others, especially Westerners, they hold that Islam can contribute to the development of a universal ethics of humanism and a regeneration of spirituality in the West.

Causes of the Failure of Reformist Discourse

Although the history of Islamic reformist thinking dates back to the mid-nineteenth century, this discourse, compared both to secular and to traditional and radical

Islamic discourses, has not fared well either in attracting the masses or in gaining power. The principal reasons for this failure, as gleaned through the chapters in this volume, are listed below.

1. *The interruption of the normal processes of political evolution in key Muslim countries because of war and intense external competition to determine the trajectory of Muslim countries' socioeconomic and politico-cultural evolution.* For example, as noted by Recep Senturk in Chapter 7, the collapse of Ottoman power at the end of World War I ended internal reform in Turkish Islam. In Iran, World War I subverted the fledgling parliamentary process that might have facilitated a gradual reform of many aspects of Islamic law.

Later, as Muslim countries were turned into laboratories for experimentation with socialist and capitalist models of development, East–West competition limited possibilities for the development of indigenous ideas on these issues. In particular, the socialist challenge worked in favor of conservative religious elements, which were able to label as materialist and atheist anyone who challenged their orthodoxy. Moreover, Islamic reformist discourse lost its own early liberal tendency and became, as in the discourse of Ali Shariati, a revolutionary ideology with totalitarian tendencies. This version, too, caused alarm both among the clergy and among Muslim governments, and even in ostensibly "revolutionary Muslim" Iran it ultimately worked to the benefit of a more conservative discourse.

The great powers' support for repressive governments and, worse, the instrumentalization of Islam as a weapon to fight communism, as was done in Afghanistan, plus the use of conservative and literalist Islam to counter revolutionary Islam, have also seriously damaged the cause of reformist Islam.

2. *The magnitude of Muslim countries' development challenges and the temptation of rapid modernization.* These factors led to the emergence of secular modernizing governments of various stripes, which believed in a top-down process of change and modernization. They had little patience for debate and consensus-building and had strong authoritarian and even totalitarian tendencies. Under these circumstances, any reformist discourse on Islam could have little chance of success, as these governments actively worked to weaken Islam, as in Turkey, or co-opted the malleable segments of conservative clergy, as in most Muslim countries.

3. *The rise of ethnocentric nationalism as a political ideology parallel to authoritarian modernization.* At least at the elite level, this phenomenon reduced the salience of Islam as a component of identity and source of political legitimacy, thus undermining the maturing and spread of Islamic reformist discourse, which offered an alternative to both secularizing modernist projects and the intellectually stagnant traditional Islam.

4. *The bureaucratization of religious establishments in most Muslim countries, the appropriation of Islam by Muslim governments, and, worse, the governments' pandering to conservative Islam in exchange for political quietism.* The result has been the lack of independent religious leaders enjoying popular credibility and capable of developing new and more relevant interpretations of Islamic injunctions.

5. *The failure of modernizing projects and the polarization of Muslim societies.* The failure of the secular modernizing projects led to a revival of interest in Islam as a social and political frame of reference. However, because of the lack of space for political debate, and influenced by decades of regimentizing modernization in either its socialist or capitalist version, the Islamic alternative that emerged was also totalitarian in its aspiration and simplistic in its reform project. It, too, did not leave room for disagreement and dissent. Moreover, it saw reformist Islam as an even greater threat to its prospects for success.

6. *The complexity and the inaccessibility of reformist discourse to the masses.* For any discourse to succeed, it must garner an adequate audience. Because of its complexity, its emphasis on continued questioning and critique, and its tolerance of diverse opinion and open debate, reformist Islamic discourse has not fared well against more simplistic secular and Islamic discourses that offer easy solutions and comforting certainties and promise a utopian future.

7. *The animosity of both secular purists and conservative and radical Muslims toward reformist Islam and its proponents.* Since discourse is inevitably related to power, Muslim reformists are disliked and are subject to suspicion and animosity by both groups. Secular purists view the reformists as being no different from Islamists, while Islamists accuse the reformists of being secularists who want to subvert Islam from within. As discussed in the case of Turkey, secularists have seen Muslim reformists as their more formidable rival because they cannot be dismissed as either obscurantist or terrorists.

8. *The lack of cohesiveness and adequate organization among reformists.* Despite the emergence of Islam-based reformist parties in many Muslim countries in recent years, most Muslim reformers are still largely individual, often lay, scholars without grassroots organizations. Many of them, particularly those of Maghrebin origin, live outside their own countries. This situation is due to a number of factors, notably the repressive nature of most Muslim regimes, which do not allow viable party politics and open debate. For example, in the run-up to the March 2008 parliamentary elections in Iran, barriers were erected against reformist candidates by conservative elements within the Iranian government and other bodies responsible for examining and ratifying the candidacy of individuals running for parliament. This process prevented their active participation in the elections. In Morocco in February 2008, the supposedly reformist Islam-based party al-Badil al-Hadri, which was legally allowed to take part in political activities, was banned, and its leader, Mustapha Moatasim, was arrested by the Moroccan authorities on charges that he had links with al-Qaeda. And in March 2008, Turkish secularists launched a constitutional effort to ban the ruling party and deprive its leaders, Recep Teyyip Erdogan and Abdullah Gul, Turkey's prime minister and president, respectively, from engaging in political activities for five years, on charges that they pursued anti-secular policies.[2] These examples indicate the still-limited space for free political activity in Muslim states, both secular and Islamic, and concerns about the commitment of Islam-based parties to the democratic process; the pressure by

conservative religious organizations and by Islamists who accuse the reformists of apostasy; the absence of a positive sociopolitical agenda among most of the reformists; and finally, as the above-noted case of the Moroccan party illustrates, the double game of some Islam-based political groups. Their behavior generates apprehension on the part of governments toward any political party with an Islamic referent or background and provides them with a strong pretext to limit the activities of even truly reformist Islam-based parties.

9. The limited grounding of many lay reformist thinkers in Islamic sciences and hence their limited credibility with the religious masses, who tend to believe more readily in even modestly educated traditional clergy than in reformist thinkers.

10. The excessively unorthodox positions of some reformist thinkers on issues such as the nature of the Qur'an or the prophetic revelation, which raises questions about their commitment to Islam and hence challenges their right to interpret Islamic sources.

11. The ambivalence of the great powers toward reformist Islam. This ambivalence derives from the fact that Islamic reformism does not mean cultural or political capitulation to the dominant order. On the contrary, reformist thinkers aspire to intellectual and political independence, albeit within an interdependent world and with an open flow of ideas. In its endeavor to develop an Islamic version of modernity by generating internal reform within Islam, reformist Islam ultimately poses a potent long-term challenge to the intellectual and hence political dominance of the current global order.

Outlook for Reformist Islam

This list of factors responsible for the lack of success of the Islamic reformist discourse thus far points to the considerable challenges that reformist thinkers and movements face, to varying degrees in different countries, in making their discourse acceptable to broader audiences and translating these ideas into action and concrete reforms. For example, there is no indication that Muslim governments are going to allow freer and more open debate. Even those countries that periodically allow a limited form of electoral politics firmly control the process and can reverse it at will. The continuation of this policy, together with the exclusion of reformist and moderate Muslims from the political game, not only retards the maturation and expansion of reformist Islam, but could even lead to a reversal of reformist and moderate trends. Nor is there any indication that governments are willing to forgo their control of the religious field of debate or of religious establishments. This, too, does not bode well for the future course of reformist Islam. Meanwhile, conservative and radical Muslims as well as ultra-secularists all remain inimical to Muslim reformists and continue to see them as serious rivals. Moreover, no major changes can be expected in the behavior of great powers toward the Muslim world. After the brief enthusiasm for democracy promotion in the aftermath of

9/11, they have reverted to a policy of sticking with their trusted, even if repressive, government allies.

Yet, in light of the following factors, the picture is not all bleak:

- First, because of the communications revolution, today's reformists are better able to get their message across to the people, even though their audience is still limited.
- Second, reformist thinkers today, at least in some countries such as Iran, include in their ranks senior clerics with solid religious and scientific credentials and hence have considerable authority with the masses.
- Third, ideas now travel more effectively across ethnic and linguistic boundaries, somewhat mitigating the impact of repressive governmental policies. Consequently, reformist discourse is acquiring a transnational character.
- Fourth, networks of reformist thinkers and activists are being formed.

Finally, the most important factor working in favor of reformist trends is the bankruptcy of current systems in the Muslim world and most Muslims' disaffection with simplistic and utopian narratives and projects, whether secular or Islamic.

Islam cannot be eliminated from the Muslim world; nor can conservative or radical Islam provide answers to Muslims' current problems and questions. Yet Muslims must resolve their dilemmas, and reformist Islam offers the most promising way to do so.

The question is how long it might take for all concerned to realize this and do what is needed to advance the reformist discourse. It will fare better in an open atmosphere of debate. At least in the long run, it will benefit from democratization in Muslim societies. The more this process of political opening is delayed, the more polarized Muslim societies will become, and no reformist or moderate discourse will have any chance of success. Rather, in those countries that have not experienced an Islamic form of government and therefore are unaware of its inadequacies, the continued exclusion of even reformist and moderate Islamic political groups could lead to their radicalization or provide a new audience for radical discourses.

For their part, Muslim reformist thinkers and activists must formulate their messages in ways accessible to the masses, work with grassroots organizations, and make their views relevant to Muslims' needs.[3] They also need to keep their messages within the tolerance of the religious masses; otherwise their intellectual musings will remain just that. The West, meanwhile, should support reformist and even moderate Muslim voices, but it should not expect reformists to do its bidding. As noted by Farish Noor, any hint of that would be the death knell for the reformists.[4] Nor should the West equate reformism with total and uncritical embrace of Western ethos or, even less, Western policies.

In short, reformists can be useful agents of change and progress in their own countries and constructive partners for the West. To realize this potential, they must keep their message within the acceptable limits of Muslims' religious sensibilities and preserve their independence from outside influence; this is essential if they are to attain credibility and legitimacy with Muslim masses.

Notes

1. In a recently published book, the Tunisian reformist thinker Mohamed Talbi makes the point that such thinkers should declare themselves as totally secular.

2. See "Morocco Bans Islamist Party over Terror Links," *Al Arabia*, available at www.alarabiya.net/save_print.php?print=1&cont_id=4593&la. On Turkey see Yigal Schleifer, "Turkey: Suit to Ban Governing Party Threatens to Plunge the Country into Crisis," EURASIANET, available at www.eurasianet.org/departments/insight/articles/eav032808_pr.shtml.

3. Following their defeat in the presidential elections of 2005, the Iranian reformists identified as one reason for their failure the excessively elitist tone of the reformist discourse and their ignoring of institutions such as mosques and religious schools.

4. Some scholars depict reformist Islam as a tool of Western domination. See Saba Mahmouud, "Secularism, Hermeneutics, and Empire: The Politics of Islamic Reformation," *Public Culture,* vol. 18, no. 2, 2006. During the Iranian parliamentary elections of March 2008, President George W. Bush's statement that "Iranian reformists have no better friend than I" was used against them by their rivals, who portrayed them as dependent on external powers. See "Transcript of an Interview of President Bush by Setareh Derakhshan of VOA's Persian News Network," available at www.voanews.com/English/2008-03-19-voa75.cfm?renderforprint=1.

Selected Bibliography

Books

Abaza, Mona. (2002) *Debates on Islam and Knowledge in Malaysia and Egypt,* London: Curzon Press.

Abderraziq, Ali. (1994) *Al-Islam wa usul al-Hukm* (L'islam et les fondements du pouvoir), translated into French by Abdou Filali-Ansary, Paris: La Découverte.

Abshar-Abdallah, Ulil. (2005) *Mejadi Muslim liberal* (Becoming a Liberal Muslim), Jakarta: Nalar.

Abu al-Futuh, 'Abd el-Mun'im. (2005) *Mujaddidun la Mubaddidun,* Cairo: Bar Press.

Abu al-Rub, Jalal. (2003) *Biography and Mission of Muhammad Ibn Abdul Wahhab,* Orlando: Medina Publishers and Distributors.

Abu Zeid, Nasr Hamed, and Esther R. Nelson, (2004) *Voice of an Exile,* Westport, CT: Praeger.

Adamiyat, Fereydoun. (1944/1945) *Amir Kabir Va Iran* (Amir Kabir and Iran), Tehran: Chapkhaneh e Payam.

———. (1346/1967) *Andisheha ye Mirza Agha Khan Kirmani* (The Ideas of Mirza Agha Khan Kirmani), Tehran: Chapkhaneh Pirouz.

———. (1340/1962) *Fakr Azadi Va Nehzat e Mashrutiat* (The Idea of Freedom and the Constitutional Revolution), Tehran: Entesharat e Sokhan.

———. (1345/1975) *Fekr e Democracy e Ejtemaie dar nehzat Mashrutiat e Iran* (The Idea of Social Democracy in Iran's Constitutional Movement), Tehran: Payam.

Ahmad, Feroz. (2003) *Turkey: The Quest for Identity,* Oxford: Oneworld.

Al-Ahmad, Jalal. (1979) *Dar khedmat va khayanat e rowshankeran* (On the Contributions and Betrayals of Intellectuals), Tehran: Kharazmi.

Al-Ahnaf, Mustapha, et al. (1991) *L'Algérie par ses islamistes,* Paris: Karthala.

Al-'Alwani, Taha Jabir. (1993) *Ijtihad,* London: International Institute of Islamic Thought.

Al-Attas, Syed Naquib. (1986) *A Commentary on the Hujjat al-Sadiq of Nur al-Din al-Raniri,* Kuala Lumpur: Ministry of Culture.

Al-Faruqi, Isma'il. (1982) *Islamization of Knowledge,* Herndon: International Institute of Islamic Thought.

———. (1961) *On Arabism: 'Urubah and Religion—An Analysis of the Fundamental Ideas of Arabism and of Islam at Its Highest Moment of Consciousness,* Amsterdam: Djambatan.

Algar, Hamid. (1969) *Mirza Malkum Khan: A Study in the History of Iranian Modernism.* Berkeley: University of California Press.

———. (2002) *Wahhabism: A Critical Essay.* New York: Islamic Publications International.

Al-Houni, Mohamed Abd El Motaleb (2004) *L'impasse arabe-Les Arabes face à la nouvelle stratégie américaine,* Paris: L'Harmattan.

Al-Jabri, Mohamed. (1999) *Arab-Islamic Philosophy: A Contemporary Critique,* Austin: University of Texas Press.

———. (1994) *Introduction à la critique de la raison arabe*, Paris: La Découverte.

Al-Jourshi, Salah Eddin, et al. (1989) *Al-Muqadadimat al-nadhariyya al-Taqq dumiyyin* (The Theoretical Bases of the Progressive Islamists), Tunis: Dar al-Buraq li al-Nashr.

Al-Na'im, Abdullahi Ahmed. (1990) *Toward an Islamic Reformation: Civil Liberties, Human Rights and International Law*, Syracuse, NY: Syracuse University Press.

Al-Nayhum, al-Sadiq. (1991) *Nihnat Thaqafat Muzawara: Sawt al-Nas am Sawt al-Fuqaha* (The Affliction of a Forged Culture: The Voice of the People or the Voice of the Clerics), Beirut: Riad el-Rayyes Books.

Arberry, A.J. (1942) *A History of Sufism*, London: Longmans, Green and Company.

———. (1953) *The Mysteries of Selflessness* (Translation of Rumuz-e-Bekhudi), London: John Murray.

Arkoun, Mohammed. (1984) *Essais sur la pensée islamique*, 3rd ed., Paris: Maisonneuve-Larose.

———. (1992) *L'Islam-Approche critique*, Paris: J. Grancher.

———. (1986) *L'Islam, morale et politique*, Paris: Desclée de Brouwer.

———. (1997) *La pensée arabe*, 5th edition, Paris: P.U.F.

———. (1993) *Penser l'islam aujourd'hui*, Algiers: Laphomic/ENAL.

———. (1984) *Pour une critique de la raison islamique*, Paris: Maisonneuve-Larose.

Ayubi, Nazih. (1991) *Political Islam: Religion and Politics in the Arab World*, New York: Routledge.

Bakhash, Shaul. (1978) *Iran: Monarchy, Bureaucracy and Reform Under Qajars, 1858–1896*, London: Ithaca Press.

Barlas, Asma. (2002) *Believing Women in Islam: Unreading Patriarchal Interpretations of the Qur'an*, Austin: University of Texas Press.

Barton, G. and G. Fealy, eds. (1996) *Nahdlatul Ulama, Traditional Islam and Modernity in Indonesia*, Clayton: Monash Asia Institute.

Baubérot, Jean. (2004) *Laïcité 1905–2005: Entre Passion et Raison*, Paris: Seuil.

Bellah, Robert N. (1970) *Beyond Belief: Essays on Religion in a Post-Traditional World*, New York: Harper and Row.

Bencheikh, Ghaleb. (2001) *Alors, c'est quoi l'islam?* Paris: Presses de la Renaissance.

———. (2005) *La laïcité au regard du Coran*, Paris: Presses de la Renaissance.

Bencheikh, Ghaleb and Philippe Haddad. (2002) *L'islam et le judaïsme en dialogue: salam shalom*, Paris: Editions de l'Atelier.

Bencheikh, Soheib. (1998) *Marianne et le Prophète, l'islam dans l'espace laïque*, Paris: Grasset.

Bennabi, Malek. (1970) *Vocation de l'islam*, 2d ed., Ouled Fayet, Tipaza: Société d'Edition et de Communication.

Bennigsen, Alexandre and Chantal Lemercier-Quelguejay. (1967) *Islam in Russia*, New York: Praeger.

Bentounés, Cheikh Khaled. (2006) *L'homme intérieur à la lumière du Coran*, Paris: Pocket.

———. (2002) *Pour un islam de paix*, Paris: Albin Michel.

———. (2006) *Vivre l'islam: Le soufisme auourd'hui*, Paris: Albin Michel.

Benzine, Rachid. (2004) *Les Nouveaux Penseurs de l'Islam*, Paris: Albin Michel.

Berger, Peter L. (1999) *The Desecularization of the World*, Washington DC: Ethics and Public Policy Center.

Biggar, N. and J.S. Scott, eds. (1986) *Cities of Gods*, Westport, CT: Greenwood Press.

Bilgrami, H.H. (1966) *Glimpses of Iqbal's Mind and Thought*, Lahore: Orientalia.

Boland, B.J. (1971) *The Struggle of Islam in Modern Indonesia*, The Hague: Martinus Nijhoff.

Charfi, Abdelmadjid. (2004) *L'Islam entre le message et l'histoire*, translated from Arabic by André Ferré, Paris: Albin Michel.

Charfi, Mohamed. (2005) *Islam and Liberty: The Historical Misunderstanding*, London: Zed Books.

———. (1998) *Islam et liberté, le malentendu historique*, Paris: Albin Michel.

Chebel, Malek. (2002) *Le sujet en islam*, Paris: Seuil.

———. (2002) *L'imaginaire arabo-musulman*, Paris: P.U.F.

———. (2005) *L'islam et la raison, le combat des idées*, Paris: Perrin.

———. (2004) *Manifeste pour un islam des lumières*, Paris: Hachette.

———. (2003) *Rencontre avec Marie de Solenne, Islam et libre arbiter—la tentation de l'insolence*, Paris: Editions Dervy.

Cragg, Kenneth. (1965) *Counsels in Contemporary Islam*, Edinburgh: Edinburgh University Press.

Crook, Stephen. (1991) *Modernist Radicalism and Its Aftermath: Foundationalism and Anti-Foundationalism in Radical Social Theory*, London and New York: Routledge.

Crotty, William J., ed. (2005) *Democratic Development and Political Terrorism: The Global Perspective*, Boston: Northeastern University Press.

Dahlen, Ashk. (2001) *Deciphering the Meaning of Revealed Law: The Surushian Paradigm, Shi'i Epistemology*, Stockholm: Elanders Gotab.

Dessouki, Ali E. Hilal, ed. (1982) *Islamic Resurgence in the Arab World*, New York: Praeger.

Djilali, Soufiane. (1993) *Que veut le P.R.A.? Histoire d'une démocratie refuse*, Algiers: Co-Edition Microedit-PRA.

Donohue, John J. and John L. Esposito, eds. *Islam in Transition: Muslim Perspectives*, 2nd ed., New York: Oxford University Press, 2007.

Efendi, Mustafa Sabri. (1373/1954) *Dini Müceddidler: Türkiye İçin Necat ve İtila Yollarında Bir Rehber*, Istanbul: Evkaf Matbaasi.

Effendi, Djohan and Ismed Natsir, eds. (1981) *Pergolakan pemikiran Islam: Catatan harian Ahmad Wahib* (The Effervescence of Islamic Thought: The Diary of Ahmad Wahib), Jakarta: LP3ES.

Eisenstadt, Schumel N. (1987) *Patterns of Modernity, Volume 2: Beyond the West*, New York: New York University Press.

Eliade, Mircea, ed. (1987) *The Encyclopedia of Religion*, New York: Macmillan.

Eshkevari, Hassan Yussefi. (1379/2000) *Shariati va Naqd–e–Sonnat* (Shariati and the Critique of Tradition), Tehran: Ghazal.

———. (1377/1998) *Nowgarai-e-Dini* (Religious New Thinking) Tehran: Qasideh.

Esposito, John L., ed. (1983) *Voices of Resurgent Islam*, New York: Oxford University Press.

———. (1995) *The Oxford Encyclopaedia of the Modern Islamic World*, New York: Oxford University Press.

Esposito, John L. and John O. Voll. (2001) *Makers of Contemporary Islam*, New York: Oxford University Press.

Federspiel, Howard M. (2001) *Islam and Ideology in the Emerging Indonesian State: The Persatuan Islam (PERSIS), 1923 to 1957*, Leiden: Brill.

Filali-Ansary, Abdou. (2001) *L'islam est-il hostile à la laïcité?* Paris: Sindbad.

———. (2005) *Réformer l'islam? Une introduction aux débats contemporains*, Paris: Editions la Découverte.

Forester, E.M. (1962) *Mohammed Iqbal: Two Cheers for Democracy*, London: Harcourt.

Fourset, Caroline. (2004) *Frère Tariq*, Paris: Grasset.

Gellner, Ernest. (1981) *Muslim Society*, Cambridge: Cambridge University Press.

Gerschenkron, Alexander. (1965) *Economic Backwardness in Historical Perspective*, New York: Praeger.

Gheissari, Ali. (1998) *Iranian Intellectuals in the Twentieth Century*, Austin: University of Texas Press.

Gibb, H.A.R. (1947) *Modern Trends in Islam,* Chicago: University of Chicago Press.
Güler, İlhami. (1998) *Allah'ın Ahlakiliği Sorunu: Ehl-i Sünnetin Allah Tasavvuruna Ahlaki Açıdan Eleştirel Bir Yaklaşım,* Ankara: Ankara Okulu.
———. (2003) *İman Ahlak İlişkisi,* Ankara: Ankara Okulu Yayınları.
———. (2004) *Özgürlükçü Teoloji Yazıları,* Ankara: Ankara Okulu.
———. (2002) *Politik Teoloji Yazıları,* Ankara: Kitabiyat.
———. (1999) *Sabit Din Dinamik Şeriat,* Ankara: Ankara Okulu Yayınları.
Habermas, Jürgen. (1991) *The Philosophical Discourse of Modernity,* Cambridge: MIT Press.
Hefner, Robert. (2000) *Civil Islam: Muslims and Democratization in Indonesia,* Princeton: Princeton University Press.
Held, David. (1980) *Introduction to Critical Theory,* Berkeley: University of California Press.
Hillman, Michael, ed. (1990) *Iranian Culture: A Persianist View,* Lanham, MD: University Press of America.
Hinnebusch, Raymond A. (1985) *Egyptian Politics Under Sadat,* Cambridge: Cambridge University Press.
Holt, John P., et al., eds. (1970) *Cambridge History of Islam,* Volume II, Cambridge: Cambridge University Press.
Hourani, Albert. (1962) *Arabic Thought in the Liberal Age,* Cambridge: Cambridge University Press.
Hunter, Shireen T., ed. (2002) *Islam, Europe's Second Religion: The New Social, Cultural, and Political Landscape,* Westport, CT: Praeger.
———. (2004) *Islam in Russia: The Politics of Identity and Security,* Armonk: M.E. Sharpe.
———. (1988) *The Politics of Islamic Revivalism: Diversity and Unity,* Bloomington: Indiana University Press.
Hunter, Shireen T. and Huma Malik, eds. (2005) *Modernization, Democracy and Islam,* Westport, CT: Praeger.
Hurgronje, Christiaan Snouck. (1931) *Mekka in the Latter Part of the 19th Century,* Leiden, Brill.
Iqbal, Javid. (2000) *Zinda-Rud: Life of Iqbal,* Lahore: Iqbal Academy.
Iqbal, Muhammad. (1936) *Zarb-e-Kalim,* Lahore: Shahik Gulam Ali and Sons.
Izutsu, Toshihiko. (1959) *The Structure of Ethical Terms in the Koran: A Study in Semantics,* Tokyo: Keio Institute of Philological Studies.
Jahanbakhsh, Forough. (2001) *Islam, Democracy and Religious Modernity in Iran (1953–2000), From Bazargan to Soroush,* Leiden: Brill.
Jahanbegloo, Ramin, ed. (2004) *Iran: Between Tradition and Modernity,* Lanham, MD: Lexington Books.
Kaddache, Mahfoud. (2003) *L'Algérie des Algériens de la préhistoire à 1954,* Paris: Edition Méditerranée.
Kadivar, Muhsen. (1376/1998) *Daftar er Aql: Majmoueheye Maqalat e Falsafi alami* (The Book of Reason: A Collection of Philosophical Theological Articles), Tehran: Entesharat e Etteleet.
———. (1378/ 2000) Theories of Government in Shi'i Fiqh (The Theories of Government in the Shi'i Fiqh), Tehran: Nashrini.
Kamal, Zainun, et al. (2004) *Fiqih lintas agama: membangun masyarakat inklusif-pluralis* (The Fiqh of Inter-Religious Relations: Building an Inclusive, Pluralistic Society), Jakarta: Yayasan Wakaf Paramadina.
Kamali, Mohammad Hashim. (1991) *Principles of Islamic Jurisprudence,* Cambridge: Islamic Texts Society.
———. (2001) *Speaking in God's Name: Islamic Law, Authority and Women,* Oxford: Oneworld.

Karaman, Hayrettin. (2001) *Her Şeye Rağmen,* İstanbul: İz Yayıncılık.
————. (2004) *Insan Hakları: Din, Vicdan ve Düşünce Hürriyeti,* Istanbul: Ensar Neşriyat.
————. (1998) *Laik Düzende Dini Yaşamak,* 3d ed., İstanbul: İz Yayıncılık.
Karaman, Hayrettin, et al., eds. (2003) *Kur'an-ı Kerim, Tarihselcilik ve HermenÖtik,* İstanbul: Işık Yayınları.
Katouzian, Huma. (1981) *The Political Economy of Modern Iran: Despotism and Pseudo-Modernism,* New York: New York University Press.
Kazemi, Abbass. (1383/2005) *Jameeh-e-shenasi Rowshanfekri-e-Dini Dar Iran (The Sociology of Religious Intellectualism in Iran),* editor's translation, Tehran: Entesharat-e-Tarh Now.
Keddie, Nikkie R. (1983) *An Islamic Response to Imperialism: Political and Religious Writings of Sayyid Jamal al-Din al-Afghani,* Berkeley: University of California Press.
————. (1981) *Roots of Revolution: An Interpretive History of Modern Iran,* New Haven: Yale University Press.
————. (1972) *Sayyid Jamal ad-Din al-Afghani: A Political Biography,* Berkeley: University of California Press.
Keddie, Nikkie R. and Ellie Kedouri. (1966) *Afghani and Abduh: An Essay on Religious Disbelief and Political Activism in Modern Islam,* London: Frank Cass.
Kedourie, Elie. (1992) *Democracy and Arab Political Culture,* Washington DC: Washington Institute for Near East Policy.
Khalid, Adeeb. (1998) *The Politics of Muslim Cultural Reform: Jadidism in Central Asia,* Berkeley: University of California Press.
Khaliq, Abdul. (1993) *Sir Sayyid Ahmad Khan: On Nature, Man and God, A Critique,* Lahore: Bazam-e-Iqbal.
Khan, M.A. Muqteda, ed. (2006) *Islamic Democratic Discourse: Theory, Debates, and Philosophical Perspectives,* Lanham and Boulder: Lexington Books.
Khatami, Mohammad. (1379/2000) *Ghozideh ye Sokhanranihaye Rais Jomhour Dar bareh ye Toeseh ye Siasi, Toeseh ye Eqtesadi va Amniat* (A Selection of President's Speeches on Economic and Political Development and Security), Tehran: Entesharat-Tarh-e Now.
————. (2000) *Islam, Dialogue and Civil Society,* Canberra: Centre for Arab and Islamic Studies, Australian National University.
————. (1998) *Islam, Liberty and Development,* translated by Hossein Kamaly, Binghamton: Institute of Global Strategic Studies.
————. (1380/2001) *Mardom Salari* (The Peoples' Rule/Democracy), Tehran: Entesharat e-Tarh-e Now.
————. (1379/2000) *Ruhaniat va Enqlab e Islami* (Islam, the Clergy and the Islamic Revolution), Tehran: Tarh e Now.
Khosrokhavar, Farhad. (1997) *L'islam des Jeunes,* Paris: Flammarion.
Kırbaşoğlu, M. Hayri. (1979) *Ebu Muhammed Abdullah b. Müslim İbn Kuteybe* (d. 276/889), *Hadis Müdafası,* translated by Mehmet Hayri Kırbaşoğlu, Istanbul: Kayıhan Yayınevi.
————. (1996) *İslam Düşüncesinde Sünnet: Eleştirel Bir Yaklaşım,* Ankara: Ankara Okulu Yayınları.
————. (1993) *İslam Düşüncesinde Sünnet: Yeni Bir Yaklaşım,* Ankara: Fecr Yayınevi.
————. (1980) *Muhammed Avvame, İmamların Fıkhi İhtilaflarında Hadislerin Rolü,* translated by Mehmet Hayri Kırbaşoğlu, Istanbul: Kayıhan Yayınevi.
Kotan, Şevket. (2001) *Kur'an ve Tarihselcilik,* Istanbul: Beyan Yayınları.
Kull, Ann. (2005) *Piety and Politics: Nurcholish Madjid and His Interpretation of Islam in Modern Indonesia,* Lund: Department of Anthropology and History of Religions.
Kurtzman, Charles. (1998) *Liberal Islam: A Sourcebook,* New York: Oxford University Press.
Laffan, Michael F. (2003) *Islamic Nationhood and Colonial Indonesia: The Umma Below the Winds,* London: RoutledgeCurzon.

Laqueur, Walter Z., ed. (1958) *The Middle East in Transition,* New York: Praeger.

Lerner, Daniel. (1958) *The Passing of Traditional Society: Modernizing the Middle East,* Glencoe, IL: Free Press.

Levtzion, N., ed. (1979) *Conversion to Islam,* New York: Holmes and Meier.

Little, Donald P., ed. (1976) *Essays on Islamic Civilization,* Leiden: Brill.

Lokhandwalla, S.T., ed. (1971) *India and Contemporary Islam,* Simla: Indian Institute of Advanced Studies.

Madjid, Nurcholish. (2004) *Indonesia Kita* (Our Indonesia), Jakarta: Gramedia.

———. (1992) *Islam doktrin dan peradaban. Sebuah telaah kritis tentang masalah keiman-an, kemanusiaan, dan kemoderenan* (Islam: Doctrine and Civilization. A Critical Study on Problems of Faith, Humanism, and Modernity), Jakarta: Yayasan Wakaf Paramadina.

———. (1987) *Islam, kemodernan dan keindonesiaan* (Islam, Modernity and Indonesian-ness), Bandung: Mizan.

———. (1985) *Khazanah intelektual Islam* (The Intellectual Resources of Islam), Jakart: Bulan Bintang.

Madsen, Richard and Tracy B. Strong, eds. (2003) *The Many and the One, Religious and Secular Perspectives on Ethical Pluralism in the Modern World,* Princeton: Princeton University Press.

Mahmassani, Subhi. (1961) *The Philosophy of Jurisprudence in Islam,* translated by Farhat J. Ziadeh, Leiden: Brill.

Malekian, Mustafa. (1380/2001) *Rahi Beh Rahaei: Jostarhaei dar Bab e Aghlaniat va Manaviat* (A Way to Freedom: Reflections on Rationalism and Spirituality), Tehran: Nashr e Negah e Moaser.

Malik, Hafeez, ed. (1971) *Iqbal: Poet-Philosopher of Pakistan,* New York: Columbia University Press.

———. (1980) *Sir Sayyid Ahmad Khan and Muslim Modernization in India and Pakistan,* New York: Columbia University Press.

Mardin, Serif. (1989) *Religion and Social Change in Modern Turkey: The Case of Bediüz-zaman Said Nursi,* Albany: State University of New York Press.

———. (2006) *Religion, Society and Modernization in Turkey,* Syracuse, NY: Syracuse University Press.

Masud, Muhammad Khalid. (1995) *Iqbal's Reconstruction of Ijtihad,* Lahore: Iqbal Academy.

———. (1995) *Shatibi's Philosophy of Islamic Law,* Islamabad: Islamic Research Institute.

Mas'udi, Masdar F. (1992) *Fiqh permusyawaratan/perwakilan rakyat* (The *Fiqh* of Consulta-tion and People's Representation), Jakarta: P3M–RMI–Pesantren Cipasung.

Meddeb, Abdelwahab. (2002) *La maladie de l'islam,* Paris: Seuil.

Melchert, Christopher. (1997) *The Formation of the Sunni Schools of Law, 9th–10th Cen-turies CE,* New York: Brill.

Merad, Ali. (1967) *Le Réformisme musulman en Algérie de 1920 à 1940, essai d'histoire religieuse et sociale,* Paris and The Hague: Mouton.

Mir-Hosseini Ziba and Richard Taffer. (2006) *Islam and Democracy in Iran: Eshkevari and the Quest for Reform.* London: T.B. Tauries.

Mirsepassi, Ali. (2000) *Intellectual Discourses and the Politics of Modernization: Negotiat-ing Modernity in Iran,* Cambridge: Cambridge University Press.

Muhammad, K.H. Husein. (2004) *Islam agama ramah perempuan: pembelaan kiai pesantren* (Islam, a Woman-Friendly Religion: Defense by a Pesantren Kyai), Yogyakarta: LKiS and Fahmina Institute.

Mutahari, Murtaza. (1962) *Bahsi Dar Bareh-e-Ruhaniat va Marjaiyat* (A Discussion of the Religious Establishment and the Institution of Marjaiyat "Sources of Emulation"), Tehran: Enteshar.

———. (1985) *Fundamentals of Islamic Thought: God, Man, and the Universe,* translated by R. Campbell, Berkeley: Mizan Press.

——. (1373/1994) *Islam va Moqtaziat-e-Zaman* (Islam and the Requirements of Time), Tehran: Enthesharat e Sadra.

Muzaffar, Chandra. (1979) *Protector? An Analysis of the Concept and Practice of Loyalty in Leader-Led Relationships Within Malay Society,* Penang: Aliran.

——. (2002) *Rights, Religion and Reform: Enhancing Human Dignity Through Spiritual and Moral Transformation,* London: RoutledgeCurzon.

——. (1979) *The Universalism of Islam,* Penang: Aliran.

Nair, Shanti. (1997) *Islam and Malaysian Foreign Policy,* London: Routledge and ISEAS.

Nanji, Azim, ed. (1996) *The Muslim Almanac,* New York: Gale Research.

Nasr, Seyyed Hossein. (1964) *An Introduction to Islamic Cosmological Doctrines,* Cambridge: Harvard University Press.

——. (1976) *Islamic Science: An Illustrated Study,* Chicago: Kazi.

——. (1991) *Man and Nature: The Spiritual Crisis in Modern Man,* San Francisco: HarperCollins.

——. (1996) *Religion and the Order of Nature,* New York: Oxford University Press.

——. (1992) *Science and Civilization in Islam,* New York: Barnes and Noble.

Nelson, Esther R. (2004) *Voice of an Exile,* Westport, CT: Praeger.

Noer, Deliar. (1973) *The Modernist Muslim Movement in Indonesia, 1900–1940,* Kuala Lumpur: Oxford University Press.

Noor, Farish A. (2002) *New Voices of Islam,* Leiden: ISIM.

Nordholt, H. Schulte, ed. (2006) *Indonesian Transitions,* Yogyakarta: Pustaka Pelajar.

Norris, Pipa and Roland Inglehart. (2004) *Sacred and Secular: Religion and Politics Worldwide,* New York: Cambridge University Press.

Nouri, Abdullah. (1378/1999) *Shawkaran e Eslah* (The Hemlock of Reform), Tehran: Entesharat e Tarh e Now.

Özsoy, Omer. (2004) *Kur'an ve Tarihsellik Yazıları,* Ankara: Kitabiyyat.

——. (1994) *Sünnetullah: Bir Kur'an İfadesinin Kavramlaşması,* Ankara: Fecr Yayınevi.

Öztürk, Mustafa. (2002) *Kur'an Dili ve Retoriği: Kur'an Metninin Dokusu Üzerine Tartışmalar,* Ankara: Kitabiyat.

——. (2004) *Kur'an'ın Mu'tezili Yorumu: Ebu Müslim el-İsfahani Örneği,* Ankara: Ankara Okulu.

Paret, Rudi. (1995) *Kur'an Üzerine Makaleler,* translated by Omer Özsoy, Ankara: Bilgi Vakfı.

——. (2004) *Kur'an ve Tarihsellik Yazıları,* Ankara: Kitabiyat.

Perkins, Kenneth J. (2004) *A History of Modern Tunisia,* Cambridge: Cambridge University Press.

Qutb, Sayyid. (1981) *Islam: The True Religion,* translated by Ravi Ahmad Fidai, Karachi: International Islamic Publishers.

——. (1993) *Milestones,* translated by Ahmad Zaki Hammad, Indianapolis: American Trust Publications.

Rahman, Fazlur. (1982) *Islam and Modernity: Transformation of an Intellectual Tradition,* Chicago: University of Chicago Press.

Ramadan, Tariq. (2002) *Dar ash-shahada, L'Occident, espace de témoignage,* Lyon: Tawhid.

——. (2002) *Jihad, violence, guerre et paix en Islam,* Lyon: Tawhid.

——. (2002) *La foi, la voie et la résistance,* Lyon: Tawhid.

——. (2002) *Musulmans d'Occident: Construire et contribuer,* Lyon: Tawhid.

Ramazani, R.K. (1966) *The Foreign Policy of Iran: A Developing Nation in World Affairs, 1500–1941,* Charlottesville: University of Virginia Press.

Ratnam, K.J. (1965) *Communalism and the Political Process in Malaysia,* Kuala Lumpur: University of Malaya Press.

Roff, W.R., ed. (1987) *Islam and the Political Economy of Meaning,* London and Sydney: Croom Helm.

Sachedina, Abdulaziz. (2001) *The Islamic Roots of Democratic Pluralism,* Oxford: Oxford University Press.

Sadri, Mahmoud and Ahmad Sadri, eds. and trans. (2000) *Reason, Freedom and Democracy: Essential Writings of Abdolkarim Soroush,* Oxford and New York: Oxford University Press.

Saidzadeh, Seyyed Mohsen. (1377/1998) *Zanan Dar Jameeh e Madani: Ta cheh Andazeh sahm Darand,* Tehran: Nashr e Ghatreh.

Sanson, Henri. (1983) *Laïcité islamique en Algérie,* Paris: Editions du CNRS.

Schimmel, A.M. (1963) *Gabriel's Wing,* Leiden: E.J. Brill.

Seddik, Youssef. (2006) *Coran, autre lecture, autre traduction,* Paris: L'Aube Edition.

———. (2004) *Nous n'avons jamais lu le Coran,* Paris: L'Aube Edition.

Shabestari, Muhammad Mojtajed. (1379/1997) *Hermeneutic e Ketab va Sonat,* Tehran: Entehsharat e Tarh e Now.

———. (1379/1997) *Naghdi Az Gharaat E Rasmi Az Din,* Tehran: Entesharat-e-Tarh-e-Now.

Shahin, Emad. (1997) *Political Ascent: Contemporary Islamic Movements in North Africa,* Boulder, CO: Westview Press.

Shariati, Ali. (1980) *Marxism and Other Western Fallacies,* translated by R. Campbell, Berkeley: Mizan Press.

———. (1979) *On the Sociology of Islam,* translated by Hamid Algar, Berkeley: Mizan Press.

———. (1996) *Shariati on Shariati and the Muslim Woman,* translated by Laleh Bakhtiar, Chicago: ABC Group International.

———. (1353/1973) *Ummat Va Immat,* Tehran: Hosseinieh e Irshad.

Smith, Donald Eugene, ed. (1974) *Religion and Political Modernization,* New Haven: Yale University Press.

Smith, Jane I. (2000) *Islam in America,* New York: Columbia University Press.

Smith, W.C. (1946) *Modern Islam in India: A Social Analysis,* London: Victor Gollancz.

Sodik, Mochamad. (2000) *Gejolak santri kota: aktivis muda NU merambah jalan lain* (The Urban Santri as Torchbearer: Young NU Activists Paving a New Way), Yogyakarta: Tiara Wacana.

Soroush, Abdolkarim. (1379/1990) *Farbahtar Az ideology* (More Substantive Than Ideology), Tehran: Moassesseh eye Farhangi-e-Sarat.

———. (1379/1991) *Gabz Va Bast e Theoric e Shariat* (The Theoretical Contraction and Expansion of the Shari'a), Tehran: Sarat.

———. (1378/1999) *Sarathay e Mostaghim* (Straight Paths), Tehran: Moassesseh e Farfangi e Sarat.

Strum, Philippa and Danielle Tarantolo, eds. (2003) *Muslims in the United States: Demography, Beliefs, Institutions,* Washington DC: Woodrow Wilson International Center for Scholars.

Subaşı, Necdet. (2005) *Ara Dönem Din Politikaları,* Istanbul: Küre Yayınları.

Taghavi, Seyed Mohammad Ali, *The Flourishing of Islamic Reformism in Iran: Political Islamic Goups in Iran (1941–61)* (2005), London/New York: RoutledgeCurzon.

Taha, Mahmoud M. (1987) *The Second Message of Islam,* Syracuse, NY: Syracuse University Press.

Taji-Farouki, Suha. (2004) *Modern Muslim Intellectuals and the Qur'an,* Oxford: Oxford Univerity Press in association with the Institute of Ismaili Studies.

Talbi, Mohamed. (1972) *Islam et dialogue,* Tunis: Maison tunisienne d'édition.

———. (2002) *Penseur libre en islam, un intellectual musulman dans la Tunisie de Ben Ali. Entretiens avec Jarczyk Gwendoline,* Paris: Albin Michel.

————. (2004) *Plaidoyer pour un islam moderne,* Paris: Editions de l'Aube.

Tozy, Mohamed. (1999) *Monarchie et islam politique au Maroc,* Paris: Presses de Sciences Po.

Vermeren, Pierre. (2004) *Maghreb: La Démocratie impossible?* Paris: Fayard.

Wadud, Amina. (1999) *Qur'an and Woman: Rereading the Sacred Text from a Woman's Perspective,* New York: Oxford University Press.

Ward, Ken E. (1970) *The Foundation of the Partai Muslimin Indonesia,* Ithaca: Cornell Modern Indonesia Project.

Watt, Montgomery. (1956) *Muhammad at Medina,* Oxford: Clarendon Press.

Webb, Gisela. (2000) *Windows of Faith: Muslim Women Scholar Activists in North America,* Syracuse, NY: Syracuse University Press.

Willis, Michael. (1996) *The Islamist Challenge in Algeria—A Political History,* New York: New York University Press.

Wolfson, Harry A. (1976) *The History of the Kalam,* Cambridge: Harvard University Press.

Yasin, Aktay. (1999) *Türk Dinin Sosyolojik İmkanı,* Istanbul: İletişim.

Articles

Abdallah, Najih Ibrahim. (2004) "Da'wa li al-Tasaluh ma'a al Mujtama,'" *Ubaikan.*

————. (2004) "Fatwa al-Tatar of Sheikh al-Islam Ibn Taymia: An Analytical Study," *Ubaikan.*

————. (2004) "al-Hakimiyya, Nathariyya Shar'iyya wa Ru'ya Waqui'iyya," *Ubaikan.*

————. (2004) "Hatmiyyat al-Muwajaha wa Figq al-Nata'ij," *Ubaikan.*

————. (2004) "Hidayat al-Khala'iq bayn al-Ghayat wa al-Wasa'il," *Ubaikan.*

————. (2004) "Natharat fi Hakikat al-Isti'la'bi al-Iman," *Ubaikan.*

————. (2004) "Tajdid al-Khitab al-Dini," *Ubaikan.*

————. (2004) "Tatbiq al-Ahkam min Ikhtisas al-Hukkam," *al-Jizia.*

Amira, Nora. (Spring 1998) "Le point de vue de Bennabi sur les femmes," *NAQD-Revue de Critique sociale,* Special Issue on "Intellectuels et Pouvoirs au Maghreb-Itinéraires pluriels." No. 11.

Bedir, Murteza. (2004) "Fikh to Law: Secularization Through the Curriculum," *Islamic Law and Society.* Vol. 11, No. 3.

Bouzeghrane, N. (September 21, 2004) "Interview de Ghaleb Bencheikh (Théologien)," *El Watan* (Algiers).

Castles, Lance. (1966) "Notes on the Islamic School at Gontor," *Indonesia.* No. 1.

Chalabi, El Hadi. (Spring 1998) "Un juriste en quête de modernité: Benali Fekar," *NAQD-Revue de Critique sociale,* Special Issue on "Intellectuels et Pouvoirs au Maghreb-Itinéraires pluriels." No. 11.

Dahim, Yasmina. "Entretien avec le Cheikh Khaled Bentounés-Nous ne sommes pas ce que vous croyez-I," *Revue Outre Terre.* Vol. 2, No. 3.

Eisenstadt, Schumel N. (2000) "The Reconstruction of Religious Arenas in the Frameworks of 'Multiple Modernities,'" *Millennium Journal of International Studies.* Vol. 29, No. 3.

Eshkevari, Hassan Yussefi. (Aban 1380/October–November 2001) "Islam, Azadi, Va Moderniteh" (Islam, Freedom and Modernity). *Aftab.* No. 9.

————. (Bahman 1381/January–February 2002) "MardomSalari e Dini" (Religious Democracy). *Aftab.* No. 23.

Feillard, Andrée. (1997) "Indonesia's Emerging Muslim Feminism: Women Leaders on Equality, Inheritance and Other Gender Issues," *Studia Islamika.* Vol. 4, No. 1.

Frégosi, Franck. (March 2005) "La regulation institutionnelle de l'Islam en Tunisie: entre audace moderniste et tutelle étatique," *Policy Paper.* No. 11.

Goodstein, Laurie. (June 18, 2006) "US Muslim Clerics Seek a Modern Middle Ground," *New York Times.*

Hafez, Osama Ibrahim and 'Asem abd al-Magid Mohammad. (2004) "Hurmat al-Ghuluw fi al-Din wa Takfir al-Muslimin," *Ubaikan.*

———. (2004) "al-Nuskhwa al-Tabiyn fi Tashih Mafahim al-Muhtasibin," *Ubaikan.*

———. (2004) "Taslit al-Adwa' 'ala ma waqu'a fi al-Jihad min Akhta,'" *Ubaikan.*

Hedges,Chris. (June 23, 2004) "A Muslim in the Middle Hopes Against Hope," *New York Times.*

Huntington, Samuel (Summer 1984) "Will More Countries Become Democratic?" *Political Science Quarterly.* No. 99.

Lewis, Bernard. (February 1993) "Islam and Liberal Democracy," *Atlantic Monthly.*

Munhanif, Ali. (1996) "Islam and the Struggle for Religious Pluralism in Indonesia: A Political Reading of Religious Thought of Mukti Ali," *Studia Islamika.* Vol. 3, No. 1.

Muzani, Saiful. (1994) "Mu'tazilah Theology and the Modernization of the Indonesian Muslim Community: An Intellectual Portrait of Harun Nasution," *Studia Islamika.* Vol. 1, No. 1.

Oukaci, Fayçal. (November 14, 2003) "Algérie: Code de la famille—Le chef d'un parti islamiste contre son abrogation," *Le Monde.*

———. (September 30, 2006) "Rabah Kebir fait l'autocritique du FIS dissous," *L'Expression* (Algiers).

Perlmutter, Amos. (January 21, 1992) "Islam and Democracy Simply Aren't Compatible," *International Herald Tribune.*

Rahman, Fazlur. (1967) "Implementation of the Islamic Concept of State in the Pakistani Milieu," *Islamic Studies.* Vol. 6, No. 3.

———. (1958) "Muslim Modernism in the Indo-Pakistan Sub-Continent," *The Bulletin of the School of Oriental and African Studies.* Vol. 21, No. 2.

Sadowski, Yahya. (July–August 1993) "The New Orientalism and the Democracy Debate," *The Middle East Report [MERIP].*

Sellam, Sadek. (Spring 1998) "Le Cheikh El Oqbi au Cercle du progrès," *NAQD-Revue de Critique sociale,* Special Issue on "Intellectuels et Pouvoirs au Maghreb-Itinéraires pluriels." No. 11.

Soroush, Abdolkarim. (1372/1993) "Shariati Va Jameeh e Shanassi e Din" (Shariati and the Sociology of Religion), *Kian.* No. 13.

Taji-Farouki, Suha. (2000) "Sadiq Nayhum: Introduction to the Life and Works of a Contemporary Libyan Intellectual," *Maghreb Review.* Vol. 25, Nos. 3–4.

Tammam, Hossam. (2004) "Democratic Muslim Brothers, Their Ideas, Their Maps and Their Obstacles," *al-Qahira Weekly Newspaper.*

Tincq, Henri. (November 11, 2001) "Soheib Bencheikh, mufti de Marseille: 'Ou l'islam marche avec son siècle, ou il reste à la marge de la société moderne,' Entretien avec Soheib Bencheikh, mufti de Marseille," *Le Monde.*

Vahdat, Farzin. (2003) "Post-Revolutionary Islamic Discourses on Modernity in Iran: Expansion and Contraction of Human Subjectivity," *International Journal of Middle East Studies.* Vol. 35.

Wajidi, Farid. (2003) "Syarikat dan eksperimentasi rekoniliasi kulturalnya (sebuah pengamatan awal)" (Syarikat and Its Experiment of a Cultural Reconciliation [A First Observation]), *Tashwirul Afkar.* No. 15.

Zebiri, Kate. (July–October 1993) "Islamic Revival in Algeria: An Overview," *The Muslim World.* Vol. 83, Nos. 3–4.

Zeghal, Malika. (March 2005) "Religion et politique au Maroc aujourd'hui," *Policy Paper.* No. 11.

Zoubir, Yahia H. (Summer 1996) "Algerian Islamists' Conception of Democracy," *Arab Studies Quarterly.* Vol. 18, No. 3.

———. (Spring 1998) "Islam and Democracy in Malek Bennabi's Thought," *American Journal of Islamic Social Sciences.* Vol. 15, No. 1.

————. (Summer 2005) "Libye: Islamism radical et lutte antiterroriste," *Revue Maghreb-Machrek.* No. 184.

————. (Winter/Spring 1997) "Islamist Political Parties in Algeria," *Middle East Affairs Journal.* Vol. 3, Nos. 1–2.

Papers

Abdul Bari, Muhammad. (September 20, 2006) Press Release of the Muslim Council of Britain.

Al-Wasat Party Papers. (2004) Cairo: International Shorouk.

Barton, Gregory James. (1995) "The Emergence of Neo-Modernism: A Progressive, Liberal Movement of Islamic Thought in Indonesia. A Textual Study Examining the Writings of Nurcholish Madjid, Djohan Effendi, Ahmad Wahib and Abdurrahman Wahid, 1968–1980." Thesis. Clayton: Monash University.

Effendi, Djohan. (2000) "Progressive Traditionalists: The Emergence of a New Discourse in Indonesia's Nahdlatul Ulama During the Abdurrahman Wahid Era." Thesis. Melbourne: Deakin University.

Esack, Farid. (August 1994) "Between Mandela and Man Dalla: Rethinking Kaffirs and Kafirs." Paper presented at Islam and Civil Society in South Africa: Prospects for Tolerance and Conflict Resolution, University of South Africa.

Gibril, Mohammad and Khalid al-Gindi. (n.d.) *Doubt, Oblivion and Hesitation. Hallucination, Sadness and Anguish. Insomnia, Despair and Obsession. Alienation, Frustration and Indifference. Seclusion, Fear and Personality Weakness,* Cairo: al-Raya.

————. (n.d.) *The Medicine of Heavens,* Cairo: al-Raya.

Iftikhar, Asif. (2004) "Jihad and the Establishment of Islamic Global Order: A Comparative Study of the Interpretative Approaches and Weltanschauungs of Abu'l a'la Mawdudi and Javed Ahmad Ghamidi." Thesis. Montreal: McGill University.

Marcoes-Natsir, Lies M. and Syafiq Hasyim (1997) *P3M dan program fiqh an-nisa untuk penguatan hak-hak reproduksi perempuan* (P3M and the Program of Women's Fiqh for the Empowerment of Women's Reproductive Rights), Jakarta: P3M.

Masud, Muhammad Khalid. (December 2004) "Defining Democracy in Islamic Polity." Paper presented at "The Future of Islam, Democracy and Authoritarianism in the Era of Globalization" Conference organized by the International Centre for Islam and Pluralism.

Muhammad, K.H. Husein, et al. (2006) *Dawrah Fiqh Concerning Women: Manual for a Course on Islam and Gender,* Cirebon: Fahmina Institute.

Nasr, Yasser. (2004) *Choosing One's Life Partner,* Cairo, Arij.

————. (2004) *Marriage in Islam,* Cairo: Arij.

————. (2004) *Woman Liberation, Woman, Suspicions and Responses,* Cairo: Arij.

Zein, Ahmed. (n.d.) *Love in Islam: Desire is Your Road to Paradise (The Double Error of Sensibility and Meta-Sensibility),* Cairo: al-Raya.

————. (n.d.) *How to Deal with Desire?* Cairo: al-Raya.

Electronic Resources

"Ayatullah Bojnourdi Moussavi: Shadat e Zan ba Mard barabar Ast" (Ayatullah Moussavi Bojnourdi: Woman's Testimony is Equal to that of Man." (July 27, 2006) Available at http://www.entekhab.ir.

Baghi, Emad Eddin. (February 13, 2006) "Do Faghih: Moroury Bar Didehgahay e Ayatullah Boroujerdi va Imam Khomeini" (Two Faghihs: A Look at the Perspectivers of Ayatullah Boroujerdi and Imam Khomeini). Available at http:// emrouz.info/archives/print/2006/04/029307.php.

Barouti, Hashem. (February 13, 2006) "Shariati va Marxism: Goftgoui ba Reza Alijani, Maghloub e Goftman Ghaleb naboud" (Shariati and Marxism: A Conversation with Reza Alijani). Available at http://www.sharghnewspaper.com/850331/html/v2.htm.

Dawood, Shimaila Matri. (December 2004) "We Are Not Remaking Islam." Interview with Dr. Fathi Osman. *Newsline.* Available at http//www.newsline.com.pk/NewsDec2004/religion2dec.htm.

"Ehsan Naraghi Takid Kard, Zarourat Bazghasht Eslahtalaban beh Shiveh e Khatami" (Ehsan Naraghi Emphasizes the Necessity of the Reformists' Return to Khatami's Approach). (February 13, 2006). Available at http://emrouz.info/print.aspx?ID=306.

El Hassouni, Abdelmohsin. (June 10, 2005) "Al Badil Al Hadari entre en scène," *Aujourd'hui le Maroc.* Available at http://www.aujourdhui.ma/nation-details36602.html.

Engineer, Asghar Ali. (n.d.) "Dr. Asghar Ali Engineer's Articles." Available at http://www.andromeda.rutgers.edu/%7Ertavakol/engineer/.

"Entretien avec l'islamologue tunisien Abdeljamid Charfi: Le pari sur le progrès et la raison." (May 15, 2005) Available at http://nawaatorg/portail/article.php3?id_article=572.

Eshkevari, Hassan Yussefi. (July 2006) "Shariati's Heritage and Us." Available at http://mellimazhabi.org/news/072006/2607eshgavari.htm.

Fernandes, Alberto. (May 2006) "Liberating Islam from Bondage: The Radical Democratic Discourse of al-Sadiq al-Nayhum," paper presented at the seventh Conference of the Center for the Study of Islam and Democracy. Available at http://www.csidonline.org/images/stories/pdfiles/alberto_fernandes[1].pdf.

Ghabel, Ahmad. (June 2005) "Nameh e Ahmad Ghabel beh Rahbar Jomhuri e Islam e Iran." Letter. Available at http://www.bbc.com.uk/persian/iran/story/2005/06/050601.shtml.

Khalaji, Mehdi. (July 19, 2006). "Iran's Shadow Government in Lebanon," *Policy Watch/Peace Watch.* Available at http:///washingtoninstitute.org/templateC05.php?CID=2489.

"L'islam et le statut de la femme," (February 7, 2006) *L'Humanité* (Paris). Available at http://www.humanite.fr.

Milani, Muhannad. (2006) "Shariati, Shah beit Andisheh-e-Irani: Gofto ghou ba Taghi Rahmani" (Shariati, The Peak of Iranian Thought: A Conversation with Taghi Rahmani), *Nameh,* No. 50. Available at http://nashrieh-nameh.com/article.php?articleID=821.

Montazeri, Ayatullah. (February 2006) "Har Tagyir e Mazhab Irtad Nist" (Every Change of Religion is not Apostasy. Available at http://mehdis.com/tablu/modules. php?name=news7file=article&sid=18112.

———. (April 2003) "Pasokh Beh Soalhaei Piramoun e Mojazat e Islami" (Answer to Questions Regarding Islamic Punishments). Available at http://www.amontazeri.com/Farsi/Payamha/52.htm.

———. (April 2003) "Pasokhhay e Ayatullah e Ozma Montazer beh Soalat e site e Rouz" (The Answers of the Grand Ayatullah Montazeri to the Questions of Rouz Site). Available at http://www.amontazeri.com/Farsi/Payamha/83.html.

———. (May 2004) Statement during a visit by the youth branch of the reformist group Jebehe e Mosharekat (The Participation Front). Available at http://mehdis.com/tabula/modules.sph?name=News&file=article&sid=15280.

Mouatassime, M. L. (December 2002) "L'attitude de l'Etat à notre égard viole la constitution," *Le Journal.* Available at http://membres.lycos.fr/albadil/journal_media.htm?

Movahed, Khalil. (2006). *Shariati va Ideology* (Shariati and Ideology). Available at http://www.mellimazhabi.org/news/08news2006/0508khalil.htm.

Nejad, Cyrus Ali. (August 2005) "Tajaddod khahi va Roshanfekran e Dini" (Modernity and Religious Intellectuals: A Conversation with Hassan Yussefi Eshkevari). Available at http://www.bbc.co.uk/persian/arts/story/2005/08/050812_pm-cy-eshkevari.shtml.

———. (August 2005) "Tajad khahi va Roshanfekri e Dini: Gotgu ba Hassan Yussefi Eshkevari" (Desire for Modernity and Religious Intellectuals: Hassan Yussefi Eshkevari). Available at http://www.bbc.com.uk/persian/Arts/story/2005/08/050812_pm-cy-eshkevari.shtml.

Rahardjo, M. Dawam. (May 20, 2003) "Pembaharuan pemikiran Islam: sebuah catatan pribadi" (The Renewal of Islamic Thought: A Private Note). Available at http://www. freedom-institute.org/id/index.php?page=artikel&id=121.

Sadri, Mahmoud. (1384/2005) "A Reflection on the Incompatibility of Modern Democracy and Guardianship and Messianism in Shiism" (Taamoli Dar bab e Nasazegari e Mardomsalari e Modern ba velayat va mahdaviyat dar Tashaio). Available at http://www. dsoroush.com/Persian/On_DrSoroush/p-CMO-13840529-MahmoudSadri.htm.

Sardar, Ziauddin. (September 2004) "Searching for Secular Islam," *New Humanist.* Available at http://www.newhumanist.org.uk/volume119issue5_more.php?id=964_0-32_0_C.

Zaiabadi, Ahmad. (June 2006) "Dr. Shariati va nakaramadi entekhabat dar Jameeh e nomotavazen" (Dr. Shariati and the Inefficacy of Elections in an Unbalanced Society). Available at http://www.bbc.co.uk/Persian/iran/story/2006/06/060619_mj-z-shariati-30years-on.shtml.

Index of Names

313

See the detailed table of contents on pages vii–xiii for additional assistance.

About the Editor
and Contributors

Hassan Hanafi is Professor of Philosophy at Cairo University and vice president of the Arab Philosophical Society. He has published extensively in Arabic, English, and French, and has translated works of Western philosophy into Arabic. Dr. Hanafi is a leading authority on Islam and a reformist thinker. He is very active in efforts to promote dialogue among cultures and faiths. Among his most recent publications in English are *Islam in the Modern World*, 2 vols. (Cairo, 2000) and *Cultures and Civilizations: Conflict or Dialogue?* (Cairo, 2005).

Riffat Hassan is Professor of Religious Studies and Humanities at the University of Louisville. She has taught courses on modern Islamic thought, human rights and religious traditions, women and religion, inter-religious dialogue, and Muslim ethics. Her publications include *An Iqbal Primer* (Lahore, 1979) and *Women's Rights and Islam: From the I.C.P.D. to Beijing* (Louisville, 1995). In 1999, Dr. Hassan founded the International Network for the Rights of Female Victims of Violence in Pakistan, a nonprofit organization that seeks to create worldwide awareness of the degree and nature of violence against girls and women in Pakistan and to provide direct assistance to the victims.

Shireen T. Hunter is a Visiting Professor at Georgetown University. Between 1998 and 2005 she directed the Islam Program at the Center for Strategic and International Studies in Washington DC, with which she had been associated since 1983. Her publications include: *Modernization, Democracy and Islam* (ed. and contributor) (Praeger, 2005; also translated into Arabic and Persian); *Islam in Russia: The Politics of Identity and Security* (M.E. Sharpe, 2004); *Islam, Europe's Second Religion* (ed. and contributor) (Praeger, 2002); *The Future of Islam and the West: Clash of Civilizations or Peaceful Coexistence?* (Praeger, 1998; also translated into Arabic and Persian); *Iran After Khomeini* (Washington D.C., 1992); *Iran and the World: Continuity in a Revolutionary Decade* (Indiana University Press, 1990); and *The Politics of Islamic Revivalism: Unity and Diversity* (ed. and contributor) (Indiana University Press, 1988).

Farhad Khosrokhavar is a Professor at Ecole des Hautes Etudes en Sciences Sociales in Paris, France. Dr. Khosrokhavar has published extensively on Islam in Europe and on Iran, in both English and French. His publications include *Les nouveaux martyrs d'Allah* (Paris, 2002) and *Iran: Comment sortir d'une revolution religieuse?* (with Olivier Roy) (Paris, 1999).

Farish A. Noor is currently based at Zentrum Moderner Orient (The Center for Modern Oriental Studies) in Berlin. Previously he was an Associate Fellow at the Institute for Strategic and International Studies (ISIS) in Malaysia. He has taught in France, Germany, Indonesia, Malaysia, and the Netherlands. Dr. Noor is the author of numerous works on Islam in Malaysia, including *Islam Embedded: The Historical Development of the Pan-Malaysia Islamic Party PAS, 1951–2003* (Kuala Lumpur, 2004) and *New Voices of Islam* (Leiden, 2002).

Recep Şentürk is Associate Professor of Sociology at Fatih University and a research fellow at the Islamic research center İslâm Araştirmalalari Merkezi (ISAM) in Istanbul, Turkey. He has published several articles on human rights in Islam and books on Hadith and Islam in Turkey, including *Düşünce Sosyolojisi: Tanximattan Cumhuriyete Turk Aydinlari* (Sociology of Ideas: Turkish Intellectuals from the Ottoman Reform Era to the Republic) (forthcoming).

Tamara Sonn is Kenan Professor of Religion and Professor of Humanities at the College of William and Mary. Dr. Sonn serves on the Board of Directors of the Center for the Study of Islam and Democracy (CSID). Her publications include *A Brief History of Islam* (Blackwell, 2004): *Comparing Religions Through Law: Judaism and Islam* (with J. Neusner and J. Brokopp) (Routledge, 2000); *Between Qur'an and Crown: The Challenge of Political Legitimacy in the Arab World* (Westview, 1990); and *Interpreting Islam: Bandali Jawzi's Islamic Intellectual History* (Oxford, 1996).

Martin van Bruinessen is ISIM Chair for the Comparative Study of Contemporary Muslim Societies at Utrecht University in the Netherlands. He has conducted fieldwork in Afghanistan, Kurdistan, and Indonesia. Dr. van Bruinessen helped to found the International Institute for the Study of Islam in the Modern World (ISIM) in 1998. His publications on Islam in Indonesia include *Tarekat Naqsyabandiyah di Indonesia* (Bandung, 1992) and *Kitab kuning, pesantren dan tarekat: Tradisi-tradisi Islam di Indonesia* (Bandung, 1995).

Yahia H. Zoubir is Professor of International Relations and International Management at Euromed Marseille. He has published extensively on North Africa in both English and French, serving as editor and contributor to *North Africa in Transition: State, Society, and Economic Transformation in the 1990s* (Gainesville, 1999) and as coeditor of *L'Islamisme Politique dans les Rapports entre l'Europe et le Maghreb* (Lisbon, 1996).